WITHDRAWN

# Theory and Practice of

# Psychiatric Rehabilitation

# Theory and Practice of Psychiatric Rehabilitation

*Edited by*

**Fraser N. Watts**
*Medical Research Council Applied Psychology Unit, Cambridge, UK*

*and*

**Douglas H. Bennett**
*Bethlem Royal and Maudsley Hospitals, London, UK*

*Reprinted with a Foreword*

## Psychiatric Rehabilitation for the 1990s

*by* **Geoff Shepherd**
*Fulbourn Hospital, Cambridge, UK*

**JOHN WILEY & SONS**
Chichester · New York · Brisbane · Toronto · Singapore

Copyright ©1983, 1991 by John Wiley & Sons Ltd,
Baffins Lane, Chichester,
West Sussex PO19 1UD, England

Reprinted January 1987
Reprinted, with corrections and new Foreword by
Geoff Shepherd, January 1991

*Other Wiley Editorial Offices*

John Wiley & Sons, Inc., 605 Third Avenue,
New York, NY 10158–0012, USA

Jacaranda Wiley Ltd, G.P.O. Box 859, Brisbane,
Queensland 4001, Australia

John Wiley & Sons (Canada) Ltd, 22 Worcester Road,
Rexdale, Ontario M9W 1L1, Canada

John Wiley & Sons (SEA) Pte Ltd, 37 Jalan Pemimpin #05–04,
Block B, Union Industrial Building, Singapore 2057

*Library of Congress Cataloging-in-Publication Data:*
is available   83–1055

*British Library Cataloguing in Publication Data:*

Watts, Fraser N.
  Theory and practice of psychiatric rehabilitation.
  1. Mentally ill — Rehabilitation
  I. Title    II. Bennett, Douglas H.
  362.2.0425        RC429.5

ISBN 0-471-92816-X (pbk.)

Phototypeset by Dobbie Typesetting Service, Tavistock, Devon
Printed and bound by Courier International, Tiptree, Essex

To
RUDOLF KARL FREUDENBERG
of Netherne Hospital
1908–1983

# Contents

# Contributors

DOUGLAS H. BENNETT, *Bethlem Royal and Maudsley Hospitals, Denmark Hill, London SE5 8AZ.*

JAMES L. T. BIRLEY, *Bethlem Royal and Maudsley Hospitals, Denmark Hill, London SE5 8AZ.*

JOHN GUNN, *Department of Psychiatry, Institute of Psychiatry, De Crespigny Park, London SE5 8AF.*

JOHN N. HALL, *Warneford Hospital, Headington, Oxford OX3 7JX.*

BARBARA L. HUDSON, *Department of Social and Administrative Studies, University of Oxford, Barnett House, Wellington Square, Oxford OX1 2ER.*

ROGER MORGAN, *St Wulstan's Hospital, Malvern, Worcestershire WR14 4JS.*

ISOBEL M. MORRIS, *Adult Psychology, Guy's Hospital, St Thomas Street, London SE1 9RT.*

GLENYS PARRY, *Psychology Services, Middlewood Hospital, Sheffield S6 1TP.*

GEOFF SHEPHERD, *Fulbourn Hospital, Cambridge CB1 5EF.*

PAMELA TAYLOR, *Department of Psychiatry, Institute of Psychiatry, De Crespigny Park, London SE5 8AF.*

ANTHONY P. THORLEY, *Centre for Alcohol and Drug Dependence Studies, Parkwood House, St Nicholas Hospital, Gosforth, Newcastle upon Tyne NE3 3XT.*

FRASER N. WATTS, *MRC Applied Psychology Unit, 15 Chaucer Road, Cambridge CB2 2EF.*

JOHN K. WING, *MRC Social Psychiatry Unit, Institute of Psychiatry, De Crespigny Park, London SE5 8AF.*

# Preface and Acknowledgements

The past 35 years have seen the genesis and the development of rehabilitation in psychiatry. In Netherne Hospital and Maudsley Hospital that development has been dependent on help and ideas from many people of many disciplines and many different backgrounds. The publication of this book provides an opportunity to acknowledge their contributions to our thoughts and practice.

It was the late Dr Rudi Freudenberg, Physician Superintendent at Netherne Hospital who with self-effacing generosity first offered me an opportunity to put into practice some ideas about the rehabilitation of the mentally ill which stemmed from my earlier experience. Dr Maxwell Jones had introduced me to the subject, and I was much influenced by his ideas about the rehabilitation of the neurotic unemployed at Belmont Hospital. Later, while working at Warlingham Park and the Fountain Hospitals, I was introduced to Dr T. P. Rees's work with psychotic patients and Dr L. T. Hilliard's approach to the rehabilitation of the mentally retarded child. This early thinking about rehabilitation was both broadened and straightened by the original ideas and research findings of Professor John Wing. His full-hearted support greatly helped me when I moved to the Maudsley. That move changed the direction of my rehabilitation practice and thinking, and made it difficult to continue with a book conceived in association with Dr Freudenberg. I do not altogether regret the loss of that attempt to describe our early and poorly formulated but surprisingly effective attempts at rehabilitation in the mental hospital. For rehabilitation has changed and is now no longer confined to the needs of the psychiatrically disabled with a long hospital stay, but has increased its scope to meet the needs of those patients who have never entered an institution as well as the needs of their family, friends, and workmates.

The growth of this non-institutional or community-centred rehabilitation received great encouragement and backing from Professor George Brown, Dr Jim Birley, Dr Tony Isaacs, Dr Robin Skynner, Dr Lorna Wing and her staff at the Camberwell Register. Although Dr J. P. R. Robertson of Netherne had provided helpful psychological advice, I now had the advantage of working much more closely with a number of able young psychologists, notably David Griffiths, Isobel Morris, Geoff Shepherd, and Fraser Watts, all of whom have made significant contributions to psychiatric rehabilitation which are reflected in the present volume.

It is impossible to recognize all those who, at Netherne and at Maudsley, in their day-to-day work have put ideas into practice and, in so doing, have not only helped disabled people, but have taught others and provided material for further research. Among the many who have helped I remember particularly Pat Comber (*née* Wills), Dora Coombes, Anne Coppard (*née* Constable), Maureen Cullen (*née* McQuade), Mary Day, Margaret Eden, Jan Finch, Cathy Fox (*née* Portnell), Gerry Grimmond, Christiane Haerlin, Tony Hart, Audrey Hudspeth (*née* Nicholson), Tessa Jowell, Peter Little, Wally Rogers, George Starkey, and Eileen Waller. Their work was essential. So, too, was the help of many friends and colleagues from different disciplines in this country and abroad who made valuable suggestions and offered information unobtainable elsewhere. Those who have contributed by upsetting cherished notions and forcing me to think in new ways have been Professor Bert Black, Professor Elaine Cumming, Professor John Cumming, Dr Donald Early, Professor Asmus Finzen, Dr Stephen Folkard, Dr Harley Frank, Professor Ernest Gruenberg, the late Dr Tony May, Professor David Mechanic, and Dr Carmi Schooler.

At a crucial stage in the production of the first edition misfortune disrupted my ability to contribute or edit. Fraser Watts generously shouldered the whole editorial burden and pushed matters forward to a successful conclusion, and I should like to express my appreciation to him.

We have been encouraged by the reception given to the book and are gratified that it is now appearing in a new edition. It seemed best to leave the original chapters intact and to bring the book up to date with a new foreword surveying developments during the last decade. We are most grateful to Geoff Shepherd for undertaking to write this. He has an encouraging story to tell about the continuing development of psychiatric rehabilitation.

DOUGLAS BENNETT

# Foreword

## Psychiatric Rehabilitation for the 1990s

GEOFF SHEPHERD

It is a great pleasure to have been asked to write a new Foreword to introduce this paperback edition of *Theory and Practice of Psychiatric Rehabilitation*. It is almost 10 years now since the hardback version first appeared and quickly established itself as one of the leading textbooks in the field. It is to be hoped that this new edition will reach an even wider audience and will also help shape rehabilitation services and practices in many different countries. Since the book was first published the field has moved on somewhat—although many of the original problems still face us—and it is thus timely to review the scene and to try and take a look forward into the future. It is not my intention to attempt an update of the hardback version chapter by chapter; that would be too ambitious and would probably run to another book in terms of length. Instead, I wish to take a personal look at what has been happening in the field of rehabilitation over the last few years and to try and highlight what seem to me to have been some of the important developments. It will, of course, be a personal view and will reflect my own background as a clinical psychologist and my interests in the problems of schizophrenia, service development, and evaluation. I can only beg the reader's indulgence in this respect and give an assurance that I remain aware of the privilege of my position.

### Developments in Theory

One of the things that strikes one most in rereading the original book is that it contains, perhaps for the first time, a psychologically sophisticated theory of psychiatric rehabilitation. At the heart of this is the notion that what is important in determining a person's social adaptation is the dynamic interaction between his or her disabilities and their social environment. Psychiatric rehabilitation addresses this dynamic adaptation and attempts to maximize functioning, while at the same time acknowledging the possibility of relatively fixed disabilities and the necessity of providing supportive environments. This dynamic view of the nature of psychological adaptation stands in sharp contrast to the traditional concept of rehabilitation which sees it as a process of 'throughput' whereby patients are 'rehabilitated' through attempts to improve their functioning so that they will eventually be able to lead relatively independent lives. The 'adaptive' view of rehabilitation sees attempts to improve functioning as part of the rehabilitation process, but not as synonymous with it. Thus, patients may be successfully 'rehabilitated', yet remain in a very sheltered, highly dependent setting (i.e. in hospital). Hence, a clear distinction is made between '*rehabilitation*' and '*resettlement*': successful rehabilitation may include the process of resettlement, but also it may not. The criterion of successful rehabilitation is that the individual achieves the best *adaptation* that he or she is capable of and this may, or may not, rest on significant improvements in functioning. In the most extreme cases it may only mean a reduction in the rate of deterioration. This still constitutes successful rehabilitation.

Successful adaptation is influenced by both the patient's functioning and the attitudes, expectations, and tolerances of those around them. Psychiatric disabilities are not as fixed as most physical disabilities and they can change depending upon the characteristics of the supportive environment. For example, a motivational 'disability' may be altered if a supportive relative dies, or is no longer able to continue caring for the patient. The fluid nature of functioning, disability, and adaptation is a reflection of the changing nature of social environments and the influence of life events. Carers may also become exhausted and frustrated and rehabilitation services therefore need to concern themselves as much with the maintenance of these supportive social environments—whether in hospital or outside it—as they do with the direct care of the patient.

Another important theoretical idea contained in the original introduction to this book is the distinction between '*symptoms*' and '*functioning*'. This distinction is supported by a wealth of empirical evidence which has demonstrated the relative independence of different aspects of long-term outcome (Strauss and Carpenter, 1972; 1974; 1977; Strauss *et al.*, 1977; De Jong *et al.*, 1986). This distinction is usually given some acknowledgement in psychiatry, but it constitutes a fundamental part of the rehabilitation philosophy. 'Chronic' patients, by definition, suffer with persistent and sometimes intractable symptoms and for them the goal of symptom relief is often not realistic. Instead, one has to try to help them develop their functional abilities and, at the very least, enable them to function at an optimal level *despite* their symptoms. 'Symptoms' and 'functioning' must therefore be considered as potentially independent domains.

There is also evidence of considerable 'specificity' in human behaviour, i.e. functioning is often bound up with a particular setting or person, and it may therefore be difficult to 'generalize' predictions about functioning across a range of different settings. Given the potential independence between symptoms and functioning and the phenomenon of 'specificity' within functional domains, it follows that we must target rehabilitation programmes specifically at particular areas of functioning. We cannot rely on improving functioning simply through attempts to treat symptomatology. Furthermore, we cannot expect improvements obtained in one setting to automatically transfer to others. These simple ideas have had a profound effect on the way that we think about models of service delivery and, in the last few years, there has been a number of examples of services which attempt to deliver multi-faceted 'packages' of care, based on careful assessments of individual need, working directly on 'criterion' functioning in the community (e.g. Stein and Test, 1985; Hoult, 1986).

Within the field of rehabilitation there has remained something of a difference in emphasis between English and American practitioners. In the United States there has always been a strong emphasis on skills acquisition and the importance of a skills-based approach in helping people function as independently as possible with the minimum of support (Anthony, 1979; Anthony, Cohen and Farkas, 1982; Anthony, Cohen and Cohen, 1984; Anthony and Liberman, 1986). Relatively little attention has been given to the problems of helping people adapt *despite* their disabilities (i.e. on environmental and social support issues). On the other hand, the English tradition has tended to emphasize the importance of understanding the factors which contribute to the maintenance of 'high quality', long-term care, with skills acquisition having something of a secondary focus (Garety and Morris, 1984; Allen *et al.*, 1989; Shepherd, 1984; 1985; 1988a; 1988b; 1991a). These studies attempt to address some of the central problems of how to create effective long-term care settings which will maintain functioning and avoid the build-up of traditional, institutional practices.

Theoretical ideas have also had a major influence in the area of 'handicap' (WHO, 1980), i.e. the social consequences of disability. In particular, the ideas of Wolfensberger and his colleagues on 'normalization' (Wolfensberger, 1972; Wolfensberger and Glenn, 1983), which were developed in the context of services for people with learning disabilities, have had an increasingly important impact on the thinking behind service development for people with long-term mental illnesses (e.g. Simpson *et al.*, 1984; Wainwright, Holloway and Brugha, 1988). These ideas stress the importance of the social message that services convey about those they are caring for. Thus, if the service appears to be low status, then those using it will likewise be deemed 'low status'. To counteract this we need to ensure that disadvantaged groups—and this includes those with long-term and disabling mental illnesses—have access to high status social facilities. For example, we should try to avoid large developments of low cost housing in single neighbourhoods with the resultant dangers of 'ghetto-ization'. We should also try to avoid the segregation of the psychiatrically disabled in low grade, menial and repetitive work. (This is not to say that there isn't a need for a range of simple work tasks, it is more a plea about how sheltered work settings may often *appear* boring and unattractive.) We must even be careful about the language that we use. 'Chronic' patients, 'schizophrenics', are terms that may blind us to the fact that patients are *people* first and 'patients' or 'schizophrenics' second. This may sound pedantic, but in the last ten years, patients—and their families—have quite rightly become much more sensitive to the detrimental effects of social 'labelling'. They have also come to demand a much more prominent role in service planning and evaluation and this has resulted in attempts to formulate models of service development which truly involve the key 'stakeholders' (e.g. Kingsley and Towell, 1988). Professionals have thus had to learn to listen much more carefully to the views of service users than perhaps they have done in the past and to recognize that it is not just *what* you provide that is important, but also *how* it is provided. These have been important lessons and are likely to continue to be important themes in the 1990s.

There is one final theoretical development which is worth mentioning and that is the notion that some rehabilitation interventions might themselves be of direct, therapeutic value (Strauss, 1986). The distinction between therapy and rehabilitation is a difficult one (Shepherd, 1991a) but we are accustomed to seeing rehabilitation partly in terms of helping the person to make the 'best of a bad job', rather than actually 'treating' and improving their functioning. As indicated earlier, this is an important aspect of rehabilitation, but as Strauss points out some rehabilitation interventions may actually turn out to have quite powerful, therapeutic effects. For example, interventions which emphasize the importance of helping the person make sense of their experience, help them integrate their functioning, develop strategies to deal with residual symptoms, improve engagement in daily activities, etc., may all be seen quite legitimately as 'treatments' in their own right. A simplistic model of rehabilitation may therefore emphasize its limitations more than is warranted and Strauss concludes that we should not be apologetic that 'we are only doing rehabilitation'.

### Research in Schizophrenia

Rehabilitation is concerned with all those with long-term and disabling psychiatric conditions and, as Bachrach (1988) points out, we have to consider a number of independent criteria (diagnosis, duration and disability) in any attempt to define 'chronic mental illness'. This book contains a discussion of how rehabilitation may be applied to all the major clinical syndromes, but schizophrenia remains the most important. Schizophrenia is the most common diagnosis for long-term patients both in hospital and community settings and I will therefore concentrate on reviewing developments specifically with regard to this disorder. I will examine 'stress' models, the importance of family factors in precipitating relapse, the usefulness of family interventions, the role of social supports, psychological approaches, role functioning and long-term outcome. In the past decade the changing pattern of psychiatric services has meant that the emphasis has shifted more towards the problems of the management of schizophrenia in the community and the research reflects this changing locus of care. It has not, as we shall see, altered many of the fundamental problems posed by the disorder.

Wing's chapter on schizophrenia in this book is a model of clarity and scholarship. He sketches out a view in which biological, psychological and social factors all play their part in aetiology, treatment and management. The biological basis of schizophrenia is progressively becoming clearer: there is a genetic component to the transmission of condition and various prenatal and perinatal (including viral) factors may enhance an individual's later vulnerability to developing the disorder (see Bebbington and McGuffin, 1988, Chapters 8–10). It also seems that the so-called 'positive' symptoms of schizophrenia (hallucinations, delusions, etc.) are almost certainly caused by an overactivity in dopamine receptors, hence the effectiveness of medications which interfere with dopaminergic transmission in controlling these symptoms during the acute phases.

## 'Stress' and Life Events

Notwithstanding the importance of these biological factors, as Wing makes clear, the course and outcome of schizophrenia is also profoundly affected by various psychological and social processes, including life events, family factors, support networks, and the individual's own personal reaction to their condition. There are considerable methodological problems in the study of the relationship between life events and relapse in schizophrenia, particularly in terms of the definition of illness onset, but there is now very strong evidence from studies conducted in a range of different cultures that stressful life events do tend to cluster in the two to three weeks prior to an illness episode (Day *et al.*, 1987). This confirmation of the association between 'stress' and exacerbations in the disorder is an important finding and raises the possibility that psychological 'stress management' programmes, which have proved extremely effective with other disorders, may have something to offer in the prevention or minimization of relapse in schizophrenia (e.g. Tarrier *et al.*, 1988). At present this research is still in its early stages but, at the very least, it is clear that stressful life events, particularly those that imply significant changes to the individual's usual routines, constitute important 'risk markers' and should make the practitioner cautious about imposing additional stresses (e.g. changes in medication, changes in social support networks, etc.) at around the same time. The implications of these 'stress' models of schizophrenia for psychological approaches will be taken up later.

Family Factors

The role of family factors in influencing relapse in schizophrenia is now virtually beyond doubt. In Birley and Hudson's chapter they describe the early studies by Brown and Wing and their colleagues which first showed that patients with schizophrenia who returned to households characterized by high levels of expressed emotions (EE) had a much higher risk of relapse than those returning to families who showed 'low EE'. ('EE' in this context refers to emotional overinvolvement, criticism, or overt hostility expressed by the carer towards the patient. Levels of criticism and hostility are particularly important.) There has been something of an explosion of activity with regard to 'EE' research in the last few years and, despite a few negative findings, these studies have generally confirmed the original conclusions (Kuipers, 1987; Bebbington and Kuipers, 1988; Kuipers and Bebbington, 1988). There has also been impressive cross-cultural validation of the findings. However, there is still controversy regarding the reliability of the EE construct and the precise mechanism through which it exerts its effects (Falloon, 1988; Koenigsberg and Handley, 1986; Parker et al., 1988). Much of this debate revolves around the stability of EE measures. Is 'high EE' an enduring characteristic of certain families, or is it more correctly seen as a short-term response associated with certain clinical changes in the patient? A definitive answer to this question is not possible because no one has yet reported the kind of in-depth, longitudinal studies which would be necessary to examine the detailed course of EE over time. However, the balance of the evidence suggests a more dynamic relationship between 'EE' and patients' functioning than was perhaps implied by the early studies. Two recent papers by Miklowitz et al. (1989) and Strachan et al. (1989) underline the complex, interactional nature of the transactions between carers and patients in families coping with an acute episode of illness. They found that families rated as 'low EE' at the time of the patient's admission were likely to be rated 'low EE' five to six weeks after discharge, whereas families who were 'high EE' at admission were equally likely to be rated high, or low, after discharge. Thus, 'low EE' may reflect a stable positive coping style on the part of the family, whereas 'high EE' may reflect situational stress in some families, but be an index of long-term difficulties in others. The EE ratings of the families also showed interesting parallels in the coping styles of the patients ('benign' or 'negative'). Neither were related to clinical features of the patients. 'EE' therefore remains a fundamentally important concept in the management of schizophrenia, although we do not fully understand how, or why, some families become 'high EE', nor how stable this is over time. Like major life changes, high EE is an important indicator of risk and should alert the practitioner to the enhanced danger of relapse and the need to monitor the situation more closely.

Family Interventions

Alongside the rapid growth in EE research, there has also been an increasing number of reports in recent years of clinical trials aimed at reducing EE and helping families cope better with the difficulties that they face. Few of these studies were available at the time of Birley and Hudson's original chapter, so I will briefly review them here. There is now a considerable body of evidence suggesting that it is possible to provide effective support for families and that this can significantly reduce the patient's risk of symptomatic relapse (Falloon, Boyd and McGill, 1984; Hogarty *et al.*, 1986; Leff *et al.*, 1982; 1985; Tarrier *et al.*, 1988). All these studies use slightly different techiques and some focus exclusively on those patients at highest risk, whereas others do not. Nevertheless, the consensus is clear and, despite the differences in technique, there are some obvious common elements. All the interventions contain a component which is aimed at informing both the patients and their relatives regarding what is known about schizophrenia, aetiological factors, the process of course and outcome, etc. The correct labelling of negative symptoms seems particularly important in this process as families often attribute social withdrawal, lack of interest, etc. to 'personality' rather than to 'illness'. Thus, helping families cope with some of these problems in a non-judgemental, non-critical manner may be a key factor in reducing levels of EE. A 'psychoeducational' approach is clearly useful and may be seen as a potentially effective treatment in its own right (Anderson, Hogarty and Reiss, 1980; Smith and Birchwood, 1987) although it is likely to have relatively limited effects if applied in isolation (Tarrier *et al.*, 1988). Secondly, all the interventions contain some kind of element aimed at improving communication and problem-solving abilities within the families. The approach here varies from study to study, but is mainly of a behavioural, 'social skills' type. The precise technique seems less important than the concerted effort to help families who are having difficulties in solving their interpersonal problems (hence the high EE). Finally, all the studies by their very nature also contain an element of non-specific, emotional support and this is clearly important, although once again it is not sufficient in itself. In one of the most recent studies Leff *et al.* (1989) compared the effect of a family 'therapy' approach with a simple relatives' support group. They concluded that the most cost-effective intervention might be to establish relatives' groups, combined with a few sessions of education, tailored to individual families' needs, and one or two sessions of 'therapy', preferably conducted in the patients' own homes.

These studies therefore provide convincing evidence for the usefulness of a 'family approach' in the management of schizophrenia and modern rehabilitation services should strive to contain such an element (Bernheim, 1982; Kuipers and Bebbington, 1985; Smith and Birchwood, 1990). However, the mechanism whereby such interventions exert their effects is not well understood. From the detailed analysis of the changes observed within families during the course of treatment the most likely explanation of reduced relapse rates is the reduction in levels of EE, but there remain other possibilities. For example, in most of the studies the effect of the family intervention is also to improve levels of engagement by the patient in the existing aftercare services (day care, work activities, etc.) and this will also inevitably produce reductions in levels of face-to-face contact between the patients and their relatives. It is therefore difficult to separate out the effects of reducing EE from the effects of reducing face-to-face contact and both are likely to be beneficial. It has also been suggested that high EE is less powerful as a predictor of relapse if the clinical characteristics of the patients are properly taken into account. Thus, high EE may be simply a reflection of families that are having to cope with the most disturbed patients, rather than being an independent stressor in its own right (MacMillan *et al.*, 1986). This suggestion has caused a degree of controversy (see Bebbington and Kuipers, 1988, pp. 212–214), and the balance of evidence is probably still with original EE formulation, nevertheless some degree of interaction between the patient's condition and levels of EE seems highly probable.

One of the most interesting implications to emerge from the EE literature which has, as yet, received little attention is the notion that EE concepts may be applied with equal validity to interactions between schizophrenic patients and non-family carers. Thus, Goldstein and Caton (1983) present some preliminary evidence that levels of support and criticism in residential care settings were more strongly predictive of relapse rates than was type of living arrangement *per se*. It is also clear from clinical experience that processes like the pejorative 'labelling' of negative symptoms, and increasing levels of hostility due to interpersonal difficulties, are not confined to family settings. They can occur among carers (and patients) in group homes, hostels, and, of course, hospital wards themselves. This opens the intriguing possibility that the kind of interventions developed to deal with high EE families may also have relevance in these kinds of settings. This is a particularly important issue given the increasing involvement of non-professionally trained carers in the community. Whether it is as feasible to create 'low EE' residential care settings, as it is to produce 'low EE' families, remains to be investigated.

## Social Networks and Support

The importance of the individual's network of social support is developed in the chapter by Bennett and Morris. This topic has also become an extremely popular focus of research in recent years across a wide range of psychiatric and physical disorders (Brugha, 1990; House and Landis, 1988; Parry, 1988). However, the concept of 'social support' remains poorly understood and there are a number of unresolved questions, particularly with regard to the most effective dimensions of support in schizophrenia. For example, how important are *subjective* as opposed to *objective* aspects of support networks? Henderson *et al.*'s (1981) work suggests that it may be the former, rather than the latter, which is more strongly associated with positive mental health. Thus, it may be more important to *feel* supported than to have access to a large number of 'friends', few of whom are perceived to be helpful. Conversely, one may feel lonely and unsupported even though 'objectively' there are plenty of friends and social contacts available. If this is also the case in schizophrenia, then it would imply that although people with schizophrenia do tend to have rather impoverished social networks, it may not be useful simply to attempt to extend their range of social contacts without paying close attention to the qualitative nature of these relationships.

What are the most important qualities of effective social support for people with schizophrenia? We have already reviewed one aspect (levels of EE) and seen how important it may be to try and achieve 'low EE' social interactions. However, apart from this very little is known about the beneficial—or harmful—qualities of social support for people with long-term mental illness. What we do know suggests that what is perceived as supportive by one individual may not be perceived as supportive by another. For example, some individuals may benefit from the presence of a close, confiding relationship as in the classic work of Brown and Harris (1978) on the social origins of depression in women. On the other hand, as Bennett and Morris note in their chapter, Mitchell and Birley (1983) found a category of long-term attender for community support who seemed to need 'company *without* intimacy', i.e. non-intrusive, low key, social contact. These tended to be the single, male schizophrenics. A similar point is made by Harris *et al.* (1986) who discuss the range of social support needs observed in long-term patients receiving a case management service in the community. Using the classification developed by Sheets *et al.* (1982), they hypothesize three different sub-groups of patients—'system dependent', 'high energy/high demand', and 'high functioning'. They suggest that the first type is most suited to 'institutional' networks (i.e. those that allow the individual to share physical space with few demands for mutuality or inter-dependency), these are most like the 'company-without-intimacy' group identified by Mitchell and Birley. The second type they suggest is most suited to 'fraternal' networks (i.e. a mix of patient and non-patient members, with high group cohesiveness, but also high peer group pressure). While the third type they suggest requires 'integrated' networks (i.e. a heterogenous mix of people, largely outside the context of psychiatric services, with a variety of interconnections). Harris *et al.* discuss the role of each kind of network and how each may be facilitated. Their ideas are very speculative, but nevertheless they provide some useful indications as to how social support interventions might be tailored more precisely to the needs of individual patients.

This theme is also taken up in a fascinating study by Breier and Strauss (1984) who described the changes in social support needs in a small group ($n = 20$)

patients recovering from a psychotic episode. Their results suggested that during the initial phases of recovery the most important need was for social supports that helped the individual reintegrate their personality and functioning. Hence, ventilation of feelings, reality testing, material help, social approval, problem solving and constancy were the priorities. After this 'convalescence phase', the individual then moved into a 'rebuilding phase' in which motivation, reciprocal relating with others, and monitoring of symptoms became more important. As with Harris *et al.*'s work, the reliability and validity of Breier and Strauss' concepts may be challenged, but they add a potentially important dimension to the complex issue of how to adequately individualize social support interventions. Thus, not only may different people have different social support needs, but these needs may vary within each individual over time. Hence, rehabilitation programmes need to provide not just individualized care, but also care that is carefully monitored and adjusted according to the individual's changing circumstances.

Fostering good social support in order to improve the management of a complex condition like schizophrenia is, of course, based on an implicit assumption that deficiencies in social supports are somehow 'causal' of exacerbations in the disorder and this assumption is debatable. It is not clear whether the observed problems in social networks (qualitative or quantitative) are *causes* or *consequences* of the disorder itself and, given the methodological problems in separating the two sets of concepts, this is perhaps not surprising. Probably the safest conclusion is that they interact with one another. Certainly, it is unlikely that there is a simple, unidirectional relationship between them. One possible hypothesis regarding the relationship between social support and illness is that support acts as a 'buffer' to reduce the effects of undue stress, i.e. social support is most important when the individual is facing adversity of some kind (Alloway and Bebbington, 1987). This has obvious relevance in schizophrenia where, as indicated earlier, the role of stressful life events in precipitating relapse has already been established. Improving social supports may therefore serve to protect the person with schizophrenia, especially when they are also subject to excessive life change, or adverse life events.

Psychological Approaches

Improving social support must depend, at least to some extent, on improving the social and interpersonal skills of the patient himself or herself. Hence, we may now turn to questions of the effectiveness of various kinds of skills training approaches in rehabilitation. Skills training is a very important element of most rehabilitation programmes (particularly in the United States) and the range of skills-based treatment packages is continually proliferating. However, the fundamental problems with skills training still remain, particularly the issues of individualization of care and of 'generalization', i.e. transferring improvements outside the immediate treatment setting (see Liberman *et al.*, 1986; 1987; Shepherd, 1983; 1988c). Liberman *et al.*, (1987) put it like this, 'while it has been amply demonstrated that behavioural training produces incremental improvements in social competence, the data are far less convincing that such interpersonal strengthening actually reduces the probability of relapse or symptom exacerbation and increases community tenure and quality of life'. I tried to address this issue in one of my own chapters in this book ('Interpersonal Relationships') and suggested that the main strategy for improving generalization is an attempt to make the treatment setting as much like 'ordinary life' as possible. The more artificial the setting, the less likely improvements are to transfer. Making the treatment sessions more 'real' may mean varying their time and place, conducting more sessions *in vivo*, placing a greater emphasis on 'homework' assignments, etc. But, fundamentally, it means being prepared to work 'backwards' from the problems of the client's everyday life in order to identify which skills are most relevant and important rather than starting out *a priori* with a number of assumptions about what skills he or she needs to survive (Shepherd, 1990). This 'criterion-oriented' approach thus solves the problem of generalization by working around it, and implies that skills training is only going to be useful when it is already clear how, and where, the person is going to be able to use their new skills. The principles of working directly in the community, and of individualizing care as much as possible, have thus led away from the application of traditional, ward-based programmes (see the chapter by Hall) towards the kind of more radical, individually-centred, community programmes mentioned earlier (e.g. Stein and Test, 1985; Hoult, 1986) and these have proved extremely effective. It should be noted they do *not* generally use a formal skills training approach; whether the introduction of skills training technology would actually add anything to their effectiveness remains an interesting question.

For the future, skills training clearly still has a place in the treatment and rehabilitation of people with schizophrenia, but it should be used rather more critically than has been the case in the past. Again, as I tried to make clear in my chapter, successful social functioning doesn't only depend upon the possession of certain skills, it also depends on motivation, judgement and flexibility, regarding when and how to deploy those skills. These more 'cognitive' factors are still somewhat neglected in the skills training literature. There have been attempts to provide more rigorous experimental investigations of the cognitive deficits associated with schizophrenia (e.g. Spaulding *et al.*, 1986), but as yet these have yielded little of very practical value. Similarly, there have been attempts to train patients directly in perceptual, decision-making, or general 'problem solving' skills (Hollin and Trower, 1986), but again the effects have been rather limited. While the importance of cognitive factors in determining skills difficulties are clearly acknowledged, our ability to significantly influence them through psychological means therefore remains severely restricted.

Nevertheless, the recognition of the crucial importance of these factors represents a considerable shift in thinking compared with 10 years ago. There has also been a much more explicit recognition of the active contribution of the patient himself or herself to monitoring and adjusting their own performance in the light of changes in the social environment. Skills training can therefore no longer be seen as something that is done *to* the person in a static, or stable, environment. It is something that must be done *with* the person, and in recognition of the need to continually monitor and adjust the input according to a changing situation. Once again the dynamic nature of adaptation, and the limitations of 'throughput' models, are highlighted.

The interest in 'cognitive behavioural' approaches marks a more general shift within clinical psychology and has produced a number of attempts to apply psychological interventions directly to the treatment of psychotic symptoms (Hemsley, 1985; Heinrichs, 1988; Birchwood, Hallett and Preston, 1988, Chapter 17). These approaches reflect a fundamental assumption that it is possible to apply techniques which are standard in the treatment of neurosis (e.g. anxiety management, cognitive behaviour therapy, etc.), to people who are suffering with psychotic disorders. They have paved the way for attempts to encourage the patient to become much more actively involved in the management of his or her own condition through 'self-monitoring' and 'self-control' techniques. Thus, researchers such as Falloon and Talbot (1981), Breier and Strauss (1983) and Tarrier (1987) have identified stimulus 'triggers', habitual responses, and spontaneous coping strategies which are commonly used by psychotic patients to deal with fluctuating levels of positive symptoms. Apart from the fascinating (and rather humbling) insights that these data give into the experiences of people living with psychosis, a number of important general conclusions emerge. For example, a significant proportion of the patients reported quite clear stimulus antecedents to their psychotic symptoms and also some degree of 'self control' over their effects. These 'self control' devices consisted of various psychological and social 'interventions' such as self-instruction, relaxation, distraction, etc., and the choice of strategies seemed highly idiosyncratic, i.e. two different people might employ totally contradictory strategies to deal with the same kind of symptomatic problem. In general, the more strategies employed by a given individual the more likely they are to be of benefit. This kind of information is now beginning to be used to build up careful, highly individualized, programmes for symptom control, based on personal coping strategies (e.g. Fowler and Morley, 1989). The results are very much at a preliminary stage, but they represent an interesting new development.

Of course, such an approach will not be feasible with all patients, neither is it yet established that 'self control' strategies will actually be effective in postponing or preventing relapse. Nevertheless, even if they turned out to be only partially effective, they would still mark a radical shift in our thinking about the management of schizophrenia. It makes the problems of managing schizophrenia much more like the problems of managing a chronic physical condition like diabetes or coronary heart disease, where the aim is to help the sufferer, wherever possible, to take responsibility for managing their *own* condition with, of course, the assistance of appropriate professional back-up. We have seemed reluctant to use this approach in psychiatry, often claiming that it would only harm, or distress people to talk to them directly about 'schizophrenia'. People with schizophrenia lack 'insight', so it is said, and hence it is unrealistic to ask them to take responsibility for managing their own condition. There is some truth in these statements, but the reality is that we have made very little effort to provide schizophrenic patients with the information and support that they would require in order to take responsibility for managing their own conditions, even some of the time. It is also worth remembering that lack of 'insight', 'irresponsibility' and failure to heed professional advice, are not unknown among people with chronic physical conditions, yet this does not deter us from attempting to involve them as fully as possible in the management of their own conditions. Patients (and their families) remain the greatest experts on their conditions and the most important allies in their treatment. Perhaps there are other reasons why we have been so reluctant to share our knowledge with those who have potentially the most to benefit; if so one may hope that these attitudes will change over the next few years.

## Occupational Functioning and Long-term Outcome

The final area we need to consider is occupational functioning and its implications for long-term outcome in schizophrenia. The long-term outcome of schizophrenia is largely dependent on the successful treatment and management of the so-called 'negative' symptoms and this has emerged as an important area in its own right (Shepherd, 1988b). This book is unusual in devoting four chapters to a specific discussion of the importance of social roles, including one by Fraser Watts on 'Employment'. These chapters reflect the general orientation towards a 'functional', rather than a 'symptomatic', perspective. Successful social adaptation depends upon the person's ability to function in key social roles (friend, partner, worker, parent, etc.), and social and occupational functioning are of central importance. We have already discussed the importance of social support and attempts to make quantitative and/or qualitative improvements in people's social networks, but by contrast to the explosion of interest in families and social support, attempts to improve occupational functioning remain a somewhat neglected field. Morgan's chapter on industrial therapy in the mental hospital unfortunately reflects what is now largely a forgotten era. As services have moved away from the mental hospital, so the traditional, hospital-based, workshops have closed and often nothing has been put in their place. Work is still as important as it ever was in the rehabilitation of people with long-term mental health problems (Pilling, 1988; Shepherd, 1989b) but the opportunities to work, especially for the most disabled clients, are probably less now than when the book was first written. Of course, there are examples of innovative and exciting work projects in the community and of 'transitional employment' schemes (i.e. temporary or part-time placements for psychiatrically disabled people in open employment settings) but the provision of work opportunities for people recovering from mental illness is generally poor and often extremely uneven. Some of the reasons why this might be so emerge in a paper by Harding *et al.* (1987) where they report on a survey of staff and client attitudes in vocational rehabilitation facilities in New Haven (Connecticut). They identify a range of issues giving rise to problems including low status, conflicting priorities, poor support, etc. Most importantly, they note the clash of cultures between 'clinically-oriented' and 'work-oriented' professionals. They suggest that the former tend to give priority to the treatment of pathology, viewing work as just occupation, while the latter tend to be more interested in people's abilities and view work as of direct, therapeutic value. This brings us back to the debate on the relationship between 'therapy' and 'rehabilitation' mentioned earlier and to the possibility of conflict, rather than complementarity, between 'symptomatic' and 'functional' perspectives. Harding *et al.* conclude with a plea for a more integrated approach which takes due account of both clinical *and* functional needs. How this might be achieved will be addressed later when we consider developments in service provision.

Before ending this section, I will briefly review some of the recent studies on the long-term outcome of schizophrenia since these confirm the central importance of role functioning and provide a useful context within which the effect of rehabilitation may be evaluated. McGlashan (1988) and Angst (1988) provide excellent summaries of these studies in the United States and Europe respectively. They note some difficulties in interpretation due to inconsistencies in diagnosis, but a number of common findings emerge. For example, the importance of certain well-established prognosic factors (age of onset, gender, levels of premorbid functioning) are confirmed, as are the historical continuities in functioning first identified by Strauss *et al.* (1977). Some new variables (e.g. treatment resistance to conventional medication) also seem to be important prognostically. Most importantly, the myth of schizophrenia as 'dementia praecox' is finally destroyed. People with schizophrenia do *not* show an inevitable, progressive deterioration in functioning. Although it is a chronic and disabling condition, and the outcome does tend to be worse than in most other psychiatric disorders, with higher mortality and physical morbidity, nevertheless the outcome is still highly variable. There is also quite strong evidence that the positive symptoms themselves tend to 'burn out', or at least to plateau, some 5 to 10 years after the condition first appears.

These long-term studies also confirm the influence of socio-cultural factors on outcome. It has already been established that the outcome of schizophrenia tends to be more favourable in 'developing', as opposed to 'developed' countries (World Health Organization, 1979) and most of the speculation as to why this should be so centres around the increased occupational opportunities and social support networks that might be available in such cultures (Cooper and Sartorius, 1977; Warner, 1985). Just as outcome is affected by such factors across cultures, so there is also strong evidence that it is similarly affected *within* different cultures over time. Thus, McGlashan notes (p. 532) that the outcome in small, urban settings, where there was greater incentive — and greater opportunity for employment — was superior to that in inner city settings, where obtaining and keeping work was more difficult. Small, stable communities offer a better base for providing continuity of care and this also clearly makes a difference. However, McGlashan emphasizes the importance of 'stable and unlimited' continuity of care if it is to be really effective. Such is the nature of good rehabilitation services. Recovery from schizophrenia thus depends on a process of social reintegration, which in turn depends not only on the person's abilities with regard to social role performance, but also on the opportunities offered for social role functioning by a particular culture. What we need to do now is to review the range of services that might be required to help people achieve their potential for social reintegration and then to maintain it.

### The Changing Pattern of Psychiatric Services

Since this book first appeared the overall pattern of psychiatric services in most countries has continued to change quite substantially. Douglas Bennett describes in his chapter on 'The Historical Development of Rehabilitation Services' some of the developments that occurred in mental hospitals after the Second World War. In the last 10 years, most countries have continued to move away from a dependence on the mental hospital — particularly as a locus for long-term care — and towards a more community based pattern of provisions. Thus, between 1960 and 1985 there was a reduction in beds in mental hospitals in the United Kingdom and Italy of around 50 per cent, and in the United States a reduction of almost 80 per cent (Jones, 1988, p. 101). This policy has been the subject of considerable controversy. All over the world, voices have been raised objecting that 'community care' too often means 'community neglect' and that hospitals cannot, and should not, be closed until an adequate range of services exists to replace them. Governments have been accused of using community care simply as a device to reduce public expenditure in the light of ever increasing health service budgets and families have been suspicious that all community care means for them is greater burdens with less help. These criticisms often contain more than a grain of truth. The adequacy of community care varies greatly both within and between countries and it is difficult to generalize; nevertheless the dramatic reduction in mental hospital provision has not usually been matched by a commensurate increase in good quality community services. Despite the existence of clear descriptions of 'model programmes' (Bachrach, 1980) and a wealth of guidance contained in a variety of policy statements and planning documents (e.g. DHSS, 1975; 1985; MIND, 1983, Brown and Parrish, 1987; Pepper, 1987; Turner and TenHoor, 1978) 'deinstitutionalization' has often led to long-stay patients simply being moved from large institutions in hospitals to small institutions in the community (Goldman, 1983; Audit Commission, 1986). Worse still, some have found themselves excluded from services altogether and ended up in shelters for the homeless, prisons, or the streets. Where community services have been developed, they have often not been targeted on those in greatest need and have failed to provide an effective alternative for those who have been most affected by the reduction in mental hospital provision (Mollica, 1983).

The reasons for these apparent failures are complex. Obviously, lack of resourcing plays a part, although it is often the case that it is not so much an absolute shortage of money, but a difficulty in transferring money from one service system to another (Mechanic and Aiken, 1987; Mangen, 1988). Professional attitudes and training are also important and, as we have seen already, it is often difficult to foster a positive attitude towards working with the long-term mentally ill. Within traditional service systems established ways of working also die hard and large institutions have an inherent conservatism which makes change difficult and slow. In our 'quick fix' culture there are few individuals who are prepared to put in the considerable time and effort required to build up new services and even fewer managers and administrators who are prepared to wait around for the results. This means that, despite the many theoretical descriptions of 'model programmes', there are relatively few good, working examples. Without being able to *see* effective community services in action, it is difficult to convince sceptical professionals (and managers) of their value. Without many working examples it is also difficult to train new staff.

But times do seem to be changing. Recently, there have been a number of reviews which appear to give community care a cautious, though guarded, welcome (e.g. Bachrach and Lamb, 1989; Mulkern and Manderscheid, 1989; Thornicroft and Bebbington, 1989). These papers are still quite critical, but they acknowledge some of the successes, as well as documenting the failures, of community programmes. They also attempt, in a constructive way, to identify some of the lessons that have emerged from the experiences so far. Thus, it does seem possible to provide services for the most disabled patients in the community, but it is not easy. In addition to all the usual range of facilities (hostels, group homes, workshops, day services, family supports, etc.) there also need to be effective mechanisms for coordinating and monitoring care and for integrating administrative and financial structures at a local level. If all these are present, community care can work and there is quite strong evidence that both patients and their families prefer to be treated in the community, rather than in hospital. There has also been a reevaluation of the need for 'asylum' for small numbers of long stay patients and some interesting ideas about the role of brief, inpatient admission in the management of long-term patients in the community. We shall now examine some of these issues in greater detail, beginning with the future of the mental hospital itself.

## The Future of the Hospital

In the UK, as in many other countries, the large, old mental hospitals have become increasingly uneconomic to run. Inpatient numbers have reduced, but staffing levels and running costs have continued to be high and thus the 'unit costs' (i.e. costs per patient) have steadily increased. Given that the policy was meant to increase the money spent on community services, this is somewhat ironic. The rundown of the mental hospitals has also resulted in a concentration of morbidity among the remaining residents. As the less severely disabled patients have been 'creamed off', so those remaining are increasingly elderly, with many years of institutional life behind them. They often become socially isolated, and have high rates of physical, as well as psychiatric, problems (e.g. Levene *et al.*, 1985; Ford *et al.*, 1987; Shepherd, 1989c). Resettlement of this population in the community is difficult because of the complex range of services that they require with high levels of supervision, intensive rehabilitation, access to day care, social supports, etc. As people have grappled with these problems of providing for the 'old' long-stay, two different kinds of solutions have emerged.

The first we may call a 'dispersed' model. This is probably the most common approach and attempts to provide care in a number of small units, usually using conversions of ordinary housing, dispersed throughout the community, with a number of different agencies (hospital, social services, voluntary sector and private) involved. The advantages claimed are that smaller units will lead to greater individualization of care; a wider range of agencies will involve more non-professional staff, thus reducing the danger of 'institutional' practices; and that the service will offer greater integration and accessibility to the community, thus enhancing the 'image' of the chronic mental patient and reducing stigma. The disadvantages are the high initial capital costs; the potential problems with community resistance to setting up residential projects for large numbers of patients (often resulting in the creation of 'psychiatric ghettos' in areas where low cost housing is available); the high revenue costs to run such a service because of the diseconomies of scale resulting from the small size of units; the problems of staff training and support; and variability in the standards of care, with the accompanying dangers of creating isolated, 'mini-institutions' in the community.

On the other hand, a 'centralized' option aims to redevelop domestic scale housing on an existing hospital site, with the additional introduction of other community facilities, e.g. shops, library, leisure amenities, etc. (see Wing and Furlong, 1986; Jones, 1988, pp. 146–150). The advantages claimed for a centralized approach are the relatively low initial capital costs (because the land is usually already owned by the hospital); the potential economies of scale, both with regard to staffing and support services (e.g. day facilities); the deployment of an existing pool of experienced and committed staff; and community acceptance, because of a longstanding psychiatric presence on the site. The disadvantages are the strong sense of stigma and negative social value associated with mental hospital sites; the dangers of a loss of individuality due to large size; the perpetuation of traditional institutional practices due to the presence of old-fashioned staff attitudes; and the lack of accessibility and remoteness of some mental hospitals.

Both models therefore have their advantages and disadvantages and both merit consideration depending on local factors such as the availability and price of land and housing, public transport facilities, the siting of the existing mental hospital, etc. Unfortunately, there is very little empirical evidence which would allow one to choose between the two. Of course, the choice may be constrained by financial considerations, since both options obviously involve considerable capital investment (this may be easier to schedule with the centralized model). There are particular dangers with the 'centralized' model, since it is tempting to use the mental hospital site just because it is available. Good quality provision in the community will be expensive to establish and maintain, but there are significant advantages. However, providing the mental hospital site is not too remote, and the capital can be found for new buildings, then small, domestic scale accommodation can be built on existing sites and 'good' institutions may be created from 'bad'. Despite the dangers of expediency, given the hasty and badly planned way in which many hospitals have already been run down, a careful reconsideration of the merits of centralized redevelopment is not a bad thing. As a House of Commons Select Committee report commented, 'We recommend that no mental illness or mental handicap hospital site be disposed of without explicit consideration being given to the possible redevelopment of suitable parts for mental disability services, and that any redevelopment should have to be justifiable solely on the intrinsic merits of the proposals, and not rely simply on the availability of the land' (House of Commons, 1985, para. 208). We may hope that the problem of how to care for large numbers of 'old' long-stay patients will not recur in the future.

## The Care of the 'New' Long-stay

Despite the growth in community services, small numbers of patients continue to accumulate who appear to need a level of resources and professional expertise which is usually only found in hospital wards. These patients are evident in most countries, although their numbers vary considerably depending on local practices and the availability of alternative provisions in the community. In Britain, the 'new' long-stay (NLS) and are usually defined as: (a) aged between 18 and 65,

(b) continuously in hospital for between 1 and 5 years, and (c) individuals for whom it has not been possible to find alternative accommodation outside hospital, despite repeated attempts to do so. They are thus distinguished from the 'old' long-stay patients by the fact that their periods of continuous hospitalization are of relatively recent origin and from other long-term patients, most of whom are maintained in the community, by the fact that they remain in hospital for long periods of time, despite repeated efforts to discharge them. Average prevalence rates tend to be around 15–20 per 100 000 (Jennings, 1982). Clinically, they tend to be a fairly heterogenous group. Typically they have poorly controlled symptomatology—most commonly schizophrenia—they show disruptive behaviour and high levels of dependency, with considerable social disabilities. A detailed report of their clinical and social characteristics has been provided in a national survey by Mann and Cree (1976).

In both the UK and the US a number of reports have appeared in the last few years of attempts to provide a specialized service for such patients (e.g. Lehman et al., 1987; Bedell and Ward, 1989) but the best developed concept is probably the British 'ward-in-a-house' or 'hospital hostel' model (Bennett, 1980). This attempts to combine the best features of high quality hospital care (e.g. good staffing levels, well-trained professionals, highly individualized programmes, etc.) with the best features of community-based residential units (e.g. small, 'non-institutional' in appearance, easy access to public amenities, etc.). Furthermore, it provides care for as long as the individual requires it, if necessary indefinitely. It was designed to provide a new model for the mental hospital of the future: small, personalized, and integrated with the local community, instead of being large, impersonal and remote.

Three of these new facilities have now been established and each has been carefully evaluated (Garety et al., 1988; Gibbons, 1986; Gibbons and Butler, 1987; Goldberg et al., 1985; Hyde et al., 1987; Wykes, 1982; 1983). All the units deal exclusively and specifically with the new long-stay as defined above. They are all relatively well-staffed, with the full range of psychiatric professionals, including psychiatrists, psychologists, nurses and occupational therapists. All the patients receive intensive and highly individualized care in a setting which resembles an ordinary home as much as possible where an attempt is made to be flexible and to arrange routines and practices so that they reflect the needs of the residents, rather than the needs of the organization. Residents are generally given much greater responsibility for choosing how they will live and what they will do compared with a traditional hospital ward, but alongside this greater responsibility and freedom, greater demands are also made and each resident is given an individual programme with carefully structured staff attention and encouragement to help them meet these expectations. Contact with the community is encouraged and residents may visit local shops, cafes, pubs, etc. alone, or accompanied if necessary. In all the units it is accepted that the rates of progress may be slow and that for some patients this may be their permanent home.

The units obviously differ quite a lot in size—from around 12 to 20 places. They also differ in location, with two being very close to the hospital and one being rather further away. The detailed mode of operation also varies slightly with greater or lesser emphasis being placed on carrying out general tasks within the house itself as opposed to leaving the house to attend day care in the local community. It is possible to summarize the outcome data as follows:

(1) All the units seem to be effective in improving the social functioning and activity levels of residents compared with matched controls receiving care on a general acute admission ward or in a traditional mental hospital.

(2) 'Negative' symptoms of schizophrenia (social withdrawal, apathy, poor motivation) show more improvement than 'positive' symptoms (delusions, hallucinations, etc.).

(3) Residents have more contact with the community than do controls.

(4) Residents (and their families) tend to report greater satisfaction with their living situation than do controls.

(5) Most rapid improvement tends to occur within the first 6 months and continue up to 3 years. After that the rate of improvement slows down, although the initial gains are maintained.

(6) A proportion of residents (up to 50 per cent) may gain sufficient independence to move on to a less intensively staffed setting, but this may take up to 3 years.

(7) In terms of the process of care, the individual programmes seem to be effective in promoting high levels of staff–patient interaction and high levels of client engagement in structured activities, with conversely low levels of time spent doing nothing.

(8) The costs of the units compare favourably with keeping the patients on a general acute admission ward, but they are probably more costly than traditional mental hospitals.

(9) A greater proportion of the costs are spent on direct, 'therapeutic' activities, i.e. less goes on 'indirect' services such as catering, cleaning, administration, etc.

(10) Not all new long-stay patients are suitable for care in these kinds of settings and some (approx. 10 per cent) have to be returned to the mental hospital because they are too disruptive, or because they find the situation too demanding. These individuals tend to show particularly high levels of dangerous, 'acting out' behaviour.

Thus, the 'ward-in-a-house' concept seems to be effective in creating a new kind of 'asylum' for the small number of new long-stay patients for whom other kinds of residential care do not seem to be an option. At the same time, these units are effective in maintaining—sometimes even improving—functioning and not isolating patients from the demands and routines of ordinary life. There are a number of ways in which this can be achieved, but the common elements seem to be the application of detailed, individual programmes in a high quality, small, non-institutional setting. Under such conditions, even the most disabled patients can improve with regard to their social functioning, even though they may remain symptomatically quite active. Of course, the 'ward-in-a-house' is not a panacea. Some patients are unable to respond to the degree of structure and the closeness of ordinary community life—although these are a minority. The units are expensive to run, but they are cost-effective if a sufficiently long-term view is taken. They are not an easy solution, but they do provide hope for some of the most severely disabled, young patients.

## Inpatient Care for the Long-term Mentally Ill

Most long-term patients can be maintained for most of the time in the community. However, even in the best community services some patients will suffer relapses from time to time which will necessitate admission to hospital (or something very like it). The community-based treatment programmes of Stein and Test (1985) and Hoult (1986) mentioned earlier still make some use of inpatient admissions. For example, in Hoult's study 40 per cent of the community treatment group were initially admitted to hospital (compared with 96 per cent of controls). But, over the twelve months of the study, the experimental group spent on average only 8.4 days in hospital, compared with 53.5 days for the controls. Inpatient care is still used therefore, but it is minimized. To achieve this minimal use of inpatient care requires not only assertive, 'outreach' work by a highly flexible and well organized staff team, but also very close cooperation from the inpatient units themselves. A useful model for the organization of inpatient and outpatient services has been suggested by Tyrer (1985). He makes an analogy between a psychiatric service and a beehive: the hospital base should thus be sited within easy reach of a well-defined catchment area with sub-units (day hospitals, community mental health centres, etc.) actually located within the areas themselves. Then, psychiatric workers—like the bee—may spend most of their time in the community, working with clients in their own environment, but not losing their contact with their home base (the 'hive'). In this way the worker continues to have access to a wide range of treatment options (everything from simple counselling to hospital admission) and avoids the situation of isolated 'crisis teams' who have no option but to keep people in the community. In places where there are well-developed 'community treatment' services, experience suggests that it is still then necessary to set up specialized teams to deal with the most severely mentally ill (Hoult, 1990, personal communication).

When long term patients are admitted to hospital, we must be very clear about what can, and cannot, be achieved. Lamb (1988) discusses the aims and opportunities of inpatient· care and suggests that the first task is to help the patient (and their relatives) to understand why the admission has been necessary and how he or she can best be prepared for life outside the hospital. From the beginning the emphasis is therefore on how the admission can be used to improve and maintain adaptation in the community. Next, there is the goal of symptom stabilization—this usually involves adjustments to medication—combined with individual counselling to deal with personal problems and those of a practical nature. Lamb recommends concentrating on 'here-and-now' issues and not aiming to achieve major personality changes. He also stresses the usefulness of 'third party' informants, not only for the light that they can shed on the reasons for admission, but also because of their help in making realistic plans for discharge. He recommends that once the individual discharge plans have been formulated, they should be followed up by regular liaison meetings with the patient's family (where appropriate) and with other community agencies.

Of course, in some cases inpatient admission can be avoided by using a day hospital facility and there has been considerable interest in recent years in 'acute' day treatment (see Rosie, 1987; Holloway, 1988; Creed et al., 1989; Shepherd, 1989a; 1991b, in press). It is generally agreed that day hospitals can provide an effective alternative to admission for a significant number of selected cases. Admission to a day facility can also substantially reduce lengths of inpatient admissions. Social functioning tends to be better in patients treated in a day setting and day care is generally less expensive than inpatient care, although as it tends to go on longer costs may converge over time. Day care is therefore useful as an alternative to admission in certain cases, but it is *not* a substitute for inpatient care. The limits of day care have really yet to be fully explored and it remains a rather under-used option.

One of the problems which still persists is the relationship of acute day treatment settings to inpatient facilities and here the work of Gudeman and his colleagues (Gudeman et al., 1983; Gudeman and Shore, 1984) is interesting. They describe a service where both elements work closely together, two day hospitals provide the core of the service, with back-up from either a small, fully staffed, intensive treatment unit, or a minimally staffed dormitory hostel (the 'Inn'). All patients are admitted initially direct to the day hospital programme where their needs are assessed by a comprehensive, multidisciplinary team. If they require more intensive, highly supervised care they can be transferred to the intensive treatment unit, although their care remains the responsibility of the day hospital team. If not, then they remain in the day hospital. The 'Inn' facility offers social care for people who require respite, or 'time out' from a difficult living situation, but who do not really need intensive treatment in hospital. The authors claim that this system ensures better continuity of care and, by emphasizing the provision of primary treatment in the day hospital, discourages dependency on inpatient care. They present some data to support the notion that these arrangements can reduce the use of inpatient care by almost two-thirds, while increasing the numbers in day care by about the same amount. Most of the patients (approximately 80 per cent) needed inpatient admission at some time, but the mean length of stay was only 9.9 days (and 22.7 days in the day hospital). These changes led to savings in staff costs of around 13 per cent. Gudeman *et al.*'s work thus provides an interesting complement to the direct, community based treatment of Stein and Hoult and others. It shows how unnecessary admissions can be avoided, and lengths of admission limited by an integrated system which encourages close working between inpatient and community teams. All these approaches change the traditional balance between hospital and community services so that the hospital becomes a back-up to the community, rather than the other way around. The continuity of clinical responsibility across community and inpatient settings seems to be the key organizational factor in enabling this to occur.

## Residential and Day Care Facilities in the Community

Most people are now agreed that a comprehensive range of residential provisions, preferably in the form of ordinary housing stock, is a vital element in community services for the long term mentally ill (Lovett, 1984; Carling and Ridgeway, 1985; Garety, 1988). These reviews stress the need for a range of different levels of supervision to cater for different levels of dependency and the need to strike a balance between 'transitional' housing, where the client is meant to gain in independence and eventually move on to less supported accommodation, and permanent placements that the person can really regard as their home. In the past, there has often been a tendency to underestimate patients' needs for supervision and overestimate their abilities to improve. This can lead to an excess of low dependency, transitional housing and a shortage of high dependency, permanent places. If this becomes the case, then there is a danger that those with the greatest difficulties, and the least 'potential', will not be accepted by the community services and will be forced to remain in hospital.

Evaluative studies of residential provisions are rare, but there are now one or two studies in the literature demonstrating that it is possible to collect systematic self-reports on clients' subjective 'quality of life' (Lehman, 1982; Simpson *et al.*, 1989). Asking clients directly can often yield some important, though sometimes not very surprising, conclusions. For example, a strong preference for greater choice and more independent housing, rather than placement in various kinds of group living situation with very little consultation (Kay and Legg, 1986). Some attention has also been given to trying to identify those aspects of care practices and organization which seem most strongly associated with favourable outcomes in terms of residents' functioning. The work of Garety and Morris (1984) and Allen *et al.* (1989), which was mentioned at the beginning has reinforced the importance of individually-centred programmes of care and high levels of good quality (i.e. 'warm') staff–resident interactions. In addition, a large-scale survey by Nagy *et al.* (1988) of more than two hundred board and care homes in the United States suggested that small units (less than 15 residents), high staffing ratios, and a non-profit orientation, were most strongly associated with high levels of residents' participation in everyday routines and productive activities. These relationships held even after statistical adjustments for age and level of social impairment.

The importance of good quality housing provision has been highlighted by the attention that has been focused recently on the problems of mental illness among the homeless. This has received particular prominence in the United States (Baxter and Hopper, 1984; Lamb, 1984) and also, to a lesser extent, in the UK (Weller, 1989). The relationship between the policies of hospital rundown and mental illness among the homeless is a controversial one. On balance, there does not seem to be strong evidence that the reduction in mental hospital beds is directly related to an increasing number of mentally ill people among the homeless — if, indeed, such an increase can actually be proven. Except perhaps in certain specific areas (mainly inner cities) the clinical characteristics of those who are identified as mentally ill among the homeless are quite different from the characteristics of the 'old' long-stay patients who form the bulk of those who have been discharged as a result of the rundown of the mental hospitals. As we noted earlier, their fate is more likely to have been 'transinstitutionalization', or death. What is more likely is that mental illness among the homeless reflects reduced numbers of acute admission beds and inadequate follow-up arrangements after discharge (the so-called 'revolving door' syndrome). Of course, it could be argued that a major reason why the 'revolving door' is revolving so fast is that there is an overall shortage of long-stay inpatient beds. It may also be the case that hospitals are less willing to accept difficult and disturbed patients nowadays and thus they tend to end up in prisons or night shelters and are dealt with by the criminal justice system, rather than the health system (Coid, 1988). For these people, their problem is that they cannot get *in* to hospital, rather than that they have been turned out. But, fundamentally, the problem of the homeless is that they don't have homes. Neither do they have stable incomes, or sufficient financial support to manage their lives at a reasonable level. Long-term mental illness is, by its nature, often strongly associated with poverty and hence any increase of mental illness among the homeless is most likely to be attributable to changes in housing and welfare policies, rather than to changes in mental illness policies *per se*.

Finally, we must consider various kinds of long-term day support in the community. It is important to distinguish between different kinds of day care since they may be used for very different purposes (Shepherd, 1989a). In particular, the division between short term, 'treatment oriented' day hospitals and longer term, social and vocational support in day *centres* or other community projects is crucial (Rosie, 1987). In general, day services are often poorly developed and tend to be unevenly distributed within countries and this can lead to a situation where people are being kept as 'patients' in treatment oriented day hospitals, when what they need is longer term day supports which will foster their social reintegration. As well as considering what kind of day care is required, we must also try to match the content of specific day programmes to the individual client's needs. (This is a theme in my chapter 'Planning the Rehabilitation of the Individual'.) There are actually very few studies which try to do this, probably the most well known is Linn *et al.* (1979) which found that programmes offering a predominance of work and other structured activities—as opposed to 'therapy'—seemed most successful in maintaining the functioning of people with schizophrenia. This should not be surprising as we noted earlier the important psychological and social benefits of vocational rehabilitation in schizophrenia (Bennett, 1978).

There are a number of new ideas which are now around in the day care field which entail a move away from traditional day centres or sheltered workshops towards much smaller, more flexible projects, offering real work and/or a range of social supports which are more closely integrated into the local community (Patmore, 1987). For example, in Europe there is now a network of 'self-help' firms and cooperatives offering a wide range of products and services covering everything from horticulture, to printing, to manufacturing and selling toys, managing a 'city farm' and running a restaurant (FAF, 1989). Likewise, there are examples of 'drop in' clubs, 'befriending' schemes, cooperative projects with local churches, work with voluntary groups, etc. to provide a range of opportunities for integrated social support for people with long term mental illness. But, integration is not an 'all-or-nothing' phenomenon, i.e. the client may be partially integrated and use some community facilities open to non-disabled citizens, together with some specific, 'psychiatric' supports. Probably the best example of a mixture of integrated and specialized social support is the 'Fountain House', or 'clubhouse' model (Beard *et al.*, 1982). In the clubhouse, each person participates as a member on equal terms. There are paid staff, but members contribute to the club's activities through their participation in various work activities, particularly the preparation and serving of food to other members. Everyone in the club has an opportunity to work, though nobody is forced to. Thus, everyone has an important role to play and everyone is 'needed'. For those who wish to progress beyond the club, part-time 'transitional employment' positions are available with local firms and the member can gradually gain confidence until they feel ready to take on a full-time, paid job. The clubhouse is then always there in the background to provide social support while the person attempts to resume their roles in the everyday world. The clubhouse model is an outstanding example of a community based rehabilitation service which provides both social and vocational support, in integrated and special settings. It has formed a model for psychosocial rehabilitation services all over the world.

Case Management

Modern, community-based rehabilitation services are likely to consist of a number of different elements, provided by a number of different agencies, on a number of different sites. Some kind of mechanism for coordinating and maintaining continuity of care is therefore necessary. 'Case management' has emerged as one possible solution, but like many good ideas it has risked being 'oversold' and then rejected as people become disillusioned because it has failed to live up to expectations. In particular, the need for case management has often been confused with the need to provide an adequate range of community based provisions. Case management is simply a device for improving the coordination and monitoring of services, it cannot be seen as a substitute for the services themselves.

The classic description of the elements of a case management approach is to be found in Intagliata (1982). He lists six main components.

(1) A comprehensive assessment of individual needs.
(2) The development of an individualized 'package' of care to meet those needs.
(3) Ensuring that the individual gains access to these services — this may entail considerable 'outreach' work, i.e. going along with the client to the housing, or social security office, or day centre to ensure that they are able to actually obtain whatever service they need and that it conforms, as far as possible, to their expressed wishes and desires. (There is thus an element which lays emphasis on the value of 'consumer choice' in determining service provision.)
(4) Monitoring the quality of services provided and liaising with service providers if the quality or content of services does not meet what is required and, if necessary, attempting to change them, i.e. case managers may be 'proactive' in actually changing and shaping services.
(5) Adjusting levels of support according to fluctuating levels of functioning.
(6) Providing long-term commitment.

The underlying concept is therefore of one agency, usually presumed to be a single individual, who has a clearly defined responsibility to provide individualized, long-term care, in a flexible and sensitive manner. The case manager coordinates the inputs of a number of different agencies, provides consistency and commitment, and acts as an advocate on behalf of the client (and their family) to ensure that they receive the right 'package' of services. He or she also monitors the quality of services provided and ensures that continuity is maintained over time. A more recent discussion of the definition, principles and components of a case management approach is to be found in Kanter (1989).

There is only a relatively small amount of empirical evidence which addresses the question of the effectiveness of case management systems and much of this is contradictory. Thus, Franklin *et al.* (1987) evaluated a generalist approach to case management and compared it with traditional aftercare services. They found that those patients in the case management programme received more services, cost more to maintain, and had higher relapse rates, but there were no increases in assessed quality of life. Similarly, Cutler *et al.* (1987) found that case management was not effective in improving the size or diversity of social networks of schizophrenic patients living in the community, and Fisher *et al.* (1988) could find little effect of case management on improving the linkage of clients to services or on global measures of change. On a more positive note, Rapp and Wintersteen (1989) reported results from 12 case management projects where there was good evidence of reduced rates of hospitalization and high rates of individual goal attainment. They note the importance of specifying very clearly the exact nature of the case management intervention. Bond *et al.* (1988) set up case management programmes in three different community mental health centres and succeeded in reducing overall rehospitalization rates over a six month period. However, they failed to show much improvement in clients' functioning and the results were rather uneven across the three centres. Goering *et al.* (1988) working directly in the community succeeded in improving functioning over a 2-year period, but failed to affect rehospitalization. A major difference between these two studies lies in the degree to which the case managers were integrated into the clinical teams who were responsible for monitoring the patient's symptoms and taking decisions about whether or not to admit to hospital. In the case of Bond *et al.* they were fully involved, in the case of Goering *et al.* they were not. This probably accounts for the failure to affect rehospitalization rates in the latter study. Taken together, these studies underline the variability in outcome depending on what kind of case management procedure is adopted and how implementation is affected by local organizational constraints. Issues of staff training, the degree of 'assertive outreach' employed, links with inpatient units, etc. also all seem of central importance.

Notwithstanding the modest successes of case management approaches, a number of outstanding problems have emerged. Firstly, case management is predicated on a careful assessment of individual needs but, as yet, there is little agreement on exactly how this should be accomplished. The concept of 'a *need* for service' raises considerable technical and conceptual problems and standardized procedures for assessing needs are still in their infancy (see Brewin *et al.*, 1987; 1988; Brugha *et al.*, 1988). Secondly, the role of case manager combines elements of many different mental health professions—social work, nursing, psychiatry, clinical psychology, occupational therapy—and we have yet to identify the 'core skills' necessary for case managers to operate effectively. There is also the question of whether case management requires highly trained professional workers, or whether it can be delivered by relatively untrained staff. Does it depend on specific, professional skills, or general clinical skills? These kinds of problems mean that there is considerable scope for interprofessional disputes and rivalries to develop and thus it is necessary to address the familiar problems of role ambiguity and role conflict which are always present in multidisciplinary teamwork. Thirdly, it is not clear whether the case manager should simply function to link clients up to services in a rather bureaucratic 'administrative' way—a kind of 'agency broker'—or whether they should use their relationship with the client as a special kind of 'therapeutic' support. Experienced practitioners like Harris and Bergman (1987) have argued very strongly that case managers should consciously cultivate the therapeutic aspects of their relationships with clients to help them deal more effectively with their problems. This must also be the basis of any truly valid assessment of need. If this view is accepted, it has obvious implications in terms of the kinds of training and support case managers might require (Bachrach, 1989). Given all the uncertainties surrounding case management procedures there is clearly a need for good supervision to be available from experienced practitioners.

As we have noted already, some degree of teamwork is inevitable even within individually-oriented case management systems in order to resolve basic questions of the appropriate contribution of each professional and their accountability. Case managers cannot do everything by themselves and they will have to recognize clearly what they *cannot* be held responsible for, as well as what they can do. There is also a view, particularly associated with Test (1979), that case management is best seen as a team responsibility. She argues that teams may come to better decisions than individuals, are less vulnerable to sickness and holidays, and provide better protection against 'burnout'. Certainly, a case management system which does not recognize the need for good teamwork is almost bound to fail (see the chapter on 'The Management of the Staff Team' by Fraser Watts and Douglas Bennett). If case managers are to operate effectively and offer a truly individualized plan of care for each client, then they must also not be overburdened with cases. There is little empirical guidance on the question of maximum caseload size, but experience suggests that caseloads of more than about 20 clients soon become unmanageable. Case management may, therefore, impose limits on the total number of patients that a given service can take on. This is a relatively new idea in the British context.

The final dilemma for case managers is, of course, the financial one. Is their primary responsibility to the client, or to the 'system'? Should they be primarily concerned with the creation of a high quality, individually tailored service or with the efficient use of scarce resources? Of course, in the best of all worlds the two should not be in conflict, but in the real world they may be and, as Renshaw (1988) has noted, this may cause tension and problems. Some kind of balance must be struck between the competing demands of individual need and economic efficiency, but we must recognize the danger that case management *could* represent nothing more than a mechanism for simply exerting even tighter control over the allocation of resources. It would certainly be a pity if an innovation that is highly appealing on clinical grounds were to be exploited, and possibly even corrupted, by economic considerations.

Case management is not, therefore, a magic solution to the problems of coordinating and maintaining continuity of care. Neither is it a magic solution to the problems of multidisciplinary teamwork and inter-agency collaboration. It simply sets these problems in a slightly different context. This is particularly important in relation to the problem of collaboration between inpatient and community based services. Case managers are often at the heart of this process and their role is a crucial one, but they cannot be expected to solve all the problems on their own.

## Conclusions

The scene has shifted in rehabilitation in the last few years. The main 'actors' all look rather familiar, but the 'backdrops' are different. The scene is now no longer the mental hospital, it is the community hostel, the group home, the day centre, or the family home. The problems of running such long-term care settings in a therapeutic and 'non-stigmatizing' way still remain. The patients (clients, users, people), whether they are suffering with schizophrenia, or simply from years of social deprivation and disadvantage, are still struggling with the simple, everyday problems of life—friendships, jobs, money, decent housing, someone to confide in, etc. and it is little wonder that they are sometimes confused, sometimes even angry, about a system which often seems incapable of meeting these apparently simple needs. At the heart of this process lies the interactions between the people. It is the nature and quality of these interactions that constitute the rehabilitation process itself. If they are effective and supportive, rehabilitation 'works', if they are critical or neglectful, the person will deteriorate. These interactions take place within a broader social context, and sometimes even if they are effective, if they also separate the individual from the ordinary connections of life, then they will simply add to his or her sense of isolation and worthlessness. Rehabilitation is not therefore just about 'systems', or facilities. It is not even really about resources. Fundamentally, it is about people and how they behave towards one another and about the attitudes that society takes towards them. These are complicated, subtle and dynamic processes. This book attempts to reflect them. I hope that this paperback edition will introduce many more readers to this fascinating and important field.

## References

Allen, C. I., Gillespie, C. R., and Hall, J. N. (1989) A comparison of practices, attitudes and interactions in two established units for people with psychiatric disability. *Psychological Medicine*, **19**, 459–467.

Alloway, R., and Bebbington, P. (1987) The buffer theory of social support: A review of the literature. *Psychological Medicine*, **17**, 91–108.

Anderson, C. M., Hogarty, G. E., and Reiss, D. J. (1980) Family treatment of adult schizophrenic patients: A pschoeducational approach. *Schizophrenia Bulletin*, **6**, 490–505.

Angst, J. (1988) European long-term followup studies of schizophrenia. *Schizophrenia Bulletin*, **14**, 501–513.

Anthony, W. A. (1979) *The principles of psychiatric rehabilitation*. University Park Press, Baltimore.

Anthony, W.A., Cohen, M.R., and Farkas, M. (1982) A psychiatric rehabilitation treatment program: can I recognise one if I see one? *Community Mental Health Journal*, **18**, 83–96.

Anthony, W.A., Cohen, M.R., and Cohen, B.F. (1984) Psychiatric Rehabilitation. In J.A. Talbott, ed., *The Chronic Mental Patient: Five Years Later*. Grune & Stratton Inc., Florida.

Anthony, W.A. and Liberman, R.P. (1986) The practice of psychiatric rehabilitation — historical, conceptual and research base. *Schizophrenia Bulletin*, **12**, 542–559.

Audit Commission (1986) *Making a Reality of Community Care*, HMSO, London.

Bachrach, L.L. (1980) Overview: model programs for chronic mental patients. *American Journal of Psychiatry*, **137**, 1023–1031.

Bachrach, L.L. (1988) Defining chronic mental illness: A concept paper. *Hospital and Community Psychiatry*, **39**, 383–388.

Bachrach, L.L. (1989) Case management: towards a shared definition. *Hospital and Community Psychiatry*, **40**, 883–884.

Bachrach, L.L., and Lamb, H.R. (1989) What have we learned from deinstitutionalisation? *Psychiatric Annals*, **19**, 12–21.

Baxter, E., and Hopper, K. (1984) Troubled on the streets: the mentally disabled homeless poor. In J. Talbott, ed., *The Chronic Mental Patient: Five Years Later*. Grune & Stratton, New York.

Beard, J., Propst, R.N., and Malamud, T.J. (1982) The Fountain House model of psychiatric rehabilitation. *Psychosocial Rehabilitation Journal*, **5**, 47–59.

Bebbington, P., and Kuipers, L. (1988) Social influences on schizophrenia. In P. Bebbington and P. McGuffin, eds, *Schizophrenia: The Major Issues*. Heinemann Medical/Mental Health Foundation, London.

Bebbington, P., and McGuffin, P. (1988) *Schizophrenia: The Major Issues*. Heinemann Medical/Mental Health Foundation, London.

Bedell, J., and Ward, J.C. (1989) An intensive community-based treatment alternative to state hospitalization. *Hospital and Community Psychiatry*, **40**, 533–535.

Bennett, D.H. (1978) Social forms of psychiatric treatment. In J.K. Wing, ed., *Schizophrenia Towards a New Synthesis*. Academic Press, London.

Bennett, D.H. (1980) The chronic psychiatric patient today. *Journal of the Royal Society of Medicine*, **73**, 301–303.

Bernheim, K.F. (1982) Supportive family counseling. *Schizophrenia Bulletin*, **8**, 634–641.

Birchwood, M.J., Hallett, S.E., and Preston, M.C. (1988) *Schizophrenia: An Integrated Approach to Research and Treatment*. Longmans, London.

Bond, G.R., Miller, L.D., Krumwied, R.D., and Ward, R.S. (1988) Assertive case management in three CMHCs: a controlled study. *Hospital and Community Psychiatry*, **39**, 411–418.

Breier, A., and Strauss, J.S. (1983) Self control in psychotic disorders. *Archives of General Psychiatry*, **40**, 1141–1145.

Breier, A., and Strauss, J.S. (1984) The role of social relationships in the recovery from psychotic disorders. *American Journal of Psychiatry*, **141**, 949–955.

Brewin, C.R., Wing, J.K., Mangen, S.P., Brugha, T.S., and MacCarthy, B. (1987) Principles and practice of measuring needs in the long-term mentally ill: the MRC needs for care assessment. *Psychological Medicine*, **17**, 971–982.

Brewin, C.R., Wing, J.K., Mangen, S.P., Brugha, T.S., MacCarthy, B., and Lesage, A. (1988) Needs for care among the long-term mentally ill: a report from the Camberwell High Contact Survey. *Psychological Medicine*, **18**, 457–468.

Brown, G.W., and Harris, T. (1978) *Social Origins of Depression: A Study of Psychiatric Disorder in Women*. Tavistock, London.

Brown, N.B., and Parrish, J. (1987) Community support and rehabilitation of the mentally disabled in the United States. *International Journal of Mental Health*, **15**, 16–25.

Brugha, T.S. (1990) Social networks and support. *Current Opinion in Psychiatry*, **3**, 264–268.

Brugha, T.S., Wing, J.K., Brewin, C.R., MacCarthy, B., Mangen, S.P., Lesage, A., and Mumford, J. (1988) The problems of people in long-term psychiatric day care. *Psychological Medicine*, **18**, 443–456.

Carling, P.J., and Ridgway P. (1985) Community residential rehabilitation: an emerging approach to meeting housing needs. In P.J. Carling and P. Ridgway, eds, *Providing Housing and Support for People with Psychiatric Disabilities*. NIMH, Rockville, Maryland.

Coid, J.W. (1988) Mentally abnormal prisoners on remand: I — Rejected or accepted by the NHS? *British Medical Journal*, **296**, 1779–82.

Cooper, J., and Sartorius, N. (1977) Cultural and temporal variations in schizophrenia: a speculation on the importance of industrialisation. *British Journal of Psychiatry*, **130**, 50–55.

Creed, F., Black, D., and Anthony, P. (1989) Day-hospital and community treatment for acute psychiatric illness: a critical appraisal. *British Journal of Psychiatry*, **154**, 300–310.

Cutler, D.L., Tatum, E., and Shore, J.H. (1987) A comparison of schizophrenic patients in different community support treatment approaches. *Community Mental Health Journal*, **23**, 103–113.

Day, R., Nielsen, J.A., Korten, A., Ernberg, G., Dube, K.C., Gebhart, J., Jablensky, A., Leon, C., Marsella, A., Olatawura, M., Sartorius, N., Stromgren, E., Takahashi, R., Wig, N., and Wynne, L.C. (1987) Stressful life events preceding the acute onset of schizophrenia: a cross-national study from the World Health Organization. *Culture, Medicine and Psychiatry*, **11**, 123–205.

De Jong A., Giel, R., Sloof, C.J., and Wiersma, D. (1986) Relationship between symptomatology and social disability: empirical evidence from a follow-up study of schizophrenic patients. *Social Psychiatry*, **21**, 200–205.

DHSS (1975) *Better Services for the Mentally Ill*. Cmnd. 6233, HMSO, London.

DHSS (1985) *Mental Illness: Policies for Prevention, Treatment, Rehabilitation and Care*. Cmnd. 9674, HMSO, London.

FAF (1989) *Third Conference of European Firms, Cooperatives and Employment Initiatives for the Psychiatrically Disabled*. FAF e.V., Berlin.

Falloon, I.R.H. (1988) Expressed emotion: current status. *Psychological Medicine*, **18**, 269–274.

Falloon, I.R.H., and Talbot, R. (1981) Persistent auditory hallucinations: coping mechanisms and implications for management. *Psychological Medicine*, **11**, 329–339.

Falloon, I.R.H., Boyd, J.L., and McGill, C.W. (1984) *Family Care of Schizophrenia*. Guilford Press, New York.

Fisher, G., Landis, D., and Clark, K. (1988) Case management service provision and client change. *Community Mental Health Journal*, **24**, 134–142.

Ford, M., Goddard, C., and Lansdall-Welfare, R. (1987) The dismantling of the mental hospital?: Glenside Hospital Surveys 1960–1985. *British Journal of Psychiatry*, **151**, 479–485.

Fowler, D., and Morley, S. (1989) The cognitive-behavioural treatment of hallucinations and delusions: a preliminary study. *Behavioural Psychotherapy*, **17**, 267–282.

Franklin, J.L., Solovitz, B., Mason, M., Clemons, J.R., and Miller, G.E. (1987) An evaluation of case management. *American Journal of Public Health*, **77**, 74–78.

Garety, P.A. (1988) Housing. In A. Lavender and F. Holloway, eds, *Community Care in Practice*. Wiley, Chichester.

Garety, P.A., Afele, H.K., and Isaacs, D.A. (1988) A hostel-ward for new long-stay psychiatric patients: the careers of the first 10 years' residents. *Bulletin of the Royal College of Psychiatrists*, **12**, 183–186.

Garety P.A., and Morris I. (1984) A new unit for long-stay psychiatric patients: organisation, attitudes and quality of care. *Psychological Medicine*, **14**, 183–192.

Gibbons J.S. (1986) Care of 'new' long-stay patients in a District General Psychiatric Unit. *Acta Psychiatrica Scandinavica*, **73**, 582–588.

Gibbons J.S., and Butler J.P. (1987) Quality of life for 'new' long-stay psychiatric in-patients: the effects of moving to a hostel. *British Journal of Psychiatry*, **151**, 347–354.

Goering, P.N., Wasylenki, D.A., Farkas, M., Lancee, W.J., and Ballantyne, R. (1988) What difference does case management make? *Hospital and Community Psychiatry*, **39**, 272–282.

Goldberg D.P., Bridges K., Cooper W., Hyde C., Sterling C., and Wyatt R. (1985) Douglas House: a new type of hostel ward for chronic psychotic patients. *British Journal of Psychiatry*, **147**, 383–388.

Goldman, H.H. (1983) The Demography of Deinstitutionalisation. In L.L. Bachrach, ed., *Deinstitutionalisation*. Jossey Bass: San Francisco.

Goldstein, J.M., and Caton, C.L.M. (1983) The effects of the community environment on chronic psychiatric patients. *Psychological Medicine*, **13**, 193–199.

Gudeman, J.E., Shore, M.F., and Dickey, B. (1983) Day hospitalisation and an 'inn' instead of inpatient care for psychiatric patients. *New England Journal of Medicine*, **308**, 749–753.

Gudeman, J.E., and Shore, M.F. (1984) Beyond Deinstitutionalisation: a new class of facilities for the mentally ill. *New England Journal of Medicine*, **311**, 832–836.

Harding, C.M., Strauss, J.S., Hafez, H., and Liberman, P.B. (1987) Work and mental illness: I. Toward an integration of the rehabilitation process. *Journal of Nervous and Mental Diseases*, **175**, 317–326.

Harris, M., Bergman, H.C., and Bachrach, L. (1986) Individualised network planning for chronic psychiatric patients. *Psychiatric Quarterly*, **58**, 51–56.

Harris, M., and Bergman, H.C. (1987) Case management with the chronically mentally ill: a clinical perspective. *American Journal of Orthopsychiatry*, **57**, 296–302.

Heinrichs, D.W. (1988) The treatment of delusions in schizophrenic patients. In T.F. Oltmanns and B.A. Maher, eds, *Delusional Beliefs*. John Wiley, New York.

Hemsley, D. (1985) Schizophrenia. In B.P. Bradley and C. Thompson, eds, *Psychological Applications in Psychiatry*. Wiley, Chichester.

Henderson, S., Byrne, D.G., and Duncan-Jones, P. (1981) *Neurosis and the Social Environment*. Academic Press, Sydney.

Hogarty, G.E., Anderson, C.M., Reiss, D.J., Kjornblith, S.J., Greenwald, D.P., Javna, C.D., and Madoniam, M.J. (1986) Family psychoeducation, social skills training and maintenance chemotherapy in the aftercare treatment of schizophrenia. *Archives of General Psychiatry*, **43**, 633–642.

Hollin, C.R., and Trower, P. (1986) Social skills training: critique and future development. In C.R. Hollin and P. Trower, eds, *Handbook of Social Skills Training Volume 2*. Pergamon Press, Oxford.

Holloway, F. (1988) Day care and community support. In A. Lavender and F. Holloway, eds, *Community Care in Practice*. Wiley, Chichester.

Hoult, J. (1986) Community care of the acutely mentally ill. *British Journal of Psychiatry*, **149**, 137–144.

House of Commons (1985) *Second Report from the Social Services Select Committee on Community Care*. HMSO, London.

House, J.S., and Landis, K.R. (1988) Social relationships and health. *Science*, **241**, 540–544.

Hyde, C., Bridges, K., Goldberg, D., Lowson, K., Sterling, C., and Faragher, B. (1987) The evaluation of a hostel ward: a controlled study using modified cost-benefit analysis. *British Journal of Psychiatry*, **151**, 805–812.

Intagliata, J. (1982) Improving the quality of community care for the chronically mentally disabled: the role of case management. *Schizophrenia Bulletin*, **8**, 655–674.

Jennings, C. (1982) *Statistics from Eight Psychiatric Case Registers in Great Britain 1976–1981*. Southampton Psychiatric Case Register, Knowle Hospital, Hants., PO17 5NA.

Jones, K. (1988) *Experience in Mental Health*. Sage Publications, London.

Kanter, J. (1989) Clinical case management: definition, principles, components. *Hospital and Community Psychiatry*, **40**, 361–368.

Kay, A., and Legg, C. (1986) *Discharged to the Community: A review of housing and support in London for people leaving psychiatric care*. City University, London.

Kingsley, S., and Towell, D. (1988) Planning for high-quality local services. In A. Lavender and F. Holloway, eds, *Community Care in Practice*. Wiley, Chichester.

Koenigsberg, H.W., and Handley, R. (1986) Expressed emotion: from predictive index to clinical construct. *American Journal of Psychiatry*, **143**, 1361–1373.

Kuipers, L. (1987) Research in expressed emotion. *Social Psychiatry*, **22**, 216–220.

Kuipers, L., and Bebbington, P. (1985) Relatives as a resource in the management of schizophrenia. *British Journal of Psychiatry*, **147**, 465–470.

Kuipers, L., and Bebbington, P. (1988) Expressed emotion research in schizophrenia: theoretical and clinical implications. *Psychological Medicine*, **18**, 893–909.

Lamb, H.R. (1984) *The Homeless Mentally Ill — A Task Force Report of the American Psychiatric Association*. APA, Washington.

Lamb, H.R. (1988) When the chronically mentally ill need acute hospitalization: maximising its benefits. *Psychiatric Annals*, **18**, 426–430.

Leff, J., Kuipers, L., Berkowitz, R., Eberlein-Fries, R., and Sturgeon, D. (1982) A controlled trial of social intervention in families of schizophrenic patients. *British Journal of Psychiatry*, **141**, 121–134.

Leff, J., Kuipers, L., Berkowitz, R., and Sturgeon, D. (1985) A controlled trial of social intervention in families of schizophrenic patients: two year follow-up. *British Journal of Psychiatry*, **146**, 594–600.

Leff, J., Berkowitz, R., Shavit, N., Strachan, A., Glass, I., and Vaughn, C. (1989) A trial of family therapy v. a relatives' group for schizophrenia. *British Journal of Psychiatry*, **154**, 58–66.

Lehman, A.F. (1982) The well-being of chronic mental patients — assessing their quality of life. *Archives of General Psychiatry*, **40**, 1269–1276.

Lehman, A., Zastowny, T., Kane, C., DiMartino, E., Supnick, J., Schwarzkopf, S., Graef, J., and Henrichs, M. (1987) Intensive inpatient treatment of young adult chronic patients. *Psychiatric Quarterly*, **58**, 167–179.

Levene, L.S., Donaldson, L.J., and Brandon, S. (1985) How likely is it that a District Health Authority can close its large mental hospitals? *British Journal of Psychiatry*, **147**, 150–155.

Liberman, R.P., Mueser, K.T., Wallace, C.J., Jacobs, H.E., Eckman, T., and Massel, H.K. (1986) Training skills in the psychiatrically disabled: learning coping and competence. *Schizophrenia Bulletin*, **12**, 631–647.

Liberman, R.P., Jacobs, H.E., Boone, S.E., Foy, D.W., Donahoe, C.P., Falloon, I.R.H., Blackwell, G., and Wallace, C.J. (1987) Skills training for the community adaptation of schizophrenics. In J.S. Strauss, W. Boker and H.D. Brenner, eds, *Psychosocial Treatment of Schizophrenia*. Hans Huber, Toronto.

Linn, M.W., Caffey, E.M., Klett, J., Hogarty, G.E., and Lamb, H.R. (1979) Day treatment and psychotropic drugs in the aftercare of schizophrenic patients. *Archives of General Psychiatry*, **36**, 1055–1066.

Lovett, A. (1984) A house for all reasons: the role of housing in community care. In J. Reed and G. Lomas, eds, *Psychiatric Services in the Community*. Croom Helm, London.

MacMillan, J.F., Gold, A., Crow, T.J., Johnson, A.L., and Johnstone, E.C. (1986) The Northwick Park study of first episodes of schizophrenia. IV. Expressed emotion and relapse. *British Journal of Psychiatry*, **148**, 133–143.

Mangen, S. (1988) Implementing community care: an international assessment. In A. Lavender and F. Holloway, eds, *Community Care in Practice*. Wiley, Chichester.

Mann, S.A., and Cree, W. (1976) 'New' Long-stay Psychiatric Patients: A National Sample Survey of fifteen mental hospitals in England and Wales 1972/3. *Psychological Medicine*, **6**, 603–616.

McGlashan, T.H. (1988) A selective review of recent North American long-term followup studies of schizophrenia. *Schizophrenia Bulletin*, **14**, 515–542.

Mechanic, D., and Aiken, L. (1987) Improving the care of patients with chronic mental illness. *New England Journal of Medicine*, **317**, 1634–1638.

Miklowitz, D., Goldstein, M., Doane, J., Neuchterlein, K., Strachan, A., Snyder, K., and Magana-Amato, A. (1989) Is expressed emotion an index of a transactional process? I. Parents' affective style. *Family Process*, **28**, 153–167.

MIND (1983) *Common Concern*. Mind Publications, London.

Mitchell, S., and Birley, J.L.T. (1983) The use of ward support by psychiatric patients in the community. *British Journal of Psychiatry*, **142**, 9–15.

Mollica, R.F. (1983) From asylum to community—the threatened disintegration of public psychiatry. *New England Journal of Medicine*, **308**, 367–373.

Mulkern, V.M., and Manderscheid, R.W. (1989) Characteristics of Community Support Program clients in 1980 and 1984. *Hospital and Community Psychiatry*, **40**, 165–172.

Nagy, M.P., Fisher, G.A., and Tessler, R.C. (1988) Effects of facility characteristics on the social adjustment of mentally ill residents of board-and-care homes. *Hospital and Community Psychiatry*, **39**, 1281–1287.

Parker, G., Johnston, P., and Hayward, L. (1988) Parents 'expressed emotion' as a predictor of schizophrenic relapse. *Archives of General Psychiatry*, **45**, 806–814.

Parry, G. (1988) Mobilizing social support. In F. Watts, ed., *New Developments in Clinical Psychology Volume II*. BPS Books/Wiley, Chichester.

Patmore, C. (1987) *Living After Mental Illness*. Croom Helm, London.

Pepper, B. (1987) A public policy for the long-term mentally ill: a positive alternative to reinstitutionalisation. *American Journal of Orthopsychiatry*, **57**, 452–457.

Pilling, S. (1988) Work and the continuing care client. In A. Lavender and F. Holloway, eds, *Community Care in Practice*. Wiley, Chichester.

Rapp, C.A., and Wintersteen, R. (1989) The strengths model of case management: results from twelve demonstrations. *Psychosocial Rehabilitation Journal*, **13**, 23–32.

Renshaw, J. (1988) Care in the community: individual care planning and case management. *British Journal of Social Work*, **18**, 79–105.

Rosie, J.S. (1987) Partial hospitalization: A review of recent literature. *Hospital and Community Psychiatry*, **38**, 1291–1299.

Sheets, J., Prevost, J., and Rehman, J. (1982) Young adult chronic patients: three hypothesized subgroups. *Hospital and Community Psychiatry*, **33**, 197–203.

Shepherd, G. (1983) Social skills training with adults. In S. Spence and G. Shepherd, eds, *Developments in Social Skills Training*. Academic Press, London.

Shepherd, G. (1984) *Institutional Care and Rehabilitation*. Longmans, London.

Shepherd, G. (1985) Rehabilitation. In B.P. Bradley and C. Thompson, eds, *Psychological Applications in Psychiatry*. Wiley, Chichester.

Shepherd, G. (1986) Social skills training and schizophrenia. In C.R. Hollin and P. Trower, eds, *Handbook of Social Skills Training: Volume 2*. Pergamon Press, Oxford.

Shepherd, G. (1988a) Practical aspects of the management of negative symptoms. *International Journal of Mental Health*, **16**, 75–97.

Shepherd, G. (1988b) Work and rehabilitation. *Current Opinion in Psychiatry*, **1**, 217–221.

Shepherd, G. (1988c) The Contribution of Psychological interventions to the Treatment and Management of Schizophrenia. In P. Bebbington & P. McGuffin, eds, *New Initiatives in Schizophrenia*. Heineman Medical, London.

Shepherd, G. (1989a) Issues in Psychiatric Day Care. In R. Echlin, ed., *Day Care Information Pack*. GPMH, London.

Shepherd, G. (1989b) The Value of Work in the 1980's, *Psychiatric Bulletin*, **13**, 231–233.

Shepherd, G. (1989c) Research in Service Planning and Evaluation. In G. Parry and F. Watts, eds, *Behavioural and Mental Health Research: A Handbook of Skills and Methods*. Lawrence Erlbaum Associates, Hove and London.

Shepherd, G. (1990) A Criterion-Oriented Approach to Skills Training. *Psychosocial Rehabilitation Journal*, **13**, 11–13.

Shepherd, G. (1991a) The Relationship Between Therapy and Rehabilitation in Psychiatry. In G. De Isabella, W.F. Cucco and G. Sala, eds, *Psicoterapia: il rapporta tra teoria e pratica*, Franco Angeli Editore, Milano (in press).

Shepherd, G. (1991b) Day Care. In H.L. Freeman and D.H. Bennett, eds, *Principles of Community Psychiatry*. Churchill Livingstone, London (in press).

Simpson, S., Higson, P., Holland, R., McBrien, J., Williams, J., and Henneman, L. (1984) *Facing the Challenge: Common Issues in Work with People who are Mentally Handicapped, Elderly or Chronically Mentally Ill*. BABP Publications, London.

Simpson, C.J., Hyde, C.E., and Faragher, E.B. (1989) The Chronically Mentally Ill in Community Facilities: A Study of Quality of Life, *British Journal of Psychiatry*, **154**, 77–82.

Smith, J., and Birchwood, M.J. (1987) Specific and Non-specific Effects of Educational Intervention with Families Living with a Schizophrenic Relative. *British Journal of Psychiatry*, **150**, 645–652.

Smith, J., and Birchwood, M.J. (1990) Relatives and Patients as Partners in the Management of Schizophrenia: The Development of a Service Model. *British Journal of Psychiatry*, **156**, 654–660.

Spaulding, W.D., Storms, L., Goodrich, V., and Sullivan, M. (1986) Applications of experimental psychopathology in psychiatric rehabilitation. *Schizophrenia Bulletin*, **12**, 560–567.

Stein, L.I., and Test, M.A. (1985) *The Training in Community Living Model: A Decade of Experience*. Jossey Bass, San Francisco.

Strachan, A., Feingold, D., Goldstein, M., Miklowitz, D., and Neuchterlein, K. (1989) Is expressed emotion an index of a transactional process? II. Patient's coping style. *Family Process*, **28**, 169–182.

Strauss, J.S. (1986) What does rehabilitation accomplish? *Schizophrenia Bulletin*, **12**, 720–723.

Strauss, J.S., and Carpenter, W.T. (1972) The prediction of outcome in schizophrenia: I. Characteristics of outcome. *Archives of General Psychiatry*, **27**, 739–746.

Strauss, J.S., and Carpenter, W.T. (1974) The prediction of outcome in schizophrenia: II. Relationships between predictor and outcome variables. *Archives of General Psychiatry*, **31**, 37–42.

Strauss, J.S., and Carpenter, W.T. (1977) The prediction of outcome in schizophrenia: III. Five-year outcome and its predictors. *Archives of General Psychiatry*, **34**, 159–163.

Strauss, J.S., Klorman, R., and Kokes, R.F. (1977) Premorbid adjustment in schizophrenia: Part V. Implications of findings for understanding and research application. *Schizophrenia Bulletin*, **3**, 240–244.

Tarrier, N. (1987) An investigation of residual psychotic symptoms in discharged schizophrenic patients. *British Journal of Clinical Psychology*, **26**, 141–143.

Tarrier, N., Barrowclough, C., Vaughn, C., Bamrah, J.S., Porceddu, K., Watts, S., and Freeman, H. (1988) The community managment of schizophrenia: a controlled trial of a behavioural intervention with families to reduce relapse. *British Journal of Psychiatry*, **154**, 532–542.

Test, M.A. (1979) Continuity of Care. In L.I. Stein, ed., *Community Support Systems for the Long-Term Patient*. Jossey Bass, San Francisco.

Thornicroft, G., and Bebbington, P. (1989) Deinstitutionalisation — from hospital closure to service development. *British Journal of Psychiatry*, **155**, 739–753.

Turner, J.C., and TenHoor, W.J. (1978) the NIMH Community Support Program: a pilot approach to social reform. *Schizophrenia Bulletin*, **4**, 319–348.

Tyrer, P. (1985) The Hive System — A model for a psychiatric service. *British Journal of Psychiatry*, **146**, 571–575.

Wainwright, T., Holloway, F., and Brugha, T. (1988) Day care in an inner city. In A. Lavender and F. Holloway, eds, *Community Care in Practice*. Wiley, Chichester.

Warner, R. (1985) *Recovery from Schizophrenia*. Routledge & Kegan Paul, London.

Weller, M.P.I. (1989) Mental illness — who cares? *Nature*, **339**, 249–252.

Wing, J.K., and Furlong, R. (1986) A haven for the severely disabled within the context of a comprehensive psychiatric community service. *British Journal of Psychiatry*, **149**, 449–457.

Wolfensberger, W. (1972) *The Principle of Normalization in Human Services*. National Institute of Mental Retardation, Toronto.

Wolfensberger, W., and Glenn, L. (1983) *Programme Analysis of Service Systems (PASS): A method for quantitative analysis of human services*. Handbook of the National Institute of Mental Retardation, Toronto.

World Health Organization (1979) *Schizophrenia: An International Follow-up Study*. Wiley, Chichester.

World Health Organization (1980) *International Classification of Impairments, Disabilities and Handicaps: A manual of classification relating to the consequences of disease*. WHO, Geneva.

Wykes, T. (1982) A hostel-ward for 'new' long-stay patients: An evaluative study of a 'ward-in-a-house'. In J.K. Wing, ed., Long Term Community Care: Experience in a London Borough. *Psychological Medicine Monograph Supplement 2*, Cambridge University Press, Cambridge.

Wykes, T. (1983) A follow-up of 'new' long-stay patients in Camberwell 1977–1982. *Psychological Medicine*, **13**, 659–662.

PART I

*Concept and History of Rehabilitation*

Theory and Practice of Psychiatric Rehabilitation
Edited by F. N. Watts and D. H. Bennett
© 1983, John Wiley & Sons, Ltd.

# 1

# Introduction: The Concept of Rehabilitation

FRASER WATTS and DOUGLAS BENNETT

The rehabilitation of psychiatric patients is still both neglected and misunderstood. Though rehabilitation programmes have been established in many centres, the provision of rehabilitation is still patchy and inadequate. Perhaps even more serious is the fact that much of what passes as psychiatric rehabilitation betrays little understanding of the processes involved and frequently amounts to misdirected effort. Misunderstandings about psychiatric rehabilitation are partly responsible both for the patchy provision of psychiatric rehabilitation and for the limited value of such services as are provided. Rehabilitation has become associated with a set of practices and procedures which have their place, albeit a declining one, but which do not themselves *constitute* psychiatric rehabilitation. What is generally lacking is a broad conception of its aims and objectives. The result is that what passes for psychiatric rehabilitation is not so much a 'goal-directed' as a 'ritual' activity, self-justifying and hallowed by tradition. It is therefore necessary to set out as clearly as possible what we believe the objectives of psychiatric rehabilitation to be and to remove misunderstandings.

## The Person and the Environment

The essential starting point for a proper understanding of rehabilitation is that it is concerned with the individual person in the context of the environment. How a person functions will invariably be the result of the *interaction* between the capacities and dispositions that he possesses as an individual and the environment in which he lives and operates. This has been clearly recognized in the rehabilitation of people with physical impairments. Here a key part of the rehabilitation programme is often the adaptation of the physical environment so that the person concerned can function at the best level possible, for

3

example repositioning door handles so that they can be opened from a wheelchair. Psychiatric rehabilitation is also concerned with the interaction between the person and the environment, though it is generally the social rather than the physical environment that is important. This introduces an additional complication as the social environment is generally less stable than the physical one.

The influence of the environment has important implications for how the individual is assessed. It is important to avoid the fallacy of assuming that a person will function in the same way in all environments. This is a point worth labouring a little. Though it was apparent, for example, from the classic psychological research of Hartshorne and May (1928) on the 'nature of character', its implications were largely forgotten until they were rediscovered by Mischel (1968) in his influential book *Personality and Assessment*. Even now, the implications for psychiatric assessment have not been fully grasped. The essential point is that a wide range of human behaviours vary very substantially from one situation to another, and that the correlation between how people perform in two different situations is so low that it is seldom possible to make good predictions from performance in one to performance in the other. Of course, some behaviours are more stable than others, task performance is more stable than social behaviour for example, and some people are more consistent from situation to situation than others. However, this does not affect the general implication that assessment needs to be concerned with capacities and tendencies rather than fixed behaviours, with what people have the capacity to achieve under optimal circumstances and with the inadequacies they are liable to manifest under deleterious circumstances.

There also needs to be an assessment of how particular environments will interact with these potential capacities and tendencies. Among the various aspects of the environment that need to be considered are whether it provides an outlet for the skills and capacities of the person concerned, whether it avoids stressful exacerbation of potential dysfunctions by providing whatever 'shelter' is needed, and whether it provides the level of 'support' needed for the person to function at his or her best level (Bennett, 1978). Only when both personal dispositions and environmental influences are considered can a sensible rehabilitation plan be formulated.

Neglect of the contribution of the social environment to social adjustment has also led to naïvety about the extent to which performance achieved during a rehabilitation programme will subsequently be transferred to another environment. There are various bases on which such transfer *can* be expected to occur. Where people acquire new skills in the course of rehabilitation, it is reasonable to hope that they will be able to deploy these skills in different situations such as in their homes or in open employment. However, even this will depend on the similarity of the skills learned in rehabilitation to those required subsequently. There is worrying evidence, reviewed by Shepherd in Chapter 13, that new social skills do not transfer easily from one environment to another unless specific steps are taken to facilitate this. In addition to the acquisition of new skills, rehabilitation may bring about a relatively stable increase in the base level of self-confidence, or a stable reduction in the level of emotional responsiveness to certain kinds of stresses. Where this occurs there is also reason to hope that gains achieved in a rehabilitation programme will transfer to other situations.

However, it is regrettably true that many of the improvements in functioning that are achieved in the course of rehabilitation are *not* likely to transfer to other situations, and are merely a transient response to the particular characteristic of the rehabilitation environment. If you take care to 'shelter' people from aspects of a particular role which they find troublesome, they may perform very well. Similarly, if you provide them with a level of support and understanding that they are not likely to receive after the end of the rehabilitation programme, they may also for a time perform surprisingly well. However, such responses to the special characteristics of a rehabilitation environment cannot be expected to transfer to other situations. There is sufficient evidence to cause serious concern about this lack of transfer. For example, Walker and McCourt (1965) found no statistical association between patients who had activity programmes in hospital and those who were employed after discharge. Ellsworth *et al.* (1968) found that the patients who were rated as most unpleasant and hostile in hospital were thought to have the best friendship skills on discharge. Rapoport (1960) found that variables, such as adoption of the values of a therapeutic community, which correlated with improvement in the unit had no relationship with the long-term outcome.

We do not wish to minimize the efforts that have been made to facilitate transfer of improvements, both in social and occupational rehabilitation, from one environment to another, though it would be idle to pretend that such transfer is easily achieved. What is very regrettable, however, is that many of those responsible for rehabilitation programmes still seem unaware of the problem. The extent to which people's behaviour or level of functioning may be specific to a particular situation has not been adequately grasped. A sensible programme of rehabilitation must be specifically designed to prepare people for the environment in which they will eventually function, rather than simply to achieve good levels of functioning *during* rehabilitation. The requirements of these two objectives may be quite different.

### The Objectives of Rehabilitation

A common misunderstanding about rehabilitation, and one with unfortunate practical consequences, arises from the widespread failure to distinguish between the *end point* of successful rehabilitation, which is usually resettlement in independent accommodation in the community or in open employment, and the *process* of rehabilitation which involves improving levels of social adjustment. Rehabilitation should ideally be a preparation for resettlement (see Chapter 2).

The conceptual distinction between rehabilitation and resettlement has parallels in other areas of psychology, such as the distinction between social positions and social roles. Kelvin (1970, p.142) has been helpfully clear about this distinction (see also Chapter 14). A 'position' is an aspect of the structure of a social group. Thus the positions of father and mother are aspects of the social structure of a family. 'Role', in contrast, refers to the functions and behaviour associated with a position and carried out in response to the expectations that the position brings with it. In terms of this distinction, resettlement is concerned with what positions a person has in society, and rehabilitation is concerned with the level of functioning achieved. There is a further parallel with the distinction between employment and work (see Chapter 11). To be an employee is to have a position in society. Work is the execution of functions and behaviours required by employment.

One unfortunate consequence of the failure to make this distinction has been the tendency to try to rehabilitate *only* those who it is hoped to resettle. There are many patients in long-stay hospitals for whom resettlement in the community or in open employment is not a realistic objective. That does not imply, however, that they would not benefit from rehabilitation. It is possible to improve social adjustment, role performance, and autonomy even within the limited opportunities provided by a mental hospital. We submit that this is always a worthwhile objective. In any case, whether or not it should be attempted with a particular patient should be decided on the arguments for and against *rehabilitation*, not on the prospects of eventual resettlement.

Another unfortunate consequence of the failure to distinguish between rehabilitation and resettlement, and this has come close to bringing community care into disrepute, is that resettlement is sometimes carried out without any prior rehabilitation. The most extreme case of patients being discharged after many years in long-stay hospitals with a suitcase of clothes and some money for transport and lodgings is no doubt rare. However, resettlement with *inadequate* prior rehabilitation is still all too common. The widespread conceptual confusion over the distinction between rehabilitation and resettlement seems to allow some people to believe that if their patients have been resettled, then rehabilitation has been carried out.

Though it is important not to confuse rehabilitation with resettlement, rehabilitation will often be judged largely by the effectiveness with which it prepares people for resettlement. This means that at least provisional resettlement objectives are needed in order to formulate a rational rehabilitation plan. As with other kinds of interventions, there are value judgements and potential ethical problems involved in what the resettlement objectives should be. Clearly, it is of prime importance that these should be acceptable to the person seeking rehabilitation. It is not part of the legitimate aims of a rehabilitation service to impose particular objectives on people against their wishes. It is for the person concerned to decide which social positions are his or her priority. Whichever social positions are chosen, a capacity to cope with social complexity is likely to be called for, and developing such a capacity is almost always an appropriate rehabilitation objective.

Sometimes the most sensitive issues about the objectives of rehabilitation arise in connection with what *level* of functioning should be aimed at, rather than which *areas* of social functioning should be the focus of the programme. People may set objectives that are unnecessarily low simply because they lack confidence in their own abilities. Here, advice should be given about what could be achieved at the end of the rehabilitation programme, and also about the possible risks of acquiring further disabilities through not exercising what social-psychological functions remain. Other people may set unrealistically high objectives. Here advice should be given about the risks of the social adjustment being an unstable one, and of psychiatric relapse occurring as a result of being overstressed. It cannot be denied that those responsible for psychiatric services will have an interest in these questions. Stress-triggered breakdowns and secondary disabilities acquired through under functioning will have consequences for the health services and the community generally as well as for the person concerned. These interests are sufficient to justify attempting to reach agreement about the level of rehabilitation that should be aimed at.

The acceptability of resettlement objectives to the person's family and social network also has to be considered. There is a limit to the degree of 'burden' families, employers, and members of the health and social services are prepared to accept from ex-patients (Hawks, 1975). It does the patient no long-term service to encourage unrealistic expectations about this. But rehabilitation should not be seen merely as an exercise in shifting the burden of caring for patients from the health service to the community. Rather, it is an exercise in enabling patients to make the best use of their residual capacities. When ex-patients have been enabled through rehabilitation to make a positive contribution in their social roles, the question of any burden they may place on others is likely to be seen in a different perspective.

## Widening the Scope of Rehabilitation Services

We have argued that rehabilitation programmes need to be geared to the objectives that are appropriate for the person concerned, and based on a comprehensive assessment of the influences that will affect the course of rehabilitation and the objectives that it is appropriate to set (see Chapter 16). Such an assessment, when carefully undertaken, usually makes it clear what sorts of measures will be needed to help the person function at his best level. Traditionally, however, rehabilitation has been associated with a narrower range of activities. In Britain, it still often means simply providing industrial work for chronic schizophrenics in long-term mental hospitals. Currently in the United States it is often concerned with the development of a range of personal skills (Anthony, 1980) to the neglect of the impact of the social environment. We wish to argue that rehabilitation services need to broaden their horizons.

To begin with, rehabilitation needs to concern itself with a wider range of psychiatric problems. In schizophrenia there is often an acute onset which has resulted in a marked loss of social functioning. Here the task of rehabilitation is clearly to help the patient to go as far as possible towards the reacquisition of his original level of functioning, or at least to help him to make a stable adjustment at the highest level he is capable of. In many patients, especially those with neurotic or conduct problems, a satisfactory social adjustment has never been achieved. Yet these patients may well benefit from the same kind of help and facilities in establishing a satisfactory social adjustment as would a patient with an acute-onset disorder in *re*establishing a social adjustment.

Of course, this strictly ought to be referred to as 'habilitation' rather than 'rehabilitation', but the former term has little currency in the psychiatric field and it is doubtful whether there is much value, apart from semantic purity, in inroducing it. Semantic purity has in the past led to the introduction of the term 'reabled' which was eventually discovered to refer to the less pure Anglo-Saxon practice of legitimizing a bastard. Neither organizational nor scientific viewpoints suggest that the distinction between habilitation and rehabilitation is a sharp one. The position taken here is that both need to be offered to psychiatric patients, but that it is not unreasonable to continue to use the term 'rehabilitation' to cover both enterprises.

In Chapters 4 to 6, the rehabilitation of a range of non-schizophrenic patient groups is considered, patients with neurotic conditions, affective disorders, conduct problems, alcohol abuse, drug abuse, and problems that have led to legal action. We have not, however, included in this volume any consideration of the application of rehabilitation methods to the mentally handicapped, the elderly confused, and those with neurological dysfunctions. Though the principles of rehabilitation with these groups have much in common with the rehabilitation of people with functional psychiatric disorders, they also raise additional issues that go beyond the scope of the present book.

Rehabilitation also needs to be provided in other settings apart from chronic mental hospitals. One of the problems with such rehabilitation is that it is often provided unnecessarily late. There are advantages in treatment and rehabilitation running side by side throughout the time of a patient's admission. To wait until treatment is completed before considering rehabilitation can mean that the patient acquires some unnecessary secondary disabilities as a result of social inactivity whether in or out of hospital. It may also mean either that the patient's stay in hospital is prolonged unnecessarily or that he is discharged without adequate preparation and with a consequently higher risk of relapse and readmission. Rehabilitation thus needs to concern itself with acute as well as chronic patients, and to be introduced at an early rather than a late stage of their management.

Much of it can be done on an outpatient basis. Many patients do not need hospital admission, certainly not a lengthy one, and can be cared for very adequately either as outpatients or in a well-staffed day hospital. Rehabilitation of such people can be undertaken while they are living at home. The viability and usefulness of such community rehabilitation is, incidentally, a helpful demonstration that rehabilitation is not simply about discharging patients from hospital!

Finally, rehabilitation needs to be concerned about a much wider range of social functions. Too much rehabilitation in Britain is concerned with industrial employment. This is an imbalance which we have sought to redress in this book (see especially Chapters 12 and 13). However, there is a need to caution against a lack of interest in the role of *work* in psychiatric rehabilitation, though many people, such as mothers, work without being in paid employment. Work is central to the self-respect and self-confidence of many people, and an essential part of their aspirations for the resumption of a normal social life. In addition, as will be argued later (Chapters 8 and 11), work involves some very important psychological functions such as the ability to perceive the requirements of other people accurately and to be regular and dependable in social habits. In preserving someone's ability to work, a rehabilitation programme is also preserving social capacities which are important in many other roles.

When rehabilitation has advanced beyond its traditional confinements to one particular type of patient (such as schizophrenics), one particular setting (long-stay mental hospitals), and one particular activity (such as industrial work) we believe it will be apparent that the *rehabilitation approach* to psychiatric care is one that has something to contribute to a great number of those who seek help for psychiatric problems, and we would wish to see it better integrated in the general routine care of psychiatric patients.

### The Positive Orientation of Rehabilitation

It is only to be expected that among those referred for rehabilitation there will be an unusually high proportion of those with very long-standing problems, whose prognosis is poor, and about whom staff working with acute referrals have despaired. Working with such a group of patients presents a number of problems. It makes for unusual difficulties in maintaining an energetic and committed approach amongst the staff team and so makes the management of the team a particularly important matter. It is also easy to fall into a patronizing, paternalistic approach to people with long-term, intractable problems. Caring *about* patients frequently reduces to caring *for* them. To maintain sympathy and conscientious concern is something that many staff are able to achieve. However, to maintain *respect* for the people, and to help them maintain a sense of dignity, autonomy, and positive self-regard is altogether more difficult.

Hard though this is, it is clearly of great importance. There have been frequent demonstrations that people tend to respond to the expectations others have of them. Freeman and Simmons (1963) provided a convincing demonstration of the association between what families expect of their members who have long-term psychological problems and what normal social activities those people actually perform. The same will be true for the attitudes and expectations of the staff team. If staff allow themselves to have little respect for patients, and to expect little of them, this will have a disabling effect on the patients concerned regardless of how 'caring' the staff may be. Generally speaking, little will be achieved by those of whom little is expected. Traditional care services have usually had difficulty in maintaining high expectations of social performance and at the same time supporting the patient. They are usually too willing to give more support than is needed and allow expectations to fall too low. There are therefore arguments for the employment and integration of non-professionals into professional service to provide the normal social context in such areas as work, self-care, and social skills training. The more realistic the setting in which rehabilitation is conducted, the more likely it is that the patient and staff will be able to make realistic assessments and appropriate decisions about rehabilitation aims. Thus patients in community rehabilitation are more likely to have realistic ideas and expectations than those who have been sheltered for years from social reality in mental hospitals. The setting should provide clear and unambiguous norms for the patient, must provide opportunities for learning and practising the required role performance, and must selectively reward the behaviour of the patient (Brim, 1976).

Some severely disabled patients will need considerable staff effort even to maintain their functioning at its present level and to avoid further deterioration. This is a role that staff find difficult to accept because it is difficult to see what is being achieved. The further deterioration that is being prevented only becomes apparent if the effort ceases to be made. Patients who have grandiosely unrealistic aims are also difficult for staff to help, because they make it particularly difficult to provide the combination of realism and positive encouragement which rehabilitation requires. Unfortunately, staff attitudes, under the stress of trying to help difficult patients, can easily swing to either defeatism or over optimism. The hope dies hard that some patients will function even better after rehabilitation than they did before their psychiatric illness.

How patients' problems are formulated is of crucial importance in maintaining staff attitudes that are both realistic and constructive. There is danger in the use of over-general concepts such as 'personality disorder', for which the proper criteria of application are so ill-defined that many staff appear to use them more as a term of abuse than as a scientific concept (Watts and Bennett, 1978). In the formulation of problems, as in the setting of goals, it is important to avoid 'fuzzies' (see Chapter 15). We do not argue against any use whatsoever of diagnostic concepts in psychiatric rehabilitation. The concept of 'schizophrenia', for example, has enough precision in its application and is linked to a sufficient understanding of a variety of casual factors (including social ones) to seem to us to be both scientifically justifiable and practically useful. However, the vague and pejorative use of pseudo-diagnostic concepts for which neither of these claims can be made is all too common.

There is also a need to ensure that problems are formulated in terms that do not arouse misleading expectations about their temporal stability and likely time-course. 'Symptom' language can be seriously misleading from this point of view in that it frequently both fails to direct attention adequately to the extent to which problems fluctuate with personal and social circumstances and arouses unrealistic expectations about the possibility of their being removed altogether by 'treatment'. Very few of those undergoing psychiatric rehabilitation are likely to respond to treatment to this extent.

'Disability' language tends to be less misleading from this point of view, but when used loosely raises other problems. The attraction of disability language is that it does not encourage unrealistic expectations that psychiatric problems will be totally removed by treatment, and therefore focuses attention on how people can make the best adjustment given their residual and sometimes permanent disabilities. However, it may encourage the opposite problem of the nihilistic belief that treatment can achieve nothing at all. There is a tendency for the disabled, like the sick, to be stigmatized. Progress has recently been made in the clarification of disability concepts (Bury and Wood, 1978), though it has not yet been widely adopted in psychiatric rehabilitation and has not been used systematically in the present book. There is an important distinction between *disability*, which is the loss of functional ability consequent upon an impairment, and *handicap* which is the social disadvantage consequent upon disability. Shearer (1981) has argued trenchantly that it is the perceptions people have of the disabled, especially the perceptions of professionals, that determine how far they are handicapped by their disabilities. The professional services and the social network, through their attitudes, can determine how far people who have disabilities become handicapped.

As we have already said, the most distinctive and practically important aspect of rehabilitation formulations is the emphasis on positive capacities. The language of 'positive mental health' (Jahoda, 1959; Offer and Sabshin, 1966) is much less well developed and articulated than that of psychiatric problems. However, it is not difficult to develop a standard checklist to help in making a comprehensive survey of a person's personal, functional, and social resources, and indeed this can be done at the same time as screening for deficits (see Chapter 16). In doing so, however, it is important never to conclude that a person is *in*capable of doing something until it has been tried. It is one of the pleasures of working in the field of rehabilitation to be surprised by the positive capacities of people who had seemed 'hopeless'.

Having positive capacities clearly in mind is the most effective antidote to the paternalistic attitudes that develop when psychiatric services try merely to 'care for' long-term patients. Staff will treat those undergoing rehabilitation with more respect and more genuine and realistic optimism if positive attributes have been clearly identified. Rehabilitation plans built on positive capacities are also likely to arouse quite different attitudes in the wider social environment. It is generally possible to work towards a rehabilitation goal that will involve the person contributing to the well being of those around him as well as making demands of them. This, of course, is crucial for his or her self-respect. The social environment will show much greater tolerance of any residual problematic behaviour or special demands if these are balanced by a positive social contribution. An impressive example of an approach to rehabilitation that was based on an appreciation of the contribution that people with psychiatric problems can make involved the rehabilitation of a group of people with schizophrenia in a British town. They were resettled in accommodation with landladies who had themselves had drinking problems. Incidentally, that made the accommodation easier to obtain. The rehabilitees, far from being an additional burden on their landladies, ended up looking after them when they got drunk. They also had a good outcome in terms of staying well themselves. That kind of approach to rehabilitation is the best response to concern about the 'burden' of ex-patients on the community.

### Theory and Practice

Sir Aubrey Lewis, that doyen of British psychiatrists, commented in 1955 that

a great deal of rehabilitation is built up on faith, hope, and rule of thumb. We could do better than that. We could plan our programs so that they may disclose principles governing successful rehabilitation and the factors that restrict it. If one hitches one's wagon to a star, there can be a waste of energy that no community can really afford. Hence the need to define our aims in each patient, and judge the success of our method by whether we obtain that goal . . . .

That remark is regrettably all too apposite many years later. Some progress has been made in investigating the principles of successful rehabilitation, and this volume summarizes and reviews what has been discovered so far. We attach considerable importance to putting psychiatric rehabilitation on a scientific basis. Only in this way will the amateurish nature of much of what passes for rehabilitation be overcome. It will make it easier to be realistic about what can be achieved, avoiding both the unjustifiable pessimism and the fanciful optimism that can easily take over when there is no adequate knowledge basis.

In part, also, the future viability of rehabilitation *depends* on putting it on a firmer scientific basis. Lewis identified the danger that otherwise 'there can be a waste of energy that no community can really afford'. As resources become increasingly scarce, the community will not be able to afford to waste them. Unless rehabilitation is, and is known to be, a good use of resources, it will probably *not* be afforded. Increasing attention to the scientific foundations of rehabilitation will also be important in overcoming the image that it still has in some circles of being a 'Cinderella' of the psychiatric services. A fruitful exchange between researchers and practitioners is valuable in giving momentum to a specialty and in attracting able people to work in it.

The basic sciences to which rehabilitation needs to look are largely the social and behavioural sciences rather than biological sciences on which medical and much psychiatric research is based. Many of the ideas and much research reported in this book have arisen from collaboration between sociologists and psychologists on the one hand and clinicians (of various disciplines) on the other. We hope that the scientific investigation of the rehabilitation process will increasingly come to be seen as a fruitful area for applied social and behavioural research. Though we are encouraged by what has already been achieved, we do not wish to be complacent. The scientific foundations of rehabilitation have now generally been laid, but there is no area of rehabilitation in which a substantial development of research is not needed. In particular, there is an urgent need for more *evaluative* research, costly and cumbersome though programme evaluations inevitably are. We need to know how effective rehabilitation is.

It is important for the future of rehabilitation that strong links are maintained between theory, research, and practice. Any one of these without the others is likely to become moribund. We hope that in this book readers will be able to see the results of preliminary efforts to articulate the principles and processes on which rehabilitation, initially a very pragmatic activity, is based. The practice of rehabilitation can then in turn be based ever more securely on these principles.

## References

Anthony, W. A. (1978) *The Principles of Psychiatric Rehabilitation*. University Park Press, Baltimore.

Bennett, D. H. (1978) Community psychiatry. *British Journal of Psychiatry*, **132**, 209–220.

Brim, O. G. (1976) Socialization through the life cycle. In O. G. Brim and S. Wheeler, eds, *Socialization after Childhood: Two Essays*. Kreiger Publishing Company, Huntingdon.

Bury, M. R., and Wood, P. H. N. (1978) Sociological perspectives on research on disablement. *International Rehabilitation Medicine*, **1**, 24–32.

Ellsworth, R. B., Foster, L., Childers, B., Arthur, G., and Kroeker, D. (1968) Hospital and community adjustment as perceived by psychiatric patients, their families and staff. *Journal of Consulting and Clinical Psychology* **32**, Monograph Supplement, 1–41.

Freeman, H. E., and Simmons, O. G. (1963) *The Mental Patient Comes Home*. John Wiley, New York.

Hartshorne, H., and May, M. A. (1928) *Studies in the Nature of Character*. Vol. 1. Macmillan, New York.

Hawks, D. (1975) Community care: an analysis of assumptions. *British Journal of Psychiatry*, **127**, 276–285.

Jahoda, M. (1959) *Current Concepts of Positive Mental Health*. Basic Books, New York.

Kelvin, P. (1970) *The Bases of Social Behaviour: An Approach in Terms of Order and Value*. Holt, Rinehart, & Winston, London.

Lewis, A. J. (1955) Rehabilitation programs in England *Proceedings Millbank Memorial Fund Annual Conference*, 196–206.

Mischel, W. (1968) *Personality and Assessment*. John Wiley, New York.

Offer, D., and Sabshin, M. (1966) *Normality: Theoretical and Clinical Concepts of Mental Health*. Basic Books, New York.

Rapoport, R. N. (1960) *Community as Doctor: New Perspectives on a Therapeutic Community*. Tavistock, London.

Shearer, A. (1981) *Disability: Whose Handicap?* Basil Blackwell, Oxford.

Walker, R., and McCourt, J. (1965) Employment experiences among 200 schizophrenic patients in hospital and after discharge. *American Journal of Psychiatry*, **122**, 316–319.

Watts, F. N., and Bennett, D. H. (1978) Social deviance in a day hospital. *Psychological Medicine*, **132**, 455–462.

Theory and Practice of Psychiatric Rehabilitation
Edited by F. N. Watts and D. H. Bennett
© 1983, John Wiley & Sons, Ltd.

# 2

# The Historical Development of Rehabilitation Services

DOUGLAS BENNETT

The history of rehabilitation in psychiatry as in other fields of medicine seems to have three phases. It has been suggested that in the first phase little is done about the handicap and people justify this inaction by saying that little can be done (Clarke, 1962). Throughout history not only those disabled by psychiatric disorder but those disabled by physical conditions 'for which little could be done or which appeared only remotely related to the broader social needs, have usually been subjected to a variety of harsh and hideous treatments' (Straus, 1966). The history of past abuse of psychiatric patients is well known. What is less considered is that such abuse recurred in our own times when it led to the extermination of large numbers of the psychiatrically disabled in Germany (Dörner *et al.*, 1980). By and large intolerance and abuse, although prevalent in nineteenth-century Europe, was later tempered in Britain by the rise of the Evangelical Movement and Fabianism.

The moral and social concern of these movements probably signalled the onset of the second historical phase in the approach to disability. In this phase the disabled person was sheltered, his weakness conceded and allowances made for them. Services were provided by charitable or voluntary organizations, often with a religious motivation, who wished to help such deserving unfortunates as orphans, the blind, and the deformed. For the mentally ill, as for other disabled groups, various programmes were visibly directed at pauperism. The distinction 'between poverty and disability was obscure except for the fact that the able bodied poor were rarely defined as deserving' (Straus, 1966). More often than not shelter was provided in an institution. Thus Dorothea Dix, a strong-minded New England schoolteacher, was so horrified by what she saw of the conditions of the mentally ill in poorhouses, gaols, and madhouses, that she launched herself into her life's work to achieve their humane care and treatment in newly constructed asylums for the insane.

Organizations of a reformist nature laid the foundations for later rehabilitation efforts. Conolly's abolition of mechanical restraint coincided with a period of moral treatment the object of which was 'to treat the patients as far as their condition would possibly admit, as if they were still in the enjoyment of the healthy exercise of their mental faculties . . . and to make their condition as comfortable as possible' (Bockoven, 1963). A unique example of this charitable approach to rehabilitation was the formation of the Mental After Care Association in 1879 by the Reverend Henry Hawkins, Chaplain of the Middlesex Asylum at Colney Hatch. He recognized the need 'to facilitate the readmission of the poor friendless female convalescent from Lunatic Asylums into social life', by obtaining for them a change of scene and air and assisting them to obtain suitable employment (Hawkins, 1871). Failing this, he said such women's only recourse was to Poor Law Relief which usually meant readmission to the workhouse. Poor Law *laissez-faire* liberalism with its emphasis on self-help and self-reliance led to the misuse of mental hospitals. Troublesomeness instead of curability became the reason for admission to the asylum and chronic patients accumulated. Their numbers were further swollen as the population increased and workers moved from the country to urban centres. Asylums had to be enlarged and conditions deteriorated so that in 1894 Weir Mitchell exclaimed, 'upon my word, I think asylum life is deadly to the insane' (Mitchell, 1894). Reform continued alongside neglect and sometimes both were intimately related. Thus Eva Charlotte Reid, writing in 1914, said that 'work may be made a great detriment or a valuable therapeutic agent in the treatment of mental disorder, according to whether or not it is scientifically applied'. She recognized that in institutions 'where much of the hard labour is done by patients and a certain amount *must* be accomplished, the tendency is to make drudges out of the willing and efficient worker and allow to remain in complete idleness those who require to be instructed, supervised or handled with tact' (Reid, 1914). Other changes were taking place which would in time lead to greater provision for the disabled. The Webbs, in their Minority Report to the Royal Commission on the Poor Law in 1909, asserted that it should be the State's responsibility to secure 'a national minimum of civilised life open to all alike of both sexes and all classes'. This view would, of course, lead in time to the abolition of the Poor Law and to a much clearer distinction being made between poverty and disability.

## Steps Towards Rehabilitation

The manifest need for the rehabilitation of the survivors of the First World War provided the impetus for some of the first explicit attempts at psychiatric rehabilitation. The King's National Roll Scheme helped disabled ex-servicemen to secure employment and provided grants to industrial undertakings which employed them. In the United States the Soldiers' Rehabilitation Act of 1918 provided a vocational rehabilitation service for disabled veterans. The later Federal Vocational Rehabilitation Act of 1920 provided funds for disabled civilians. It is doubtful if these Acts and the British scheme were used for the disabled mentally ill. However, in 1919 Frederick Milner founded the Ex-services Welfare Society to assist shell-shocked and neurasthenic ex-servicemen. After a hesitant beginning the society flourished and provided convalescent accommodation at Leatherhead. In 1927 Mr Everett Howard and the Society's committee recognized the need for the employment of residents. A factory manufacturing electric blankets was subsequently established and traded under the name of Thermega. This pioneering venture in psychiatric rehabilitation and resettlement attracted little attention, although its benefits were recognized by Professor Mapother, the society's consultant psychiatrist, when he visited in 1929. He wrote that 'it should be the end to which treatment proper leads for all that large group who are intermediate between fitness for normal employment and fitness for none. . . . It points a moral for application in ordinary psychiatry that may well have a wide influence in the future' (Tennent, 1960). In the years between the two wars there were notable advances in the training of the war blinded and in orthopaedic rehabilitation, while the need for post-hospital reconditioning was recognized following the Report of the British Medical Assocation's Fracture Committee in 1935. The establishment of rehabilitation for the tuberculous by Penderill Varrier-Jones and German Woodhead at the Bourne Colony in 1919, before the unit moved to Papworth, is of interest as many of the problems described have since been encountered in psychiatric rehabilitation (Woodhead and Varrier-Jones, 1920; Varrier-Jones, 1943).

In psychiatry for some time before and after the First World War the main rehabilitative drive was for early treatment of the mentally ill. In the first decades of the twentieth century this was initiated in outpatient clinics at Wakefield Asylum and St Thomas's Hospital. The Maudsley Hospital in London opened in 1923 and admitted patients who were under no legal restraints and could receive individual treatment as inpatients or outpatients. The changing emphasis was also reflected in the Report of the Royal Commission on Lunacy and Mental Disorder which, in 1926, suggested not only the abolition of the traditional demarcation between physical and mental illness, but also that of the connection between the treatment of mental illness and the Poor Law (Jones, 1954). Other recommendations led to the Mental Treatment Act of 1930 which granted the status of voluntary patients to that section of the population who could not afford private treatment; it also made money available for the establishment of more outpatient clinics. New attempts to reform the hypertrophied and neglected mental hospitals received a stimulus from Germany where Dr Herman Simon used work in a programme to counter the institutionalization of patients in his hospital at Gutersloh (Simon, 1927, 1929). He saw work as part of an educative process the purpose of which was to prepare patients to return to everyday life. Interest in his work spread throughout Europe and particularly to the Netherlands. Eventually his ideas found their way to England following a visit to Holland by a delegation of British psychiatrists (Evans, 1929). In the United States, Abraham Myerson and Kenneth Tillotson established what they called the 'total push' method of treatment for 'deteriorating' patients in Boston State Hospital (Myerson, 1939; Tillotson, 1939). Myerson said that 'when a patient has been put into an institution his remaining initiative is taken from him. His social contacts become diminished; he becomes entirely passive in activities. He is immersed in, and perhaps more importantly, he lives in a "motivation vacuum".' Myerson used such methods as physiotherapy, exercise and games, better diet and vitamins. On the psychological side there was an improvement in clothing and the use of praise and blame, reward and punishment. In his last paragraph he says, 'it may be added that this sort of prison stupor is one of the dangers that threaten the hospital attendant and the hospital physician'. In Britain a Government report (Mental Deficiency Committee, 1929) suggested that the institution should no longer be 'a stagnant pool but should become a flowing lake, always taking in, always sending out'. But these changes were only a pale shadow of what was to come during and after the Second World War.

### The Stimulus of War

For the disabled the Second World War created what Straus (1966) described as 'a situation of broader social need'. The need was for manpower. A full description of the measures taken for the management of psychiatric casualties during the war is given by Ahrenfeldt (1958). It was found that many of those who had responded well to treatment subsequently relapsed after they had returned to their units and duties. Aubrey Lewis suggested a plan called the Annexure Scheme (Wittkower and Lebeaux, 1943). He felt that soldiers who failed to adjust to army conditions and developed neurotic symptoms should, if possible, be employed on the type of military work for which, within broad limits, they were more fitted. He said that 'it is not a question of being kind and grandmotherly to the man, but of making him a useful soldier of a particular kind, instead of letting him remain a useless soldier of another kind and eventually discarding him'. Aubrey Lewis also undertook a study of the resettlement of neurotic patients in civilian life. The social condition of these discharged neurotic soldiers, as revealed by his survey, was far from satisfactory, but Lewis thought that 'further development of the arrangements for co-operation between psychiatric and social, especially industrial, agencies would be likely to bring about further improvement' (Lewis, 1943). The idea was not only to attempt to modify the neurotic disability, but to foster the individual's adaptation by a change of environment. Similar efforts were made to improve the adjustment of dull and backward soldiers by transferring them to the Army's Pioneer Corps.

Further developments in rehabilitation were stimulated by the ever-present need for manpower, a feeling of moral obligation towards war casualties, and the assumption of responsibility by the Ministry of Health for hospitals in the Emergency Medical Service.

### The Third Phase of Rehabilitation

These developments marked the first steps in the transition from charitable concern to the third historical stage in the care of the handicapped, where attempts are made to modify the disability and compensate for it by developing other abilities (Clarke, 1962). In 1941 the Ministry of Labour, in conjunction with the Ministry of Health, started an interim scheme for the training and resettlement of the disabled. For the first time the process of rehabilitation flowed, without administrative hindrance, from medical treatment to industrial resettlement, as cooperation was established between the Ministry of Labour, the hospitals, and voluntary agencies. An Inter-departmental Committee on the Rehabilitation and Resettlement of Disabled Persons, better known as the Tomlinson Committee, reported in 1943. The committee examined the needs of a wide range of disabled persons, including those with neurosis and psychosis, and recommended that any scheme should be open to *all* disabled persons whatever the cause or nature of this disablement. These recommendations were embodied in the Disabled Persons' Act of 1944 which laid down a comprehensive pattern for the rehabilitation of the disabled in Great Britain. In the United States the Barden–La Follette Vocational Rehabilitation Act, approved in 1943, similarly extended rehabilitation to all disabled persons who could profit from it (Switzer, 1946). With the end of the war in Britain civilian resettlement units were established to facilitate the readjustment and resettlement of ex-prisoners of war, returning from abroad, in civilian life. The Ministry of Labour supported by the Ministry of Health established the Industrial Neurosis Unit at Belmont Hospital to examine the needs of the chronic unemployed neurotic. Dr Maxwell Jones, who had previous experience with the rehabilitation of neurotic soldiers at Mill Hill and with the resettlement of prisoners of war, was put in charge of this unit. Its aims were to rehabilitate and resettle those chronically unemployed, by reasons of neurosis, in the most appropriate job possible (Jones, 1952). Over the years the aims of the unit changed with its name; it became the Social Rehabilitation Unit in 1954 and later was renamed the Henderson Hospital, specializing in the use of community methods for the readjustment of psychopaths. At that time concepts of rehabilitation were still not firmly established. Rapoport, examining the unit's function in 1960, noted that the staff considered that they were giving treatment, which was simultaneously rehabilitation. He felt that the lack of a conceptual distinction between treatment and rehabilitation led to recurrent difficulties.

> The Unit's staff have tended to assume that treatment in the Unit is accomplished through rehabilitation to the Unit and that rehabilitation in the Unit is a dress rehearsal for rehabilitation to the outside world. Our own proposition, based on the research findings . . . is that treatment and rehabilitation aims ought to be kept distinct

for while they may be mutually reinforcing they are often independent and even conflicting (Rapoport, 1960).

In British mental hospitals there had been no explicit rehabilitation of the mentally ill, although in some hospitals doors were being unlocked and there was even talk of a return to moral treatment (Rees, 1957a). An early approach to mental hospital rehabilitation was the 'habit training' of chronic patients (Symons, 1951). This was actuated by the desire to help the mentally ill to adapt more successfully to life in hospital and to reduce the burdens of nursing care (Bennett and Robertson, 1955). Similar developments were reported in the United States (Sines et al., 1952; Galioni et al., 1953). Hospitals were recovering after the war, and conditions in many hospitals both in Britain and the United States were at a low ebb. There was considerable overcrowding and there was a lack of staff. However, it was felt that as a result of treatment with electro-convulsive therapy which began in 1945, and insulin treatment which commenced in 1952, many more patients were able to occupy themselves constructively and opportunities to do so were made available (Miller and Clancy, 1952; Chittick et al., 1961).

In Britain, Tizard and O'Connor, investigating the disabilities and rehabilitation of the mentally retarded, found that patients were still engaged in occupations which were out of date. 'Only in the protected environment of hospital could these uneconomical and outmoded methods continue' (Tizard and O'Connor, 1952). As a result, they introduced simple, paid subcontract work into these hospitals (O'Connor and Tizard, 1956). The subsequent discovery of the capacity of the mentally retarded for gainful employment led to a new interest in the aptitudes and disabilities of the mentally ill. A number of British psychiatrists visited the Continent to study the use of occupation in the treatment of chronic psychotics (Carstairs et al., 1955). Subsequently, members of the Medical Research Council (MRC) Social Psychiatry Unit established a workshop at Banstead Hospital to study the effect of psychiatric disability on work and employment. Paid industrial sub-contract work was introduced into this workshop. Its use not only provided a realistic medium for the assessment of the patients' capabilities, but was seen to benefit those who had been sitting in the wards doing nothing for years on end (Carstairs et al., 1956).

Advances in the biological therapies were slowing down and their efficacy was being questioned. On the other hand, there was a growing awareness of the influence of the social organization of mental hospital care on the adjustment of patients and a reassessment of the relative value of biological therapy and changes in the patient's social environment (Freudenberg *et al.*, 1957). At the same time as Maxwell Jones (1952) was trying to create an alternative hospital environment which would foster the adjustment of patients, other writers were drawing attention to the disabling effects of life in the traditional mental hospital (Stanton and Schwartz, 1954; Goffman, 1961). In different countries and in different hospitals new programmes for the resocialization of patients, for their remotivation and the modification of their disabilities, were being established (Greenblatt, *et al.*, 1957). What was done varied from country to country, but in outline there was an attempt to reduce disabilities, to change attitudes and to enable the patient to make full use of what residual capacity he had. These developments depended, in part, on an expansion in the number of nurses, doctors, occupational therapists, and social workers employed in psychiatry.

The gap between hospital and community was closing from both sides. In the hospital, working patients and those taking part in groups showed themselves to be more competent than they had seemed. When these changes were recognized by staff, their attitude to, and relationship with, patients was changed. The community for its part was beginning to abandon its self-imposed ignorance of the extent of mental illness and to develop a new feeling of responsibility for the mentally ill. In Britain these changes were reflected in the increase of mental hospital admissions and discharges between 1950 and 1955. Other changes were taking place. The National Health Service Act of 1948 had vested responsibility for both the general and the mental hospitals in Regional Hospital Boards, responsible in their turn to the Ministry of Health. In 1954 a Royal Commission was set up to examine the law relating to mental illness and mental deficiency. When it reported in 1957 it recommended that the law should be altered so that, whenever possible, suitable care should be provided for mentally disordered people with no more restriction of liberty or legal formality than were applied to people who needed care because of other types of illness or disability or social difficulties (Royal Commission, 1957). When these recommendations received legislative sanction in the Mental Health Act of 1959, the mentally sick and the mentally retarded, except those who denied their need for treatment, were to be given parity of care with the physically sick. Mental illness and retardation were not necessarily to be forms of social deviance warranting legal expulsion from society and detention in an institution, but illnesses which entitled their sufferers to the same medical consideration, help, or rehabilitation as the patient with a physical disease or disability. The Act made no mention of rehabilitation, but the distinction between hospital care and the use of those 'forms of treatment and training and social services which can be given without bringing patients into hospital as inpatients, or which make it possible to discharge them from hospital sooner than was usual in the past' would depend very much on the nature and extent of those patients' disabilities (Royal Commission, 1957). In the United States federally supported rehabilitation was extended in 1954 with the provision of training grants.

## Concepts of Disability and Rehabilitation

There had been many different definitions of rehabilitation (Schwartz, 1953), but these were often so generalized that it was difficult to use them in programme planning and development. Schwartz comments that 'because of the problems involved in and the disagreement about what constitutes the concept of rehabilitation' there was no clearly delineated body of rehabilitation literature as such. There were other difficulties. Most definitions of rehabilitation had as their aim the restoration of the disabled person to his former state. There was little or no criticism of this overambitious aim which even today still persists in some quarters. There was then, as now, confusion, too, between rehabilitation and resettlement, and Schwartz did question whether the aim of rehabilitation was reintegration into the community, just living outside the mental hospital, living in the community and being able to support oneself economically, or full recovery from illness.

In practical terms it was evident that with the opening of the hospital doors patients did not leave, presumably because they were unable to cope with life in the outside world. They were disabled; but even less attention had been given to concepts of disability. In the USA, Gruenberg formulated the concept of the Social Breakdown Syndrome. He believed that the disability was only partly intrinsic. In large part it was an artefact extrinsic to the illness. He saw the syndrome as analogues to cardiac decompensation and shock and described it as following one of three patterns: (a) withdrawal, (b) anger and hostility, and (c) a combination of these two (Program Area Committee on Mental Health, 1961; Gruenberg, 1967). In Britain, John Wing, a member and later the director of the MRC Social Psychiatry Research Unit, had earlier worked out his own formulation of disability. He said

the patient may be handicapped by his illness (by slowness in schizophrenia for example) and these primary disabilities may be influenced by numerous social factors. If the illness is chronic, secondary handicaps of various kinds will almost certainly develop in response to various social pressures whether the patient stays for a long time in an institution or not. These will take the form of personal attitudes or habits which prevent the attainment of optimum social functioning. Individuals who are handicapped from the start by a poor education or lack of work skills, with deprived home backgrounds or one or another kind of personality disorder, will be especially liable to accumulate extra social disadvantages and secondary handicaps. The pattern of disabilities is unique for each person but once it is worked out a rational prescription of social treatments becomes possible. (Wing, 1967)

Wing further believed that this breakdown of handicaps into their component parts was more useful, more scientific than 'to force all reactions to all disapproved social environments into one all-embracing "social breakdown syndrome".' (Wing, 1967). It can be difficult to distinguish secondary handicaps from those which are part of the disease process (Wing, 1963). Such distinctions may only be made from a consideration of the individuals' response to treatment or rehabilitation.

Members of the MRC Social Psychiatry Unit attempted to define and make precise and objective measurements of psychiatric disabilities. They found, for example, that chronic schizophrenic patients were slow on psychomotor indices, slow to learn, and showed a poor response to incentives (O'Connor *et al.*, 1956; O'Connor and Rawnsley, 1959; Topping and O'Connor, 1960; Venables and Tizard, 1956). Even when such patients responded to an incentive they rapidly relapsed when it was withdrawn (Wing and Freudenberg, 1961). In an Industrial Rehabilitation Unit (IRU) chronic schizophrenic patients were noted by their supervisors to be slow, lacking in initiative, and to have impaired capacity for independent judgement. They could not make complicated decisions and they lacked manual skill (Wing, 1960). It was recognized, too, that chronic schizophrenic patients were subject to symptomatic relapse in situations which were socially overstimulating, or understimulating. In schizophrenia disabilities were not necessarily fixed, but were responsive to changes in the social environment. Such patients have a marked tendency to withdraw socially. If there is no social stimulation this withdrawal is fostered, together with passivity, inertia, and lack of initiative. On the other hand, if the patient is overstimulated socially he may well break down and once again develop florid psychotic symptoms (Stone and Eldred, 1959; Wing *et al.*, 1964). For this reason it was realized that for such patients, and perhaps for all disabled patients, rehabilitation had to be arranged in a series of steps in which social expectations are slowly increased without causing undue stress to the patient. Secondary handicaps, too, were delineated. The longer a patient with schizophrenia has been in hospital the less likely he is to want to leave or to have any realistic plans for a future life outside (Wing, 1962). This increasing dependence is part of a syndrome of institutionalism. Normal habits are lost and maladaptive habits develop in hospital. The unfavourable opinions and attitudes of others to the patient's mental hospital stay are also shown to be secondary handicaps.

### Industrial Rehabilitation and Resettlement

In the later 1950s both in Britain and America resettlement of mental hospital patients became the main aim of psychiatric rehabilitation. But not all disabled persons can achieve this end. Many cannot be placed in employment, or, if they are disabled housewives, are not able to return to a normal domestic life. So they are not resettled, for resettlement was defined as placement in economic employment or domestic life. While resettlement is the ideal aim of rehabilitation, an improvement in adaptation which enables the disabled person to make the best use of his residual capacities in as normal a social context as possible is properly regarded as the aim of rehabilitation. Such distinction between resettlement and rehabilitation is not pedantic for confusion leads to poor rehabilitation practice. Those who confuse the aims of rehabilitation and resettlement are heard even today to say that this or that disabled person cannot be rehabilitated because he will never be able to work and earn a living in open employment. A recent survey of the patient population of London mental hospitals suggested that 'no rehabilitation was needed or possible for 40% of patients' (Bewley *et al.*, 1975). This shows a misunderstanding of the process of rehabilitation and disregards the needs of those who are most handicapped. Although not every handicapped person can be resettled, few cannot be rehabilitated. It may seem paradoxical, but the disabled can also be resettled without being rehabilitated. Many patients are discharged from hospital and placed in work without prior rehabilitation in the sense of having been helped to make the *best* possible use of their residual abilities.

Nevertheless this period, in which resettlement dominated rehabilitation thinking, was productive in so far as psychiatrists were forced to match their view of the patient's abilities and disabilities against the realities of adaptation and functioning in life outside hospital. This trend meant that for some time rehabilitation was seen in terms of discharge from hospital and the restoration of a capacity for gainful employment. This was not surprising given the difficulties faced by the mentally disabled both in mental hospitals and in the community. There were few supportive or sheltered facilities in the community and the disabled were often looked upon as a burden on the community (Bennett and Wing, 1963). If they were to be resettled and to survive in society most had to be able to earn a living. So more emphasis had to be given to their preparation for an employment role in society. Following the establishment of an experimental industrial therapy workshop in Banstead Hospital under the auspices of the Medical Research Council (Carstairs *et al.*, 1956), industrial therapy units were introduced in many mental hospitals (Kidd, 1965; Wansbrough and Miles, 1968). Even where workshops were not established there was an increasing use of 'work for pay' in former occupational therapy departments (Bennett, 1966). The work was usually contracted from industrial concerns outside the hospital and was paid at the piecework rate obtaining for normal workers in the community. It helped to reactivate long unemployed chronic patients and prepare them for subsequent resettlement in employment.

Thus Early considered that industrial therapy was the first stage of 'economic' occupational rehabilitation since it took place under more realistic conditions than those of the ward or the occupational therapy department (Early, 1965b). It introduced a new realism into patients' lives. Resettlement demanded realistic assessment of assets and disabilities. Before its introduction the expectations of patients' performance held by doctors and nurses were often unrealistically low.

There were critics of industrial work in mental hospitals (MacDonald, 1960; Bickford, 1963) and of the stress put on vocational resettlement. Some thought that while emphasis on work was legitimate for the physically disabled it was less appropriate for the psychiatrically disabled. Aubrey Lewis did not feel that this view was justified. 'The human relations involved in adjusting to work are so exacting in many cases, and the satisfactions derived from work are so great, it can hardly be denied that it is an important indicator as well as an important means of rehabilitation' (Lewis, 1955). Rehabilitation and resettlement was still a kind of folk wisdom. At this time both in England and in the USA 'a great deal of rehabilitation is built up on faith, hope, and rule of thumb. We could do better than that, we could plan our programs so that they may disclose principles governing successful rehabilitation and the factors which restrict it' (Lewis, 1955). Much early rehabilitation research was formulated in terms of resettlement. Meyer and Borgatta's (1959) attempt to evaluate an experiment in employment resettlement undertaken by the Altro workshops at Hillside Hospital in New York was one of the first. It was impaired by the difficulty of acquiring an adequate control group. In consequence, the findings suggested, but did not substantiate, the view that rehabilitation available in the Altro workshop produced positive results. The assessment of the rehabilitation of chronic patients with schizophrenia in a British Ministry of Labour IRU showed that moderately ill patients with schizophrenia were more likely to be resettled than those who were severely ill when compared with matched controls who remained in hospital (Wing and Giddens, 1959). Subsequently, twelve patients with schizophrenia were sent to the IRU and twelve matched patients attended a course of lectures, seminars, and films. Attitudes to hospital discharge improved in both groups and both groups showed significantly less social withdrawal. Neither group showed any improvement in primary handicap. In a further study (Wing et al., 1964) 45 long-stay patients with schizophrenia from two mental hospitals were sent to IRUs. Six showed an exacerbation of symptoms and it was felt that of these at least five had been inadequately prepared for the stresses of life and work in a 'near industrial' situation. The study also examined the proportion of long-stay patients with schizophrenia who were quickly resettled in the community with the special use of industrial and social rehabilitation. Further studies indicated the importance, in addition to the disabilities due to schizophrenia, of the degree of confidence with which the ex-patient approached the rehabilitation process, and the confidence which he could develop during his stay at the IRU (Wing, 1966).

These IRUs provided for the extra mural vocational rehabilitation of mental hospital patients. They not only helped the resettlement of patients but did much to change the attitude of hospital staff and the public. Their activities are described by Maxwell Jones (1956) and Goldberg (1967). These units had developed after the war in line with the requirements of the Disabled Persons' Act, 1944. This Act also required the Ministry of Labour to maintain a register of persons who were substantially handicapped by reason of their disability in obtaining or keeping employment. This included the psychiatrically disabled. It required every employer who had 20 employees or more to include amongst them 3 per cent of the registered disabled. Certain occupations such as car park attendant and lift attendant were reserved for the disabled person. It established sheltered employment in so-called Remploy factories. The Act also provided that there would be Disablement Resettlement Officers at every employment exchange to find work for the disabled.

In spite of all this provision, a Committee of enquiry on the Rehabilitation, Training, and Resettlement of Disabled Persons (1956), the Piercy Committee, said that the mentally disabled presented special problems of rehabilitation and resettlement, not only by reason of their number and variety but also because of the special statutory provision applying to them. It recognized that at that time nearly half the beds in the National Health Service hospitals were occupied by mentally ill or disabled patients, and said that the numbers involved, together with those treated as outpatients, represented a considerable problem of rehabilitation and resettlement. The committee presented an interesting classification of patients suffering from psychosis or neurosis. The first group were those whom they considered to have been highly socially trained and employable. The second group were convalescent patients whose recovery was not as complete as that of the first group, and who needed expert rehabilitation preparatory to help in getting work. Then there were patients with residual instability who were employable but needed to live under psychiatric supervision and care. Finally there were deteriorating mental patients who must remain as inpatients although some were capable of training and occupation in hospital workshops. They felt that the first group presented no special problem and could use the kind of help available for the non-disabled. They felt that for the second group, arrangements should be made with industrial rehabilitation units so that patients could attend while still living in hospital. They also felt that hostels might be useful. For the third group they thought that care might be better provided in separate hospital annexes convenient for patients' work rather than in the main hospital itself. For the fourth they recommended that simple factory work could be provided within the hospital. While these suggestions were never fully implemented they showed a growing appreciation of the range of disability in group, although not in individual terms. The report also illustrated a change in the position of the mental patient. The psychiatrically disabled were no longer seen as being isolated in the mental hospital. Instead, family doctors, some local authorities, employment services, employers, and voluntary organizations were beginning to play a part in rehabilitation and resettlement. Transitional services were developing to bridge the persisting gap between the hospital and the community. As the possibilities of successful rehabilitation were recognized, some hospitals in Britain developed comprehensive services with rehabilitation policies. In his account of mental health services in Europe, Furman (1965) described hospital rehabilitation services at Cheadle Royal Hospital near Manchester, Glenside Hospital Bristol, Netherne Hospital, Coulsdon, and St Wulstan's Hospital at Malvern. There are, of course, many other hospitals worthy of mention, but these four hospitals have been the subject, perhaps, of most research, evaluation, and report.

### Mental Hospital Rehabilitation Services in Britain in the 1960s

Cheadle Royal Hospital is one of the few mental hospitals in Britain which operates outside the National Health Service, since it remains a private hospital for fee-paying patients. It began to develop a rehabilitation service in 1957 and established an industrial unit manufacturing and marketing its own products. At that time it was perhaps the most sophisticated example of the use of industrial expertise in the organization, management, staffing, and operation of a hospital workshop, although this pattern has not been replicated elsewhere (Wadsworth *et al.*, 1962).

Glenside Hospital, built in 1863, had for years the responsibility of caring for the long-stay chronic patients in the Bristol area. Dr Early, the Physician Superintendent, felt that the success achieved by the introduction of industrial therapy during the 1950s emphasized the need for further training in the community if former long-stay patients were to take their place in open industry. Industrial work was introduced at Glenside in 1957. In January 1958, fourteen patients were doing industrial work. By December 1959 this number had increased to 385 (Early, 1960). The industries supplying the work were impressed by the quality of the finished product and felt that, with further employment training, many patients could be employed in open industry. These industrialists, together with civic dignitaries, and representatives of the Church and the unions, joined with Dr Early to establish the Bristol Industrial Therapy Organization (ITO) (Early, 1960; Early and Magnus, 1968). This was a non-profit-making company, limited by guarantee, which offered medically and industrially supervised training for employment under conditions approximating, as far as possible, ordinary factory conditions. This scheme, like that of Netherne Hospital, was not solely concerned with *vocational* rehabilitation. Early recognized that at an appropriate stage during the process of economic rehabilitation, domestic resettlement must begin: the ultimate aim being independence in the open community (Early, 1965a, 1973). Most hospitals offered a restricted gradient of increasing expectations within the hospital, so that a patient moved to a ward with less nursing supervision as his condition improved. Early recognized that this intra-hospital gradient was not complete without the provision of similar extra-hospital steps in domestic living, so that from being in hospital the patient could move to a hostel or to a training house, a supervised hostel or unsupervised hostel, lodging, bedsitting room, flat, house, hotel, or to living with his own family. Thus, under the umbrella of the ITO he sought to provide a series of working and living situations arranged in steps.

At Netherne Hospital attempts had been made to provide and evaluate 'habit training' for chronic patients (Bennett and Robertson, 1955). Later, a resettlement unit was opened for those patients who were likely to be capable of employment (Bennett et al., 1961). About the same time long-stay patients were moved to hospital villas which were run on 'milieu' lines rather than as 'therapeutic communities'. This programme of 'milieu therapy', together with the provision of industrial subcontract work and the arrangement of the wards and the workshop situation into independent 'ladders' of graded expectations, seemed to contribute to a better outcome for chronic patients with schizophrenia when they were compared with similar patients at two other hospitals studied by Wing and Brown (1970). The programmes for long-stay patients were more fully described by Freudenberg et al., (1957) and Bennett et al., (1961). In the resettlement unit it was possible to overcome some of the major restrictions of hospital life. Patients were mixed by sex as early as 1957 and were also encouraged to take more personal responsibility for themselves and for their daily lives. Most patients who were not working outside hospital worked either in a utility department, in the hospital services, or on paid industrial subcontract work. It was recognized that for resettlement the hospital team needed the support of the community services.

St Wulstan's Hospital is still the only specialized regional hospital for the rehabilitation of long-stay mental hospital patients in Britain (Morgan et al., 1965; Query, 1968). Patients were referred to St Wulstan's from twelve mental hospitals in the Birmingham region. Dr Morgan, who established the unit, accepted patients who had been in hospital 2 years, were under 55 years of age, not legally committed and not mentally retarded. The aim of the hospital programme was to foster socialization and vocational readaptation of the patients with a view of their resettlement in work outside hospital. There was no time limit on a patient's stay but the hospital had the right to select patients and to refer them back to the parent hospital when necessary. Some 85 per cent of the patients had a diagnosis of schizophrenia. The main difference from most other hospitals was that, since all the patients worked, the workshops took the place of the wards. All the nursing and other staff were to be found in the workshops and it was there, too, that the patients' notes were kept. The wards were really dormitories which were empty during working hours.

## Psychiatric Rehabilitation in the United States in the 1950s and 1960s

In the United States psychiatric rehabilitation developed more slowly. This may have been due to a different relationship between the mental hospital and the community it served (Greenblatt and Lidz, 1957). Greenblatt and his colleagues thought that 'in England where community responsibility has been considerable, it has been possible for hospitals like Warlingham Park to flourish'. They also recognized the part played by the British social welfare legislation. 'In the United States, by contrast, governmental support for rehabilitation of the mentally ill has been lagging, although determined efforts are now being made to remedy this deficit.' Even so, in 1954 Congress had passed Public Law 565 amending the Federal Vocational Rehabilitation Act and making funds available for a series of demonstration projects. Later, after Congress passed the Health Amendments Act Title V in 1956, the National Institutes of Mental Health could provide further money for the rehabilitation of the mentally ill both in hospitals and in the community. Yet in the United States in the late 1950s the main thrust had been to remove the restrictive and punitive barriers between patients and staff in the mental hospitals and to turn these custodial institutions into more therapeutic hospitals. Altro Health and Rehabilitation Services were an exception.

In 1953 their workshop had been engaged in experimental collaboration with Hillside Hospital in New York City for the rehabilitation of a few psychiatrically disabled patients (Meyer and Borgatta, 1959). Altro saw itself as providing a staging point on the transition from hospital to adjustment in the workaday world. Already at that time the staff at Altro had discovered that the mentally ill required a longer time in the workshop than other rehabilitees. Bert Black, the director, noted that 'the degree of dependency of psychiatric patients is nothing short of fantastic' when they were compared with those tuberculous and cardiac patients which the workshop had been accustomed to help. Altro continued to be committed to the rehabilitation of the mentally ill and in 1963 reported on a programme of rehabilitation initiated in 1958 in cooperation with Rockland State Hospital (Black, 1963). As a result of that study various guides to the assessment of patients for rehabilitation were proposed. Manhattan State Hospital opened a sheltered workshop in 1958 and other State hospitals, such as Medfield in Massachusetts and Middletown in Long Island, followed in 1962. The PROP Shop at Boston State Hospital and the CHIRP Programme which grew out of Dr Peffer's PEP Programme at Brockton VA Hospital (Knudson, 1959), used subcontract work from outside suppliers. Like their British counterparts, those involved in these programmes (which are discussed in more detail by Black, 1970) stressed the importance to patients of working for pay (Peffer, 1956).

Throughout the United States in the 1930s, centres had been established in a number of cities by the Jewish Vocational Services to meet problems of religious discrimination in the private employment services. With the establishment of public employment services and a gradual change in the attitude towards Jewish job applicants, the primary purpose of these services faded. They turned to the task of helping the more severely disabled young handicapped. These centres provided a programme somewhat similar to, but substantially different from, that of the British IRU. Not many of the programmes seem to have run long into the 1960s. In general it seems to have been concluded that, while the results of their efforts were superior to those of the State hospitals in securing competitive employment for their psychiatrically disabled clients, the percentage of people getting jobs was small—about 25 per cent. They felt that their programmes were more successful in promoting the discharge than in promoting the employment of former patients. Their model of rehabilitation for psychiatrically ill patients embraced preparation in an institutional setting, a transitional phase with a community orientation, and, finally, a phase of community integration. They recognized that continued support from staff would be necessary if their clients were going to develop and maintain their role performance, and achieve the final goal of community integration. With the passage of time these services have changed. Some have maintained a rehabilitation interest, while others have redirected their efforts to group psychotherapy or community psychiatry.

### From Hospital to Community

It was difficult in the late 1950s to appreciate that the mental hospital was already in decline. Yet as a result of a number of trends, doubtless including the more vigorous rehabilitation and resettlement of hospital patients, the population of these institutions in the United States and in Britain was decreasing (Tooth and Brooke, 1961; Brill and Patton, 1962). The gap between the mental hospital and the community was being bridged by the disabled patients who were resettled, by the introduction of 'normal' roles with paid employment in mental hospitals, and by the involvement of extra-mural services and resources. The possibility and necessity of transferring patients and rehabilitation to the community were underlined in both rhetoric and research. Dr T. P. Rees, a pioneer of the 'open' hospital, said

the time has come when we should ask ourselves seriously whether the interests of the mentally ill are best served by providing more psychiatric beds, building bigger and better mental hospitals. Perhaps we should concentrate our efforts on treating patients within the community of which they form part and teach that community to tolerate and accept their idiosyncrasies . . . Has not the time arrived when psychiatrists should see more patients in their own homes, within the family setting rather than in the more artificial atmosphere of the outpatient department or of the psychiatric observation ward? (Rees, 1957b)

Such views led psychiatrists and others to consider how many hospital residents could adjust to community life. To this end they began to survey hospital patient populations. One study examined more than a thousand patients who had been continuously resident for 2 years or more. At that time a hospital stay of 2 years was generally accepted as an index of disability (Cross *et al.*, 1957). Two thirds of the male and three quarters of the female patients had been in hospital for 10 years or more. Many patients did not show any serious behaviour problems and retention in hospital often seemed to depend on social and other factors unrelated to the severity of the illness. The disabilities were considered in terms of the amount of nursing supervision required. Garratt *et al.*, (1957) studying an even larger number of Birmingham residents in mental hospitals, classified the patients according to the type of facilities required for their care. Only 13 per cent were thought to need the full resources of a hospital while 55 per cent needed limited hospital services. Again, the assessment was in terms of care needed, and, of course, there is a big difference between that and the abilities needed to function in the community. However, these studies did direct attention to, and stimulate interest in, those patients who were most likely to be resettled or more likely to respond to whatever rehabilitation was available.

Wing and Brown (1970) compared the disabilities of patients with schizophrenia in three mental hospitals using Wing's (1961) 'simple and reliable' classification of schizophrenia. They showed the difference in the distribution of disabilities in those hospitals. Thus while Hospital A had 40 per cent of patients who were moderately disabled, Hospital C had 23 per cent; 26 per cent of patients in Hospital A showed poverty of speech or were mute, compared with 56 per cent of patients with that disability in Hospital C. A further survey of the functional handicaps of a sample of 150 long-stay schizophrenic patients at Netherne Hospital showed that 45 per cent were moderately ill but only 13 per cent of that sample appeared likely to be able to hold down stable jobs and be discharged from hospital within a few months (Catterson *et al.*, 1963).

There was still uncertainty about the effects which former patients would have on their families and others, and talk of 'burden on the community'. Certainly, a considerable proportion of discharged patients who had been in hospital at least 2 years, three quarters of whom suffered from schizophrenia, were found to be a liability in the community at the time of follow-up (Brown *et al.*, 1958). It was reckoned that 60 per cent of discharged patients were moderately disturbed or had severely strained relations with their families (Waters and Northover, 1965; Wing *et al.*, 1964). At first disabilities were regarded as being fixed and stable following rehabilitation; but it was soon recognized that overstimulation in the family situation, as in the hospital environment, had an influence on symptomatic relapse as well as on the role performance of the disabled person (Freeman and Simmons, 1958). Brown *et al.*, (1958) showed that patients who went to live in lodgings with their siblings were more likely to stay out of hospital than those who went to live with parents or wives or in large hostels. Brown subsequently demonstrated that these results could not be entirely explained in terms of more severely ill patients returning to their parental home. He formulated the view that schizophrenic patients could not tolerate strong feelings of like or dislike. In a subsequent paper (Brown *et al.*, 1962) it was shown that such patients were more likely to relapse in homes where there were strongly expressed emotions and a high degree of contact with the key relative. At that time the only solution appeared to be to place the patient in another environment, preferably in a hostel, or to reduce the amount of time which he or she spent with the family. There was little thought of working with such families. Doubtless such views were reinforced by the follow-up study of Stringham (1952). Of 33 patients discharged after an average stay in hospital of 12 years, 24 were still in the community 2 years later. Only half of these were self-supporting. There were many factors favouring successful community adjustment, but two of the most important were having gainful employment and living away from home. Goldberg (1966) showed that the work performance of patients living with parents was worse than that of patients living with other kin or in lodgings. The finding that life in the parental home for the patient with schizophrenia compared badly with other settings was widely accepted; Simmons and Freeman (1959) showed that mothers were more tolerant than wives while Freeman and Simmons (1958) showed that more patients were considered unwell who lived in parental rather than conjugal homes. In spite of these interesting findings, little was done at this time in terms of family rehabilitation, for in Britain and the United States personal social services in the community were rudimentary. In 1958 Harris said that in Britain 'Local authorities have some sort of service for the supervision of the mental defectives and services of widely varying standards and completeness for the care of old people. None, as far as I know, made any substantial provision for the psychotic discharged from hospital' (Harris, 1958). Communication and continuity of treatment between the duly authorized officers who were responsible for removing certified patients to hospital and the few psychiatric social workers and psychiatrists were very inadequate (Lawson, 1966). Follow-up was woefully inadequate. Parkes *et al.*, (1962) showed that, of 100 male schizophrenic patients discharged from mental hospitals in the London area, only 4 patients were visited by a social worker during the follow-up year.

## Community Rehabilitation

In Britain the movement of the care and rehabilitation of the psychiatrically disabled from mental hospitals to the community was given impetus by the Royal Commission on the Law Relating to Mental Illness and Mental Deficiency and in America by the Report of the Joint Commission on Mental Illness and Health. The views of the commissions were surprisingly similar. Both believed that the objective of the modern treatment of people with major mental illness was to enable them to maintain themselves in the community in as normal a manner as possible. The Joint Commission urged that aftercare and rehabilitation were essential parts of the service to mental patients, and that various methods of achieving this rehabilitation should be integrated in all forms of service; among them day hospitals, family care, convalescent nursing homes, rehabilitation centres, work services, and ex-patient groups. In practice provision did not match these worthy sentiments, in either Britain or the United States. In the two countries the community response was somewhat different. In Britain there was a new Mental Health Act in 1959, while the legislative response in the United States was President Kennedy's Community Mental Health Centres Act of 1963. The chief aims of the American approach were to provide services in the community, to locate facilities reasonably near the patient's home, and to provide a comprehensive range of services. Further aims were to make services immediately available and easily accessible and to provide continuity of care until rehabilitation was completed. By 1973 community mental health centres were already providing the services for 23 per cent of inpatient and outpatient episodes in mental health facilities. While psychiatric care in this country and in the United States was moving outside the hospital and nearer the patient's home, rehabilitation still remained in the mental hospital. There seemed to be difficulties in reformulating rehabilitation. Perhaps this was not surprising. Rehabilitation had too often been equated with the resettlement of former mental hospital patients or even with their discharge from hospital. It was also difficult, when the mental hospitals had been considered one of the major causes of psychiatric disability, to concede the need for the rehabilitation of those patients who had never had that institutional experience. There were difficulties, too, because in many areas community services which are the necessary infrastructure for rehabilitation had yet to be provided. Even in the absence of adequate community facilities, enthusiasm generated by the success of physical treatments had led to the earlier discharge of partially recovered or unrecovered patients. The development of outpatient and domiciliary services, day hospitals and psychiatric units in general hospitals, meant that many patients were being treated without ever being admitted to a mental hospital.

Whether it was or was not recognized, we were entering a new phase of rehabilitation provision. This was called 'early' rehabilitation by Gastager

(1969) to distinguish it from 'late' rehabilitation in the mental hospital where considerable effort had to be expended in reversing the effects of past neglect. In early rehabilitation the disabled patient would not have had a long hospital stay. He might not have been in hospital at all. The disabilities, too, were different; less severe and less extensive, although less stable and more responsive to stress. Since the handicaps were not so gross, they alone were unlikely to determine the outcome of rehablitation. The patient's adaptation would also be determined by his adaptative capacity as indicated by his adjustment before disablement, by his coping capacity, and by the social support upon which he could draw. Little attention had been paid to these aspects of rehabilitation.

In spite of the recognition of psychiatric disability by the Tomlinson and the Piercy Committees, rehabilitation still meant physical rehabilitation in the minds of the public and the remedial professions. It was only during the late 1960s and early 1970s, with the establishment of psychiatric units in general hospitals, that psychiatric rehabilitation was first considered in the context of general medicine. The Department of Health had encouraged the development of psychiatric outpatient, day-patient, and inpatient services in general hospitals. At first it was thought that a substantial part of psychiatric inpatient care would have to be undertaken in the traditional mental hospital, but eventually it was decided that the general hospital psychiatric unit, in cooperation with the other parts of the health service and the social services, would replace the mental hospital. While there were, and are, doubts about this plan, the Central Health Services Council nevertheless set up a subcommittee on rehabilitation in 1968 to consider the future provision of rehabilitation services in the National Health Service and particularly in the District General Hospital (Standing Medical Advisory Committee on Rehabilitation, 1972). The report of this subcommittee, commonly known as the Tunbridge Committee, noted the lack of interest in, or recognition of the importance of, rehabilitation and the failure to appreciate that psychiatric and geriatric patients have the greatest need for this approach. Most importantly, it noted that psychiatric rehabilitation had in the past been directed to those patients whose primary psychiatric disabilities were aggravated by the secondary social disabilities of institutionalism. In future we would need to provide for those with unstable psychiatric disabilities who had spent only a short time in the hospital environment. It anticipated that, in time, district general hospitals would have psychiatric departments designed to meet the needs of the local population, and that each department would have a day hospital attached. While the committee's report received little attention from the Department of Health, it stimulated some thought about the similarities and differences between physical and psychiatric rehabilitation, and the nature of the differences between psychiatric and physical disability and between the physical and social environment (Bennett, 1978). The distinction between physical and psychiatric rehabilitation is clear. The psychiatrically disabled person has difficulties in performing roles in the social environment while the physically disabled has difficulty in performing tasks in the physical environment. It was recognized, of course, that there was some overlap between task performance and role performance; even so, their separation did something to clarify the aims of psychiatric rehabilitation.

Several studies, reviewed by Criswell (1968), showed that transitional facilities in the community did not influence the role performance of many patients. Patients who were 'fairly well' when entering a halfway house were 'well' when leaving and those who were 'sick' on entering did not improve. Criswell concluded that 'we are setting our sights too high if we are thinking of rehabilitation of marginally employed mental patients as a permanent return to full participation in the open community'. Certain patients may achieve this but many will not. A controlled study of rehabilitation in a British day hospital, using a sample of patients drawn from the catchment area population, showed no significant difference in outcome between the experimental and the control group when this was measured in terms of patients' attitudes, disabilities, and social performance (Griffiths, 1974; Stevens, 1973; Wing et al., 1972). It was obviously easier to improve the functioning of those who, in the mental hospital, had had no opportunity to adapt, than of those who, in the community setting, had not been able to adapt. It is likely that in any process of rehabilitation the adaptation of some patients will be improved while that of others will not.

With the move to the community the aim of rehabilitation began to change. Resettlement was no longer the main aim and rehabilitation was no longer solely the process of improving or restoring the function of the disabled person. The studies of Wing et al. (1972) and those quoted by Criswell (1968) throw considerable doubt on the view that psychiatric rehabilitation is a process of change in competence such as had been thought to take place in the mental hospital. Instead, it is a process of what Criswell calls 'accommodation'. This means that the professionals involved in rehabilitation have to be more concerned with the everyday 'real life' problems of people with mental illness. The disabled patient in the community often has difficulties in establishing and maintaining successful mutually interdependent relationships with others. Rehabilitation requires adjustment in the individual's social environment in terms of both his primary and secondary support systems (see Chapter 10). Thus the non-handicapped members of the system as well as the disabled person have to make adjustments. This is necessary because the social stresses in those systems exacerbate disabilities, while social supports are needed to buffer such stresses and to maintain acceptable role performance. It is not always easy for the disabled psychiatric patient or for relatives and friends to make these adjustments because patients have often shown behaviour which has alienated them from those family and friends. Alternatively, the family may be so critical or rejecting that life with them is not a desirable rehabilitation aim. For similar reasons disabled psychiatric patients often have difficulty in finding somewhere to live or reasonable employment (Ebringer and Christie-Brown, 1980). While employment is no longer a major goal of rehabilitation, it is a desirable aim for those who can achieve it. If the disabled person is not employed, occupation is essential, for, in schizophrenia at least, intrinsic disabilities are much influenced by an increase in the amount of time spent doing nothing (Wing and Brown, 1970).

The move to community rehabilitation has made other changes. It has broadened the aims of rehabilitation to include not only the vocational but also interpersonal and residential adjustment. It has indicated the need for 'combined operations'. There has to be an accommodation between the handicapped and the non-handicapped both within and outside the family. There has to be cooperation between staff and patient, since rehabilitation is not something that is 'done' to or for someone. There is a need for communication between staff in the multidisciplinary teams, between different forms of service such as residential, day, and inpatient care, as well as between medical and social, statutory and voluntary agencies. These changes have in turn directed attention not only to the individual's specific needs and very specific patterns of disability and ability, but also to the very specific demands and supports of the individual's environment. In early community rehabilitation, therefore, there has been a move away from the routine 'blunderbuss' rehabilitation of large groups of patients, practised formerly in the mental hospital, to the 'individual' approach which is emphasized in many chapters of this volume. It follows that in community rehabilitation there is a need 'for more study of the mental patient and his interaction with the non-handicapped, to find out what happens in such situations and how conditions can be altered to enable the sick and well to get along with mutual satisfaction' (Criswell, 1968). In Britain there is a continuing move to day hospital treatment which has not been pursued so actively in the United States and in other parts of the world. In 1960 there were fewer than 50 day units, providing under 2,000 places, by 1976 this had risen to 400 units with over 15,000 places (Carter et al., 1978). Day hospital rehabilitation exemplified Criswell's concerns, for patients are in the treatment world for, at most, 40 hours of the week; for at least part of the other 128 hours they are interacting with non-handicapped people. The recognition of his situation led Bennett et al. (1976) to adopt a family approach in a psychiatric day hospital. Although some of the principles of family therapy method were used, the family approach did not conform to any clear theoretical classification. The therapeutic responses to the patient's needs, therefore, extend beyond periodic family therapy to include daily group discussions and individual psychotherapy where appropriate. In preparation for work there is a need for rehabilitation staff to understand the real-life demands of the employment situation. In spite of the long history of vocational rehabilitation it is perhaps significant that initially little attention was given to the attitudes of employers to hiring the mentally ill (Olshansky *et al.*, 1958; Wansbrough and Cooper, 1980). There have been many more studies about halfway houses and other forms of residential care. While the value of psychiatric and other forms of traditional expertise in the care of psychiatric patients has been questioned, community residential care provided by Local Authority services has only offered a limited alternative to mental hospital care. One reason for this might be that treatment and clinical expertise have largely remained based in the psychiatric hospital so that facilities in the community have had only limited therapeutic strategies. In a study of hostels for psychiatric patients Ryan (1979) found that, although they provided a satisfactory unrestricted social milieu, staff lacked technical expertise and methods of coping with difficult behaviour or of developing the social functions of the residents.

Nevertheless, in the United States, psychologists and social workers are playing an ever greater part in rehabilitation and, in particular, in the development of community psychosocial rehabilitation. Since rehabilitation in the United States became a condition· of Federal financial support, in community and mental health centres there has been a more rapid development of psychosocial rehabilitation units. These centres are not new. Fountain House, the pioneer unit in New York, opened in the 1950s. The aim of such centres is to assist former psychiatric patients in their community adjustment. They variously seek to support patients, prepare them for employment, and provide residential care (Beard *et al.*, 1963). Probably the most comparable programme in Britain is that of the Psychiatric Rehabilitation Association in Bethnal Green and Tower Hamlets (Wilder, 1979). The growth of these centres and of other Local Authority day centres in the community does not necessarily prevent the desocialization which occurred in the mental hospitals. Studies of hostels and Local Authority day centres have revealed institutional practices (Shepherd and Richardson, 1979; Carter and Edwards, 1975). There is a growing interest in the provision of non-institutionalizing environments (King *et al.*, 1971; Otto and Orford, 1978).

Today rehabilitation is taking place at an earlier stage in the development of disability, and is more concerned with the prevention of disability in institutions. It is also locally based but, even so, the development of rehabilitation outside the hospital has been slow.

### References

Ahrenfeldt, R. H. (1958) *Psychiatry in the British Army in the Second World War*. Routledge & Kegan Paul, London.

Beard, J. H., Pitt, R. B., Fisher, S. H., and Goertzl, V. (1963) Evaluating the effectiveness of a psychiatric rehabilitation program. *American Journal of Orthopsychiatry*, **33**, 701–712.

Bennett, D. H. (1966) Future trends in psychiatric occupational therapy. In *Proceedings of the IVth International Congress of the World Federation of Occupational Therapists*. Excerpta Medica Foundation, London.

Bennett, D. H. (1978) Social forms of psychiatric treatment. In J. K. Wing, ed., *Schizophrenia: Towards a New Synthesis*. Academic Press, London.

Bennett, D., Fox, C., Jowell, T., and Skynner, A. C. R. (1976) Towards a family approach in a psychiatric day hospital. *British Journal of Psychiatry*, **129**, 73–81.

Bennett, D. H., Folkard, S., and Nicholson, A. K. (1961) Resettlement unit in a mental hospital. *Lancet*, **2**, 539–541.

Bennett, D. H., and Robertson, J. P. S. (1955) The effects of habit training on chronic schizophrenic patients. *Journal of Mental Science*, **101**, 664–672.

Bennett, D. H., and Wing, K. K. (1963) Sheltered workshops for the psychiatrically handicapped. In H. Freeman and J. Farndale, eds, *Trends in the Mental Health Services*. Pergamon, London.

Bewley, T., Bland, J. H., Ilo, M., Walch, E., and Willington, G. (1975) Census of mental hospital patients and life expectancy of those unlikely to be discharged. *British Medical Journal*, **1**, 671.

Bickford, J. A. R. (1963) Economic value of the psychiatric patient. *Lancet*, **i**, 714–715.

Black, B. J., ed. (1963) *Guides to Psychiatric Rehabilitation: A Co-operative Program with a State Mental Hospital*. Altro Health and Rehabilitation Services, Inc., New York.

Black, B. J. (1970) *Principles of Industrial Therapy for the Mentally Ill*. Grune & Stratton, New York.

Bockoven, J. S. (1963) *Moral Treatment in American Psychiatry*. Springer, New York.

Brill, H., and Patton, R. E. (1962) Clinical-statistical analysis of population changes in New York State mental hospitals since the introduction of psychotropic drugs. *American Journal of Psychiatry*, **119**, 20–35.

Brown, G. W., Carstairs, G. M., and Topping, G. (1958) Post-hospital adjustment of chronic mental patients. *Lancet*, **ii**, 685–689.

Brown, G. W., Monck, E. M., Carstairs, G. M., and Wing, J. K. (1962) Influence of family life on the course of schizophrenic illness. *British Journal of Preventive and Social Medicine*, **16**, 55–68.

Carstairs, G. M., Clarke, D. H., and O'Connor, N. (1955) Occupational treatment of chronic psychotics. *Lancet*, **ii**, 1025–1030.

Carstairs, G. M., O'Connor, N., and Rawnsley, K. (1956) Organisation of a hospital workshop for chronic psychotic patients. *British Journal of Preventive and Social Medicine*, **10**, 136–140.

Carter, J., and Edwards, C. (1975) *National Day Care Study: Pilot Report*. National Institute for Social Work, London.

Carter, J., Edwards, C., Anderson, J., and Jones, V. (1978) *Adult Day Care: Selected Reading*. National Institute for Social Work, London.

Catterson, A. G., Bennett, D. H., and Freudenberg, R. K. (1963) A survey of longstay schizophrenic patients. *British Journal of Psychiatry*, **109**, 750–757.

Chittick, R. A., Brooks, G. W., Irons, F. S., and Deane, W. N. (1961) *The Vermont Story: Rehabilitation of Chronic Schizophrenic Patients*. Vermont State Hospital, Burlington.

Clarke, A. D. B. (1962) Constructing assets in the severely subnormal. *Lancet*, **i**, 40–42.

Committee of Inquiry on the Rehabilitation, Training, and Resettlement of Disabled Persons (1956) (Piercy Committee). *Report*. HMSO, London.

Criswell, J. K. (1968) Considerations on the permanence of psychiatric rehabilitation. *Rehabilitation Literature*, **29**, 162–165.

Cross, K. W., Harrington, J. A., and Mayer-Gross, W. (1957) A study of chronic patients in a mental hospital. *Journal of Mental Science*, **103**, 146–171.

Dörner, K., Haerlin, C., Rau, V., Schernus, R., and Schwendy, A. (1980) *Der Krieg Gegen Die Psychisch Kranken*. Psychiatrie-Verlag, Rehrburg, Loccum.

Early, D. F. (1960). The Industrial Therapy Organisation (Bristol). *Lancet*, **ii**, 754–757.

Early, D. F. (1965a) Domestic resettlement. In H. Freeman, ed., *Psychiatric Hospital Care*. Bailliere, Tindall, & Cassell, London.

Early, D. F. (1965b) Economic rehabilitation. In H. Freeman, ed., *Psychiatric Hospital Care*. Bailliere, Tindall, & Cassell, London.

Early, D. F. (1973) Bristol Industrial Therapy Housing Association: a contribution to domestic resettlement. *British Medical Journal*, **2**, 491–494.

Early, D. F., and Magnus, R. V. (1968) The Industrial Therapy Organization (Bristol) 1960–1965. *British Journal of Psychiatry*, **2**, 1–13.

Ebringer, L., and Christie-Brown, J. W. R. (1980) Social deprivation among short-stay psychiatric patients. *British Journal of Psychiatry*, **136**, 46–52.

Evans, A. E. (1929) Report on R.M.P.A. study tour of Holland. *Journal of Mental Science*, **75**, 192–202.

Freeman, H. E., and Simmons, O. G. (1958) Wives, mothers and the post-hospital performance of mental patients. *Social Forces*, **37**, 153–159.

Freudenberg, R. K., Bennett, D. H., and May, A. R. (1957) The relative importance of physical and community methods in the treatment of schizophrenia. *Congress Report 2nd International Congress of Psychiatry*, Vol. 1, 157.

Furman, S. S. (1965) *Community Mental Health Services in Northern Europe*. US Department of Health, Education and Welfare. Public Health Service Publication No. 1407, Bethesda.

Galioni, E. D., Adams, E. F., and Tallman, F. F. (1953) Intensive treatment of backward patients. A controlled pilot study. *American Journal of Psychiatry*, **1009**, 576–583.

Garratt, F. N., Lowe, C. R., and McKeown, T. (1957) An investigation of the medical and social needs of patients in mental hospital. Part I. *British Journal of Preventive and Social Medicine*, **11**, 165–173.

Gastager, H. (1969) Frührehabilitation and Spätrehabilitation von psychosen. *Psychotherapy and Psychosomatics*, **17**, 34–41.

Goffman, E. (1961) *Asylums: Essays on the Social Situation of Mental Patients and Other Inmates*. Doubleday, New York.

Goldberg, D. (1967) Rehabilitation of the chronically mentally ill in England. *Social Psychiatry*, **2**, 1–13.

Goldberg, E. M. (1966) Hospital, work and family: a four year study of young mental hospital patients. *British Journal of Psychiatry*, **112**, 177–196.

Greenblatt, M., Levinson, D. J., and Williams, R. H. (1957) *The Patient and the Mental Hospital*. Free Press, Glencoe.

Greenblatt, M., and Lidz, T. (1957) The patient and the extra-hospital world: some dimensions of the problem. In M. Greenblatt, D. J. Levinson, and R. H. Williams eds., *The Patient and the Mental Hospital*. Free Press, Glencoe.

Griffiths, R. D. P. (1974) Rehabilitation of chronic psychotic patients. *Psychological Medicine*, **4**, 316–325.

Gruenberg, E. M. (1967) Social Breakdown Syndrome—some origins. *American Journal of Psychiatry*, **123**, 1481–1489.

Harris, A. (1958) General adult psychiatric services outside the mental hospital. *Hospital and Health Management*, **21**, 405–407.

Hawkins, H. (1871) A plea for convalescent homes in connection with asylums for the insane poor. *Journal of Mental Science*, **17**, 107–116.

Interdepartmental Committee on the Rehabilitation and Resettlement of Disabled Persons (1943) (Tomlinson Committee) *Report*. HMSO, London.

Jones, K. (1954) *Lunacy Law and Conscience 1744–1845*. Routledge & Kegan Paul, London.

Jones, M. (1952) *Social Psychiatry: A Study of Therapeutic Communities*. Tavistock, London.

Jones, M. (1956) Industrial therapy of mental patients still in hospital. *Lancet*, **ii**, 985.

Kidd, H. B. (1965) Industrial units in psychiatric hospital. *British Journal of Psychiatry*, **111**, 1205–1209.

King, R. D., Raynes, N., and Tizard, J. (1971) *Patterns of Residential Care*. Routledge & Kegan Paul, London.

Knudson, A. B. C. (1959) Rehabilitation of the mentally ill in the Veterans Administration. In *Rehabilitation of the Mentally Ill*. American Association for the Advancement of Science Publication No. 58, Washington.

Lawson, A. R. L. (1966) *The Recognition of Mental Illness in London*. Maudsley Monograph No. 15, Oxford University Press, London.

Lewis, A. J. (1943) Social effects of neurosis. *Lancet*, **i**, 167–170.

Lewis, A. J. (1955) Rehabilitation programs in England. *Proceedings Millbank Memorial Fund Annual Conference*, 196–206.

MacDonald, E. M. (1960) *Occupational Therapy in Rehabilitation*. Bailliere, Tindall, & Cox, London.

Mental Deficiency Committee (1929) *Report*. Board of Education and Board of Control. HMSO, London.

Meyer, H. J., and Borgatta, E. F., (1959) *An Experiment in Mental Patient Rehabilitation*. Russell Sage Foundation, New York.

Miller, D. H., and Clancy, J. (1952) An approach to the social rehabilitation of chronic psychotic patients. *Psychiatry*, **15**, 433–443.

Mitchell, S. W. (1894) Address before the fifteenth annual meeting of the American Medico-Psychological Association. *Transactions of the American Medico-Psychological Association*.

Morgan, R., Cushing, D., and Manton, N. S. (1965) A regional psychiatric rehabilitation hospital. *British Journal of Psychiatry*, **111**, 955–963.

Myerson, A. (1939) Theory and principles of the 'total push' method in the treatment of chronic schizophrenia. *American Journal of Psychiatry*, **95**, 1197–1204.

O'Connor, N., Jeron, A., and Carstairs, G. M. (1956) Work performance of chronic schizophrenics. *Occupational Psychology*, **30**, 153–164.

O'Connor, N., and Rawnsley, K. (1959) Incentives with paranoid and non-paranoid schizophrenics in a workshop. *British Journal of Medical Psychology*, **32**, 133–143.

O'Connor, R. N., and Tizard, J. (1956) *The Social Problems of Mental Deficiency*. Pergamon, London.

Olshansky, S., Grob, S., and Malamud, I. (1958) Employers' attitudes and practices in the hiring of ex-mental patients. *Mental Hygiene*, **42**, 391–401.

Otto, S., and Orford, J. (1978) *Not Quite Like Home: Small Hostels for Alcoholics and Others*. John Wiley, Chichester.

Parkes, C. M., Brown, G. W., and Monck, E. M. (1962) The general practitioner and the schizophrenic patient. *British Medical Journal*, **1**, 972–976.

Peffer, P. A. (1956) Motivation of the chronic mental patient. *American Journal of Psychiatry*, **113**, 55–59.

Program Area Committee on Mental Health of the American Public Health Association (1961) *A Guide to Control Methods for Mental Disorder*. American Public Health Association Inc., New York.

Query, W. T. (1968) *Illness, Work and Poverty*. Jossey-Bass, San Francisco.

Rapoport, R. N. (1960) *Community as Doctor*. Tavistock, London.

Rees, T. P. (1957a) Back to moral treatment and community care. *Journal of Mental Science*, **103**, 303–313.

Rees, T. P. (1957b) Some observations on the psychiatric patient, the mental hospital and the community. In M. Greenblatt, D. J. Levinson, and R. H. Williams, eds, *The Patient and the Mental Hospital*. Free Press, Glencoe.

Reid, E. C. (1914) Ergotherapy in the treatment of mental disorders. *Boston Medical and Surgical Journal*, **171**, 300.

Royal Commission on the Law Relating to Mental Illness and Mental Deficiency 1954–1957 (1957). HMSO, London.

Ryan, P. (1979) Residential care for the mentally disabled. In J. K. Wing, and R. Olsen, eds, *Community Care for the Mentally Disabled*. Oxford University Press, London.

Schwartz, C. G. (1953) *Rehabilitation of Mental Hospital Patients*. Public Health Monograph No. 17, Washington.

Shepherd, G., and Richardson, A. (1979) Organisation and interaction in psychiatric day centres. *Psychological Medicine*, **9**, 573–579.

Simmons, O. G., and Freeman, H. E. (1959) Familial expectations and post hospital performance of mental patients. *Human Relations*, **12**, 233–242.

Simon, H. (1927) Aktiviere Krankenbehandlung in der Irrenanstalt I. *Allgemeine Zeitschrift für Psychiatrie*, **87**, 97.

Simon, H. (1929) Aktiviere Krankenbehandlung in der Irrenanstalt II. *Allgemeine Zeitschrift für Psychiatrie*, **90**, 69.

Sines, J. O., Lucero, R. J., and Kauman, G. R. (1952) A state hospital total push program for regressed schizophrenics. *Journal of Clinical Psychology*, **8**, 189–193.

Standing Medical Advisory Committee on Rehabilitation (1972) *Report of a Sub-Committee* (Tunbridge Report). HMSO, London.

Stanton, A. G., and Schwartz, M. S. (1954) *The Mental Hospital*. Basic Books, New York.

Stevens, B. C. (1973) Evaluation of rehabilitation for psychotic patients in the community. *Acta psychiatrica Scandinavica*, **49**, 169–180.

Stone, A. A., and Eldred, S. H. (1959) Delusion formation during the activation of chronic schizophrenic patients. *Archives of General Psychiatry*, **1**, 177–179.

Straus, R. (1966) Social change and the Rehabilitation Concept. In M. B. Sussman, ed., *Sociology and Rehabilitation*. American Sociological Association in collaboration with the Vocational Rehabilitation Administration, Washington.

Stringham, J. A. (1952) Rehabilitating chronic neuro-psychiatric patients. *American Journal of Psychiatry*, **108**, 924–928.

Switzer, M. E. (1946) Rehabilitation and mental handicaps. *Mental Hygiene*, **30**, 390–396.

Symons, J. J. (1951) The nursing of the deteriorated patient. *Mental Health*, **11**, 18–21.

Tennent, T. (1960) The sheltered workshop. In the Annual Report of the Ex-Services Mental Welfare Society, London.

Tillotson, K. J. (1939) The practice of the 'total push' method in the treatment of chronic schizophrenia. *American Journal of Psychiatry*, **95**, 1204–1213.

Tizard, J., and O'Connor, N. (1952) The occupational adaption of high-grade mental defectives. *Lancet*, **2**, 620–623.

Tooth, G. C., and Brooke, E. M. (1961) Trends in the mental hospital population and their effect on future planning. *Lancet*, **i**, 710–713.

Topping, G. G., and O'Connor, N. (1960) The response of chronic schizophrenics to incentives. *British Journal of Medical Psychology*, **33**, 211–214.

Varrier-Jones, P. (1943) *Papers of a Pioneer*, ed. P. Fraser. Hutchinson, London.

Venables, P. H., and Tizard, J. (1956) Performance of functional psychotics on a repetitive task. *Journal of Abnormal Social Psychology*, **53**, 23–26.

Wadsworth, W. V., Wells, B. W. P., and Scott, R. F. (1962) The organization of a sheltered workshop. *Journal of Mental Science*, **108**, 780–781.

Wansbrough, N., and Cooper, P. (1980) *Open Employment after Mental Illness.* Tavistock, London.

Wansbrough, S. N., and Miles, A. (1968) *Industrial Therapy in Psychiatric Hospitals.* King Edward VII's Hospital Fund for London, London.

Waters, M. A., and Northover, J. (1965) Rehabilitated long-stay schizophrenics in the community. *British Journal of Psychiatry*, **111**, 258–267.

Wilder, J. (1979) *Aids to Community Care.* Psychiatric Rehabilitation Association, London.

Wing, J. K. (1960) A pilot experiment on the rehabilitation of long-hospitalized male schizophrenic patients. *British Journal of Preventive and Social Medicine*, **14**, 173–180.

Wing, J. K. (1961) A simple and reliable sub-classification of chronic schizophrenia. *Journal of Mental Science*, **107**, 862–875.

Wing, J. K. (1962) Institutionalism in mental hospitals. *British Journal of Social and Clinical Psychology*, **1**, 38–51.

Wing, J. K. (1963) Rehabilitation of psychiatric patients. *British Journal of Psychiatry*, **109**, 635–641.

Wing, J. K. (1966) Social and psychological changes in a rehabilitation unit. *Social Psychiatry*, **1**, 21–28.

Wing, J. K. (1967) The concept of handicap in psychiatry. *International Journal of Psychiatry*, **3**, 243.

Wing, J. K., Bennett, D. H., and Denham, J. (1964) *Industrial Rehabilitation of Long-stay Schizophrenic Patients.* Medical Research Council Memorandum No. 42, HMSO, London.

Wing, J. K., and Brown, G. W. (1970) *Institutionalism and Schizophrenia.* Cambridge University Press, London.

Wing, J. K., and Freudenberg, R. K. (1961) The response of severely ill chronic schizophrenic patients to social stimulation. *American Journal of Psychiatry*, **118**, 311–322.

Wing, J. K., and Giddens, R. (1959) Industrial rehabilitation of male chronic schizophrenic patients. *Lancet*, **ii**, 505–507.

Wing, L., Wing, J. K., Stevens, B., and Griffiths, D. (1972) An epidemiological and experimental evaluation of industrial rehabilitation of chronic psychotic patients in the community. In J. K. Wing, and A. M. Harley, eds, *Evaluating a Community Psychiatric Service: The Camberwell Register 1964–71.* Oxford University Press, London.

Wittkower, E. D., and Lebeaux, L. (1943) The Special Transfer Scheme: an experiment in military psychiatric vocational re-employment. *Medical Press*, **209**, 366–368.

Woodhead, G. S., and Varrier-Jones, P. C. (1920) *Industrial Colonies and Village Settlements for the Consumptive.* Cambridge University Press, London.

# PART II

*Clinical Syndromes*

Theory and Practice of Psychiatric Rehabilitation
Edited by F. N. Watts and D. H. Bennett
© 1983, John Wiley & Sons, Ltd.

# 3

# Schizophrenia

JOHN WING

## Clinical Considerations

### Introduction

The principles of rehabilitation expounded in Chapter 1 apply broadly to all psychiatric disorders but the details of their application vary from one clinical condition to another. A great deal, therefore, depends on repeated clinical assessment. This is particularly true of schizophrenia, in which the course is not stable like that of, say, Down's syndrome, or progressive like severe dementia, or intermittent like manic-depressive psychosis, but can take any of these forms and even move from one to another. The major part of this chapter will be devoted to a consideration of the acute and chronic manifestations of schizophrenia and of the factors that precipitate, maintain, improve, or prevent them, since these factors are of central importance in long-term rehabilitation and management. Less specific factors contributing to social disablement, and methods of rehabilitation which apply to all chronic disorders, will be considered in detail in other chapters, and we shall here be concerned only with features that are particularly important in schizophrenia. Because the central topic of the book is rehabilitation we shall concentrate on the chronic or frequently relapsing disorders which necessitate long-term contact with socio-medical services.

### Use of the Term 'Schizophrenia'

The term 'schizophrenia' covers a large central group of conditions, probably not homogenous in terms of cause, and of unknown pathology, which are recognized in the acute phase by the description and elaboration of certain kinds of abnormal subjective experiences, including those called by Kurt

Schneider 'symptoms of the first rank'. Other paranoid delusional syndromes which cannot be explained as part of a manic or depressive or organic psychosis are often included under the same rubric, although there is provision in the International Classification of Diseases (World Health Organization, 1974) for separate classification. Patients with acute catatonic symptoms but no schizophrenic or paranoid symptoms are rarely encountered nowadays but they, too, in the absence of a clear organic aetiology, are likely to be included as having a subvariety of schizophrenia. Difficult-to-classify conditions, such as recurrent stupor or recurrent excitement without more specific symptoms, are also often called schizophrenic.

In addition, there are chronic behavioural and subjective manifestations which lead some clinicians to make a diagnosis of schizophrenia even in the absence of the acute delusional and hallucinatory phenomena. Flatness of affect and 'thought disorder' are the chief symptoms, but they are difficult to define except where severe (in which case there is usually a history of acute delusional and hallucinatory episodes), and the practice of using them as the sole basis for diagnosis introduces the possibility of a large measure of unreliability between different clinicians. Moreover, the methods of treatment and rehabilitation suitable for more central forms of schizophrenia are not necessarily applicable to the so-called pseudo-neurotic or pseudo-psychopathic varieties.

The pros and cons of diagnosing schizophrenia have been extensively discussed elsewhere (Strömgren and Wing, 1973; Wing, 1978a, 1978b) and will not be further considered here, except to point out that the term should not be used simply for any chronic condition that does not respond to prolonged treatment. Obvious as this may seem, it is not uncommon to find people with chronic obsessional neurosis, long-term personality disorders, Asperger's syndrome, Kanner's syndrome, or the sequelae of diseases such as encephalitis, given the label 'schizophrenia' and treated as such, although the rehabilitation problems are often very different.

In the rest of this chapter, the term will be used fairly broadly to include the central schizophrenic syndromes, the paranoid psychoses, and the severe chronic impairments that often accompany or follow them. Mild behavioural or affective deficits occurring in the absence of a history of more florid episodes are excluded.

Factors Influencing Acute Onset and Relapse

Acute psychotic episodes are the most visible and easily recognizable features of schizophrenia and even when short-lived they cause much suffering, disturbance, and inconvenience to patient and relatives. Any information of possible preventive value is therefore very important. Known precipitating factors include drugs such as alcohol, amphetamine, and bromide, diseases such as cerebral tumour, temporal lobe epilepsy, and porphyria, and natural conditions such as childbirth. In most cases no such factor is found but social and personal precipitants do seem to be quite frequent. Although research into such matters is methodologically difficult and the results cannot be called conclusive, there is reasonable evidence for the importance of at least three kinds of environmental factor.

The first of these consists of events that are found personally disturbing by the patient, not necessarily only those that appear threatening or unfavourable such as a loss or an illness, or are unpleasant and depressing like witnessing a street accident, but also those that are exciting or arousing such as winning the pools or being promoted at work (Brown and Birley, 1970). This diversity of precipitating events is much broader than is found in depression or anxiety states and means that prevention, short of living in a very sheltered and restricted environment, is difficult to achieve. It is important to bear in mind, however, that people who have had one attack of schizophrenia have a lower stress tolerance than average, and that the consequence of stressful events can be a further disastrous psychotic episode.

The second kind of precipitating factor arises from close personal relationships, particularly those that are critical, dominating, and intrusive, which occur in about 40 per cent of families at the time of relapse (Brown, *et al.* 1972; Vaughn and Leff, 1976a). The number of critical comments made by a key relative about a patient can be counted reliably and has been found to be closely associated with subsequent relapse, particularly if there is a high degree of face-to-face contact between patient and relative and if no medication is being taken. The latter two factors are potentially modifiable and thus offer a practical possibility for preventive action in the case of a patient living in a 'high-emotion' home. Counselling highly critical relatives may also be helpful, particularly since the criticisms usually involve aspects of the· patient's personality — social unresponsiveness, lack of motivation to work, etc. — which are not seen by relatives as part of an illness and for which no allowances may be made (Freeman and Simmons, 1963; Vaughn and Leff, 1976b). The patient, too, can to some extent avoid highly intrusive relationships once their unfavourable effect is recognized. The implications for counselling will be considered later.

The third type of precipitating factor is iatrogenic. The occasional reactivations of delusions and hallucinations when a patient is put under too much pressure in a rehabilitation programme or discharged prematurely is well-known in hospital practice and has been observed in systematic research studies (Goldberg *et al.*, 1977; Stevens, 1973; Stone and Eldred, 1959; Wing *et al.*, 1964). The way that rehabilitation programmes are planned and implemented is therefore of great importance.

The common link between these three types of precipitating factor may be an increase in stress or anxiety. Clearly, this is non-specific, in the sense that 'stress' is experienced by everyone in day-to-day life and may lead to a wide variety of psychiatric symptoms or to successful coping without the appearance of symptoms at all. The specific feature is the vulnerability of people with schizophrenia to break down with acute psychotic or lower-order symptoms (and this can also occur, of course, without any obvious precipitating factors being involved). We do not know the nature of the vulnerability although psychophysiological studies suggest that the arousal system is involved. Schizophrenic patients tend to have a higher heart rate, higher sweat gland activity, and slower habituation in the rate of spontaneous fluctuations in skin conductance than normal, and the degree of arousal is correlated with degree of slowness, underactivity, and flatness of affect. Recent observations suggest that this arousal has different characteristics in patients from high-emotion and low-emotion homes (Tarrier *et al.*, 1979; Venables and Wing, 1962). Whether a sudden increase in level of arousal is a mediating factor between a non-specific environmental stress and a specific exacerbation of florid symptoms, and, if so, what the mechanism might be, requires further investigation.

Factors Influencing the Development of Chronic Impairments

The nature of the psychological deficit in schizophrenia has long been discussed by psychologists and psychiatrists. Jung was one of the first to point out a problem in attention. Chronically handicapped patients show a 'passive registration of events which are enacted . . . but all that requires attention passes without heed' (Jung, 1906). He quoted an experiment by Stransky in which subjects were asked to talk on a given topic without paying any attention to what they were saying, thus producing incoherent speech. Lack of attention and its concomitant apathy and poor motivation, together with an incoherence of thought and speech (said to be due to 'loosening of the associations') were the two features regarded by Eugen Bleuler as necessary and sufficient for a diagnosis of schizophrenia. There has, however, been very little effort to relate the two symptoms to each other theoretically.

The so-called negative symptoms (the 'clinical poverty syndrome') are very familiar to clinicians: emotional blunting, slowness of thought and movement, underactivity, lack of drive, poverty of speech, and social withdrawal. The lack of ability to communicate through non-verbal means is particularly striking. Severely affected patients have a flat, monotonous voice and expressionless face, use few gestures, and have a stiff and unnatural posture and gait. They may understand the emotional connotations of what is going on around them but they cannot communicate this understanding or engage in ordinary two-way social intercourse. This is precisely the syndrome complained of (in other terms — 'lazy, self-centred, unwilling to try') by critical relatives, who do not realize that patients are impaired by an 'invisible' disability. When it is complicated by incoherence of thought and therefore of speech, the difficulties of communication are indeed extreme. Most of the behavioural problems encountered in schizophrenic patients can be understood when these multiple disabilities, together with the liability of acute psychotic experiences, are considered in relation to the environment in which the patient lives.

Clinicians used to regard an increase in the poverty syndrome as an inevitable concomitant of schizophrenia and called it 'deterioration'. Some psychologists thought they had demonstrated that deficit increased with time (Babcock, 1933), but in fact there is very little evidence for this theory (Foulds and Dixon, 1962; Kendig and Richmond, 1940). If there is a genuine intellectual impairment it is present at the time of first examination.

The problem of the severity of negative impairments cannot be separated from the problem of reactivity to environmental factors. Much of the early work on motivation was carried out in somewhat artificial laboratory conditions, but the introduction of rehabilitation workshops into mental hospitals allowed assessment in a more realistic environment. An important observation was that the improvement due to practising simple tasks, which takes the form, in normal people and in those severely retarded with Down's syndrome, of a 'learning curve', was not negatively accelerated as is typically found in normal subjects, but showed only slow, linear improvement (O'Connor et al., 1956). One workshop experiment is worth describing in a little detail because it illustrates, albeit with severely impaired long-stay schizophrenic patients 'in the old days', a number of points that remain vital for an understanding of rehabilitation today. Two matched groups worked at a simple assembly task in adjacent workshops. They were all living in a resocialization villa in a hospital renowned for its pioneering work in rehabilitation. Supervision and encouragement was given by the charge nurse of one of the groups, once a baseline of production had been established, but not by the charge nurse of the other, who remained passive, just giving out and collecting work. (Both nurses were well-known and trusted by patients.) There was a sharp increase in output of the experimental group and *decrease* in output of the controls (who could hear what was going on next door). The increase did not take the form of a learning curve as would be expected, but of a once-and-for-all increment which was maintained until the nurse was asked to resume the passive behaviour of the baseline condition, when output fell immediately, while that of the control group rose. The exercise was then repeated, this time introducing social stimulation into both workshops, with a similar immediate improvement in output, accompanied, of course, by a decrease in aimless wandering, empty fidgeting, or staring into space (Wing and Freudenberg, 1961).

Several basic features of severe negative schizophrenic impairments should be noted. First, improvement in one situation does not necessarily generalize to other settings. (In this case, the changes in workshop behaviour were not accompanied by changes in ward behaviour.) Second, the response was immediate and continued only as long as the stimulation was kept up. When it was withdrawn there was an immediate relapse. This was not a learning effect. It could be said that the nurses were passively exercising functions which the patients were unable to exercise actively for themselves, in the hope that the functions would eventually return. This is an excellent and fundamental principle of rehabilitation. Third, the improvement in performance and behaviour was due to social stimulation from a trusted person. Fourth, it is quite difficult for nurses to respond to withdrawn, slow, and unspontaneous patients with the active stimulation they need, because social approaches seem to be unrewarded. (This is precisely the problem complained of by critical relatives.)

A broader survey of long-stay schizophrenic patients in three large psychiatric hospitals enabled these conclusions to be generalized (Wing and Brown, 1970). Social poverty of the hospital environment was found to be associated with clinical poverty in the patients. Improvement or deterioration in the former was accompanied by improvement or deterioration in the latter. One of the most important environmental factors was found to be the length of time that the patient was allowed to spend doing absolutely nothing. In one of the hospitals studied the *average* waking time without any kind of activity or occupation, even watching television, was over 5½ hours; 24 per cent of the patients in this hospital were mute and showed other symptoms of the clinical poverty syndrome in severe form, compared with 6 per cent and 14 per cent in the other two hospitals. These are symptoms that earlier were regarded as fundamental and immutable.

There is considerable evidence that social understimulation has the same harmful effect on schizophrenic patients in non-hospital settings; in fact, the length of time spent doing nothing can be of the same order among unemployed patients living at home as in a hospital with a poor social environment (Brown et al., 1966). Some forms of alternative residential accommodation, particularly unsupervised group homes, can even promote inactivity (Ryan, 1979), while the lives of destitute men can be completely isolated (Leach and Wing, 1980). The simple fact of not being in hospital is no guarantee that the environment will not be harmful.

Lesser degrees of negative impairment can still be very disabling. Groups of long-stay schizophrenic patients who entered courses at the units now called Employment Rehabilitation Centres were selected because most were not severely impaired by contrast with other patients. At the centre, however, they seemed slow, plodding, lacking in initiative, and unsociable by contrast with their physically disabled colleagues (Wing, 1960; Wing et al., 1964).

An underlying disorder of thought also contributes to disablement. When the disorder is marked, the patient finds it difficult, without intense concentration, to keep to an intended line of thought and speech, and may appear completely incoherent. Only relatively routine work, requiring little thought, then remains unaffected. All forms of communication and activity can be disturbed. Minor forms of the symptom are quite common and are very puzzing to relatives, friends, workmates, and employers.

Hemsley (1978) provides a useful discussion of chronic cognitive impairments in schizophrenia and of behaviours which can be understood as an attempt to adapt to or cope with these impairments. He emphasizes that operant procedures applied to patients without understanding their basic impairments may either fail or actually result in making symptoms worse.

## Frequency and Course of Schizophrenia

The effect of the environmental factors discussed above, and the use of medication to shorten acute episodes and prevent relapse, mean that it is difficult to delineate a 'natural' history of schizophrenia. Nevertheless, there are regularities which are relevant to planning rehabilitation services. The expected rate during adulthood, in most countries where careful studies have been carried out, is about 1 per cent. The figure is higher in areas where a broader definition of schizophrenia is used, such as the USA. The incidence in the UK is 0.10–0.15 new cases per 1,000 total population per year and the 1-year prevalence about 0.3–0.4 per 1,000. The difference between the two latter rates indicates the chronic nature of the disorder. The rates vary from one district to another but do give planners an approximate idea of expected numbers.

The influence of modifying factors should also be taken into account. Onset is rare in childhood, though there are a few prepubertal cases, mostly male. The male predominance continues up to the mid-30s when incidence rates become higher in women. Since early onset, before the personality has had time to mature, is associated with a more chronic course, it is not surprising that male patients are less likely to be married than female and that men are commoner among the small long-stay groups still accumulating in hospitals. An early age of onset is more associated with 'hebephrenic' forms of schizophrenia and a later onset with paranoid forms.

Another important factor is the presence of adverse 'pre-morbid' characteristics. People who develop an acute attack of florid schizophrenia are more likely during childhood to have shown a poor school performance, social withdrawal, and abnormal behaviour than their contemporaries (Hanson et al., 1976; Robins, 1970; Watt and Lubensky, 1976). It is well known that an insidious, as opposed to an acute, onset is associated with a poor outcome. One of the chief factors predictive of a favourable social course in the International Pilot Study of Schizophrenia was the absence of marked social withdrawal before onset. The only clinical factor of importance was that the predominant type of symptom at the time of initial examination tended to be again predominant at the time of any psychotic relapse, though it did not predict whether or when relapse would occur (World Health Organization, 1979; see also Brown *et al.*, 1966 Zubin, 1967).

A study of 111 patients first admitted to three English mental hospitals in 1956 and followed up 5 years later showed that 56 per cent had recovered socially, 34 per cent were to some degree socially disabled but out of hospital, and only 10 per cent were inpatients. Overall, about one quarter of the admission cohort were still severely disabled. The figures have probably improved somewhat since then, but it is clear that a substantial proportion of schizophrenic disorders run a chronic or intermittent course which is why rehabilitation programmes are so important (Brown *et al.*, 1966).

A crude estimate of the numbers of patients with *chronic* schizophrenia who are in touch with hospital services, or living in hostels or group homes, or attending day centres can be derived from psychiatric case registers. For Camberwell, an inner suburb of London, the prevalence is about 170 per 100,000 population. About half of this figure is accounted for by patients who have been in hospital for more than 1 year.

Before turning to consider rehabilitation there are still two types of problem factor, other than impairment, that need to be considered in relation to schizophrenia, although neither is specific to it. One is social disadvantage, the other is adverse personal reaction.

## Social Disablement

### Introduction

We have seen that frequent relapse with acute psychotic episodes, or the development of chronic impairments, or both, are likely to lead to social disablement, and that age of onset, sex, 'pre-morbid' personality, and environmental overstimulation or understimulation may give clues to the prognosis. The importance of 'pre-morbid' abnormalities makes it particularly difficult to evaluate the extent to which the other two factors, each of which can itself cause, as well as exacerbate, social disablement, play a part in determining the course of schizophrenia. A good clinical history, taken from a good informant, is of great value in making the distinction.

### Social disadvantage

We are here principally concerned with the ways in which deprived or hostile social environments, lack of opportunity to develop vocational or social skills, stigma, poverty, unemployment, homelessness, and similar unfavourable experience before and after the onset of schizophrenia, can lead to the development of an unnecessary degree of social disablement, which can be corrected or to some extent prevented. Clinical impairments can, of course, be very severe, even in the best social environment that can be devised, and supervene even in an individual who has had a fortunate or privileged childhood and adolescence. In such a case, impairment is the chief cause of social disablement, but these impairments may themselves lead to social disadvantage and thus to extra disablement, unless preventive measures are instituted.

This interaction is particularly obvious in people who had a poor social history, extending into childhood, before the first onset. Apart from poor school performance, they may already have set up adverse personal relationships in the family, have few social skills or supports, no vocational qualifications, and an unsatisfactory record at work, and may have moved away from home into isolated areas of town. The extensive literature on epidemiological research into such factors has recently been reviewed by Cooper (1978). A 'drift' rather than a 'breeder' hypothesis seems most plausible. However, it is important to take into account what sociologists call 'deviance amplification' ('disability amplification' is a better term in the present context), which is summed up in the biblical text: 'from him that hath not shall be taken away even that which he hath'. At a time of high unemployment rates, even someone with mild impairments will be at a disadvantage. The effect of these social deficits, serious enough in themselves, can be multiplied many times by the personal reaction of the patient.

## Adverse Personal Reactions

How people react to social disadvantage, or to the impairment of schizophrenia, at any given level of severity, varies greatly from individual to individual, but, in the absence of special protective factors, exposure to such adverse experiences is likely to lead to depression, despair, overdependence, and, eventually, lack of motivation for self-help. The opinions of important people in the disabled person's socal environment — relatives, workmates, friends, caring professionals — and also public attitudes more generally, become reflected in self-attitudes. Some degree of dependence is inevitable when serious impairment is present. A congenitally deaf child must rely on others to teach him to talk and help him to communicate. Someone with severe schizophrenia may be wise to restrict his close contacts and his confidence to a few people whom he can trust not to be rejecting or overintrusive. That is being realistic and sensible. But often the reaction goes too far and an unnecessary element of 'secondary' disability is added to those that cannot be helped. The acceptance by the handicapped person of limitations that are not actually necessary is the essence of secondary disablement. This extra element is the one that needs to be prevented or corrected.

A very clear-cut example is 'institutionalism', at the heart of which is a gradually acquired contentment with life in the institution which culminates in the individual no longer wishing to live any other. This can happen even to midly impaired patients (Wing, 1962; Wing and Brown, 1970). Individual variation is probably as great as in a prisoner-of-war camp, where some people will take great risks to escape while nothing would induce others to try. Schizophrenic patients can show great determination to leave hospital even when there is little help available from outside, although preserved social ties are, of course, very important (Brown, 1959). But even a moderate degree of affective blunting, social withdrawal, or 'thought disorder' can act as the nucleus of a crystal upon which institutionalism grows. Schizophrenic patients are particularly vulnerable. (A similar process can occur in the mentally retarded and in those of 'inadequate personality'.)

A combination of understimulating social conditions, which patients came to appreciate because of the protection from external stresses, with the attitude of professional people (and any relatives who stayed in contact) who did not expect someone with schizophrenia to be able to cope outside a sheltered setting, was sufficient to explain part of the large accumulation of long-stay inpatients in the mental hospitals of former days. Many of the social factors responsible, and the best means of correcting them, have been described by clinicians (Barton, 1959; Bennett, 1975; Freudenberg, 1967) and will be considered in more detail elsewhere in this book.

Very few patients stay for long periods (i.e. a year or more) in hospital nowadays (only 5 per cent of those admitted during a year, according to register figures, about one quarter of whom are diagnosed as schizophrenic). These 'new' long-stay patients tend to be very much more impaired than in the past and adopt institutional attitudes rather more quickly than in the past (Mann and Cree, 1976). A similar process occurs in all the alternative services. There is a substantial 'new' long-stay group in hostels, group homes, day hospitals, and day centres, many of whom are content to stay where they are rather than aspire to become self-supporting (Edwards and Carter, 1979; Hassall and Cross, 1972; Hewett et al., 1975; Leach and Wing, 1980; Ryan, 1979) in spite of the fact that many of the new settings have an avowedly rehabilitative aim.

Adverse reactions can develop among people who remain at home. Some 20 per cent of schizophrenic patients admitted to three hospitals in 1956 left home during the subsequent 5 years and did not return (Brown et al., 1966). Divorce is much commoner among schizophrenic patients (particularly men) than in the general population. The secondary problems arising from unemployment, solitary living, poverty, and even destitution, can cause an attitude of despair and then apathy.

One of the most rewarding aspects of rehabilitation practice is to observe the gradual restitution of morale and self-confidence in someone whose social disablement had been considered to be due, perhaps entirely, to 'intrinsic' factors. It is never safe to make this assumption without some reservation although, in some cases, the cost-benefit equation is very difficult to balance.

## The Process of Rehabilitation in Schizophrenia

### Introduction

In the first two sections of this chapter, the three main factors contributing to social disablement in schizophrenic patients—impairments, social disadvantage, and adverse personal reactions—and the environmental factors that tend to exacerbate, maintain, prevent, or improve them, have been considered. In practice, it may be difficult to distinguish the elements from each other, particularly if a patient is first seen after there has been a long and poorly documented history of social failure. In a properly organized rehabilitation service, however, there will have been plenty of opportunity to observe the patient in a variety of social environments and responding to a variety of social pressures. This long-term knowledge is invaluable in planning a realistic programme of aid. The emphasis in what follows is placed on elements of the programme that are especially important for those with chronic schizophrenia. Other chapters deal with more general features.

### Assessment

The value of assessment is to determine the severity and chronicity of disablement and its main causes, to discover what talents might be developed, to lay down a plan of rehabilitation, to allocate the appropriate professional help to patient and relatives, and to monitor progress and update the plan as necessary. It is sometimes not understood that a good clinical, social, and personal history is just as essential as a basis for rehabilitation and management as it is for treatment. The way the patient has reacted in the past gives pointers to how he or she will react in future, what interventions are likely to be successful, and how the interventions should be made. In the clinical assessment, as well as describing the acute and chronic impairments of schizophrenia and whether they have been related to environmental pressures, inquiry should be made about the common depressive and other neurotic symptoms. These may deserve attention in their own right, since some patients are disabled more by social phobias, for example, than by delusions or hallucinations or slowness and inactivity. These phobias are usually rooted, however, in the communication difficulties common in schizophrenia and should not be dealt with solely by routine behavioural methods. The rate of suicide is greater in schizophrenia than in most psychiatric disorders, with the exception of uncomplicated depression, and the act is often a desperate response to what is experienced by the patient as a long series of unsuccessful struggles against the problems created by acute episodes, chronic impairments, and social disadvantage.

The social assessment is as important as the clinical, since it covers factors in the social environment (particularly if the patient is living with relatives) that are particularly likely to be harmful or protective. The attitudes and responses of relatives to the patient being at home, to personal relationships, to symptoms and impairments, and to medication, need to be assessed. Relatives who cope successfully with disturbed or withdrawn behaviour can teach professionals a great deal. At the same time, the problems that relatives themselves experience must be sympathetically reviewed (Creer and Wing, 1974). Schizophrenia may sometimes result in a stable disability which presents problems similar to those of severe mental retardation. The relative then knows the extent to which responsibility must be taken for the patient. But this is not the common course. Still less is chronic schizophrenia like a stable physical disability such as blindness where, apart from the dependence necessitated by the condition, the patient can take full responsibility for himself. The schizophrenic process tends to fluctuate, with the patient sometimes able to function normally or with only moderate restriction but at other times requiring considerable supervision and care. This creates great difficulties for relatives especially when the patient has little insight into the fluctuations. Furthermore, there is a tendency, over the years, if the family does not break up, for relatives and patient to reach an accommodation with each other. This is particularly true when a single (or separated) patient lives with elderly relatives (often a widowed mother). Thus there are special features of family life and social and vocational adjustment that require specific assessment as well as the more general factors which are taken into account whatever type of psychiatric condition is involved.

The same is true of the extended assessment of behaviour and attitudes that is made in a rehabilitation unit. The influence of the setting in which observations are made should be taken into account. Behaviour and performance seen in a protected environment may not be matched where expectations are closer to those found in open employment or at home. This is why it is necessary to have a range of units available with greater and lesser degrees of shelter, and why assessment must be a continuous process rather than restricted to one initial period of observation. The special characteristics of behaviour that need to be taken into account are described in the two previous sections. In addition, a more general assessment of occupational, domestic, self-care, and leisure-time skills, deficits, and potentialities, as discussed in Chapters 11–13, will be undertaken.

The assessment of self-attitudes is particularly important in schizophrenia and presents certain special difficulties. A patient who displays good work skills in a rehabilitation workshop, for example, may insist on taking jobs that are apparently lower than his capacity, perhaps as a night-watchman rather than as a skilled fitter. The reason might be that he is underconfident; i.e. not simply that he lacks confidence but that there is good reason to believe that he could realistically have more confidence in his ability to obtain and hold down a higher level job. In that case, the plan of rehabilitation would be to introduce him gradually to more and more realistic settings, so that he can demonstrate to himself and others what his abilities are. This is the same principle used in the rehabilitation of the physically disabled (Wing, 1966). On the other hand, the patient's own assessment might already be a realistic one if he has found, for example, that time-pressures and the need to keep up social relationships with workmates and supervisors have made him confused, anxious, and unhappy, as can be the case when thought and speech disorder is present. Social withdrawal can be protective in such situations and, although there is a temptation to take it too far, professional staff should be aware of the importance of 'invisible' impairments and alive to the possibility that the patient's self-attitudes may have a rational basis. The patient's experience of and reactions to medication similarly need careful assessment since this can provide information that is vital for future management. This principle holds true across the whole range of self-attitudes and responses to environmental events and circumstances.

## Formulating the Plan of Rehabilitation

The process of assessment forms the basis for a plan of rehabilitation and, more generally, long-term management. Target problems are selected, in order of priority; realistic goals are set in collaboration with patient, relatives, and other relevant people; progress is monitored and discussed with those concerned; and new goals adopted as necessary. The overall aim is a gradual reduction of dependence through the use of a wide range of options for progress, but only to the point where increasing demands actually begin to have harmful effects. The ladder model of rehabilitation described in Chapter 8 implies that there must be resting places for those who cannot make steady progress to the top, and that a satisfactory 'settlement' is reached when the patient's potential assets are realized as fully as possible, even if this falls short of complete independence. The aim is to maintain this optimum condition and to prevent deterioration or relapse.

## Counselling Schizophrenic Patients

The main techniques used in rehabilitation are described elsewhere in this book but some special features of one fundamental method, counselling, need to be considered. In part, the course of schizophrenia is determined by the attitudes and expectations of patients, relatives, and other important people in the patient's social environment. Those whose ability to communicate with others is very severely impaired have little chance to achieve a satisfactory outcome unless others take many decisions for them, but that is not the most difficult type of problem. Most people with schizophrenia are not severely impaired all the time but their insight tends to fluctuate or be impaired. The acute symptoms of schizophrenia carry a peculiar conviction to most of those who experience them, which resists the scepticism of relatives or professional helpers. Since many patients have, in addition, always been somewhat detached from social opinion and the first onset often occurs during the rebellious teens, it is not surprising that patients find themselves at odds with their relatives and society more generally and unwilling to accept advice. Sometimes it is only after prolonged experience and suffering that patients begin to understand some of the factors that make matters better or worse, and that they can help themselves.

Attitudes to medication provide an example. Three highly intelligent professional people who contributed to a volume of essays on experiences of schizophrenia each said that they found medication dampening and depressing although they were grateful for the relief it brought from acute symptoms (Wing, 1975). Up to one third of patients with schizophrenia do not persist with medication (Hirsch *et al.*, 1973). Serious attention given to explanations about the drugs available, the use of other drugs to minimize side-effects, the circumstances under which the dose may need to be varied, and the effects of discontinuing medication under different conditions of stress, may prove very helpful, particularly if the patient's own experience is used in illustration.

Some patients learn eventually to recognize situations which make them feel worse and which might trigger episodes of relapse. One said: 'There is a sensitivity in myself and I have to try to harden my emotions and cut myself off from potentially dangerous situations. . . . When I get worked up I often experience a slight recurrence of delusional thoughts.' He avoided arguments on topics that made him emotionally upset. Another found that sometimes, when sitting in a subway train, he noticed the eyes of another passenger begin to radiate. Then he would deliberately turn his attention to something else; in fact, he had evolved a relaxation technique in order to deal with such occasions. Another only experienced hallucinatory voices last thing at night, when his attention began to wander before he went to sleep, but he knew that he would not act on them and quite enjoyed them. A very bright girl chose her men friends among people who were not her intellectual equals because she did not get so involved with them and found she could control the situation better.

Social withdrawal is a technique that can be consciously manipulated by patients and used in a specific way to avoid situations they find painful. It is important that they know the dangers of going too far, since understimulation carries its own risk of increasing morbidity. A degree of external social stimulation is necessary for ordinary social functioning. Nevertheless, being withdrawn is often found preferable to being forced into unwanted social interaction. Work that is within the patient's competence and not too socially exacting is a great help, but other people do not always recognize how exhausting many patients find a full-time job, even of this kind.

The degree of *insight* required to use these techniques sensibly is uncommon and some patients take them too far. Many never attain this degree of control; severity of illness is an important factor and it can vary independently of the quality of the social environment. Nevertheless, many could achieve more insight if they were given help.

Rehabilitation is not simply a matter of prescribing services but of finding the right way to use them. The more active the patient's participation and the deeper his understanding of the problems he faces, the greater the likelihood of progress.

## Counselling Relatives

The role of relatives as caring agents is often not understood by professionals, who thereby fail to learn from the expertise of those who cope well (and who may have learned to do so by trial and error in default of useful advice being available). The traditional patient–doctor or client–social worker relationship may also prevent professionals from accepting opportunities for useful collaboration with relatives in the care of patients. When most people with schizophrenia tended to become long-term inpatients relatives were relieved of their responsibility. Now they need all the help they can get. Nurses often prove the most sympathetic helpers since they themselves take over the responsibility for patients from relatives from time to time and are in a position to understand the problems of management that can arise from day to day.

One of the commonest complaints of relatives is that they do not receive practical advice on how to react to deluded or withdrawn patients, what to do when a patient refuses to claim benefits or to take the medication prescribed, or even how to deal with the patient's jealousy of a normal sibling (a problem quite frequently met with in the case of chronic physical disability). The counselling expertise that has long been available to the families of people with diabetes or multiple sclerosis rests, of course, on a securer foundation of knowledge about the nature of the disabilities involved, but there is now quite a substantial body of knowledge about schizophrenia which is not always applied.

All the topics raised when counselling patients are likely to be important also to relatives. Both overstimulation and understimulation have to be avoided. Relatives have to learn (as nurses do) that it is rarely useful to argue with a deluded patient (though this is not the same as agreeing with them); that it is possible to go so far in trying to motivate a slow and apathetic individual but that pushing too hard may induce a protective withdrawal or a florid relapse; that what appears to be laziness or selfishness may actually be disability; and that sometimes it is unreasonable to expect a cure. Some of the factors that, with help, can be controlled by relatives are the following: creating an accepting and non-critical environment, providing social stimulation without undue intrusion, keeping expectations realistic, coping with fluctuating insight, responding to odd ideas or behaviour, understanding affective blunting and social withdrawal, knowing what to expect from medication, learning to use the medical and social services, helping to foster the patient's confidence and self-knowledge (Creer, 1978; Priestly, 1979; Wing, 1977).

A voluntary organization, the National Schizophrenia Fellowship, has sponsored a number of useful projects designed to highlight these problems and suggest solutions to them. There are branches in many parts of the United Kingdom and help from caring professionals is much appreciated (Creer and Wing, 1974; National Schizophrenia Fellowship, 1974, 1979; Priestly, 1979).

Rehabilitation Services: the Need for Continuity

The network of medical, social, and voluntary services needed in every health district in order to ensure the optimum rehabilitation of schizophrenic patients, and to prevent a drift into solitary and substandard living conditions or even destitution, has been set out in a memorandum by a Working Party of the Royal College of Psychiatrists (1980). Other chapters of this book deal with the various units needed and with their size, staffing, functions, and coordination. What must be emphasized here, in relation to the problems of schizophrenia, is the need for skilled and experienced staff, for continuity of advice and care (which means a high degree of collaboration between the staff of different agencies), for rapid help at times of emergency including at night and at weekends, and for a welcoming, positive, and flexible attitude. Above all, what is required is time. An occasional 10-minute outpatient consultation with a junior doctor who changes every few months is rarely sufficient for counselling. It may not even give time for a proper consideration of medication and gives no feeling of security and support to patient or relatives between visits.

Conclusion

Schizophrenia still quite frequently develops into a chronically  disabling or relapsing condition, but sufficient knowledge is available to reduce much social disablement. When a survey was made of relatives' problems, it was found that most people had experienced some part of the service working well at some time and were full of praise for its effectiveness. If all staff and all agencies reached the standards of the best, chronic schizophrenia would still occur but the satisfaction and the quality of life of patients and relatives would be greatly improved.

## References

Babcock, H. (1933) *Dementia Praecox: A Psychological Study* Science Press, New York.

Barton, R. (1959) *Institutional Neurosis*. Wright, Bristol.

Bennett, D. H. (1975) Techniques of industrial therapy, ergotherapy and recreative methods. In K. P. Kisher, J.-E. Meyer, C. Müller, and E. Strömgren *Psychiatrie der Gegenwart*, eds, *III*. Springer-Verlag, New York.

Brown, G. W. (1959) Social factors influencing length of hospital stay of schizophrenic patients. *British Medical Journal*, **2**, 1300–1302.

Brown, G. W., and Birley, J. L. T. (1970) Social precipitants of severe psychiatric disorders. In E. H. Hare and J. K. Wing, eds, *Psychiatric Epidemiology*. Oxford University Press, London.

Brown, G. W., Birley, J. L. T., and Wing, J. K. (1972) Influences of family life on the course of schizophrenic disorders: A replication. *British Journal of Psychiatry*, **121**, 241–258.

Brown, G. W., Bone, M., Dalison, B., and Wing, J. K. (1966) *Schizophrenia and Social Care*. Oxford University Press, London.

Cooper, B. (1978) Epidemiology. In Wing (1978b).

Creer, C. (1978) Social work with patients and their families. In Wing (1978b).

Creer, C., and Wing, J. K. (1974) *Schizophrenia at Home*. National Schizophrenia Fellowship, 79 Victoria Road, Surbiton, Surrey, KT6 4NS.

Edwards, C., and Carter, J. (1979) Day services and the mentally ill. In J. K. Wing and R. Olsen, eds, *Community Care for the Mentally Disabled*. Oxford University Press, London.

Foulds, G. A., and Dixon, P. (1962) The nature of intellectual deficit in schizophrenia: III. A longitudinal study of the subgroups. *British Journal of Clinical and Social Psychology*, **1**, 199–207.

Freeman, H. E., and Simmons, O. G. (1963) *The Mental Patient Comes Home*. John Wiley, New York.

Freudenberg, R. K. (1967) Theory and practice of the rehabilitation of the psychiatrically disabled. *Psychiatric Quarterly*, **41**, 698–710.

Goldberg, S. C., Schooler, N. R., Hogarty, G. E., and Roper, M. (1977) Prediction of relapse in schizophrenic outpatients treated by drug and sociotherapy. *Archives of General Psychiatry*, **34**, 171–184.

Hanson, D. R., Gottesman, I. I., and Heston, L. L. (1976) Some possible childhood indicators of adult schizophrenia. *British Journal of Psychiatry*, **129**, 142–154.

Hassall, C., and Cross, K. W. (1972) Psychiatric day-care in Birmingham. *British Journal of Preventive and Social Medicine*, **26**, 112–120.

Hemsley, D. R. (1978) Limitations of operant procedures in the modification of schizophrenic functioning. *Behaviour Analysis and Modification*, **2**, 165–173.

Hewett, S., Ryan, P., and Wing, J. K. (1975) Living without the mental hospitals. *Journal of Social Policy*, **4**, 391–404.

Hirsch, S. R., Gaind, R., Rohde, P. D., Stevens, B. C., and Wing, J. K. (1973) Out-patient maintenance of chronic schizophrenic patients with long-acting fluphenazine: double-blind placebo trial. *British Medical Journal*, **1**, 633–637.

Jung, C. G. (1906) *The Psychology of Dementia Praecox*, trans. A. A. Brill. Nervous and Mental Diseases Monographs, 1936.

Kendig, I., and Richmond, W. V. (1940) *Psychological Studies in Dementia Praecox.* Edwards, Ann Arbour, Mich.

Leach, J., and Wing, J. K. (1980) *Helping Destitute Men.* Tavistock, London.

Mann, S., and Cree, W. (1976) 'New' long-stay psychiatric patients: a national sample of 15 mental hospitals in England and Wales, 1972/3. *Psychological Medicine,* **6,** 603–616.

National Schizophrenia Fellowship (1974) *Living with Schizophrenia.* 79 Victoria Road, Surbiton, Surrey KT6 4NS.

National Schizophrenia Fellowship (1979) *Home Sweet Nothing.* 79 Victoria Road, Surbiton, Surrey KT6 4NS.

O'Connor, N., Heron, A., and Carstairs, G. M. (1956) Work performance of chronic schizophrenics. *Occupational Psychology,* **30,** 1–12.

Priestly, D. (1979) Helping a self-help group. In J. K. Wing and R. Olsen, eds, *Community Care for the Mentally Disabled.* Oxford University Press, London.

Priestly, D. (1979) *Tied Together with String.* National Schizophrenia Fellowship, 79 Victoria Road, Surbiton, Surrey KT6 4NS.

Robins, L. N. (1970) Follow-up studies investigating childhood disorders. In E. H. Hare and J. K. Wing, eds, *Psychiatric Epidemiology.* Oxford University Press, London.

Royal College of Psychiatrists (1980) *Psychiatric Rehabilitation in the 1980s: Report of Rehabilitation Working Party.* Royal College of Psychiatrists, London.

Ryan, P. (1979) New forms of residential care for the mentally ill. In J. K. Wing and R. Olsen, eds, *Community Care for the Mentally Disabled.* Oxford University Press, London.

Stevens, B. (1970) Frequency of separation and divorce among women aged 16–49 suffering from schizophrenia and affective disorders. *Psychiatrica Scandinavica,* **46,** 136–140.

Stevens, B. C. (1973) Evaluation of rehabilitation for psychotic patients in the community. *Acta Psychiatrica Scandinavica,* **49,** 169–180.

Stone, A. A., and Eldred, S. H. (1959) Delusion formation during the activation of chronic schizophrenic patients. *Archives of General Psychiatry,* **1,** 177–179.

Strömgren, E., and Wing, J. K. (1973) Diagnosis and distribution of schizophrenia. In *The International Pilot Study of Schizophrenia.* Volume 1. World Health Organization, Geneva.

Tarrier, N., Vaughn, C., Lader, M. H., and Leff, J. P. (1979) Bodily reactions to people and events in schizophrenics. *Archives of General Psychiatry,* **36,** 311–315.

Vaughn, C. E., and Leff, J. P. (1976a) The influence of family and social factors on the course of psychiatric illness. *British Journal of Psychiatry,* **129,** 125–137.

Vaughn, C. E., and Leff, J. P. (1976b) Schizophrenia and family life. *Psychology Today,* **10,** 13–18.

Venables, P. H., and Wing, J. K. (1962) Level of arousal and the sub-classification of schizophrenia. *Archives of General Psychiatry,* **7,** 114–119.

Watt, N. F., and Lubensky, A. W. (1976) Childhood roots of schizophrenia. *Journal of Consulting and Clinical Psychology,* **44,** 363–375.

Wing, J. K. (1960) A pilot experiment on the rehabilitation of long-hospitalised male schizophrenic patients. *British Journal of Preventive and Social Medicine,* **14,** 173–180.

Wing, J. K. (1962) Institutionalism in mental hospitals. *British Journal of Social and Clinical Psychology,* **1,** 38–51.

Wing, J. K. (1966) Social and psychological changes in a rehabilitation unit. *Social Psychiatry,* **1,** 21–28.

Wing, J. K. ed. (1975) *Schizophrenia from Within.* National Schizophrenia Fellowship, 79 Victoria Road, Surbiton, Surrey KT6 4NS.

Wing, J. K. (1977) The management of schizophrenia in the community. In G. Usdin, eds, *Psychiatric Medicine*. Brunner, Mazel, New York.

Wing, J. K. (1978a) *Reasoning About Madness*. Oxford University Press, London.

Wing, J. K. (1978b) *Schizophrenia: Towards a New Synthesis*. Academic Press, London.

Wing, J. K., Bennett, D. H., and Denham, J. (1964) *The Industrial Rehabilitation of Long-stay Schizophrenic Patients*. Medical Research Council Memo. No. 42, HMSO, London.

Wing, J. K., and Brown, G. W. (1970) *Institutionalism and Schizophrenia*. Cambridge University Press, London.

Wing, J. K., and Freudenberg, R. K. (1961) The response of severely ill chronic schizophrenic patients to social stimulation. *American Journal of Psychiatry*, **118**, 311–322.

World Health Organization (1974) *Glossary of Mental Disorders and Guide to their Classification*. World Health Organization, Geneva.

World Health Organization (1979) *Schizophrenia. A Two-Year Follow-up of Patients Included in the IPSS*. John Wiley, London.

Zubin, J. (1967) Classification of the behaviour disorders. *Annual Review of Psychology*, **18**, 373–401.

Theory and Practice of Psychiatric Rehabilitation
Edited by F. N. Watts and D. H. Bennett
© 1983, John Wiley & Sons, Ltd.

# 4

# Neurotic, Affective, and Conduct Disorders

FRASER WATTS and DOUGLAS BENNETT

The rehabilitation of schizophrenics is much better understood than that of other groups of psychiatric patients. The historical reasons for this are clear. Schizophrenic patients, more than any other group, used to be admitted to hospital and kept there indefinitely in the absence of any effective treatment. The most immediate problem facing psychiatric rehabilitation when it was first introduced was the large number of long-term schizophrenic inpatients. The rehabilitation of other groups is always likely to be conducted more as part of a community psychiatric service than in a long-term mental hospital. It is only now that community rehabilitation facilities are being developed that the issues raised by non-psychotic patients are being properly considered. The lack of attention to long-term neurotic patients is no doubt also related to the fact that they are a less conspicuous drain on resources.

Many non-psychotic psychiatric problems either respond to treatment or show spontaneous remission within a reasonable period of time. When this happens, many aspects of social adjustment also improve without any specific interventions directed to this end. The patients concerned will often have been off work or out of their social roles for a relatively short time, and this naturally makes it much easier for them to resume normal social functioning. However, this is not always the case. The kind of chronic neurotic patients who are most likely to need rehabilitation have problems in their social circumstances, functioning, and adjustment (Sylph *et al.*, 1969) that seem to go beyond the temporary consequences of their neurotic problems.

Some areas of social functioning are more likely than others to improve when the primary psychiatric problems recede. Rehabilitation services need to be based on sound information about which aspects of social functioning can be expected to improve spontaneously and which cannot. Some such information is available, but it is a key question on which more work is needed. Naturally, rehabilitation efforts need to be especially concentrated on those areas of social functioning that are least likely to improve without specific attention.

More information is also needed about the extent to which efforts to improve the social functioning of neurotic patients may also indirectly help to overcome their primary presenting problems. Too often a sequential model is used in which an attempt is made to 'treat' the primary problem with physical or psychological methods (or both). Only after this is rehabilitation considered, and even then only for those patients who have strikingly failed to return to their previous level of social functioning. The interrelationship between primary psychiatric problems and difficulties in social adjustment is such that often it is as reasonable that the main effort should be directed at the former as the latter, using the kind of methods and facilities that a psychiatric rehabilitation service provides.

In view of the extent to which neurotic and affective psychiatric problems are precipitated and maintained by social stress, it is particularly important to consider what stresses the patient is being exposed to, what support he or she is receiving from the social environment, and to what extent he or she is personally equipped, both in general personal resources and specific skills, to cope with the prevailing social stresses. Some such models of stress and coping have emerged from a number of workers (e.g. Mechanic, 1974; Pearlin and Schooler, 1978) and will be discussed in detail in Chapter 14. It will already be clear, however, that there is much more to the rehabilitation of neurotic psychiatric patients than the acquisition or reacquisition of specific skills. Little will be achieved unless the rehabilitation plan is firmly based on an examination of the 'fit' between the patient and his social environment, and unless it considers a wide range of personal skills, capacities, and attitudes.

Employment is a less central focus of rehabilitation with neurotic than with schizophrenic patients, not because it is less important, but because it presents fewer problems for these patients (Sandler, 1952; Shupe *et al.*, 1966). For example, Shupe *et al.* found that there were relatively few differences in the work ratings on the Work Performance Inventory for patients with 'psychoneurotic disorders' or 'psychophysiological reactions' than for their matched controls. However, 'holds up under pressure' and 'gets along with others' were two items on which these patient groups got significantly poorer ratings. In contrast, schizophrenic patients received poorer ratings than their matched controls on a wide range of items. The role problems of many neurotic patients are concentrated more in interpersonal and domestic roles than in employment, and this needs to be reflected in the focus selected for rehabilitation effort. However, the potential importance of employment for neurotic patients should not be underestimated. For example, Brown and Harris (1978) found that women who have jobs are less vulnerable to depression. This can be attributed to the central role of employment in providing a social network, independence, financial resources, self-respect, etc. (See Chapter 11).

## Depressed Patients

A very substantial proportion of the neurotic patients who are potential candidates for rehabilitation are depressed. In some cases this depressed mood occurs in the context of other psychiatric problems; in others it is the major presenting problem. The severity of the depression may vary from a mild disturbance of mood to an affective psychosis. How people react to their feelings of depression will depend on their assumptions and beliefs about it (Rippere, 1977). Similarly, the reactions of clinicians to complaints of depression depend on prevailing assumptions. It is noteworthy that an increase in the diagnosis of depression coincided with the introduction of antidepressant drugs (Hare, 1974). Psychiatrists have also become more willing to try to manage cases of depression in a flexible and community-based way.

The main focus of rehabilitation is naturally on the patients' adjustment in social roles. Depression is typically accompanied by a marked impairment in role performance. Weissman and Paykel (1974) found that this is most severe in work (whether open employment or housework) and in the major domestic roles associated with marriage and parenthood. Frequently the patients' subjective sense of impairment is even greater than the objective reduction in the level of performance. Many patients' role performance improves as their mood state returns to normal and no specific rehabilitation measures will be thought necessary. However, long-standing problems of interpersonal friction and poor communication tend to be less exacerbated by an acute depressive episode, but also to show less spontaneous improvement as mood state returns to normal (Weissman and Paykel, 1974). Similarly, Altman and Wittenborn (1980) found that recovered depressives still had poor self-esteem, an unhappy outlook, narcissistic vulnerability, helplessness, and low confidence. It should be noted that both these studies focused solely on depressed women; less is known about how depression affects the role performance of men.

Miller (1975) has provided an authoritative review of psychological performance in depression. Though depressives have been shown to be impaired on a variety of tasks, such impairments have seldom been shown to be a unique feature of depression. In assessing the psychological impairment of the individual patient it is important to take objective measures, in view of the fact that depressed patients systematically underestimate their performance. Two common impairments, difficulties in concentration and retardation of performance, will be discussed here to illustrate how they can be approached in rehabilitation.

Difficulties in concentration are prominent among the complaints of depressed patients, though it is a problem that is found in many anxiety states. In a psychometric study (Giambra and Traynor, 1978) depression was found to correlate with reported distractability and slow mentation rate. It is likely that the memory deficit that has sometimes been found in depression (Henry *et al.*, 1973) is secondary to a basic problem in concentration or registration. Poor initial registration results in poor recall. This registration deficit can be seen theoretically as a tendency to process material (such as instructions about how to do a new job) largely at an acoustic rather than a semantic level. The words are heard but their meanings are not adequately registered. There is some evidence from work with normal subjects that anxiety is associated with poor 'semantic processing' (Mueller, 1976). Following this formulation, there is a rationale for the use of strategies to improve the level of semantic processing in the rehabilitation of depressed patients, such as asking patients tacitly to paraphrase work instructions as they listen to them. Patients may also have difficulty in sustaining concentration for a required span of time. A graded training approach in which they practice sustaining concentration for gradually increasing periods of time can be useful here.

Retardation is another important performance deficit in depression, though it is also not unique to depression. There is some evidence for retardation in both intellectual and motor speed (Miller, 1975) though the latter is more pronounced. Payne and Hewlett (1960) suggested that retardation might be due to cognitive interference. Miller (1975), in contrast, has suggested a motivational explanation. Consistent with the cognitive interference view, it has been suggested that external distraction, by drawing patients' attention away from their internal preoccupations, can improve their speed of performance. The main support for this comes from an experiment by Foulds (1952). Patients with depressed, anxious or obsessional states all showed a degree of improvement in the speed of motor performance that was not matched by more extroverted groups of patients, hysterics, and psychopaths. An alternative approach would be to use cognitive methods to reduce interference from distracting thoughts. It is known that under test conditions (e.g. Wine, 1978) anxious subjects spend an excessive proportion of time worrying about their performance. This can also be true for depressed patients. Meichenbaum (1977) has developed methods of training people to identify such maladaptive and redundant 'self-talk' and to replace it with self-talk directing attention back to the problem in hand and suggesting that it can be tackled effectively. Some depressed patients find this a useful aid in their rehabilitation.

Specific attention to these problems may well speed recovery from depression, even though such problems of poor concentration and retarded performance may eventually improve without it. Many patients find the cognitive impairments of depression deeply distressing and take them as evidence that they are 'going out of their minds'. This fear tends to maintain their depressed state. Further, such cognitive impairments can prevent patients from participating in potentially satisfying activities, and the deprivation of satisfaction that results can also maintain the depressed state. The benefits from helping patients to overcome cognitive impairments as soon as possible can thus be considerable.

However, the social adjustment problems of depressed patients are by no means confined to the consequences of such specific impairments in psychological performance. Even in the work role, difficulties in social relationships are likely to be at least as important. It should be remembered that many depressed patients have a long-standing difficulty with establishing close personal relationships. There is now a good deal of evidence that having an intimate, confiding, non-hostile relationship is critical in enabling people to survive experiences that might otherwise lead to depression (Lowenthal and Haven, 1968; Brown and Harris, 1978). Conversely, hostile relationships predispose a person to depression, Leff and Vaughn (1980) were able to show that it is the combination of a hostile, unsupportive relationship with a close relative and a potentially stressful life event that is likely to precipitate depression. Anything that can be done to help patients to achieve a close, confiding relationship will not only be inherently worthwhile, but will have an important role in reducing the risk of further periods of depression. The skills necessary for establishing such relationships are apparently difficult for many patients to acquire. However, deficiencies in the relevant skills may also be compounded by ambivalent motivation. Many depressed patients are extremely cautious about engaging in the self-disclosure that is a necessary part of a confiding relationship, lacking the necessary trust and confidence.

It has already been remarked that personal relationships interact with life events in predisposing people to depression. Social events have an important role both in precipitating a depressive episode and in determining its course. There is typically greater than the normal concentration of potentially threatening life events in the months preceding a depressive episode (Paykel, 1974; Brown et al., 1975; Leff and Vaughn, 1980). These are usually events that represent loss and disappointment to the person concerned and are often prolonged (Brown and Harris, 1978). In addition, Lewinsohn and Graf (1973) have demonstrated an association between depressed mood and a low level of pleasant life events.

Behavioural approaches to depression (e.g. Wilcoxon et al., 1976; Eastman, 1976) emphasized the importance of restoring the level of satisfaction in the lives of depressed patients. Beck (Beck et al., 1979) has made a useful distinction among satisfying experiences between those involving 'pleasure' and those involving a sense of 'mastery'. There may have been an insufficient emphasis on the latter in some behavioural work on depression. It is one of the basic assumptions of rehabilitation theory that social competence and effectiveness are very important in enabling patients to cope with stress and so improve their prognosis. This naturally leads to an attempt to restore a sense of mastery to depressed patients.

There is some evidence that depressed patients are more abnormal in their response to failure than to success. This is true, for example, as far as self-esteem (Flippo and Lewinsohn, 1971) and expectations for the future (Wener and Rehm, 1975) are concerned. Depressed patients may be unusually demoralized by their failures. Seligman (1975) has described the sense of 'learned helplessness' characteristic of depression in which people begin to feel hopeless about all attempts to solve problems. It is an important objective of the rehabilitation of depressed patients to help them to unlearn this feeling of helplessness. The preliminary evidence of Teasdale (1978) suggests that it is not sufficient to recall past successes. Fresh achievements are needed to offset the experience of repeated failure.

There can be a variety of explanations for patients experiencing a low level of success or satisfaction, and the interventions that are appropriate will depend on the reasons that obtain with the individual patient concerned. It may be either the individual or the social environment that is mainly responsible. An individual may not have the necessary skills to elicit the 'satisfactions' or 'successes' that are potentially available, or the environment may be such that the opportunities for obtaining them are very low. The interventions that flow from these two possibilities need more careful consideration.

Lewinsohn (Libet and Lewinsohn, 1973; Youngren and Lewinsohn, 1980) has been a strong advocate of teaching depressed patients the social skills necessary to achieve a greater degree of satisfaction in their lives. However, as Shepherd (Chapter 13) emphasizes, these cannot necessarily be identified with the kind of micro-level skills, such as maintaining appropriate eye contact, that have been the focus of much so-called social skills training. Probably it would be more relevant, for example, to focus on difficulties in communicating some kinds of emotional material. The ability to achieve moderate levels of expression of annoyance rather than going to one extreme or the other is a crucial skill for some depressed patients to acquire in forming deeper personal relationships. Also very important are the skills necessary to establish new social contacts and sources of satisfaction. Costello (1972) has pointed out that people with limited skills are particularly vulnerable to the loss of one source of satisfaction because they do not have the skills or resources to create alternatives. However, at least some such people will prove to have the skills necessary to *maintain* fresh sources of satisfaction, provided they are given help in developing them after a loss.

It is also necessary to consider what direct interventions in the social environment may be necessary in addition to measures taken with the individual patient. In some cases there will be features of the environment that are serving to maintain depressive behaviour; in other cases there will be a lack of incentives for the depressed patients to resume normal social functioning. Liberman and Raskin (1971) report an impressive intervention following these principles. The husband of a depressed patient was asked to reduce the level of sympathetic attention he gave to his wife's depressed behaviour and instead to show this when his wife carried out her previous normal social functions. This simple intervention produced a marked reduction in depressed behaviour and a corresponding improvement in social functioning.

In the rehabilitation of the depressed patient it will usually be helpful to involve the patient's family. The relationship between a patient's depression and an unsatisfactory family situation is complex, and it is often not clear which is cause and which is effect (Brisoe and Smith, 1973). Adopting a family approach to the social management of depression (Bennett *et al.*, 1976; Bennett, 1982) does not necessarily involve undertaking family therapy. A family conference is always useful in assessing the social context of the problem and the patient's level of functioning. Also, the patient and family members are given the opportunity to express their perceptions of the illness, their expectations of treatment, and their hopes for the future (Deykin *et al.*, 1971).

Sometimes it will be useful to go beyond the family and involve other important members of the patient's social network (Speck and Attneave, 1973). The social network is especially important for unmarried patients. Though the family is often the arena in which patients' interpersonal problems manifest themselves, it can also provide support. Single people are more prone to depression (Pearlin and Johnson, 1977) and show a poorer recovery from it (Burke *et al.*, 1967). If the patient cannot be helped to find a supportive network in the community it may be necessary for the psychiatric services to provide him or her with one (see Chapter 10). Some married patients also need help in finding independent social networks. Depressed patients and their spouses tend to spend an abnormally large amount of time together (Nelson *et al.*, 1970) and it can be important for them to disengage to some extent and find independent sources of social satisfaction.

Finally, some comment is needed about the implications for rehabilitation of the periods of manic behaviour that alternate with depression in some patients. Very little attention has been given to the social management of manic-depressive psychosis. Perhaps because it has been widely assumed to have a biological basis, the social aspects have been thought to be unimportant, though of course this would not be a justified inference. With schizophrenia there has been less difficulty in recognizing the interaction of biological and social factors.

The most important social measures to be taken during periods of manic behaviour are preventive. Patients frequently do things in manic periods that destroy their relationships and social standing with their employers and their families. A patient who dissipates his marital savings in a burst of manic behaviour will not readily be forgiven by his spouse. Equally, employers can quickly become so exasperated with the irresponsibility of a manic patient that they would never reemploy him. To prevent this happening it is necessary to monitor patients carefully and to intervene to remove car keys and cheque books, admit to hospital, or whatever is necessary to prevent the patient concerned damaging his future social prospects too seriously (Bennett, 1982).

There is also a role for self-regulation by manic patients of their own behaviour, though this has been insufficiently explored. Rankin (1973) reports an experimental investigation of pressure of speech in a manic patient. This revealed that the degree of abnormal talking varied considerably between situations. The patient was made aware of the kinds of situations in which he was liable to reveal socially unacceptable pressure of speech, such as relatively unstructured situations where a large number of people were present. This provided him with an opportunity of regulating his own manic behaviour by controlling the situation in which he placed himself. The value of self-regulation methods with manic patients deserves to be more fully explored.

### Phobic and Obsessional Patients

Recent years have seen major advances in the treatment of phobic and obsessional patients by behavioural methods. These methods have as their central objective the modification of abnormal phobic avoidance behaviour or compulsive rituals, together with the emotions and cognitions surrounding them. The value of these methods is now well established, and they feature in the proper management of the vast majority of phobic and obsessional patients.

In addition to their central objectives, they may have secondary effects on patients' social adjustment. The rehabilitation team will need to assess in each individual case how much spontaneous improvement in social adjustment can be expected to take place as a result of direct modification of the target symptom. Where necessary, additional measures will need to be taken to help patients regain a better social adjustment.

The series of studies by Marks and his colleagues of the treatment of phobic patients by behavioural methods, which have a 4-year follow-up (Marks, 1971), illustrate the secondary effects on social adjustment which are important in rehabilitation. They looked at five areas of social adjustment (work, leisure, sexual activity, family relationships, and other relationships). Unfortunately, the ratings of adjustment obtained in these areas were of limited reliability and produced inconsistent findings. The results may underestimate the extent to which successful behavioural treatment facilitates subsequent social adjustment, as the data provided relate to all patients treated, not just to those treated successfully. It emerged that work and leisure adjustment showed some spontaneous improvement following behavioural treatment of the phobia, but that this is less true of sexual, family, and other relationships. It is these latter areas, therefore, that are likely to require specific remedial efforts.

It is not surprising that phobias should interfere with work adjustment. Agoraphobics are restricted by not being able to travel to a suitable job, and are thus confined to the limited range of jobs available within easy access of home. Social phobics have anxieties about interaction with their co-workers. Starting a new job and meeting a completely new set of people is especially difficult for them. Working in a large open workshop with many people can also be problematic. Once these restrictions of the phobia on the scope for employment have been removed it can be expected that work adjustment will improve. The same is true of leisure adjustment, as many leisure activities are interfered with directly by phobic avoidance behaviour.

It is interesting that relationship problems are less likely to improve as a result of behavioural treatment of a phobia. There is now growing evidence for a close connection between relationship difficulties and phobic problems, illustrated for example by Hafner's (1977) work on the influence of marital relationship on the prospects for success of the behavioural treatment of agoraphobic patients. The implication of this is that specific attention to the marital relationship is likely to be needed to achieve improved adjustment in this area. Further, such marital work may actually be *necessary* if the phobia itself is to be effectively treated. Just as treatment of the phobia can indirectly improve social adjustment, so measures designed to improve patients' social adjustment can increase their prospects of overcoming the phobia. Again, this is perhaps especially true of agoraphobia, which shows more spontaneous fluctuation in severity than do simple phobias (Snaith, 1968). It is likely that these are related to changes in social circumstances relevant to the social adjustment of the patients concerned.

In considering the rehabilitation of obsessional patients, a distinction needs to be made between obsessive–compulsive neurosis and obsessional personality. The empirical relationship between the two is not close (Slade, 1974). Obsessional personalities are much more common and present as an obstacle to rehabilitation much more frequently. Sandler and Hazari (1960) describe the obessional personality as follows:

an exceedingly systematic, methodical and thorough person, who likes a well-ordered mode of life, is consistent, punctual and meticulous in his use of words. He dislikes half-done tasks, and finds interruptions irksome. He pays much attention to detail and has a strong aversion of dirt.

It is clear that such personality traits can create difficulties in many social roles, both for the patient and for those with whom he has to work. A job in which it is necessary to respond to unexpected events is highly stressful for the obsessional personality. Equally, excessive and apparently unnecessary efforts to keep everything tidy may become exasperating both for work colleagues and for family. There are many patients who have such obsessional traits, but who do not have any specific obsessional ruminations or compulsive rituals.

Compulsive behaviour, such as cleaning rituals, tends to interfere more directly with domestic than with work roles. For example, a housewife with even mild obsessional symptoms can find the task of keeping her house acceptably clean an overwhelmingly demanding one. Moreover, her efforts to achieve extreme cleanliness can be a source of friction within the family. Behavioural methods of modelling and response prevention (Rachman and Hodgson, 1980) represent the most effective treatment approach to this problem, and are usually a prerequisite to effective rehabilitation. Obsessional checking is another symptom that can seriously interfere with social functioning. For one thing, checking gas-taps, light switches, and so on before leaving the house can become such a time-consuming business that it becomes difficult for severely obsessional patients to get to work at the beginning of the day. Again, treatment of the symptoms is essential before rehabilitation can be attempted.

As with phobic patients, the direct treatment of obsessional patients has more effect on work and leisure functioning than on other areas of adjustment such as personal and family relationships (Marks *et al.*, 1975). Stern and Marks (1973) describe an obsessional patient whose marital problems had not been affected by an attempt to treat her rituals and ruminations directly. Indeed, the obsessions themselves had shown little response to treatment. They went on to use a 'contracting' approach to reducing this patient's marital discord. This not only improved the marital relationship but, interestingly, also resulted in a marked improvement in the rituals, though regrettably not in the ruminations. Of course, one can never know how typical such an individual patient is, but it shows that there are at least some obsessional patients in whom attempts to improve social functioning are of more value than direct treatment of the obsessional problems.

Beech and Vaughn (1978, Chapter 9) discuss the ways in which obsessional patients may need help with work, leisure, social activities, family interaction, marital relationships, and sexual functioning following treatment. They point out, for example, that removal of compulsive rituals leaves considerable time that can be filled with recreational or other social activities, and that patients may need help in finding suitable alternative pursuits. The rituals will presumably be less likely to recur if the time has been filled with satisfying activities. The removal of an obsessional approach to the upbringing of children may similarly reveal a deficit in more normal, flexible skills of family interaction that the patient may need to acquire. Specific help may also be needed in overcoming the strained relationships that may have built up in the family as a result of obsessional symptoms.

More commonly, however, a rehabilitation team will be faced with the impact on role adjustment of the meticulous approach to tasks that characterizes obsessional personalities. These problems arise most clearly in occupational rehabilitation. There are a variety of factors that can slow down the performance of obsessional patients. When a decision is involved, they tend to go on collecting additional or repeated information well beyond the point that most people regard as necessary (Milner et al., 1971; Volans, 1976). This reflects the need for certainty that generally characterizes the cognitive performance of obsessionals. Similarly, obsessionals tend to check their work more frequently than others would find necessary, and to do so exceptionally slowly and thoroughly. In as far as this arises from anxiety about making mistakes it is possible to adopt a graded approach to the desensitization of this anxiety by gradually increasing the speed of performance and hence the risk of making mistakes.

Rachman (1974) has emphasized that the slow performance of obsessionals is not just a consequence of time spent checking, but represents a primary disability. It may well be as characteristic of obsessional personalities as of patients with classical obsessional neurosis. Rachman has demonstrated the relative slowness of obsessional patients compared to other neurotic patients in tasks such as digit cancellation (crossing out all the fours in a series of digits) and arithmetic problems. The difference in speed was greatest when there was no pressure to work quickly. When the obsessional patients were pressed to work as quickly as possible, through monitoring of their speed and regular time checks, they mostly speeded up substantially. This suggests that these patients may be able to learn to work at a greater speed consistently. Interestingly, however, two of the series of ten obsessional patients Rachman studied were slower under these conditions of time pressure. The tasks that Rachman studied may not have been of the type at which obsessionals are slowest. Reed (1977) found that obsessional patients were slowest, in comparison to other neurotic patients, in doing an 'inductive' letter series test, though they were faster on a more deductive mental arithmetic test. The fact that obsessionals are at their slowest with open-ended tasks should be remembered in vocational guidance.

The reports of obsessional patients suggest that another factor that may impair their performance is their difficulty in dividing attention between different things. Many familiar tasks are performed automatically and the information involved is processed at a tacit rather than a conscious level. Obsessional patients sometimes describe what appears to be a distrust of this style of information processing. Unless they are consciously aware of what they are doing, they cannot feel sure that they have done the task correctly. There is evidence that normal subjects can improve their capacity for divided attention with training and practice (Spelke et al., 1976) and it would be interesting to investigate the response of obsessional patients to such training.

Though it is reasonable to hope that through developing such ideas it will become possible to do more to remedy the deficiencies in obsessional patients' performance, it is to be expected that in many cases there will be some residual obsessional traits that defy treatment. The important issue, then, is whether or not the patient is able to 'cope' with his obsessionality in the sense of being able to find a pattern of social adjustment that is effective, acceptable to others, and tolerable to himself. This depends in part on tolerance of anxiety. For a patient not to check as much as he would wish, for example, may cause him considerable anxiety. Whether patients' performance in a particular social role is acceptable to others may depend on their ability to tolerate this. It is also important that patients should attempt roles that stress them as little as possible in such ways. Jobs vary considerably in the extent to which it is necessary to leave one task half-completed and turn to something else. This should be a major consideration in vocational guidance with obsessional patients.

### Patients with Conduct Disorder

The rehabilitation of patients with conduct disorder is little understood. There was some interest in this field in the immediately postwar years, but it was not sustained. The rehabilitation of such patients was a central concern of the Neurosis Centre established at Belmont Hospital in 1947 (Jones, 1952; Rapoport, 1960), which in turn developed from work on the rehabilitation of ex-servicemen after the war (Jones, 1946). Jones says that the population at Belmont consisted of 'chronic neurotics and character disorders of a kind usually considered unsuitable for treatment by psychotherapy or physical methods' and included 'inadequate and aggressive psychopaths, schizoid personalities, sexual perversions and the chronic form of psychoneurosis'.

The problems of reliably identifying and classifying patients with disorders of social conduct have not yet been solved. The field has been clouded by imprecisely defined terms such as that of 'psychopathic personality' which Lewis (1974) has aptly called a most elusive category. From the point of view of rehabilitation such concepts have little value, and it is best to concentrate on identifying the specific areas where deviant social behaviour has become apparent. This approach has been adopted by a number of workers (Robins, 1966; Gunn and Robertson, 1976; Watts and Bennett, 1978).

Watts and Bennett carried out a survey of social deviance among the psychiatric patients attending a rehabilitation-orientated day hospital and identified four main areas of deviant conduct. The first was concerned with family roles (care of children, marital conduct, and sexual conduct), the next with social integration (social isolation and an unsettled life), the third with antisocial behaviour (contact with the law, abuse of drugs and alcohol, self-poisoning, and self-mutilation), and the last with violence (to people or property). In women, poor conduct in family roles was a particularly bad prognostic sign as far as benefiting from the day hospital was concerned. In men, self-mutilation was the only individual area of conduct significantly associated with a poor outcome of the day hospital admission, though the total number of areas of deviant conduct was also important. Some of these areas of deviant conduct are considered in detail in other chapters (viz. contact with the law in Chapter 6, abuse of drugs and alcohol in Chapter 5, and poor performance in domestic roles in Chapter 12).

With patients with conduct disorder the distinction between primary psychiatric symptoms and the secondary handicaps in social functioning that follow from them is less relevant than when applied to schizophrenic patients. With conduct disorders the primary presenting problem is itself in the area of social adjustment. Very often these patients have never made a satisfactory social adjustment. The problem is one of completing their primary adjustment rather than simply helping them with secondary readjustment after a psychiatric episode. The methods of psychiatric rehabilitation may be helpful in enabling them to do so, but in this context they should strictly be called habilitation rather than rehabilitation.

Nevertheless, there are cases where a distinction can usefully be made between working on a focal problem such as a sexual deviance and working on more general problems of establishing a network of social roles. As with other disorders, there are complex interrelationships. However, there is a growing recognition, at least in the field of sexual deviation, that unless 'normal' sexual interests have been established the prospects for eliminating 'deviant' ones are poor. Indeed, once 'normal' interests are established, 'deviant' ones may decline without any further treatment (Barlow and Abel, 1976). If the same is true for other areas of conduct disorder, it argues for the general importance of the efforts to establish a normal social adjustment for these patients, which is the aim of the rehabilitation approach.

There seem to be particular problems in gaining the cooperation of socially deviant patients in a rehabilitation programme. These difficulties go beyond value judgements regarding the area of deviance itself. Jones *et al.* (1956) describe the difficulties they had at Belmont in persuading patients with character disorders to show any interest or enthusiasm for the industrial workshop. They finally solved the problem by getting patients to work on the improvement of living conditions in the bomb-damaged building in which the unit was housed, instead of doing production work. It seems to be particularly important for these patients to see the value of the work they undertake in a rehabilitation programme and identify with those who will benefit from their efforts.

The difficulties that 'personality disorder' patients have with the work role should not be underestimated. Shupe *et al.* (1966), comparing such patients with matched controls, found significantly poorer performance on many items of the Work Performance Inventory (holds up under pressure, gets along with others, respects authority, quality of work, ambition, absenteeism, adjusts to new situations, safety-minded, shows initiative). Evans and Moloney (1974) found that work difficulties among patients in an adolescent unit were highly correlated with disturbed behaviour and poor tolerance of frustration. Employment makes demands for cooperative social behaviour that many patients with conduct disorders seem to be unable to meet.

It is with these general characteristics of work behaviour that conduct disorder patients most need help, and the main benefit they derive from rehabilitation often comes from the practice they obtain in meeting the general structural requirements of a work role (see Chapter 11) rather than from practising particular skills. However, with this group of patients, it is often not possible to get them to approach the role seriously unless the content is acceptable to them. Patients generally tend to regard rehabilitation workshops as 'unrealistic' work settings in the sense that they are very different from open employment (Kyrou, 1969). Such perceptions seem to be particularly important for socially deviant patients.

The rehabilitation of these patients is less a matter of teaching skills than of modifying attitudes. It is argued in Chapter 14 that increasing self-confidence is one of the crucial processes in rehabilitation. There seems to be a significant group of socially deviant patients for whom any progress whatsoever in rehabilitation is critically dependent on bringing about an improvement in the patient's self-esteem. In planning the rehabilitation of such patients it is important to identify areas of functioning where some gain will be possible, and which will have the maximum impact on self-esteem. As with the household improvements at Belmont, this may lead to concentration on areas that are not important in their actual *content* for post-rehabilitation functioning. For example, there are a number of socially inadequate patients for whom gains in arithmetic are critical in rehabilitation, solely because of their impact on self-esteem, but not because the skills would be required in any subsequent employment.

For other conduct disorder patients, the development of satisfactory relationships with colleagues and supervisors is the central issue in rehabilitation. One is often dealing here with general difficulties in relationships that manifest themselves in a variety of settings. The rehabilitation programme offers an area in which some social learning can take place. For example, a patient described as having a 'borderline' personality may have strong and apparently insatiable needs for support and approval from other people, and have great difficulty in accepting the occasional criticism which is an inevitable part of any social role. The first requirement here is to get a common understanding with the patient of the nature of the problem. Once this is achieved there is some hope that he or she will be able to recognize that emotionally frustrating situations in the rehabilitation programme are a learning opportunity and not gratuitous punitiveness on the part of the staff.

As with other kinds of patients, changes in a conduct disorder patient's social network can make a critical difference to rehabilitation. It is a striking clinical observation that when such patients eventually marry, their work record often changes dramatically. The combination of support and responsibilities that marriage brings can change both the patient's attitude to employment and his capacity for it.

These aspects of rehabilitation, finding the work meaningful, gaining in self-confidence, and learning to tolerate stressful role relationships, are particularly important in the rehabilitation of conduct disorder patients. But it cannot be concealed that our understanding of the issues involved is at a very early stage. The systematic development and evaluation of appropriate rehabilitation programmes for psychiatric patients with conduct disorders is still largely something for the future.

## References

Altman, J. H., and Wittenborn, J. R. (1980) Depression-prone personality in women. *Journal of Abnormal Psychology*, **89**, 303-308.

Barlow, D. H., and Abel, G. G. (1976) Sexual deviation. In W. E. Craighead, A. E. Kazdin, and M. J. Mahony, eds, *Behaviour Modification: Principles, Issues and Applications*. Houghton Mifflin, Boston, Mass.

Beck, A. T., Rush, A. J., Shaw, B. F., and Emery, G. (1979) *Cognitive Therapy of Depression*. John Wiley, Chichester.

Beech, H. R., and Vaughan, M. (1978) *Behavioural Treatment of Obsessional States*. John Wiley, Chichester.

Bennett, D., Fox, C., Jowell, T., and Skynner, A. C. R. (1976) Towards a family approach in a psychiatric day hospital. *British Journal of Psychiatry*, **132**, 441-449.

Bennett, D. H. (1982) Social and community approaches to treatment of depression. In E. S. Paykel, ed, *Handbook of Affective Disorders*. Churchill-Livingstone, Edinburgh.

Briscoe, C. W., and Smith, M. D. (1973) Depression and marital turmoil. *Archives of General Psychiatry*, **29**, 812-817.

Brown, G. W., Brolchain, M. N., and Harris, T. (1975) Social class and psychiatric disturbance among women in an urban population. *Sociology*, **9**, 225-254.

Brown, G. W., and Harris, T. (1978) *Social Origins of Depression: A Study of Psychiatric Disorder in Women*. Tavistock, London.

Burke, L., Deykin, E., Jacobson, S., and Haley, S. (1967) The depressed woman returns. *Archives of General Psychiatry*, **16**, 548-553.

Costello, C. G. (1972) Loss of reinforcers or loss of reinforcer effectiveness. *Behaviour Therapy*, **3**, 240-247.

Deykin, E. Y., Weissman, M. M., and Klerman, G. L. (1971) Treatment of depressed women. *British Journal of Social Work*, **1**, 277-291.

Eastman, C. (1976) Behavioural formulation of depression. *Psychological Review*, **83**, 277-291.

Evans, J., and Moloney, L. (1974) Adolescents and work difficulties. *British Journal of Psychiatry*, **124**, 203-207.

Flippo, J. R., and Lewinsohn, P. M. (1971) Effects of failure on the self-esteem of depressed and non-depressed subjects. *Journal of Consulting and Clinical Psychology*, **36**, 151.

Foulds, G. A. (1952) Temperamental differences in maze performance: II The effect of distraction and electroconvulsive therapy on psychomotor retardation. *British Journal of Psychiatry*, **43**, 33–41.

Giambra, L. M., and Traynor, T. D. (1978) Depression and daydreaming: an analysis based on self-ratings. *Journal of Clinical Psychology*, **34**, 14–25.

Gunn, J., and Robertson, G. (1976) Psychopathic personality: a conceptual problem. *Psychological Medicine*, **6**, 631–634.

Hafner, R. J. (1977) The husbands of agoraphobic women and their influence on treatment outcome. *British Journal of Psychiatry*, **131**, 289–294.

Hare, E. H. (1974) The changing content of psychiatric illness. *Journal of Psychosomatic Research*, **18**, 283–289.

Henry, G. M., Weingartner, H., and Murphy, D. L. (1973) Influence of affective states and psychoactive drugs on verbal learning and memory. *American Journal of Psychiatry*, **130**, 966–971.

Jones, M. (1946) Rehabilitation of forces neurosis patients to civilian life. *British Medical Journal*, **1**, 532–535.

Jones, M. (1952) Industrial rehabilitation of mental patients still in hospital. *Lancet*, **ii**, 985–986.

Jones, M., Pomryn, B. A., and Skellern, E. (1956) Work therapy. *Lancet*, **i**, 343–344.

Kyrou, N. (1969) An evaluation of the success of a rehabilitation workshop in appearing realistic to the patients who are working in it. Unpublished MSc dissertation, University of London.

Leff, J. P., and Vaughn, C. E. (1980) The influence of life events and relatives' expressed emotion in schizophrenia and depressive neurosis. *British Journal of Psychiatry*, **136**, 146–153.

Lewinsohn, P. M., and Graf, M. (1973) Pleasant activities and depression. *Journal of Consulting and Clinical Psychology*, **41**, 261–268.

Lewis, A. (1974) Psychopathic personality: a most elusive category. *Psychological Medicine*, **4**, 133–140.

Liberman, R. P., and Raskin, D. E. (1971) Depression: a behavioural formulation. *Archives of General Psychiatry*, **24**, 515–523.

Libet, J. M., and Lewinsohn, P. M. (1973) Concept of social skills with special reference to the behaviour of depressed persons. *Journal of Consulting and Clinical Psychology*, **40**, 304–312.

Lowenthal, M. F., and Haven, C. (1968) Interaction and adaptation: intimacy as a critical variable. *American Sociological Review*, **33**, 20–30.

Marks, I. M. (1971) Phobic disorders for years after treatment: a prospective follow-up. *British Journal of Psychiatry*, **118**, 683–688.

Marks, I. M., Hodgson, R., and Rachman, S. J. (1975) Treatment of chronic obsessive–compulsive neurosis by in-vivo exposure. *British Journal of Psychiatry*, **127**, 349–364.

Mechanic, D. (1974) Social structure and personal adaptation: some neglected dimensions. In G. V. Coelho, D. A. Hamburg, and J. E. Adams, eds, *Coping and Adaption*. Basic Books, New York.

Meichenbaum, D. (1977) *Cognitive and Behaviour Modification: An Integrative Approach*. Plenum, New York.

Miller, W. R. (1975) Psychological deficit in depression. *Psychological Bulletin*, **82**, 238–260.

Milner, A. D., Beech, H. R., and Walker, V. J. (1971) Decision processes and obsessional behaviour. *British Journal of Social and Clinical Psychology*, **10**, 88–89.

Mueller, J. H. (1976) Anxiety and cue utilization in human learning and memory. In M. Zuckerman and C. D. Spielberger, eds, *Anxiety: New Concepts, Methods and Application*. Lawrence Erlbaum, New York.

Nelson, B., Collins, J., Kreitman, N., and Troop, J. (1970) Neurosis and marital interaction: II Time sharing and social activity. *British Journal of Psychiatry*, **117**, 47–58.

Paykel, E. S. (1974) Recent life events and clinical depression. In E. K. E. Gunderson and R. D. Rahe, eds, *Life Stress and Illness*. C. C. Thomas, Illinois.

Payne, R. W., and Hewlett, J. H. G. (1960) Thought disorder in psychotic patients. In H. J. Eysenck, ed., *Experiments in Personality*, Vol. 2. Routledge & Kegan Paul, London.

Pearlin, L. I., and Johnson, J. S. (1977) Marital status, life strains and depression. *American Sociological Review*, **42**, 704–715.

Pearlin, L. I., and Schooler, C. (1978) The structure of coping. *Journal of Health and Social Behaviour*, **19**, 2–21.

Rachman, S. J. (1974) Primary obsessional slowness. *Behaviour Research and Therapy*, **12**, 9–18.

Rachman, S. J., and Hodgson, R. J. (1980) *Obsessions and Compulsions*. Pentice-Hall, Englewood Cliffs, NJ.

Rankin, H. (1973) Some problems in the investigation of manic speech: a single case study. Unpublished manuscript, Institute of Psychiatry, University of London.

Rapoport, R. N. (1960) *Community as Doctor: New Perspectives on a Therapeutic Community*. Tavistock, London.

Reed, G. F. (1977) Obsessional cognition: performance on two numerical tasks. *British Journal of Psychiatry*, **130**, 184–185.

Rippere, V. (1977) Commonsense beliefs about depression and anti-depressive behaviour: a study of social consensus. *Behaviour Research and Therapy*, **15**, 465–473.

Robins, L. N. (1966) *Deviant Children Grown Up*. Williams & Williams, Baltimore.

Sandler J. (1952) Follow-up enquiry II. Statistical analysis and the concept of general adjustment. In M. Jones, ed., *Social Psychiatry: A Study of Therapeutic Communities*. Tavistock, London.

Sandler, J., and Hazari, A. (1960) The obsessional on the psychological classification of obsessional traits and symptoms. *British Journal of Medical Psychology*, **33**, 113–122.

Seligman, M. E. P. (1975) *Helplessness*. W. H. Freeman, San Francisco.

Shupe, D. R., Cole, N. J., and Allison, R. B. (1966) Job adjustments of former patients: II Specific characteristics of work performance related to psychiatric diagnosis. *Hospital and Community Psychiatry*, **17**, 178–180.

Slade, P. D. (1974) Psychometric studies of obsessional illness and obsessional personality. In H. R. Beech, ed., *Obsessional States*. Methuen, London.

Snaith, R. P. (1968) A clinical investigation of phobias. *British Journal of Psychiatry*, **114**, 673–697.

Speck, R. V., and Attneave, L. L. (1973) *Family Networks*. Random House, New York.

Spelke, E., Hirst, W., and Neisser, U. (1976) Skills of divided attention. *Cognition*, **4**, 215–230.

Stern, R. S., and Marks, I. M. (1973) Contract therapy in obsessive–compulsive neurosis with marital discord. *British Journal of Psychiatry*, **123**, 681–684.

Sylph, J., Kedward, H. B., and Eastwood, M. R. (1969) Chronic neurotic patients in general practice. *Journal of Royal College of General Practitioners*, **17**, 162–170.

Teasdale, J. D. (1978) Effects of real and recalled success on learned helplessness and depression. *Journal of Abnormal Psychology*, **87**, 155–164.

Volans, P. J. (1976) Styles of decision-making and probability appraisal in selected obsessional and phobic patients. *British Journal of Social and Clinical Psychology*, **15**, 305–317.

Watts, F. N., and Bennett, D. H. (1978) Social deviance in a day hospital. *British Journal of Psychiatry*, **132**, 455–462.

Weissman, M. M., and Paykel, E. C. (1974) *The Depressed Woman: A Study of Social Relationships*. University of Chicago Press, Chicago.

Wener, A. E., and Rehm, L. P. (1975) Depressive affect: a test of behavioural hypotheses. *Journal of Abnormal Psychology*, **84**, 221–227.

Wilcoxon, L. A., Schrader, S. L., and Nelson, R. E. (1976) Behavioural formulations of depression. In W. E. Craighead, A. E. Kazdin, and M. J. Mahoney, eds, *Behaviour Modification: Principles, Issues and Applications*. Houghton Mifflin, Boston, Mass.

Wine, J. (1978) Cognitive-attentional theory of test anxiety. In I. Sarason, ed., *Test Anxiety: Theory, Research and Application*. Lawrence Erlbaum, New York.

Youngren, M. A., and Lewinsohn, P. M. (1980) The functional relation between depression and problematic interpersonal behaviour. *Journal of Abnormal Psychology*, **89**, 331–341.

Theory and Practice of Psychiatric Rehabilitation
Edited by F. N. Watts and D. H. Bennett
© 1983, John Wiley & Sons, Ltd.

# 5

---

# Problem Drinkers and Drug Takers

---

ANTHONY THORLEY

## The Conceptual Background

During the last 20 years the fields of alcoholism and drug addiction have been undergoing major conceptual changes and it is against these changes that rehabilitation must be considered. At both academic and clinical levels alcoholism has never been a satisfactorily defined entity, and drug addiction as a diagnosis has been strained and stretched because several coexistent patterns of drug taking have been found. Both alcoholism and drug addiction have been conceptualized within a psychiatric disease model, with predictable course and life history. However, empirical evidence in both fields suggests that a disease model implying an inexorable process, with little prospect of cure or recovery, has less and less credibility and currency in treatment and rehabilitation (Gossop, 1980; Shaw *et al.*, 1978; Pattison *et al.*, 1977; Thorley, 1978, 1981a).

Although for a long while it has been self-evident that many factors contribute to cause both alcohol and drug problems, paradoxically much clinical effort has been based on a primitive, organic, reductionist, aetiological model (ranging from Alcoholics Anonymous 'allergy', through alleged primary biochemical dysfunctions to more current refinements based on endorphins) which applies to all affected persons. Consequently, the diseases of alcoholism and drug addiction, if somewhat undetermined, have been responded to by a predominant modality of treatment at the expense of strategies of rehabilitation. Often, and in particular for alcoholism, the relative failure of primitive treatments and their lack of superiority over natural processes or spontaneous remission (Orford and Edwards, 1977) have led to an emerging therapeutic nihilism.

One response to the shortcomings of the disease concept of drug addiction and alcoholism has been to refine the concept and centre it upon the problematic phenomenon of dependence (Edwards and Gross, 1976; Shaw *et al.*, 1978; Thorley, 1981a). Other alcohol related problems, less identified with dependence *per se*, are categorized by the World Health Organization (1977) as 'alcohol related disabilities', but to date an approach to these disabilities outside a health remit has not been elaborated in a way that informs strategies of rehabilitation. It would appear, therefore, that no disease-orientated, dependence-orientated, or reductionist model can do justice to the variety and complexity of the phenomena that present. Narrow disease models are an impediment in multidisciplinary or non-medical treatment settings, and are least applicable in the non-medical statutory rehabilitation agencies which predominate in the United Kingdom (Thorley, 1981).

More practical and empirical is a problem-orientated, hence task or service-orientated model (Thorley, 1980a), based on the implicitly multidisciplinary umbrella term of 'problem drinker'. A problem drinker is defined in a report issued by the Department of Health and Social Security (DHSS) as 'any person who experiences social, psychological or physical problems as a consequence of his or her own repeated drinking of alcohol or the repeated drinking of others' (DHSS, 1978). The final phrase boldly implies the need for services for helping members of families of problem drinkers. Elsewhere I have proposed a similar definition of 'problem drug taker' which avoids labels such as drug addict and drug dependent and utilizes the three elements of problematic drug use outlined below.

A *problem drug taker* is any person who experiences psychological, physical, social or legal problems related to intoxication, and/or regular excessive consumption, and/or dependence as a consequence of his or her own use of drug or chemical substances excluding alcohol or tobacco. (Thorley, 1980b)

I have described elsewhere (Thorley, 1980a) how a problem-orientated model of alcohol and drug problems informs a rehabilitative and treatment approach. It requires a careful assessment of the system of antecedent and consequent factors (see Figure 5.1) in medical, social, and legal modalities, together with the specific pattern of drug taking or drinking. This is the system which is open to intervention and change, treatment and rehabilitation. The pattern of problematic drinking or drug taking may fall into three interrelated (but not mutually exclusive) elements: intoxication, regular excessive consumption, and dependence. Each of these three elements produces its own characteristic problems which fall into medical, social, and legal categories (Thorley, 1982).

It is clear that alcohol and drug problems are not seen here implicitly as diseases, although physical pathology may be present, but as patterns of behaviour leading to a variety of problems of personal and social functioning. Often the three basic elements overlap to give a composite, but in planning

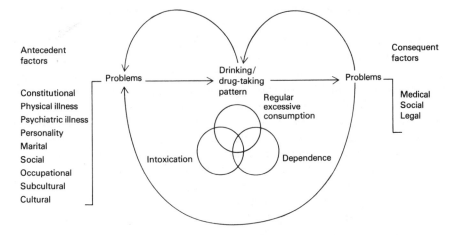

Figure 5.1   An explanatory system for alcohol or drug problems

rehabilitation and treatment it is most instructive to identify the contribution of each element to the whole. Here the model avoids fitting people into diagnoses of alcoholism or drug addiction with their implicit symptomatologies and outcome, and concentrates on the variety of the individual's problems and the implication of a variety of relevant responses.

## Clarifying Treatment and Rehabilitation

An enduring problem in the alcohol and drug fields has been the technical and often obscure distinctions made between treatment and rehabilitation. This issue is discussed more fully elsewhere in this book, but alcohol and drug problems raise issues of their own which required clarification.

We may define *treatment* as the response in a specific modality (e.g. chemotherapy, psychotherapy, behaviour therapy) to specific symptoms and problematic behaviours. In this setting the patient is usually seen to have a disease or illness which responds to treatment, and a sick role is implicit and appropriate. Classically, the patient in the sick role may not be (or feel) accountable for his symptoms or problems. This is true for manic-depressive psychosis or schizophrenia, but it is much less so for alcohol or drug problems where clearly there is a powerful volitional element, personal responsibility is implicit, and determinism plays a less predominant role (Robinson, 1972). To date, as outlined above, models of alcoholism and drug addiction have stressed illness and disease and this has encouraged patients strongly to embrace the sick role and so avoid, or only obliquely acknowledge, accountability. Nowhere is this more evident than within Alcoholics Anonymous (Robinson, 1979) where alcoholism as a disease can never fade, or remit. The drinking alcoholic can only become 'dry alcoholic', 'sober alcoholic', or 'recovering alcoholic'. Here the sick role is implicit and life-long! A similar implicit fixity of essential pathology is suggested by the idea of transfer of dependence in drug takers. 'Once a drug addict always a drug addict': the heroin addict may give up heroin, but will transfer his dependence to barbiturates or alcohol or safer tranquillizers, and so in essence is still a drug addict. Ideas of fixity in drug takers predominate in spite of evidence to the contrary (Thorley, 1978). A further paradox arises in the treatment of drug problems by 'maintenance' prescriptions of opiates or benzodiazepine tranquillizers given by general practitioners, or psychiatrists in drug clinics. In the sick role the patient's expectation of the prescribed drugs is that they will cure his addiction or problem; often, as many observers have acidly pointed out, they only add to his problem and extend his drug career. These, then, are powerful and enduring images of the sick role in alcoholism and drug addiction and they must necessarily be confronted in any radical reevaluation of treatment (Robinson, 1972; Thorley, 1980a).

In contrast to treatment, *rehabilitation* is a much more active and extended process, with the patient or client being encouraged to shed the passivity of the sick role and to take responsibility himself for his improved functioning. One of the attractions of the rehabilitation of problem drinkers and drug takers, compared with other patient groups in general psychiatry, is that given time and well coordinated agencies, complete reintegration into society is possible without any residual handicap, except perhaps the deviant role of being abstinent from alcohol! How, then, does rehabilitation relate to treatment?

The view of treatment presented in this account suggests responses which in general are likely to be short-term. Thus detoxification, medical responses to intoxication-related trauma, and social work responses to marital or family crisis are all treatment strategies commonly carried through within 2 or 3 weeks. Rehabilitation implies a longer-term response, less related to the short-term amelioration of symptoms, and more aligned to a long-term relearning of new skills and coping mechanisms. Traditionally, the need for rehabilitation presumes that there is some residual personal or social dysfunction (if not handicap) remaining *after* treatment. In responses to handicap, or personal or social dysfunction, the traditional sick role with its implied patient compliance and non-accountability is less appropriate than a therapeutic process involving personal responsibility and self-determination. A combination of these responses, leading to increased social integration, personal effectiveness, and independence, is encompassed within the term 'rehabilitation'.

The United Nations Division of Narcotic Drugs, viewing drug problems more as a chronic handicap than a chronic disease, usefully suggests that for drug takers

Rehabilitation is the process of helping individuals to establish a state in which they are physically, psychologically and socially capable of coping with situations encountered, thus enabling them to take advantage of the opportunities that are available to other people in the same age group in society. (United Nations, 1978)

This definition is just as apt for problem drinkers, and it is to be noted how emphasis is placed on the process of social reintegration. Clearly, for many disturbed clients this integrative element of rehabilitation is less reintegration than primary integration: *habilitation* rather *re*habilitation.

Most authorities identify two essential elements in the rehabilitation process for problem drinkers and drug takers. There are processes centred on the *individual* and processes concurrently centred on the *environment* in which the individual is learning new skills. We may denote the two basic processes as follows:

(a) To enable problem drinkers/drug takers to utilize personal resources and so modify attitudes, behaviour, and skills in order to achieve a stable and fulfilling way of life with minimal or no alcohol-or drug-related problems.
(b) To provide the graded social supports and agencies required to facilitate the development of the individual so as to establish or reestablish problem drinkers/drug takers in the community in roles which they find more stable and fulfilling than those related to their previous alcohol or drug use.

Clearly, if rehabilitation is to work, the individual and environmental processes of development must be optimized and dovetailed in an active programme, graded over time, which increases individual competence and limits problems.

Now that some of the essential differences between treatment and rehabilitation as applied to alcohol and drug problems have been outlined it remains to examine the present and future optimal relationship between these two basic responses. If management is to be seen as the overall coordination of treatment and rehabilitation, then for alcohol and drug problems a change in the emphasis of management appears to be required.

In the past, and commonly at present, treatment (e.g. hospital-based) has been the predominant helping response. Short-term measures have often only produced limited success. Contact with agencies concerned primarily with long-term rehabilitation (e.g. community-based hostels) has been tenuous, with coordination fragmentary and disorganized. This situation would be reflected in A and B in Figure 5.2, where A would be the view from a clinic and B the view from a hostel. However, and particularly in the United Kingdom with regard to alcohol services, there is in some areas a degree of integration between treatment and rehabilitation (e.g. C or D) but usually it is with a medical treatment model as the predominant modality. However, rehabilitation is now being seen as playing a major part in recovery and being

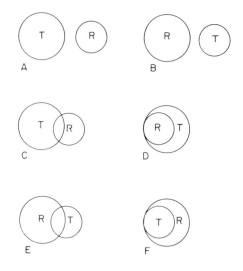

Figure 5.2    Models of the interrelationship between rehabilitation (R) and treatment (T) for problem drinkers and drug takers

of greater overall significance. In much of medicine, where disease predominates and short-term treatment is to the fore, models such as C and D are common: rehabilitation is seen as a component of treatment. Many authorities would see model D as the predominant one in psychiatry today. However, for alcohol and drug problems (and arguably for much else in psychiatry), seen less as short-term treatable diseases and more as chronic handicaps or behaviour disorders, a model which has rehabilitation as the primary response may be most appropriate (e.g. E or F).

This primary emphasis on rehabilitation is supported by the time-scale of recovery (often 2–3 years), the inappropriateness of illness and a chronic sick role, and the predominant non-medical multidisciplinary approach of personnel in the field. In the rehabilitation services, medical skills and attitudes may be less relevant than a model of social case work, occupational or remedial therapy, or psychological learning theory. The non-statutory ('voluntary') rehabilitation agencies are the fastest growing area of response in the UK and are actively encouraged by the government (e.g. Department of Health and Social Security, 1978). The United Nations (1978) Narcotics' Division recognizes a temporal distinction or continuum between, first, treatment leading to rehabilitation, and, second, social reintegration, and this approach would be closest to model E. In the USA, reflecting the predominance of non-medical personnel, especially in drug services, many agencies use model F, and in both the drug and alcohol field this model has growing adherents in the UK (e.g. Federation of Alcoholic Residential

Establishments, 1978; D.H.S.S. 1982). Here rehabilitation becomes the central task for the services, with treatments making up essential components. It is an approach which radically confronts the problem of chronic alcoholism and drug addiction and suggests a basic shift in emphasis for the future. It is rehabilitation, therefore, which should be in the centre of our thinking as we consider individual assessment and specific services.

### Principles of Assessment and Management

The assessment and management of problem drinkers and drug takers must necessarily take into account the two basic elements of rehabilitation: the individual's potential response and resources in the environment. As indicated above, it is useful always to have rehabilitation in mind whatever the service setting. Thus good treatment must anticipate and look to rehabilitation, and good rehabilitation must reflect or even actively integrate treatment. For instance, the patient or client who is undergoing detoxification treatment can be actively introduced and encouraged to affiliate to a network of rehabilitation services: in fact, detoxification which is not a prelude to such affiliation is a poor form of treatment. General principles of treatment will not be dwelt upon here; basic accounts have been provided by Madden (1979), Murray (1979), and Thorley (1979) and the enduring problem of client motivation and specific treatment techniques relevant to alcohol problems has been explored in detail by Thorley (1980a).

Assessment of the individual is best carried out against the kind of system outlined in Figure 5.1. A basic history from and discussion with the client will identify the pattern of problems, symptoms, and dysfunctions which the client and worker must place in some kind of order or priority and agree to attend to. Rehabilitation, even more than treatment, depends crucially on negotiation between doctor/worker and patient/client about the meaning and basis of the problems and the agenda for dealing with them (Scheff, 1968). As problems and dysfunctions are often ranged across medical, social, and legal areas, it makes sense where a multidisciplinary team is present to allow each member to make his contribution to the assessment of individual dysfunction and potential. Past levels of functioning and stability are as important as current functioning and need to be taken into account when realistically planning for the future. Many patients entering rehabilitation tend to look to the good times in the past: 'If only I could be like I was ten years ago I would be fine.' In truth there are caveats in a backward-looking approach because something in that idealized past may have led to the chaos of the present. Rehabilitation should, therefore, be forward-looking.

Concomitant with this general assessment of functioning will be an analysis of the current pattern of drinking or drug taking and the way specific problems emerge from the pattern. For instance, chronic excessive consumption of alcohol (possibly in the absence of dependence or intoxication) may lead to financial debt as well as liver damage. This may relate to homelessness or offences of theft. Rehabilitation must take into account the most realistic goals with regard to future use of alcohol or drugs. Thus abstinence may be a first goal in the process of detoxification, but how realistic is it to plan future overall rehabilitation in an alcohol or drug free setting? In spite of the criticism of observers, many drug takers rehabilitation in the context of carefully monitored 'maintenance' or slowly reducing drug prescriptions (Wille, 1981), and there is much evidence that many drinkers will slowly achieve stability and harm-free status without total abstinence. The distinction between harm-free alcohol or drug use and abstinence as a goal is an important one in planning rehabilitation, and Thorley (1980a) has examined some of the factors relevant to the right choice for problem drinkers. Rehabilitation can occur from a basis either of abstinence or of harm-free alcohol or drug use, and there is no place here for dogmatic attitudes. Too many patients have inevitably failed because of unrealistic goals imposed upon them by the doctor or worker instead of attaining mutual agreement about a realistic goal as a first priority. It is vital, therefore, to be realistic about goals without being pessimistic. It is also useful to create a structure to the process of rehabilitation by identifying with the client short-, mid-, and long-term goals regarding all the problems being tackled. Rehabilitation, like treatment, is valued much more if the patient or client can see the purpose and meaning of it: cognitive elements are always vital in change.

Whilst it is possible for client or patient to have a dramatic flight into abstinent stability or a 'spontaneous' remission, this cannot be relied upon, and thus the functional and developmental needs of the individual have to be matched against the provision of local resources. In general local resources are more useful that distant ones as this allows for closer work with the patient's spouse, family, or occupational base. However, in some circumstances, moving away from a problematic subculture or disturbed family can be a crucial element in management. Hence a dry hostel or house is not only a residential resource for the non-domiciled drinker or drug taker who has shown he can manage abstinence with support. It is also relevant for the inappropriately domiciled, such as clients who risk almost certain relapse if they return to spouse or family but who may benefit immeasurably from a period in a dry house before attempting a return home. Most specialist residential units are in fact dry, but non-specialist agencies often allow a reasonable degree of drinking and should be utilized when a non-abstinent goal is agreed upon. Non-abstinent goals are sometimes tolerated or actively encouraged in specialist day centres and day hospitals, and these are especially valuable in areas of heavy cultural drinking where the client is under great pressure to drink. In general, environmental facilities should be used in a coordinated and graded way. Close supervision, possibly in a residential setting, should lead to less supervision and more independence. Finally, it must be remembered that no one is totally independent of support and that many socially reintegrated clients will need nominal support from social worker or volunteers for many years.

It is clear from the complexity of the system that the management of integrated rehabilitation and treatment requires coordination and some kind of identifiable guiding agent or person who will help the patient or client to keep his progress and present and future goals in perspective. Initial assessment carried out by a multidisciplinary team must be coordinated into a recipe or plan which both client and agency clearly understand. If in time the plan involves other agencies the strategies and goals must be clearly communicated. Case conferences with all relevant agencies present (including the client!) are just one practical model to use. The guiding agent or coordinator should be someone who will not move on but will provide continuity and perspective over the 2–3-year period of rehabilitation: a probation officer, social worker, general practitioner, or hospital consultant are obvious candidates. At any one time in the programme, team members other than the coordinator may have a closer or more therapeutic relationship, but matters of teamwork are dealt with more explicity elsewhere in this book (Chapter 15). Management must be flexible and allow for mutual renegotiation of the goals of rehabilitation.

Finally, management should not allow for the concept of absolutely 'hopeless cases'. It is necessary to be realistic about unmotivated individuals apparently set on self-destructive careers and about the paucity of overworked resources. However, the attitude of the agency workers makes a big difference to the outcome of a negotiated contract. The idea of 'hopeless cases' can be overworked and provide a slippery slope towards client exclusion and general nihilism. Clients adopt workers' nihilism just as they take up workers' enthusiasm and hope. A successful client career in rehabilitation is like a successful career in medicine or social work: it needs to be managed with care and concern for the individual, and with not a little enthusiasm.

### Services for Problem Drinkers

Treatment Effectiveness and the Basis for Rehabilitation

Since the Second World War it has been recognized that an international increase in alcohol consumption has been accompanied by a striking rise in alcohol problems, and currently in the United Kingdom it is accepted that up to 5 per cent of the adult population are problem drinkers (Plant, 1982).

For many years the predominant approach to these alcohol problems has been the medical treatment of alcoholism married to an abstinence outcome goal. However, modern thinking accepts that harm-free drinking outcomes are equally or even more appropriate. Personal and social effectiveness, accommodation stability, and employment are also relevant aspects of outcome (Costello, 1980; Heather and Robertson, 1981).

Early results of treatment programmes were unspectacular, reflecting narrow treatment models and poor service coordination, but a survey of more recent studies shows that treatment programmes offering a wide base of therapies and techniques can expect a 50 per cent success rate at 1 year follow-up (Costello *et al.*, 1977). Programmes which have individualized therapy with a strong behavioural component can show success rates of over 70 per cent after 3 years follow-up (Sobell and Sobell, 1978; Caddy *et al.*, 1978).

In spite of certain methodological reservations, the vast follow-up studies conducted under the auspices of the Rand Corporation in the USA provide important evidence which suggests that treatment is superior to random processes (Armor *et al.*, 1978; Polich *et al.*, 1980). Significant differences were found between the percentage in remission in the high-treatment and no-treatment groups, though the specific effect of treatment in producing high remission rates must remain in doubt because the patients were not originally randomly assigned to treatment intensities (Polich *et al.*, 1980; Heather and Robertson, 1981). In spite of being controversial (Hodgson *et al.*, 1980), the Rand studies provide evidence of naturalistic remission processes, the unlikelihood of sustained stability in remission, and the significance of formal treatment and rehabilitation programmes.

Costello (1975a, 1975b) has provided a comprehensive review and analysis of the effectiveness of a variety of treatment methods drawn from many studies and agencies, such as those involved in the Rand studies, and found that the most effective programmes had the following characteristics:

(a) A well-organized treatment philosophy that was implemented in consistent and logical fashion.
(b) Inpatient resources for medical care and non-medical rehabilitation.
(c) An aggressive post-discharge follow-up.
(d) Collateral counselling and participation, e.g. marital and/or family therapy and support.
(e) Aggressive outreach and coordination with community agencies to facilitate rehabilitation.
(f) Adjunctive use of disulfiram chemotherapy.
(g) Behaviourally orientated therapies in addition to traditional psycho-dynamic group and individual therapies.

Clearly, there is no single effective form of treatment (Thorley, 1980a; Plant, 1982). Good results require a coordinated system of treatments in a wider rehabilitation perspective.

Detoxification Services

Detoxification represents a complexity of services and techniques having only one aim in common: to remove alcohol from the client so as to allow his body to detoxify. Thus detoxification may not require hospitalization or medical supervision, and specialized detoxification centres reflect a variety of orientations and service concerns. Unfortunately, they tend to be the focus of unrealistic expectations that they can incidentally ameliorate a variety of related social, legal, and medical problems.

Reports from the highly developed Ontario Detoxification System (Annis *et al.*, 1976; Smart, 1978) show that clients stay in a detox centre on average for 4 days, and only a small proportion of clients make further contact with rehabilitation services. Detoxification appears to have little influence on later drinking behaviour, and the expectation that the service would be a viable alternative to the 'revolving door' of the court system has been disappointed (Smart, 1978). Similarly, in Scotland, Hamilton (1979) found that 'detoxification' patients had not benefited as regards their alcohol dependence, or episodes of drunkenness; though their periods of abstinence were longer. However there was evidence of significant improvements in accommodation and self-reported quality of life, and it is probable that physical and mental health improved.

In England two experimental detoxification centres were set up in the mid-1970s in response to the Home Office recommendations on habitual drunken offenders (Home Office, 1971). The Manchester Detoxification Centre was set up in a purpose-built hospital unit with direct access to an alcoholism treatment unit in the same building and a well-developed network of hostels and community projects. The Leeds Detoxification Centre is community based and was grafted onto an existing residential rehabilitation project for the single homeless (St Anne's Shelter, 1980). Both projects have a very similar remit, reflect medical and social models of response, and are undergoing current evaluation. Preliminary information on the clients of these centres has been provided by Hore (1980) and Otto *et al.* (1979). It is important to avoid prior judgement whilst these pioneering detoxification projects await full research evaluation, but certain cautious conclusions can be drawn. It appears that too much has been asked of detoxification centres, in Britain partly due to unclear thinking in the Home Office report on Habitual Drunken Offenders (1971) regarding the relationship between alcohol dependence, homelessness, and habitual drunken offenders and a presumed unitary client group. Detoxification centres have shown clearly that they do not serve any single group and that the needs are more complex and beyond any single agency.

Hospital Services

There are similar limitations to hospital-based services. Admitting patients for 'drying out' and 'patching up' medical or surgical problems and discharging them into almost certain relapse and further medical problems is of little value to the patient and probably not cost-effective. General hospital staff have to recognize and treat the underlying alcohol problem more energetically, for instance by utilizing lay counsellor sessions in the hospital (North East Council on Alcoholism, 1981), and so affiliate patients to the wider treatment and rehabilitation service network (Thorley, 1980a). Similarly, the admission of problem drinkers in a general psychiatric setting is often less than satisfactory. Brief admissions for detoxification treatment that imply non-accountability by the patient, with inadequate follow-up, is a formula for poor results. The remedy, as with general medical hospitals, is to reduce extended admissions, amplify outpatient and community follow-up, and liaise effectively with other services which minimize the sick role.

Alcoholism Treatment Units

The need for a more explicit specialist psychiatric hospital unit for problem drinkers, developed from postwar experience in the USA, and in the UK at Warlingham Park Hospital by Dr Max Glatt, has been critically examined by Orford and Edwards (1977). They comment that this abstinence-orientated, inpatient treatment formula was recommended before any strong scientific evidence had been produced showing that such a formula was effective. None the less, many Alcoholism Treatment Units (ATUs) were set up, and by 1975 there were more than 30 in England and Wales. A lively debate has sprung up, and ATUs have been roundly criticized for remaining inpatient orientated, narrow in their range of treatments, selecting only verbally skilled middle-class patients, barely relating with other alcohol agencies, and, most significantly, failing to demonstrate their effectiveness (Department of Health and Social Security, 1978; Federation of alcoholic Residential Establishments, 1978; Glatt et al., 1979). In fact, ATUs and their services come in all shapes and sizes and this caricature may be unfair to units which have developed abstinent and non-abstinent drinking goals, outpatient and day-patient departments, a wide variety of treatment approaches including behavioural techniques, and coordinated their activities effectively with community agencies.

As community services for rehabilitation and treatment grow more numerous and complex, the alleged specific effectiveness of an ATU becomes more elusive and difficult to measure. Research on their effectiveness has been well reviewed by Hore (1976), and other important evaluations of ATU programmes have been published by Costello et al. (1980) and Sobell et al. (1980). These studies provide evidence that by utilizing a variety of treatment techniques involving abstinent and harm-free drinking goals, the ATU multidisciplinary team can have considerable therapeutic power. If at present ATUs have the richest service resources, it is arguable that the patients they take on should be the most complex and problematic: difficult cases that other services cannot manage.

## Outpatient and Day Care Services

Virtually all the treatment modalities possible in the developed ATU are possible in an outpatient or day care setting, and a considerable body of work has emerged showing that specialist outpatient services are as effective as ATU inpatient admissions (e.g. Edwards and Guthrie, 1967). Extending this work, Orford and Edwards (1977) described how 100 problem drinking men, and their wives, were seen in an intensive multidisciplinary 3-hour outpatient assessment followed by a 30-minute interactive advice session, and then randomly allocated to two equal groups. One group was offered no further treatment from the centre. The other 50 couples were offered every kind of facility the centre could offer: inpatient detoxification and ATU treatment, outpatient follow-up, and social work for the wives. Twelve months after the initial assessment and advice session, 60 per cent of both groups had improved, and there were no differences between the groups in drinking behaviour, drinking-related problems, assessment of improvement, and social adjustment. There have been many criticisms of this study (Orford, 1980), and those with a natural scepticism have used the apparent ineffectiveness of concerted treatment to develop a therapeutic nihilism (Kendell, 1979). However, rather than proving that treatment does not work, the study raises fundamental questions about what exactly effective treatment consists of. It shows that outpatient contact with highly experienced staff and some kind of follow-up is therapeutically beneficial and almost certainly more cost-effective than inpatient services.

Many ATUs have taken heed of these findings and developed outpatient and day-patient services at the expense of inpatient beds. Day hospitals and day centres can provide rehabilitation and treatment with the patient or client still living in the real situation of his home and community and thus avoid some of the disadvantages of an intensive sick role.

## Residential Community Projects

Hostels for alcoholics have been in existence for over 40 years although the first significant projects in the United Kingdom were only opened in 1960. These early projects were set up to provide secure accommodation for homeless and rootless men so that rehabilitation through abstinence might be possible. Cook (1975) has described the history of hostels for problem drinkers in the 1960s, how the predominant disease model of alcoholism legitimized this rehabilitative thrust, and how psychodynamic group psychotherapy was found to be less satisfactory for the homeless, rootless client group than basic support.

Otto and Orford (1978) carried out a detailed investigation into the administration, structure, and working of a number of London hostels and provided a useful model of the function of rehabilitation in such settings.

The task of the small hostel . . . is that of social influence. Depending upon the age of residents, and the nature of their problems, this task may be best construed as one of socialisation, or alternatively as one of providing improved skills and resources. In either case, the key concern is that of creating a hostel social environment characterised by cohensiveness and shared philosophy. (Otto and Orford, 1978, p.37)

Although the effectiveness of hostel rehabilitation was barely demonstrable, by the mid 1970s there was a considerable expansion of alcohol hostels in the United Kingdom following important Department of Health and Social Security (1973) circular 21 on the *Community Services for Alcoholics*. In 1974 the Federation of Alcoholic Residential Establishments (FARE) was set up. A further development has been for some hostels to work on eclectic group therapy and social work counselling lines, thus appealing to those clients (such as patients leaving ATUs) who are not necessarily homeless and rootless but who are inappropriately domiciled for further effective recovery and rehabilitation (Turning Point, 1980).

During the same period as these United Kingdom developments were taking place, the Addiction Research Foundation in Canada began a most extensive study of hostel projects and detoxification services in Ontario (Ogborne, 1978a). General follow-up data of residents suggested that extended abstinence was rare but that a significant proportion had increased periods of abstinence and less problematic drinking. None of the studies concerned had randomly allocated experimental and control groups, but one study comparing detoxified project residents and matched non-resident controls found that the hostel group reduced their drinking significantly and had fewer post-programme arrests than the controls (Annis and Liban, 1976). Ogborne and his colleagues (1980) also found that although Alcoholics Anonymous orientated houses tended not to select 'skid row' clients, retention rates of different types of clients were not influenced by the intensity of the programme or the particular house ideology. Much of this research suggests that, given a basic hostel provision, non-specific factors rather than specific treatments or service provision account for most of the improvement.

The Bon Accord community is a well researched pioneering experimental rehabilitation project for male, single, homeless and rootless problem drinkers ('skid row' alcoholics) set in the Ontario countryside (Collier and Somfay,

1974). The project approaches change in the men's attitudes and way of life from a behavioural and counselling standpoint, with a phased programme not unlike those of some drug therapeutic communities. Follow-up results of Bon Accord residents show a number of positive effects, less behaviour associated with skid row life, and fewer periods of uncontrolled drinking. Drunkenness offences dropped significantly in the 12 months after discharge, but whereas in the year prior to Bon Accord men averaged 3.7 detoxification admissions, in the year after discharge this increased to an average of 7.2 admissions, a feature unrelated to length of stay (Ogborne and Clare, 1979). These may appear paradoxical findings, but it is to be remembered that part of rehabilitation is tertiary prevention: teaching damaged clients to make the best use of services.

Harm-free drinking programmes and so-called 'wet' hostels as opposed to traditional dry houses present a tantalizing alternative and some of these complex issues have been investigated in the United Kingdom by the Alcoholic Rehabilitation Research Group at Birmingham in conjunction with projects run by a non-statutory agency 'Aquarius'. Three new residential units were established, all bringing professional expertise into a self-help model, and using a programme of 'personal skills training'. A comparison was made between two houses, one taking clients aiming for controlled drinking and the other aiming for abstinence. However, four residents from each house controlled their drinking for 9 months, and two in the abstinence house abstained for 9 months, as did two residents from the controlled drinking house (Yates, 1980). The striking feature of these preliminary results is the similarity in outcome from the two houses in spite of different approaches. It was found that the controlled drinking house had double the episodes of disruptive drinking compared with the abstinence house, and the controlled drinking programme was more easily managed from the day counselling centre (Norris, 1981). The significance of this pioneering study is that it raises familiar questions regarding the nature of effective residential treatment. Here controlled drinking goals were less effective than abstinence goals. Residential experience in either house enabled about half of each group to manage at least 3 months of controlled drinking, and yet analysis of the post-discharge drinking careers revealed immense variety and status changes only tenuously related to treatment modalities.

A decade of evaluative research into the functions and effectiveness of hostels for problem drinkers has only provided modest evidence of any specific effects on specific client groups. Most of the effects are non-specific and compare best with even less well understood naturalistic processes. Paradoxically, research into the long-term impact of alcohol projects compares unfavourably than equivalent research into residential projects for drug takers discussed later in this chapter. The absence of random allocation and control groups remains a basic stumbling block to understanding both process and effectiveness. Finally, if research in this area is disappointing, it must be remembered that it is also in its infancy and that after 10 years' work we still barely understand the nature of problem drinking, the nature of treatment, the nature of rehabilitation, or the social function of stable accommodation. Little wonder there is much to clarify.

### Skid Row: The Alcoholics Recovery Project Model

Inner urban areas have been repositories for destitute and rootless vagrant men and women since time immemorial. Vagrants, or the single homeless and rootless, are a heterogeneous group of men and women, some wanderers, some problem drinkers, many mentally ill, and even more socially eccentric (Archard, 1975; Cook, 1979). The role of alcoholism as a disease component of modern vagrancy is highly developed and Bahr (1973) has indicated that 'uncontrollable alcoholism gained currency in the 1950s and to some extent replaced uncontrollable wanderlust and congenital laziness as the primary characteristic of the homeless man'.

In this historical context 'skid row' is a relatively new term in the United Kingdom; it is derived from the inner city haunts, institutions, and ways of life of the vagrant alcoholic in the USA. Archard (1975, 1979) has expertly described the British skid row world in a pioneering and revealing participant observation study. The world of drinking men, their values and their relationship with society's caring and legal institutions, skippering (living rough in abandoned or empty property), their distinctions between down-and-outs and dossers, between meths and jake drinkers, is essential reading for anyone who takes the subject seriously.

It is important to appreciate that general services for the homeless and rootless exist in which catering for the homeless problem drinker is only a component of the work. Leach and Wing (1978) carried out evaluative action research at the St Mungo Community Trust housing project for vagrant men, with a view to lengthening a client's stay on the assumption that such longevity was evidence of change and rehabilitation. A new client assessment procedure was introduced which led to a dramatic improvement in long-stay occupancy so that through lack of movement, due to absence of further rehabilitation facilities, no further admissions became possible (Leach and Wing, 1978; Leach, 1978). Several important points arise from this study. First, action research can improve the function of rehabilitation agency. Second, a non-specialist agency allowing appropriate drinking can become a significant force in stablizing some destitute men with drinking problems. Third, without further related projects such as sheltered workshop schemes, group homes, and supported bedsits and flats, movement of clients through the residential project is clogged up and rehabilitation becomes limited.

The Alcoholics Recovery Project in South London has evolved over the last

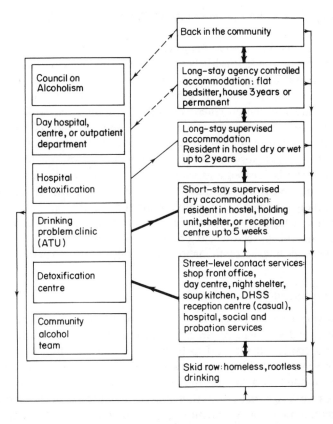

Figure 5.3 The structure of the rehabilitation network for single, homeless problem drinkers. The lines indicate the frequency with which channels are used, heavy lines being the most used.

12 years as an integrated specialist network of agencies which attempt to provide a ladder of rehabilitation (see Figure 5.3) and this model is being increasingly adopted in other cities (Cook, 1975). The model allows a realistic timescale for rehabilitation as clients may take several years after entering the service network to achieve stable recovery. The homeless and rootless have profound problems in affiliating to treatment services through conventional means, owing to lack of stable accommodation, so special street projects allowing undemanding and easy contact have to be developed. If strong demands are made clients drop out and disaffiliate from the network. A man may visit a shop front office daily for months and drink gallons of tea before asking staff for help with drying out. At this stage, clients are introduced to hospital or other detoxification services and are subsequently discharged to a dry holding unit or similar project which allows further recovery, provides

social work support, and permits motivation to be assessed for a committed period of abstinence in long-stay accommodation.

These long-stay residential projects differ greatly in type and size, as discussed previously, and it is likely that in the future more halfway houses will offer harm-free drinking programmes. Clients are encouraged during a stay, often in excess of 1 year, to extend their socialization into the wider community and seek employment or work in a sheltered workshop. Many projects then offer secure agency controlled long-stay flatlets, bedsitters, or houses where clients can live for several years, or indefinitely, with some degree of social work support. If clients have a crisis or episode of problem drinking they can be treated and stabilized in hospital whilst sickness benefits pay the rent of their room. Sometimes this arrangement can be made through private landlady schemes, but usually, without secure accommodation, a man in crisis will lose his privately rented room, become homeless, and run a high risk of more significant relapse and a return to skid row. Finally, a few clients can make the step to normal accommodation and be fully integrated in the community.

### Alcoholics Anonymous and Alanon

The fellowship of Alcoholics Anonymous (AA) is the best documented and most widespread self-help organization in the world (Robinson, 1979). It is present as a central ideological influence, or as an adjunct, at all points of intervention in the rehabilitation network. It continues, of its very essence, to be closely wedded to a disease model of alcoholism and the need for total abstinence to presage recovery. Almost every town has a weekly meeting, and the only requirement for AA membership is a desire to stop drinking. Here the problem drinker can find acceptance, fellowship from fellow sufferers, a clear ideology, and guidelines for resocialization and rehabilitation. Various studies have shown that the average AA member is likely to be middle class and not otherwise deviant in race, criminality, or social identity save for his alcoholism. Due to its anonymous nature, the representation of all problem drinkers within AA, and the success rate, remain elusive (Bebbington, 1976), but Baekeland et al. (1975) estimate that the overall success rate is 34 per cent. In the UK, Robinson (1979) has surveyed AA groups and found that members appear to benefit most from active participation in AA organization and administration. It is clear that AA does not suit everyone, but it is an organization that all problem drinkers should try (more than once!), and for those it does help, its impact is inestimable.

Spouses, family members, and teenage children of problem drinkers can get support and counsel for themselves at Alanon and Alateen meetings which, like those of AA, are held in many centres. These two self-help organizations are separate from AA but broadly share its ideology and see their work as complementary.

Occupation and Rehabilitation

Many problem drinkers develop problems at work, deterioration of efficiency, and ultimately poor employment records. Returning to work or getting a job after a long period of unemployment becomes a crucial part of rehabilitation. Many problem drinkers such as the homeless are always borderline as far as long-term reemployment is concerned, and the most significant single factor in employment success will be the overall level of employment in local industry. Areas of the country with high indices of problem drinking tend to be areas of high unemployment (Kilich and Plant, 1981) and this severely constrains effective rehabilitation.

Increasing attention is being paid to types of occupation in the aetiology of problem drinking and the impact of high-risk occupations, such as brewery workers, on subsequent drinking careers (Plant, 1979; Hore and Plant, 1981). Occupational stability, often highly correlated with stable accommodation and domestic life, is a powerful prognostic factor in the successful recovery of problem drinkers. Yet problem drinkers in the work setting tend to have high absenteeism and sickness rates, more industrial accidents than average, and loss of efficiency and productivity (Hore and Plant, 1981). Thus companies are increasingly encouraged to set up alcohol programmes or 'company policies' which combine relevant health and safety education for the whole work force with a provisional procedure to identify the problem drinker through work efficiency related criteria. They can then offer him treatment, or sick leave from work in order to seek treatment and rehabilitation, with an in-built guarantee of resumed employment following recovery. Company alcohol policies are well tested in the USA (Dunkin, 1981), and are increasingly utilized in the UK. Experience in the USA has shown that up to 10 per cent of a total workforce may utilize the programme in a 4-year period! Success rates in terms of recovery and return to work are high, commonly in excess of 60 per cent of workers who use the company policy, and are extremely cost-effective. On average, for every dollar per year spent on programme facilities, 5 dollars per year are saved in reduced absenteeism and increased productivity (Dunkin, 1981).

The Community Alcohol Team in a Pattern of Services

The variety and complexity of services for problem drinkers have gradually developed over the last 20 years in response to a massive problem in terms of numbers and of extent of need and a realization that recovery and rehabilitation commonly take place over several years. In the UK the Advisory Committee on Alcoholism has set out its model of an integrated pattern of services for problem drinkers (Department of Health and Social Security, 1978). It is clear from the foregoing account that such complexity, and the inevitable disparity between needs and resources, both in terms of projects and trained personnel, necessitate coordination and facilitation if the services are to work effectively. These can be provided by a community-based, multidisciplinary Community Alcohol Team (CAT). The CAT was set up in a fertile experimental project to establish an integrated community response to problem drinkers in an urban area, and is emerging as an important element in any network of services (Shaw *et al.*, 1978).

## Services for Problem Drug Takers

### The Size of the Problem

Various accounts have described the development of a drug problem in the United Kingdom, culminating in the opening of drug clinics for regularized opiate prescription in 1968 and the Misuse of Drugs Act regulations of 1971 (Judson, 1973; Plant, 1981; Thorley, 1979). The predominance of opiates as an international index of drug misuse has always made the prevalence of opiate drug takers of importance. Bewley (1968) estimated the prevalence as being 4 per 100,000 of the adult population, and between 1970 and 1975 the number of addicts officially known to the Home Office remained around 2,000. Since 1976 there has been a rapid increase in the numbers so that at the end of 1979 the number was close to 3,000. This official figure has long been recognized as an underestimate and a national figure closer to 20,000 opiate drug takers is widely accepted as being more appropriate. Increase in illegal international drug trafficking, customs seizures, and the relative stability of street prices of illegal heroin all suggest that a rising prevalence of opiate drug takers in the 1980s is inevitable, and will bring the relatively low United Kingdom prevalence more in line with Europe and North America (D.H.S.S., 1982; Moser, 1974; Thorley, 1981c).

Almost all drug takers are multiple drug users, occasionally using barbiturates, amphetamines, hallucinogens, cannabis, and alcohol. However, in the 1970s an important and problematic group of multiple drug takers emerged, individuals who may not by physically dependent on any one drug, but have many medical and social problems from concurrent psychological dependence on several (Thorley, 1979). This group, estimated in the United Kingdom as many tens of thousands, constitutes a major problem for large city accident and emergency departments (Ghodse, 1976).

Widening the perspective of problem drug taking still further, it appears that cannabis use is increasing to a point where, though illegal, it is accepted by a considerable minority as an acceptable drug for recreational use. What burden morbidity from intoxication and, more important, morbidity from long-term regular consumption (Nahas and Paton, 1979) will bring to the services in the next 10 years is impossible to estimate, but it may be considerable. Much the same arguments apply to increasing problems of vapour inhalation and solvent misuse (Watson, 1980).

Finally, it is important to consider the iatrogenic contribution to the current national drug problems. Benzodiazepines and similar tranquillizers and hypnotics, once considered relatively harmless, are now viewed with increasing caution as reports of dependence problems are made (Murray *et al.*, 1981; Tyrer, 1980). Hindmarch (1981) has identified that for each person there are 26 unused, previously prescribed, pills or tablets in bathroom cabinets, and many of these are psychoactive drugs. Lader (1981) has estimated that there may be 300,000 people in the United Kingdom who have some degree of dependence on benzodiazepine tranquillizers.

Thorley (1981c) has speculated that as tobacco use diminishes and mean per capita alcohol consumption plateaus, there may be much more generalized drug use and problems in the 1980s. The United Kingdom has an increasing drug problem, and certainly one which only will be unsatisfactorily served by existing levels of treatment and rehabilitation services.

What Happens to Drug Takers?

Follow-up studies of physically dependent opiate drug takers have established that at least 10 per cent are drug-free after 1 year, 25 per cent are drug-free after 5 years, and 40 per cent are abstinent after 10 years, and that each year 2–3 per cent of a sample will die of a drug-related cause (Thorley, 1981d). These figures, derived from a variety of international studies up to 1970, reflect primitive treatment strategies and virtually no coordinated rehabilitation, and therefore are the closest data we have to a spontaneous remission rate (Waldorf and Biernacki, 1979). It can be argued that if treatment and rehabilitation are to be effective they must demonstrate an improvement on these follow-up figures. Thorley (1981c) has reviewed longitudinal studies of British drug takers attending clinics since 1968 and found a significant improvement in recovery rates compared with the 'spontaneous' rates above, and discussed the contribution made by treatment agencies. Stimson and his colleagues (1978) have found that a 7-year follow-up of 128 British heroin addicts with a 97 per cent contact rate reveals that 36 per cent are opiate free, and that relapse is unlikely after 6 months' abstinence. Wille (1978; 1981) has examined the treatment and rehabilitation careers of the drug-free group and has identified several basic common patterns of improvement.

This important work on careers of recovery amplifies similar findings from Sweden (Frykholm, 1979). One group of opiate drug takers in Wille's study achieved abstinence in the community whilst receiving reducing legal opiate prescriptions as long-term drug clinic outpatients (mean time of attendance 4.1 years). Here social stability, exemplified by significant personal relationships, accommodation, and employment, appeared to be essential before abstinence was achieved. A more chaotic group, unable to develop social stability, only achieved abstinence in more controlling institutional settings such as prison or hospital. Back in the community this group was very vulnerable to relapse before social stability could be integrated with an abstinent life-style. Following opiate abstinence, both groups showed a temporary compensatory excessive use of alcohol, cannabis, or other drugs but there was no evidence of long-term transfer of dependence. It is significant that many abstinent subjects in Wille's study drew attention, amongst other factors, to the effective contribution of drug clinics and therapeutic community personnel and treatment methods.

Two major North American follow-up studies have attempted to evaluate treatment and rehabilitation effectiveness by following up drug takers who have passed through one of a variety of rehabilitation or treatment modalities: assessment only and no treatment; outpatient detoxification; methadone maintenance; therapeutic community; drug-free outpatients (Bale *et al.*, 1977; Sells and Simpson, 1980; Simpson *et al.*, 1979). These studies, like the Rand follow-up on problem drinkers, can be criticized simply because the samples are not necessarily representative of US problem drug takers in general and because there was often no random allocation of patients into each treatment group (Bale, 1979; Maisto and Cooper, 1980). Notwithstanding these important reservations, the results from both studies suggest that therapeutic communities, drug-free outpatients, and methadone maintenance programmes produce higher rates of abstinence from illegal drugs and higher rates of employment and a greater reduction in criminality as compared with detoxification or assessment only. Though it is necessary to consider these studies with caution, there is a weight of evidence emerging which suggests that long-term treatment and rehabilitation strategies are significantly more effective than random processes.

Detoxification Services

It is clear that in isolation detoxification has only a limited influence on long-term outcome. Nevertheless, for many drug users, it is a necessary prelude to a successful rehabilitation career. Some drug clinics offer a detoxification service through their inpatient beds or day-patient facilities, but the majority are unable to serve the large number of multiple drug takers that present.

Since 1978 the experimental City Roads Project in London has attempted to fill this service gap and so provide assessment, detoxification, and links with further residential rehabilitation projects for chaotic multiple drug takers. There is a 24-hour service staffed by nurses and social workers and referrals come from many sources including self-referrals. Following initial referral and assessment, the project offers a 3-week residential stay during which there is primary medical care, detoxification (using a liquid phenobarbitone regime for barbiturate dependence), counselling, and social work. The mean length of stay is 14 days, and 38 per cent of all residents are referred at some time for further residential rehabilitation such as to a therapeutic community. The project staff hope that such a breathing space and preparation will enable residents referred on to therapeutic communities to be less likely to drop out at an early stage, and further research will evaluate this potential influence (Glanz et al., 1980). There appears, however, to be little doubt that this service is a real benefit to chaotic multiple drug takers, and this suggests the need for wider application of this model in other large cities with similar client groups.

## The Role of the Drug Clinic

Since its inception in 1968 the specialized drug clinic, usually in a psychiatric setting, has been seen, somewhat unfairly, as the central response to the British drug problem (Thorley, 1979; West, 1978). The drug clinic using outpatient and inpatient facilities and the resource of a multidisciplinary team is in a strong position to provide a broad assessment of the drug taker's problems and provide treatment and rehabilitation (Thorley, 1979). Unfortunately, treatment in the past has centred too much on the transaction of the legal opiate prescription to the detriment of other treatment techniques, and some clinics have become somewhat isolated from other drug agencies and rehabilitation projects (Stimson and Oppenheimer, 1982). In the opinion of some drug agency workers rehabilitation can only happen in a drug-free environment, and therefore opiate prescribing (like US methadone maintenance programmes) is viewed with suspicion. Abstinence may be an ideal setting for personal change and growth, but many individuals can only make the change within the context of a legal opiate prescription and therapeutic support, perhaps over several years in an outpatient setting (Newman and Whitehill, 1979; Stimson et al., 1978; Wille, 1981).

The Rehabilitation of Metropolitan Addicts (ROMA) housing projects have developed a philosophy and service of community residential rehabilitation of drug takers in receipt of a clinic prescription (Rehabilitation of Metropolitan Addicts, 1977). Clients here are encouraged first, to, find personal and social stability through employment and secure accommodation. From this base of stability some individuals become stable drug takers for many years, and others voluntarily choose abstinence, a pattern of rehabilitation and recovery supported by Wille's findings (Wille, 1981).

The full role of the drug clinic set in the wider and more complex world of problem drug taking rather than in the narrower world of heroin addiction has yet to be developed. Like the alcoholism treatment unit, the drug clinic may have to work more in a community service perspective closely coordinated with other developing drug services.

## Day Hospitals and Centres

There is a definite role for day care services in the rehabilitation of drug takers (Bernsten, 1976), but experience has shown, certainly in the UK, that the programme and rules of the centre must be carefully worked out and adhered to. In the early 1970s, several drug clinics and non-statutory agencies extended their outpatients' facilities into a day care programme. Some allowed for the facility of injection on the premises, a so-called 'fixing room', and many offered individual and group counselling, occupational therapy, and workshop facilities. Most projects, however, found that group activities with patients or clients who were still actively drug taking were complicated by the predominance of the powerful drug subculture, negative 'street talk', illegal possession, and drug dealing, and consequently few day projects have survived. Experience at Parkwood House Day Hospital in Newcastle has shown that abstinent drug takers with continuing personal problems, including that of potential relapse, can be rehabilitated in a group setting and affiliated to residential projects if appropriate (Thorley, 1981b).

The rehabilitation of active drug takers from a day centre or clinic can be more satisfactory and effectively carried out using behavioural contract techniques in addition to supportive counselling (Boudin, 1980), or by community visits and therapeutic work in a family and domiciliary setting (Thorley, 1981b).

One innovative day centre which has found a successful formula, the Lifeline Project in Manchester, avoids drug subculture contamination through adherence to a strict abstinence rule. Founded in 1971, project workers see their role as identifying and challenging negative attitudes in the client, either through direct confrontation from staff, or through peer group pressures. The aim is to assist attenders to become aware of their own potential capacity to live without drugs. Access to the day programme is only by being drug-free, either through hospitalized detoxification, or through daily affiliation to the project's 'shop front' (Lifeline, 1980). The programme offers a wide variety of group and individual work and utilizes a good deal of internal structure not unlike that found in therapeutic communities. Recognizing the value of assessing and preparing day attenders for the right kind of residential rehabilitation, the project has developed a 2-week multifacility induction programme which is proving to be a significant advantage in placing clients. Early evidence suggests that clients so prepared are less likely to drop out ('split') and more likely to maintain high achievement rates in a therapeutic community (Lifeline, 1980).

## Street Services and Community Projects

Problem drug takers using illicit drugs are often very suspicious of statutory agencies and commonly experience lack of understanding and rejection from poorly informed workers. Hence there is an important role for more informal agencies of contact and affiliation. At a statutory level many local educational authorities have unattached youth workers who can be a crucial source of support for some chaotic individuals. Other non-statutory specialist agencies, such as Release and Lifeline, offer advice, support, counselling, and affiliation to other services in the rehabilitation network. The Hungerford Centre is almost the only detached social work project working directly with drug takers in London's West End, an area always associated with a high prevalence of homeless young people with multiple drug problems. In 1979, 86 per cent of the Hungerford's clients had no legal supply of drugs, and this reflects a strong illegal drug market, overloaded drug clinics, and unpreparedness on the part of this client group to use them (Turning Point, 1980). Clearly, street agencies play an essential part in drug services, similar to that of shop fronts and night shelters for alcohol services, and like them they need to be more systematically developed as a service (Yates, 1979).

## Residential Rehabilitation Projects

Residential rehabilitation projects for problem drug takers come in a wide variety of forms and philosophies. The more specific drug therapeutic communities and concept houses have a rich history of their own, but derive essentially from projects like Synanon, Daytop, and Phoenix House which were established in the USA in the 1960s (Glaser, 1981). These pioneering communities have had wide publicity and occasional notoriety, but the essential principles of a specialist service have endured and evolved into structure programmes of integrated and coordinated rehabilitation (Hinshelwood and Manning, 1979). A therapeutic community is essentially a closed system of residents and staff creating a unique culture based on security, hierarchy, and structured growth in which a client can make significant changes of personal attitude and behaviour.

Essentially, what takes place in the early treatment phases of the programme is a stripping away of a resident's self defeating and antisocial behaviours, which are then replaced by a more personally and socially acceptable life style. The values that are imparted to the resident relate to honesty with self and others, and communal concern and responsibility as opposed to pre-occupation with self. The later phases, re-entry, serve as a testing ground, a point at which the resident must then learn to apply to his day-to-day living on the outside that which he has been taught in the therapeutic community. (Collier and Hijazi, 1974)

One of the enduring problems of therapeutic communities has been the reentry phase. So often it has appeared that the client who has 'graduated' from the full programme, often of 1–2 years' duration, has only been prepared for one role: a drug-free worker in another therapeutic community (Hart, 1972; Wilson, 1980)! Many communities, now more aware of relevance to the outside world, have more structured reentry phases with secure outside accommodation from which clients can get out to employment but still have access to the community in the evenings and at weekends: a true 'halfway' house.

The processes of client change have always been clear to therapeutic community workers, but only in the last few years has objective evidence of change been presented. A major problem is the high rate of client dropout, or splitting: up to 80 per cent within 3 months in many projects. Clearly, to improve a graduation rate of 5–15 per cent many factors could be altered: client selection, degree of obligation (as in Court Orders), induction programmes (such as Lifeline), and the basis and structure of the house programme and reentry. Many houses have examined these factors and replaced a philosophy of rigid hierarchical achievement through confrontation techniques with a more flexible hierarchy and a wider range of individual and group activities, and so improved 'splittee' rates (Ogborne, 1978b; Phoenix House, 1980).

Work carried out in the Ley Community in Oxford has shown how clients who stay in the programme for more than 6 months tend to become less personally disturbed and more extroverted. Similarly, long stays (in excess of 6 months) were associated at follow-up with less criminality and less tendency to drug use or injection practice (Wilson and Mandelbrote, 1978; Wilson, 1978). Similar studies in the USA have shown that therapeutic community graduates improve most, as compared with other treatment and rehabilitation modalities, in terms of reducing drug taking and criminality, and unemployment (Bale et al., 1977; Sells and Simpson, 1980). Other studies have confirmed that dropouts also improve, but have higher levels of psychopathology than graduates, the degree of overall improvement being related to the length of time spent in the programme (De Leon et al., 1973; De Leon, 1977; De Leon et al., 1979; Romond et al., 1975). Many of these studies do not involve random allocation or control groups, but taken as a whole they provide important evidence for the effectiveness of rehabilitation.

In summary, therapeutic communities and drug rehabilitation houses are coming of age. The crudeness of early programmes is being refined, dropout rates are reducing, effectiveness seems likely to be increasingly demonstrated, and reentry programmes are being made more relevant as projects work more closely with other agencies in the wider community.

## A Pattern of Drug Services

It is clear, as with alcohol services, that the treatment and rehabilitation of a wide variety of problem drug takers require a network of coordinated agencies operating within a perspective of rehabilitation (D.H.S.S., 1982). Although such patterns have been described elsewhere (Bernsten, 1976), as yet no network of drug services has been developed in the United Kingdom. However, as is clear from this account, the basic building blocks of such a service already exist and are being evaluated: affiliation and street agencies, detoxification services, holding units for intensive assessment and induction programmes, day care programmes, drug clinic services, residential rehabilitation projects and therapeutic communities, employment, and sheltered housing schemes. The role of the statutory youth counselling and social services, particularly in response to the vapour inhalation problems of minors, is only just beginning to be explored (Dixon, 1981). There is clearly much work to do in the next 10 years, and the report of the Advisory Council on the Misuse of Drugs on *Treatment and Rehabilitation* (D.H.S.S., 1982) must be viewed as a significant strategic plan for statutory and non-statutory authorities to use in improving local services for problem drug takers.

## References

Annis, H., Giesbrecht, N., Ogborne, A., and Smart, R. (1976) *The Ontario Detoxification System.* Addiction Research Foundation, Toronto.

Annis, H., and Liban, N. (1976) *A Follow-up Study of Halfway Houses Residents and Matched Non-resident Controls.* Addiction Research Foundation, Toronto.

Archard, P. (1975) *The Bottle Won't Leave You: A Study of Homeless Alcoholics and their Guardians.* Alcoholics Recovery Project, London.

Archard, P. (1979) *Vagrancy, Alcoholism and Social Control.* Macmillan, London.

Armor, D. J., Polich, J. M., and Stambul, H. B. (1978) *Alcoholism and Treatment.* Report R-1739-NIAAA, Rand Corp., Santa Monica, Calif.

Baekeland, F., Lundwall, L. K., and Kissin, B. (1975) Methods for the treatment of chronic alcoholism: a critical appraisal. In Y. Israel, ed., *Research Advances in Alcohol and Drug Programs*, Vol. 2. John Wiley, New York.

Bahr, H. M. (1973) *'Skid Row'.* Oxford University Press, Oxford.

Bale, R. N. (1979) Outcome research in therapeutic communities for drug abusers: a critical review 1963-1975. *International Journal of the Addictions*, **14**, 1053-1074.

Bale, R. N., Van Stone, W. W., and Zarcone, V. P. (1977) Two year follow-up results from a randomised comparison study of methadone maintenance and therapeutic communities. Paper presented to National Drug Abuse Conference, San Francisco.

Bebbington, P. E. (1976) The efficacy of Alcoholics Anonymous: the elusiveness of hard data. *British Journal of Psychiatry*, **128**, 572-580.

Bernsten, K. (1976) Treatment of drug addicts: a six years' experiment. *Bulletin on Narcotics*, **28**, (i), 9-24.

Bewley, T. H. (1968) Recent changes in the incidence of all types of drug dependence in Great Britain. *Proceedings of Royal Society of Medicine*, **62**, 175-177.

Boudin, H. M. (1980) Contingency contracting with drug abusers in the natural environment: treatment evaluation. In Sobell *et al.* (1980).

Caddy, G. R., Addington, H. J., and Perkins, D. (1978) Individualized behaviour therapy for alcoholics: a third year independent double-blind follow-up. *Behaviour Research and Therapy*, **16**, 345-362.

Collier, D. F., and Somfay, S. A. (1974) Ascent from Skid Row. *The Bon Accord Community 1967–1973.* Addiction Research Foundation, Toronto.

Collier, M. V., and Hijazi, Y. A. (1974) A follow-up study of former residents of a therapeutic community. *International Journal of the Addictions,* 9, 805–826.

Cook, T. (1975) *Vagrant Alcoholism.* Routledge & Kegan Paul, London.

Cook, T. (1979) *Vagrancy: Some New Perspectives.* Academic Press, London.

Costello, R. M. (1975a) Alcoholism treatment and evaluation. I. In search of methods. *International Journal of the Addictions,* 10, 251–275.

Costello, R. M. (1975b) Alcoholism treatment and evaluation. II. Collation of two year follow-up studies. *International Journal of the Addictions,* 10, 857–868.

Costello, R. M. (1980) Alcoholism treatment effectiveness: slicing the outcome variance pie. In G. Edwards and M. Grant, eds, *Alcoholism Treatment in Transition.* Croom Helm, London.

Costello, R. M., Baillargeon, J. G., Biever, P., and Bennett, R. (1980) Therapeutic community treatment for alcohol abusers: a one year multi-variate outcome evaluation. *International Journal of Addictions,* 15, 215–232.

Costello, R. M., Biever, P., and Baillargeon, J. G. (1977) Alcoholism treatment programming: historical trends and modern approaches. *Alcoholism: Clinical and Experimental Research,* I, 311–318.

De Leon, G. (1977) Therapeutic community dropouts, 5 years later: preliminary findings on self-reported status. *Proceedings of Second World Conference of Therapeutic Communities at Montreal.* Lausanne, ICAA.

De Leon, G., Andrews, M., Wexler, H. K., Jaffe, J., and Rosenthal, M. S. (1979) Therapeutic community dropouts: criminal behaviour five years after treatment. *American Journal of Drug and Alcohol Abuse,* 6, 253–271.

De Leon, G., Skodol, A., and Rosenthal, M. S. (1973) Phoenix House: changes in psychopathological signs of resident drug addicts. *Archives of General Psychiatry,* 28, 131–135.

Department of Health and Social Security (1973) *Community Services for Alcoholics.* Department of Health and Social Security, London.

Department of Health and Social Security (1978) *Advisory Committee on Alcoholism: The Pattern and Range of Services for Problem Drinkers.* Department of Health and Social Security, London.

D.H.S.S. (1982) *Treatment and Rehabilitation.* Report of the Treatment and Rehabilitation Working Group of the Advisory Council on the Misuse of Drugs. HMSO, London.

Dixon, A. (1981) Working with problems of drug and solvent misuse: materials relevant for training social workers and other disciplines. Report to Council for Education and Training in Social Work.

Dunkin, W. S. (1981) Policies in the United States. In Hore and Plant (1981).

Edwards, G., and Gross, M. M. (1976) Alcohol dependence: provisional description of a clinical syndrome. *British Medical Journal,* i, 1058–1061.

Edwards, G. and Guthrie, S. (1967) A controlled trial of in-patient and out-patient treatment of alcohol dependence. *Lancet,* I, 555–559.

Federation of Alcoholic Residential Establishments (1978) *Community Services for Alcoholics.* Report of FARE Working Party at the House of Commons, April–October 1978. Federation of Alcoholic Residential Establishments, London.

Frykholm, B. (1979) Termination of the drug career: an interview study of 58 ex-addicts. *Psychiatrica Scandinavica,* 39, 370–380.

Ghodse, A. H. (1976) Drug problems dealt with by 62 London casualty departments. *British Journal of Preventive and Social Medicine,* 30, 251–256.

Glanz, A. H., Jamieson, A., and MacGregor, S. (1980) *City Roads: Interim Evaluation Report.* Department of Health and Social Security, London.

Glaser, F. B. (1981) The origins of the drug-free therapeutic community. *British Journal of Addiction*, **76**, 13–26.

Glatt, M. M., Grant, M., Hodgson, R., O'Leary, B., Shaw, S., Taylor, D., and Thorley, A. (1979) Comments on 'The pattern and range of services for problem drinkers'. *British Journal of Addiction*, **74**, 115–133.

Gossop, M. (1980) Drug dependence: the mechanics of treatment evaluation and the failure of theory. In J. R. Eiser, ed., *Social Psychology and Behavioural Medicine*. John Wiley, New York.

Hamilton, J. R. (1979) Evaluation of a detoxification service for habitual drunken offenders. *British Journal of Psychiatry*, **135**, 28–34.

Hart, L. (1972) Milieu management for drug addicts: extended drug subculture or rehabilitation? *British Journal of Addiction*, **67**, 291–301.

Heather, N., and Robertson, I. (1981) *Controlled Drinking*. Methuen, London.

Hindmarch, I. (1981) Too many pills in the cupboard. *New Society*, **55**, 142–143.

Hinshelwood, R. D., and Manning, N. (1979) *Therapeutic Communities: Reflections and Progress*. Routledge & Kegan Paul, London.

Hodgson, R., Nathan, P. E., Hay, W. M., Moos, R. H., Finney, J. W., Cronkite, R. C., and Room, R. (1980) Comments on the Rand report: a four-year follow-up. *British Journal of Addiction*, **75**, 343–360.

Home Office (1971) *Habitual Drunken Offenders*. HMSO, London.

Hore, B. D. (1976) *Alcohol Dependence*. Butterworth, London.

Hore, B. D. (1980) The Manchester detoxification centre. *British Journal of Addiction*, **75**, 197–205.

Hore, B. D., and Plant, M. A. (1981) *Alcohol Problems in Employment*. Croom Helm, London.

Judson, H. F. (1973) *Heroin Addiction in Britain*. Harcourt Brace Jovanovich, London.

Kendell, R. E. (1979) Alcoholism: a medical or a political problem? *British Medical Journal*, **i**, 367–371.

Kilich, S., and Plant, M. A. (1981) Regional variations in the levels of alcohol related problems in Britain. *British Journal of Addiction*, **76**, 47–62.

Lader, M. (1981) Benzodiazepines: panacea or poison? Paper in Symposium Report: 'Psychiatric drugs in perspective: problems, prescribing and priorities' ed. K. Davison. *Journal of Royal Society of Medicine*, **74**, 461.

Leach, J. (1979) The evaluation of a voluntary organization attempting to resettle destitute men: action research with the St. Mungo Community Trust. In T. Cook, ed., *Vagrancy: Some New Perspectives*. Academic Press, London.

Leach, J., and Wing, J. K. (1978) The effectiveness of a voluntary service for helping destitute men. *British Journal of Psychiatry*, **133**, 481–492.

Lifeline (1980) *Multifacility Induction: the First Six Months*. Lifeline Project, Manchester.

Madden, J. S. (1979) *A Guide to Alcohol and Drug Dependence*. John Wright, Bristol.

Maisto, S. A., and Cooper, A. M. (1980) A historical perspective on alcohol and drug treatment outcome research. In Sobell *et al.* (1980).

Moser, J. (1974) *Problems and Programmes Related to Alcohol and Drug Dependence in 33 Countries*. World Health Organization, Geneva.

Murray, R. (1979) Alcoholism. In P. Hill, R. Murray, and A. Thorley *Essentials of Postgraduate Psychiatry*. Academic Press, London.

Murray, R., Ghodse, A. H., Harris, C., Williams, D., and Williams, P., eds (1980) *The Misuse of Psychotropic Drugs*. Royal College of Psychiatrists, Gaskell, London.

Nahas, G. G., and Paton, W. D. M. (1979) *Marihuana: Biological Effects*. Pergamon, London.

Newman, R. G., and Whitehill, W. B. (1979) Double-blind comparison of methadone and placebo maintenance treatments of narcotic addicts in Hong Kong. *Lancet*, **ii**, 485–488.

Norris, H. (1981) The Aquarius Project. Alcoholics Rehabilitation Research Group, Birmingham University (personal communication).

North East Council on Alcoholism (1981) *Annual Report 1981*. North East Council on Alcoholism, Newcastle upon Tyne.

Ogborne, A. C. (1978a) Recidivism among clients of half way houses. *Drug and Alcohol Dependence*, **3**, 216–217.

Ogborne, A. C. (1978b) Program stability and resident turnover in residential rehabilitation program for alcoholics and drug addicts. *British Journal of Addiction*, **73**, 47–50.

Ogborne, A. C., and Clare, G. (1979) A note on the interface between a residential alcoholism centre and detoxification centres. *British Journal of Addiction*, **74**, 283–288.

Ogborne, A. C., Wiggins, T. R., and Shain, M. (1980) Variations in staff characteristics, programmes and recruitment practices among half way houses for problem drinkers. *British Journal of Addiction*, **75**, 393–404.

Orford, J. (1980) Understanding treatment: controlled trials and other strategies. In G. Edwards and M. Grant *Alcoholism Treatment in Transition*. Croom Helm, London.

Orford, J., and Edwards, G. (1977) *Alcoholism: A Comparison of Treatment and Advice, with a Study of the Influence of Marriage*. Maudsley Monograph No. 26. Oxford University Press, Oxford.

Otto, S., Hashimi, L., Leadbitter, J., and Shaw, S. (1979) Leeds community based detoxification centre: an interim report. Detoxification Evaluation Project, Maudsley Hospital, London.

Otto, S., and Orford, J. (1978) *Not Quite Like Home: Small Hostels for Alcoholics and Others*. John Wiley, London.

Pattison, E. M., Sobell, M. B., and Sobell, L. C. (1977) *Emerging Concepts of Alcohol Dependence*. Springer, New York.

Phoenix House (1980) *Annual Report, 1980*. Phoenix House, London.

Plant, M. A. (1979) *Drinking Careers: Occupation, Drinking Habits, and Drinking Problems*. Tavistock, London.

Plant, M. A. (1981) *Drugs in Perspective*. Hodder & Stoughton, London.

Plant, M. A., ed. (1982) *Drinking and Problem Drinking*. Junction Books, London.

Polich, J. M., Armor, D. J., and Braiker, H. B. (1980) *The Course of Alcoholism: Four Years after Treatment*. Rand Corporation, Santa Monica, Calif.

Rehabilitation of Metropolitan Addicts (1979) *Annual Report, 1977*. Rehabilitation of Metropolitan Addicts, London.

Robinson, D. (1972) The alcohologist's addiction: some implications of having lost control over the disease concept of alcoholism. *Quarterly Journal of Studies on Alcohol*, **33**, 1028–1042.

Robinson, D. (1979) *Talking out of Alcoholism: The Self-help Process of Alcoholics Anonymous*. Croom Helm, London.

Romond, A. A., Forrest, C. K., and Kleber, H. D. (1975) Follow-up of participants in a drug dependence therapeutic community. *Archives of General Psychiatry*, **32**, 369–374.

St Anne's Shelter (1980) *St Anne's Shelter and Housing Action, Annual Report 1979–80*. St Anne's Shelter, Leeds.

Scheff, T. (1968) Negotiating reality: notes on power in the assessment of responsibility. *Social Problems*, **16**, 3–17.

Sells, S. B., and Simpson, D. D. (1980) The case for drug abuse treatment effectiveness. *British Journal of Addiction*, **75**, 117–132.

Shaw, S., Cartwright, A., Spratley, T., and Harwin, J. (1978) *Responding to Drinking Problems*. Croom Helm, London.

Simpson, D. D., Savage, J., and Lloyd, M. R. (1979) Follow-up evaluation of treatment of drug abuse during 1969 to 1972. *Archives of General Psychiatry*, **36**, 772–778.

Smart, R. G. (1978) The Ontario detoxification system: an evaluation of its effectiveness. In J. S. Madden, R. Walker, and W. H. Kenyon, eds, *Alcoholism and Drug Dependence: A Multidisciplinary Approach*. Plenum Press, New York.

Sobell, L. C., Sobell, M. B., and Ward, W. (1980) *Evaluating Alcohol and Drug Abuse Treatment Effectiveness: Recent Advances*. Pergamon, New York.

Sobell, M. B., and Sobell, L. C. (1978) *Behavioural Treatment of Alcohol Problems: Individualized Therapy and Controlled Drinking*. Plenum Press, New York.

Stimson, G. V., and Oppenheimer, E. (1982) *Heroin Addiction: Treatment and Control in Britain*. Tavistock, London.

Stimson, G. V., Oppenheimer, E., and Thorley, A. (1978) Seven year follow-up of heroin addicts: drug use and outcome. *British Medical Journal*, **i**, 1190–1192.

Thorley, A. (1978) How natural is the natural history of opiate drug dependence? *British Journal of Addiction*, **73**, 229–232.

Thorley, A. (1979) Drug dependence. In P. Hill, R. Murray, and A. Thorley, eds, *Essentials of Postgraduate Psychiatry*. Academic Press, London.

Thorley, A. (1980a) Medical responses to problem drinking. *Medicine* (3rd series), no. 35, 1816–1822.

Thorley, A. (1980b) What is meant by rehabilitation? Internal paper presented to treatment and rehabilitation working group of the Advisory Council on the Misuse of Drugs, Home Office, London.

Thorley, A. (1981a) *Alcohol Dependence and the Alcohol Dependence Syndrome: Emergence of a Concept and its Potential Utility in Treatment and Rehabilitation Services*. New Directions in the Study of Alcohol Group. Booklet No. 1, 1–27.

Thorley, A. (1981b) *Parkwood House Alcohol and Drug Problem Service: Hand Book for Professional Workers*. Parkwood House, Newcastle.

Thorley, A. (1981c) Drug problems in the United Kingdom: retrospect and prospect. Paper in Symposium Report 'Psychiatric drugs in perspective: problems, prescribing and priorities', ed. K. Davison. *Journal of Royal Society of Medicine*, **74**, 461.

Thorley, A. (1981d) Longitudinal studies of drug dependence. In G. Edwards and C. Busch, eds, *Drug Problems in Britain: A Review of Ten Years*. Academic Press, London.

Thorley, A. (1982) The effects of alcohol. In Plant (1982).

Turning Point (1980) Turning Point: The helping hand organization. *Annual Report 1979–1980*. Turning Point, London.

Tyrer, P. (1980) Dependence on benzodiazepines. *British Journal of Psychiatry*, **137**, 576–577.

United Nations (1978) *Resource Book on Measures to Reduce the Illicit Demands for Drugs*. UN Division of Narcotic Drugs, Geneva.

Waldorf, D., and Biernacki, P. (1979) Natural recovery from heroin addiction: a review of the incidence literature. *Journal of Drug Issues*, **2**, 281–289.

Watson, J. M. (1980) Solvent abuse by children and young adults: a review. *British Journal of Addiction*, **75**, 27–36.

West, D. J. (1978) *Problems of Drug Abuse in Britain*, ed. D. J. West. University of Cambridge Institute of Criminology, Cambridge.

Wille, R. (1978) Preliminary communication: cessation of opiate dependence: processes involved in achieving abstinence. *British Journal of Addiction*, 73, 381–384.

Wille, R. (1981) Case studies I. Natural processes of recovery. In G. Edwards and G. Aris, eds, *Drug Dependence in Socio Cultural Context*. World Health Organization, Geneva.

Wilson, D. (1978) The effect of treatment in a therapeutic community on intravenous drug abuse. *British Journal of Addiction*, 73, 407–411.

Wilson, D. (1980) Addiction therapist: a transient status passage in drug rehabilitation. *International Journal of Addictions*, 15, 927–930.

Wilson, D., and Mandelbrote, B. (1978) The relationship between duration of treatment in a therapeutic community for drug abusers and subsequent criminality. *British Journal of Psychiatry*, 132, 487–491.

World Health Organization (1977) *Alcohol Related Disabilities*, ed. G. Edwards, M. M. Gross, M. Keller, J. Moser, and R. Room. Offset Publication No. 32. World Health Organization, Geneva.

Yates, F. (1980) *The Aquarius Project*. Alcoholics Rehabilitation Research Group, Birmingham University, Birmingham.

Yates, R. (1979) Street level services: options for services to drug users in the 1980s. *Proceedings of SCODA Annual General Meeting 1979*. SCODA, London.

Theory and Practice of Psychiatric Rehabilitation
Edited by F. N. Watts and D. H. Bennett
© 1983, John Wiley & Sons, Ltd.

# 6

# Rehabilitation of the Mentally Abnormal Offender

JOHN GUNN and PAMELA TAYLOR

This chapter will be concerned with some of the special problems relating to psychiatric patients who come into conflict with the law. It will deal only with the adult patients. Some legal issues are discussed, but legal issues are different for each country in the world, and the points made here refer to England and Wales.

The general principles of rehabilitation for the patient who has been processed by the criminal court at some stage have a lot in common with those used for his law-abiding counterpart. The techniques employed will depend on age, diagnosis, personality structure, social skills, social assets, and financial assets in precisely the same way that all rehabilitation is dependent upon these features. Where there are distinctions between the offending and non-offending patient populations then these are related to the way in which problems are distributed within the two populations, the facilities available to the two categories, and the psychosocial effects of the legal process. For example, an offender patient population may have a predominance of patients suffering from personality disorders or subnormality, which means that something slightly more ambitious than ordinary rehabilitation is being aimed at because an improvement in life-style is being sought rather than a return to a pre-morbid level of function. In addition, there will be a proportion of such patients who have spent a good deal of time in closed and authoritarian institutions of one sort or another and will have secondary problems as a result of that experience. The other features which are sometimes prominent in a group of mentally abnormal offenders are stigma and chronicity. These problems will therefore have to be kept very much in mind in constructing any rehabilitation programme for offenders. However, before considering such special problems there are several ordinary rehabilitation techniques which should be emphasized.

(1) It is important to avoid continuing the history-taking procedure as a mere information-collecting exercise. From the outset emphasis should be placed on building an effective doctor–patient relationship for at least two reasons. Mentally abnormal offenders probably have a higher dropout rate from therapy than other psychiatric patients. Secondly, psychotherapy in some form is going to provide the basis of treatment for almost all the patients and the early interviews form an important phase of that psychotherapy. Finesinger (1948) stresses these points and outlines some of the steps in the initial development of the relationship, as well as the progression to more specific psychotherapeutic intervention.

(2) The value of defining intermediate as well as ultimate goals in therapy is also emphasized by Finesinger. The problem-oriented method of recording information about patients (Weed, 1968) which is gaining popularity may be especially helpful in organizing the material obtained so that both patient and therapist can comprehend the extent of the task ahead and agree about priorities. A list of personal problems, and a list of social problems, together with possible realistic solutions, are drawn up and discussed.

(3) It is insufficient to note the patient's psychopathology, and his failings. It is also important to establish the nature and strength of his personality and social assets. These assets are the cornerstones of any rehabilitation programme. Almost every patient has some characteristics which help him to survive and adapt, and these should be fostered at the expense of his maladaptive characteristics.

(4) Crisis intervention is a cliché phrase that most psychiatrists have subscribed to, but it is of particular importance when dealing with patients who are antisocial at times of stress and who show long-term potential for antisocial behaviour. It is very demanding and requires the therapeutic team to be constantly available. It may require rapid admission to hospital without too many 'democratic' debates about the merits of such an admission. It requires a network of interrelated professional advisers each of whom will be prepared to undertake difficult tasks at short notice. It may be necessary, for example, for a domiciliary visit to be carried out, or for an employer to be interviewed and reassured, or for an urgent visit to be made to a prison or police station.

(5) In the same way that crisis intervention is regarded as part and parcel of ordinary psychiatric practice so is supportive psychotherapy. Here again, however, genuine supportive work is demanding and skilled (Stafford-Clark, 1970). Patients require regular support, sometimes on a weekly basis, and sometimes for many years.

An element of supportive psychotherapy which is sometimes underestimated is the patient's expectation of long-term support. As far as the offending behaviour is concerned, one of the few factors which has been demonstrated to be effective in prevention is a supportive relationship with a relative, friend, or professional adviser (West, 1963). If a patient wishes (and it really must be left to the patient's choice) for such a longer-term relationship this may mean keeping in touch with him as he moves in and out of the formal clinical arrangements. For example, he may move to another part of the country, or, if he is an offender, he may well end up in prison or a Special Hospital. During these times a relationship can be preserved, very largely, by correspondence. This seemingly trivial and obvious point is often neglected, and patients who have done reasonably well in an outpatient setting but who relapse, re-offend, and then go into an institution are clearly at a moment of maximum need. It is extremely common for that to be the point of rejection by neglect though the contact and potentially beneficial relationship could be preserved by a regular, infrequent exchange of letters. It is possible that a legal sanction, such as a probation order with a condition of medical treatment, is helpful in cementing a long-term relationship in some cases as it implies commitment from both parties.

(6) Rogers's Client Centred Therapy (Rogers, 1961) seems particularly valuable for this group of patients, and was developed during his work with delinquent children. He identifies the main criteria of a helping relationship as:

(a) genuiness and transparency, in which the helper behaves naturally and does not disguise his real feelings;
(b) warm acceptance of and respect for the client as a separate individual;
(c) a sensitive ability to see the client's world and self-image as he sees them.

Many offender patients are characterized by extraordinarily low self-esteem and can only begin to develop as they feel valued. The therapeutic relationship may be the first in which they have ever experienced this. The warmth and regard, however, is for the individual rather than all aspects of his behaviour. Rogers stresses the need for continued contact with two important kinds of reality: the therapist's feelings about the patient's activities, and the patient's view of himself and his relationships.

(7) The emphasis on confronting the patient with his own responsibility for his behaviour is the core of 'reality therapy'—another technique that has been applied with some success to offenders. Glasser (1965) describes work with delinquent girls. In the setting of a school providing work and vocational programmes, the girls were held wholly responsible for their behaviour and not allowed to account for it, and thereby excuse themselves, on such grounds as emotional upset, maltreatment by mother, neglect by father, and discrimination by society. Again, however, emphasis was also placed on warm, positive respect for the individual and the girls were allowed to stay in the programme, despite irresponsible acts, until they were ready to leave.

(8) Finally, the value of group psychotherapy for any population containing a preponderance of patients with personality disorders must be emphasized. So

many of these people do not respond well to an individual analytic approach to their problems, but they do seem to gain support and insight from seeing their own difficulties reflected in other individuals whose problems are in the same broad area (Gunn *et al.*, 1978). Furthermore, patients with personality problems are often particularly deficient in relating to groups of people. This means that the type of group and the point in treatment at which it is offered are important decisions to make. To plunge someone who is anxious about groups into the nerve-racking experience of a formal psychotherapy group may simply drive him from the clinic completely. Individual sessions and quasi-social groups may be important preliminaries.

## Legal Process

A unique problem for the offender or an accused patient is involvement in the legal process. There are the problems associated with the remand period when the patient is awaiting trial. The remand may have to be spent in custody thus interfering with family life and either jeopardizing or ruining a job or career. The remand period may be prolonged, creating its own persistent anxieties. Some patients will not consider a detailed examination of their problems until the trial is over as they are too preoccupied with defending themselves. Some psychiatrists believe that the patient's motivation is too much influenced by his need for mitigation. One patient, who suffers from mild dementia, chronic alcoholism, and chronic anxiety, waited, on bail, for over 2 years for his trial for arson and fraud. During this period his health deteriorated and he required two admissions to hospital. He was found guilty and sent to prison for 12 months. Now, after his release, constructive rehabilitation can begin, partly because he was not abandoned during that phase when the more obviously constructive work was impossible.

Part of the rehabilitation process for the mentally abnormal offender, therefore, is to protect the patient from the most negative aspects of the legal process, helping to ensure that everything is done to speed up a trial and a decision of sentence and that, if possible, patients are remanded on bail so that family connections and job can be kept intact until a court takes a deliberate decision to jeopardize these by imprisonment.

Another aspect of this involvement with the legal process is the fact that a number of patients will have legal restraints applied to them after their trial, for example they may be on a probation order with a condition of medical treatment (see below). This will inevitably affect the doctor–patient relationship and every effort must be made to get the patient to understand how far the doctor sees himself as a controlling agency and how far a normal medical adviser. Doctors and circumstances will vary, but the issue should not be ignored as the uncertainty can be harmful to successful treatment.

## Stigma

The mentally abnormal offender has to overcome the double stigma of being both mad and bad. A moment's reflection on the phrase 'criminal lunatic' will give some idea of the force of this categorization. Stigma causes problems in two ways. First, it has an effect on people who come into contact with the patient. Employers, for example, are less likely to take criminal lunatics on to their books than they are, say, disabled ex-soldiers, even when the offender patient is more suitably qualified for the job in hand. Secondly, feeling both mad and bad can have a crushing effect on the patient's self-esteem. It ensures, for example, that he is isolated whether he is in hospital or in prison; some patients don't want him because he is bad, other prisoners don't want him because he is mad.

The first problem has to be tackled by education. There is education in the general sense to improve the level of understanding amongst the community. More important, however, for the particular individual is the careful supplying of accurate information to friends, relations, employers, and other significant people in his life. Sometimes the patient is unwilling for information to be imparted and his wishes have to be respected, but with time, and in the course of his own psychotherapy, he should come to see the benefits for him of allowing others to have accurate information. No effort should be spared to ensure that those in close contact with a patient understand the nature of his problems, and the course of action to take if they believe things are beginning to go wrong again.

## Problems of Institutions

### Special Hospitals

A small number of mentally abnormal offenders are sent to security hospitals, known in Britain as 'Special Hospitals'. There are four in England and Wales—Broadmoor, Rampton, Moss Side, and Park Lane—and an equivalent hospital at Carstairs in Scotland. These hospitals are separate from the NHS regional system and are run directly by a special health authority for the Secretary of State for Health. They provide a special secure facility for patients who are deemed to be dangerous in some way. This very security makes rehabilitation more difficult when the need for the closest possible supervision is over. Furthermore, because they take dangerous patients, these hospitals carry an extra stigma all of their own.

There are three main routes out of the Special Hospitals. The patient can be discharged directly into the community, he can be transferred to a regional security unit, or he can be transferred to his local psychiatric hospital. The problems with direct discharge into the community are fairly obvious. First, the patient is moved from maximum security to no security in one step. Secondly, only a few homes are within easy reach of each Special Hospital and, therefore, rehabilitation is difficult or organize. Thirdly, outpatient supervision will have to be carried out by a local hospital the staff of which will have only limited prior knowledge of a patient they are receiving and maybe no special investment in his continued care.

Transfer to a local hospital as an intermediary step towards home also carries a problem. These days hospitals are very reluctant to take patients from Special Hospitals. To some extent this is related to the remarkable deficiencies in psychiatric facilities which have accrued over the last two or three decades, due partly to the new liberal and open door policies in psychiatric hospitals which rule out moderate security or supervision, and partly to attitudinal problems amongst doctors and nurses who sometimes stigmatize the Special Hospital patient in the same way that the general public does.

It is also important to provide effective linkage between Special Hospitals and local psychiatric facilities. To achieve this it will probably be necessary to provide a graded security service, with intermediate tiers between local psychiatric facilities and Special Hospitals. Problems that are too complex for local facilities to manage can be referred to the next level. Furthermore, the process can operate in reverse, thus providing a proper rehabilitation route for offender patients no matter what level they have been maintained at during the acute phase of their illness. The graded security service proposed by South East Thames Regional Health Authority (Gunn, 1977; South East Thames Regional Health Authority, 1979) is a good example of this tiered approach.

Prisons

In recent years British prisons have accumulated an increasing number of mentally abnormal offenders (Orr, 1978). Within the prison system there are several types of psychiatric facility: inpatient units, visiting psychiatrists, and a number of specialized therapeutic communities such as Grendon which have been established for the treatment of personality disordered men (see Gunn *et al.*, 1978, for a fuller account).

The problem for the mentally abnormal prisoner is that he is always discharged abruptly from a secure environment to a relatively unwelcome outside world, and there is really no possibility of him being gradually integrated into the National Health Service facilities. He may be referred to a local psychiatric clinic, but he will then often be dealt with by a doctor whom he regards as a stranger, and who may not have much interest in his particular problems; or even worse, to a service that tried and failed to help him in the past and is now understandably reluctant to have him back again.

As with the patients leaving Special Hospitals the answer to these problems lies in a change of medical policy. The setting up of tiered services like those mentioned above will go a long way towards enabling ordinary psychiatric services to take a bigger proportion of the mentally abnormal offenders than they do at present. This will mean that more people will be able to receive their treatment within the Health Service, in the first place, thus obviating the need for 'therapeutic' imprisonment.

All institutions create secondary difficulties because of the structure inherent in institutional life. Perhaps the fundamental problem which many mentally abnormal offenders have is a lack of internal controls; the contrast between prison life and liberty is particularly great for them. Furthermore, prisons usually also create a special hostile culture between inmate and prison officer. The effects of this culture have been called 'prisonization' by Clemmer (1940). One of the main characteristics of this secondary state is fairly intense negative attitudes towards professionals and other figures in authority who could be expected to assist with rehabilitation after imprisonment. There is evidence that therapeutic communities such as Grendon ameliorate this institutional effect to a large extent (Gunn *et al.*, 1978). However, very few prisoners are able to experience this type of facility.

The Home Office, on the advice of its Parole Board, has the power to release some offenders some time after they have served one third of the sentence imposed. (Most prisoners are released, in any case, after they have served two thirds of their sentence.) This arrangement can be used by the Home Office to ensure that a particularly mentally abnormal offender, who has been in prison, goes to a clinic and sees a social worker for the early phase of his release, for such conditions can be imposed as part of the parole licence granted to him. An arrangement of this sort is not unlike the aftercare arrangements made for patients leaving hospital on a restriction order (see below), except that the parole licence has a predetermined end point, equivalent to two thirds of the sentence imposed, unless the prisoner is serving life when it is an indefinite licence.

## Compulsory Hospital Admission

A mentally abnormal offender, like any other mentally abnormal person, may be subject to compulsory admission under the British Mental Health Act. He may, of course, be subject to the ordinary provisions of the Act which can be applied by two doctors and a relative (or a social worker in lieu of a relative) if it is considered to be in the interests of the patient's health or safety, or necessary for the protection of other people, that he should be detained, and in the case of psychopathic disorder or mental impairment treatment is likely to prevent a deterioration of his condition. However, special provisions also apply to those who have been convicted by a criminal court and are liable to punishment by imprisonment.

Once a patient has been convicted of a crime, it is not necessary for a relative to acquiesce in his admission, and the criterion for admission is simply suitability rather than danger to self or others. An additional restriction can also be made on such a patient by the courts, after the hospital order has been agreed, if the court is satisfied that the public needs protection from the patient; then the court can remove the power of discharge from the doctor and give it to the Home Secretary under a so-called restriction order.

A few Special Hospital consultants sometimes welcome the addition of a restriction order to a patient's hospital order because this then means that when the patient is eventually discharged from the hospital he is likely to remain on licence to the Home Office for an indeterminate period, usually under the care of both a doctor and a social worker, until the Home Office is satisfied that he is fully recovered. What little evidence there is about the effectiveness of supervision suggests that statutory aftercare is more successful than voluntary, and that probation officers do slightly better than other kinds of social workers (Home Office/DHSS, 1975).

Clearly, then, the offender-patient is often dealt with more paternalistically than is the case with other psychiatric patients. Those taking such powers against a patient must remember that the restraints applied have their own implications for rehabilitation when that time comes. The patient must be very carefully appraised of his rights under the Mental Health Act, which include the possibility of challenging his detention by applying to a Mental Health Review Tribunal. For a fuller account of the issues involved the reader is referred to either the Butler Report (Home Office/DHSS, 1975), or *A Human Condition*, a special report produced by MIND (Gostin, 1977), or the Mental Health Act itself.

### Probation Order with a Condition of Medical Treatment

When the patient is convicted of an offence the court has, of course, the options of ordinary punishments which include fines, imprisonment, and the like, as well as the possibility of compulsory admission to a hospital. There is a third avenue open to the court which is sometimes underestimated. This is the probation order with a condition of mental treatment. The advantages of this order are considerable. The patient has to be motivated for treatment and express that motivation in court. Most importantly, the court still has some sort of sanction to apply if things go wrong, for if the offender becomes in breach of his probation order, or if for any other reason the probation officer feels that the order should be reviewed, the patient can be brought back to court and if necessary resentenced for the original offence.

The order is sometimes regarded as of little value because it has been used in trivial cases where nobody takes it very seriously. In order to avoid any misuse of this particular law, it is probably better to reserve probation orders with a condition of medical treatment for the more serious offender. It is of particular importance that the probation officer, doctor, and client fully understand one another before the court hearing. Each must understand his or her responsibilities and each must be aware of the procedures which will be adopted if things go wrong. As the order proceeds there should be frequent communication between doctor and probation officer (telephones are quite sufficient) to ensure that each is mindful of the other's strategy.

## Voluntary Organizations

So far we have been concerned with official services. No medical or social work team should, however, forget that a great deal of the difficult work with rejected and despised populations is taken on by voluntary organizations who receive few funds and little credit for the work they undertake. They will, for example, sometimes take on the patient who is 'too ill to be admitted to hospital'! Every part of the country has its own volunteer groups. The services offered by such bodies include accommodation, advice, support, or simply a place to go in the evenings. The National Association for the Care and Resettlement of Offenders produces a booklet which gives the names and addresses of all the voluntary bodies they are aware of who offer services to offenders.* Most of the organizations do not, of course, expect to provide specialist psychiatric facilities but inevitably they pick up a proportion of mentally abnormal people. Brief mention of four such voluntary projects will illustrate the range of assistance which is available. All these examples come from South London; other areas could produce an equally interesting list.

(a) Effra House, a residential long-stay hostel, specially designed to provide accommodation for brain damaged and mentally disturbed men who have been in trouble with the law, particularly those leaving prison.
(b) Alcoholics Recovery Project, a large organization comprising three hostels, two shop fronts, and a new careers scheme, which aims to employ a few recovered alcoholics as social workers in the alcoholism field.
(c) Circle Clubs, run by the Circle Trust: non-residential evening and weekend facilities to which men and women can drift for a cup of tea, a game of darts, a film show, or perhaps counselling and advice from the project staff.
(d) The South London Wives Group run by the Circle Trust provides support for the families of men who have been sent to prison. Its stated aim is 'to

*Obtainable from NACRO, 169, Clapham Road, London SW9 0PU.

try and help families of prisoners . . . so that the husband on release has a home to return to and a better chance to resettle into normal life' (Crosthwaite, 1972).

Any medical or social work team working with mentally abnormal offenders should be fully acquainted with, and in contact with, the voluntary groups in the locality concerned. It is sometimes possible for professional staff to note a gap in the services and, with a group of colleagues, to launch a voluntary project of their own.

### Case Report

The following clinical example illustrates a few of the principles outlined above. A 26-year-old woman was referred by her general practitioner because of very disturbed behaviour which included repeated self-injury, recurrent episodes of window or furniture smashing, disinhibited sexual behaviours, sleeplessness, enuresis, and abuse of medication. The precipitant of referral was an episode of running through the streets naked, for which she claimed amnesia. She had in the past received a diagnosis of personality disorder and in the absence of psychotic features or signs of classical mental illness this diagnosis remained appropriate, except in so far as it failed to assist us in defining her problems or planning a programme of treatment.

Her history in more detail revealed that she was placed in care at the age of 10 months. She had spent much more time away from the family than her four siblings and was very conscious of this difference. She was expelled from school at the age of 12 after much truanting and a fight with the teacher, and was admitted to a residential child guidance clinic. After the superintendent of the clinic left she deteriorated, kicking, punching, and biting members of the staff, and was removed to a remand home. She started thieving, was placed on probation for theft, but was soon in breach and sent to an approved school. Soon, regarded as unmanageable, she was moved to an adult mental hospital when still only 13. Abnormal EEGs were recorded and epilepsy diagnosed. At the mental hospital she continued to attack staff and other patients and set fire to her room, which precipitated her transfer to a Special Hospital, Rampton. Inevitably her education suffered.

At Rampton her violence continued for some time but when she was 18 she was discharged by a Mental Health Review Tribunal. A few months later she was back in a mental hospital on an order, where she claims to have been raped. Soon after she absconded but she then attacked a lavatory attendant and was returned to Rampton for a further 5 years.

After leaving Rampton she found accommodation and a job but was soon in trouble for an assault on the police. Fortunately, a probation order was made and a custodial sentence averted, but she had several changes of supervising officer and her disruptive behaviour continued. She became pregnant. At the insistence of her mother who regarded her as insane she had an abortion, against her own wishes. A breach of the probation order took her to the probation hostel, her home at the time of referral. While there she met her boyfriend, now her husband. He had serious problems of his own, but her main concern about the relationship was her lack of sexual feelings for him and the intrusion of homosexual feelings, directed in particular at one of the wardens at the hostel.

At the point of referral, then, her problems were legion and were better listed as fully as possible rather than lumped under a single heading of personality disorder. The following summarize the problems demanding attention at referral:

(1) possible organic brain disorder or epilepsy;
(2) sleeplessness;
(3) enuresis;
(4) abuse of prescribed drugs;
(5) institutionalism;
(6) poor education;
(7) poverty of personal relationships:
    (a) lack of parenting,
    (b) previous absence of any long-term relationships,
    (c) excessively demanding behaviour in professional relationships,
    (d) aggressive tendencies;
(8) sexual problems
    (a) unresolved feelings about the rape,
    (b) inability to form satisfactory heterosexual relationships,
    (c) homosexual conflicts,
    (d) disinhibited behaviour;
(9) unresolved grief over the abortion;
(10) impulsive behaviours:
    (a) destructive towards self,
    (b) destructive towards property,
    (c) aggressive towards other people,
    (d) abrupt withdrawals from difficult situations, for example breach of probation;
(11) accommodation;
(12) employment;
(13) criminal behaviours.

It must be emphasized that she also presented with considerable strengths which included:

(1) high motivation towards treatment;
(2) determination to communicate, especially with the therapist, e.g. she

wrote lengthy if ungrammatical letters whenever she could not talk face to face;

(3)  she related warmly and affectionaly;

(4)  she had a strong sense of loyalty, e.g. despite constant rejections by her family she had maintained contact with them and attempted to improve relationships;

(5)  in trying to build a stable relationship with her boyfriend, she showed tolerance of his difficult behaviours.

Reassured that physical investigations were not a preliminary to her readmission to hospital she allowed these to take place. In the absence of psychotropic drugs her EEG was normal. We were able to exclude the diagnosis of epilepsy or organic basis for the enuresis. Tight controls of medication were established. Clear limits were set for tolerance of impulsive behaviour, while key professionals offered to be readily available at her times of crisis.

The most striking effects of years in institutions were her difficulties with financial and other practical management. Much of the 2 years of intensive therapy was spent under the threat of eviction for erratic payment of rent. A substantial amount of the assistance she received from social workers and probation officers was directed towards educating her about coping in the community. Perhaps surprisingly, the criminal behaviours abruptly ceased at the beginning of the programme.

Her general personal relationships and the more specific sexual problems improved with exploration, simple interpretations, and education. It soon became clear, for example, that much of her lesbian feeling was better interpreted as a search for the physical maternal warmth that she had never received; she had little difficulty in accepting that idea and working with it. Perhaps the single most important feature was that for the first time in her life most of the caring figures remained constant for 2 years, and she had the strength on her side not to abandon them at difficult times in therapy.

A desired pregnancy further improved her behaviour and her attitudes markedly, but her delivery revived the horrific fantasies and guilt she had had about her abortion. She was delighted with her baby, as was her husband, but soon the child started to vomit and lose weight. There was doubt about whether the child would survive. A milk allergy was diagnosed, and the baby began to thrive on special food, but by this time the baby had spent 6 weeks in hospital and the mother–child relationship had suffered. On release the baby was irritable and crying constantly. She interpreted this as evidence both of her inability to mother and of the child's hatred of her, and became extremely tense. The paediatric unit responded well to this with occasional admission, as there was some concern on her part as well as ours that as she became more tense she might attack the child.

This new crisis reactivated many of the old problems, which in turn coloured the new issues. Not only, for example, did she fear loss of her child by death but its removal by authority figures and its placement in institutions. Not least of the difficulties was the fact that more than 20 key workers were involved in her care at one stage. Maintaining communication and clear lines of responsibility demanded a lot of attention. Staff and patient alike had to negotiate carefully the setting of the new limits, given the presence of the baby. The crisis was finally alleviated to a large extent by an admission to the mother and baby unit in her local psychiatric hospital. During that time she was weaned from overdependence on some of the many workers who had become involved, and after 1 month she was discharged with the child and went back to her husband, where, under supervision, the childminder became the key figure in consolidating the improving mother–child relationship.

In summary, for this woman the diagnosis 'personality disorder' covered a very large number of medical, interpersonal, and practical social problems. Her strengths, together with coordination of a multidisciplinary approach towards these identified problems, have achieved much. A year after the birth of her child she is still in the community, she is no longer considered dangerous, she is not offending, her baby has survived, and her domestic life has reached a reasonable equilibrium.

## Acknowledgements

We would like to thank Dr Paul Bowden for helpful comments, and Miss Kathy Coomes and Mrs Maureen Bartholomew for secretarial skills and patience.

## References

Clemmer, D. (1940) *The Prison Community*, Holt, New York.

Crosthwaite, A. (1972) Voluntary work with families of prisoners. *International Journal of Offender Therapy and Comparative Criminology*, **16**, 253–259.

Finesinger, J. E. (1948) Psychiatric Interviewing 1. Some principles and procedures in insight therapy. *American Journal of Psychiatry*, **105**, 187–195.

Glasser, W. (1965) *Reality Therapy*. Harper & Row, New York.

Gostin, L. O. (1977) *A Human Condition. Volume Two: The Law Relating to Mentally Abnormal Offenders*. National Association of Mental Health, London.

Gunn, J. (1977) Management of the mentally abnormal offender: integrated or parallel. *Proceedings of the Royal Society of Medicine*, **70**, 877–880.

Gunn, J., Robertson, G., Dell, S., and Way, C. (1978) *Psychiatric Aspects of Imprisonment*. Academic Press, London.

Home Office/DHSS (1975) *Report of the Committee on Mentally Abnormal Offenders*. HMSO, London, Cmnd. 6244.

Orr, J. H. (1978) The imprisonment of mentally disordered offenders. *British Journal of Psychiatry*, **133**, 194–199.

Rogers, C. R. (1961) *On Becoming a Person*. Houghton Mifflin, Boston.

South East Thames Regional Health Authority (1979) *Secure but not Secured*. Sethra, Croydon.

Stafford-Clark, D. (1970) Supportive psychotherapy. In J. H. Price, ed., *Modern Trends in Psychological Medicine Vol. 2*. Butterworths, London.

Weed, L. C. (1968) Medical records that guide and track. *New England Journal of Medicine*, **278**, 593–600 and 652–657.

West, D. J. (1963) *The Habitual Prisoner*. Macmillan, London.

# PART III

*Hospital Rehabilitation*

Theory and Practice of Psychiatric Rehabilitation
Edited by F. N. Watts and D. H. Bennett
© 1983, John Wiley & Sons, Ltd.

# 7

# Ward-based Rehabilitation Programmes

JOHN HALL

## Ward-based Rehabilitation Schemes

The ward is the basic organizational unit within the psychiatric hospital. It is the location of many routine domestic and clinical procedures. It is the home of most residents who have been in hospital for some time.

Many administrative procedures are ward-based. These include the issue and continuing care of clothing, for example the sorting of clothes for 'foul', 'standard', or 'private' laundering. The more handicapped patients may not be able to manage their own money so cigarettes and sweets purchased for their consumption are kept in the ward office and distributed by ward staff.

The daily sequence of washing, dressing, bedmaking, etc., takes place on the ward. Many of these daily activities take place in no other location, so that the physical layout of a ward becomes a key determinant of the ease with which long-stay patients carry them out. Indeed, simply paying attention to 'normalizing' the washing and toilet facilities of a ward may lead to significant improvements in self-care skills.

Many medical procedures occur on the ward. A significant proportion of the patients on a long-stay ward may be on some form of maintenance psychotropic medication, often requiring up to four doses a day. A small proportion of the patients may fail to take their medication as prescribed, so that blood serum levels of a drug, for example, may need to be regularly checked  Some of the patients will also require medical and nursing attention for intercurrent infections or chronic physical conditions, such as epilepsy.

Visitors and relatives often visit patients on the ward, so the individual ward is the only part of the entire hospital that visitors will see. The visitors may often see the nurse in charge of the ward as their main point of contact in any dealings with the hospital. The importance of the ward staff is enhanced by the support, or even informal therapy, that they provide for relatives. This applies especially to the minority of relatives who maintain close, long-term contact with the hospital, many of whom have problems of their own.

### The Hospital Context of the Ward

Despite the significance of the ward as a location for rehabilitation, the ward is but one part of the whole institution and service. Frequently, there are organizational constraints which hamper the freedom of action of ward staff. A hospital is a complex organization. 'It does not have a single line of authority and does not fit classical descriptions of bureaucratic organizations. . . . The actual disposition of authority and power differs from hospital to hospital and depends on a host of organizational and personal factors' (Brown, 1973). Though patients tend to receive better care where individual wards are given maximum autonomy within the organization, there are a variety of ways in which this autonomy can be restricted. Many hospitals have budgetary arrangements for catering, laundry, and other supplies that are a major source of frustration and inconvenience to ward staff. At times the work of the ward will be affected by inspection by an external agency such as the Health Advisory Service in Britain, or the possibility of a scandal may bring pressure from the Authority responsible for the hospital. Sudden changes in agreed catchment populations, in local employment, or in patterns of referral and admission of various client groups (e.g. the elderly) may alter the levels of age and handicap within a hospital in a relatively short period. While the focus of this chapter is rehabilitation based on a ward, it is essential to recognize that what happens in any ward is at least partly dependent upon a range of economic, clinical, and administrative decisions beyond the control of ward staff.

It is possible to become so concerned with the limitations of institutional care that the few advantages of the larger psychiatric hospital can be overlooked. Because of the size of most psychiatric hospitals it is possible to have at least some degree of specialization of function for individual wards. The hospital may well provide a range of facilities and specialized staff that are not readily available to smaller, dispersed units. Ward staff can thus selectively use these facilities to complement the facilities available on the ward. By virtue of the large number of staff employed, the worst consequences of absenteeism or sickness can be overcome and, more positively, it is easier to build up a group of staff with special and extended experience.

### The Physical Characteristics of Wards

The majority of long-stay psychiatric patients live in hospitals which are both old and large. Since newer psychiatric units in General Hospitals tend to cater for the more acutely ill patients, very few chronic patients are in wards designed in recent years. This is reflected in the average number of patients in wards for chronic patients. In Britain the Department of Health and Social Security's (DHSS) own statistics (1976) indicate a norm of 30 beds per ward for admission patients, and 50 beds for 'other patients'.

Apart from the sheer size of some wards, they may also be designed and constructed in a way that makes them difficult to alter. Reflecting the treatment ideology of past generations, wards may be designed either as one large space, or as corridors joining a large number of small or single rooms. Whatever the layout, the cost of alteration and the possibly uncertain future of some psychiatric hospitals mean that desirable modifications may not be carried out. The wonder is that so many ward staff do manage to provide a genuinely 'homely friendly ward atmosphere' which is often seen as a prerequisite for any more structured rehabilitation programme (Barton, 1966).

## The Ward Staff

Kushlick *et al.* (1976) have carried out an operational analysis of the functions of various groups of direct care staff. Rather than categorize them by educational qualifications or professional origin, they have categorized them 'by the extent and nature of their contact and interaction with clients during the course of the day and night, and their contact and interaction with other people providing direct-care (DC) to clients'. On this basis nurses are 'DC 12 hours', who interact with clients, mainly in the same location, on a shift basis which extends over the full 7-day week. 'DC 2–6 hours' includes teachers and occupational therapists who run programmes during a morning and/or afternoon of the 5-day working week. This categorization implies, it may be noted, the additional responsibility of ward staff for providing activities at weekends and on public holidays. 'DC 10 minutes' includes doctors and social workers, who interact with clients in many different locations throughout the day for relatively short periods of the day. This type of analysis links groups of staff with locations, illustrating the close interdependence of staff and the physical ward in providing the setting for a ward-based programme.

The key staff of a ward are the nurses — DC 12 hours in Kushlick's notation. A ward may be visited by a range of staff, and the nurses may nominally be under the supervision or control of a consultant or nursing officer, but effectively the ward nurses run a ward. Shortage of staff is often given as the main reason why a ward programme cannot be mounted. Yet there is no doubt that in recent years the overall number of nurses per resident has risen significantly, from 24.5 nurses for each 100 residents in 1964 to 48.1 nurses for each 100 residents in 1974 (Department of Health and Social Security, 1976).

The level of training of nurses varies considerably. In general, the proportion of trained (registered or enrolled) nurses is higher in admission and specialized wards than in long-stay or rehabilitation wards. Although a national norm of 60 trained to 40 untrained nurses overall has been set, there is recent evidence that this norm is not only unmet, but the proportion of trained staff is actually falling (Department of Health and Social Security, 1974). In a long-stay ward a significant proportion of the nursing staff will usually be nursing assistants or aides. Many of these are married women, some part-timers, who may have a great personal concern for their patients but who are still essentially untrained. Since there may be relatively high turnover among the trained staff the situation can thus arise where the 'culture carriers' of the ward are a group of untrained staff who exert an influence on the patients' lives which is disproportionate to their apparent responsibilities. The significance of ward staff views, attitudes, and aspirations in shaping the therapeutic experience of patients has been discussed by Stannard (1973). Another staff group in close contact with the patients are the ward domestics and porters. They often share with the patients such tasks as washing-up and fetching ward supplies, and thus have a therapeutic potential.

It is possible for a short daily visit by a junior or a non-specialist family practitioner to be the only medical contact with patients in a long-stay ward, and for there to be very little involvement of a hospital consultant in the work of the rehabilitation ward. To remedy this there have been recommendations in Britain (Department of Health and Social Security, 1972; Murray, 1977) that every large psychiatric hospital should appoint a consultant psychiatrist with formally recognized responsibility for rehabilitation. While other staff may have contact with individual patients off the ward, it is helpful to have a named member of each of the other therapeutic professions assigned to wards, particularly where an active rehabilitation programme is planned.

The Patients

The residents of the ward are the remaining group of people involved in a ward programme. The total number of inpatients began to drop in the mid-1950s, and the patients who have remained in hospital are more handicapped than those who have left. Apart from these 'old long-stay', there is the continuing accumulation of 'new long-stay' (Wing and Hailey, 1972). In Britain it is estimated (MIND, 1974) that if new long-stay patients represented only 1 per cent of all acute patients, after only 7 years they would have filled up half of all the beds in the psychiatric units of district general hospitals. There is also a proportion of patients who use the hospital only periodically, perhaps to give relatives a rest, but are in fact highly dependent. In terms of the history of hospitalization alone, therefore, a chronic ward will include patients with widely differing patterns of continued contact with family and community, and with widely differing patterns of remaining interests and abilities.

The majority of long-stay patients are schizophrenic. While the proportion of all psychiatric patients in hospital in Britain who are schizophrenic is 44 per cent, this increases to 61 per cent for patients who have been in hospital continuously for 10–20 years (Department of Health and Social Security, 1975). The stereotypic long-stay patient is thus a 'chronic schiz.', and ward staff may respond to patients as such in the absence of any current psychopathology. A careful reappraisal of diagnosis, with the specific aim of informing ward staff, may be helpful as a prelude to initiating a ward programme. A number of diagnosis-specific characteristics of chronic schizophrenic patients have been established, such as their restricted range of attention (Silverman, 1968). The widely used classification of origins of handicap into primary, secondary, and pre-morbid (Wing, 1975) has been developed with schizophrenic subjects, and has some value with non-schizophrenic patients. However, surprisingly little is known about the diagnosis-specific response of non-schizophrenic chronic patients to rehabilitation.

Increasingly, chronic wards are becoming sex-integrated, and anecdotal evidence suggests that sex-mixing in wards improves patient morale and social functioning. However, sex differences in response to treatment and in the form of disorder or handicap abound (Phillips and Segal, 1969; Cash, 1973), and many older patients may actively dislike being on a mixed-sex ward. A mixed-sex rehabilitation ward should not, therefore, be created without careful consideration of the issues.

Depending on the internal organization of a hospital, chronic patients may be allocated to wards according to several different principles. Patients may be grouped together in divisions or sectors of the hospital depending on their original place of residence in the community. Alternatively, hospitals may be divided into 'firms' with the consultant in charge of the wards as the main organizing factor. In both of these systems a division or consultant in a smaller hospital may have a very small number of beds to accommodate the full range of psychiatric patients, and accordingly opportunities for patient selection may be very poor. Some larger hosptals may allocate long-stay patients more or less at random to any long-stay ward as vacancies occur, or may develop a comprehensive system of graded wards, with patients allocated to wards on the basis of their level of handicap (Martin, 1965).

Depending on which one of these schemes is adopted, it is possible to have a 'rehabilitation' ward which may contain a high proportion of elderly, disturbed, or even admission patients. One of the first steps in rehabilitation, irrespective of the type of regime being adopted, is to carry out at least some selection, so that the regime can be fitted to at least the majority of patients. An alternative philosophy is deliberately to mix patients with different levels of ability together, in the expectation that the more able patients will act as positive therapeutic models for the less able patients. Where this has been attempted (Lugwig et al., 1967), the improvement in the poorer patients has been balanced by a deterioration in the more able patients, so that overall there has been no benefit from such a strategy.

## Preparing for a Ward Rehabilitation Scheme

Planning a ward scheme should take into account the realities of the ward staff and patients who are likely to be involved. One of the difficulties commonly faced in initiating a ward-based scheme is the maze of statutory or merely traditional regulations which has to be traced in order to obtain something quite trivial, such as uncooked food from the hospital kitchens so that patients can cook their own breakfasts. The skill required for threading a passage through such mazes is not conventionally taught in medical or nurse training schools, so ward staff need a considerable degree of both initiative and persistence. The temptation for ward staff is to believe they can initiate change rapidly. 'Such a view is ingenuous. The fact of the matter is that organizations such as schools and hospitals will, like dragons, eat hero-innovators for breakfast' (Georgiades and Phillimore, 1975).

A knowledge of elementary organizational psychology is useful in the initial planning stages (see, for example, Hall, 1979a). This may suggest some organizational changes in the wider hospital as a prelude to planning the ward programme. These might include the grouping together of some long-stay wards under a senior nursing administrator to form a rehabilitation unit. It might be helpful to set up a joint committee with the local social services or welfare staff responsible for providing residential care, so that any necessary non-hospital accommodation can be earmarked or provided in advance.

One implication of present patterns of ward staffing is that some degree of staff training may be essential in planning a ward scheme. While training is imperative for unqualified staff, it may be necessary to carry out some training of the qualified staff who may have been trained many years previously or who may have little natural commitment to the proposed scheme. A training programme should ideally be short and related directly to the actual scheme in which the staff are to be involved. Butler and Rosenthall (1976) have described a short course, carried out on 1 day a week for 7 consecutive weeks. In England a syllabus for a 9-month course has been designed, providing for very full training in the principles and practice of rehabilitating chronic patients. The course emphasizes not only skills and knowledge, but also the importance of attitudes, which are relevant both in initially selecting nurses and as an index of change during training.

## Assessing Patients for Rehabilitation Schemes

Planning a scheme for an individual ward involves a series of preliminary choices or decisions. If some positive selection of patients for the ward is possible, it may be desirable to carry out a survey of the entire hospital population of long-stay patients (see, for example, Christie Brown *et al.*, 1977). From the results of such a survey it is possible to identify the number of patients with given levels of handicap, and of given ages and chronicity, and programmes can then be planned to meet the needs of the greatest numbers of patients. In practice, the opportunity to select an entire ward of patients without any other constraints is rare, so that a compromise has to be made between reducing the heterogeneity of the ward and making complicated transfers of patients between wards.

Consideration of ward routine indicates that some categories of activity occur most often on the ward. These include:

Self-care skills: washing, dressing
Domestic skills: keeping 'personal space' in order, washing-up
Social skills: conversation, recreation

A number of other activities *may* take place on the ward, but could equally well take place in an occupational therapy department. These might include practising budgeting skills, such as preparing a shopping list for a week, or recreation involving the use of large equipment or large spaces, such as dancing. A number of other activities might be positively contraindicated. 'Work' activities, for example, are not in general compatible with 'home', and in any case usually involve equipment not usually available on a ward if adequate simulation of a work environment is to be achieved.

For some activities the ward is thus, if not the only, at least the preferred, location for rehabilitation training. For other activities the ward may be as appropriate a setting as any other for rehabilitation. For yet other activities the ward may well appear to be the wrong setting for training. Depending upon the alternative facilities available in the hospital, some decision regarding the general goals of the ward programme must be made. For example, for more able patients goals might be determined as:

>Increasing the range of community contact.
>Increasing independent use of money.

For less able patients goals might be determined as:

>Increasing the level of self-care skills.
>Increasing the level of conversation between patients.

These general goals, to be effective, have then to be translated into specific goals, appropriate to the handicaps and assets of the patient group, comprehensible to ward staff, and capable of being objectively monitored. The aim of setting specific goals and monitoring progress is achieved by careful assessment of individual patients.

Assessment often focuses on the intended targets of the ward regime in an attempt to indicate the level of performance of the individual patient at, for example, a self-care skill such as dressing. The extent of a patient's ability will only be apparent in an environment which facilitates the maximum use of that skill. What initially appears to be a patient-centred assessment may turn out to be implicitly, if not explicitly, an assessment of the environment. The significance of the assessment environment is such that some assessment methods are concerned solely with the environment, and not with the patient at all. This approach is illustrated by a number of 'ward restrictiveness' inventories, or the Ward Atmosphere Scale of Moos (1970).

Given that an individual patient is normally the focus of assessment, the main task of assessment is seen as quantifying the degree of behavioural deficit, or the nature of behavioural deviation. This fundamental distinction between underactivity (or deficit) and overactivity (or deviation) is shown by the two factors (Social Withdrawal, and Socially Embarrassing Behaviour) of Wing's (1961) widely used ward behaviour rating scale, and by other factor analytic studies. Behavioural assets are less frequently assessed, and an excessive preoccupation with the patients' handicaps can lead to neglect of what the patient *can* do. Many chronic patients retain some skills and interests, which can be useful starting points in planning individually tailored ward programmes.

A wide range of standard assessment techniques is available. The range of methods available for chronic patients is undoubtedly narrower than for acute patients, but the most relevant method to use is some form of rating scale based on nursing observation. Examples of these scales are the 12-item scale of Wing, already mentioned, and the Nurses' Observation Scale for Inpatient Evaluation (commonly known as NOSIE) available in the standard 80-item version and in shorter modifications (Honigfeld and Klett, 1965). The popularity of rating scales is so great that discussions on assessment of chronic patients can slide into a discussion exclusively of rating methods (Klett, 1968). A number of other methods have been used, usually some form of psychiatric rating, which may be either a purely clinical judgement or a standard rating based on psychiatric observation (Hall, 1979b). Increasing use is being made of behavioural assessment methods, usually incorporating a time-sampling system with a set of behavioural codes or categories describing specific acts or positions of the patient. A number of texts on behavioural assessments are now appearing (see Haynes, 1978) which provide a comprehensive introduction to this type of assessment.

If nurse rating methods are used, then the nurses will normally need at least some basic training in assessment. This training can be incorporated into any more general course of training carried out as a preliminary to starting the ward programme. The main aims of training should be to familiarize staff with the meaning of the items and with the purely clerical aspects of completing the rating. It is not enough to assume that if a standard rating scale with acknowledged reliability is being used, reliability is ensured. Reliability in a specific setting with a specific set of raters and patients should be positively demonstrated and reliability trials should be continued for the duration of the rehabilitation scheme (Romanczyk *et al.*, 1973).

While ward staff are the most obvious assessors to use in a ward-based programme, other groups of people may be involved. If patients are attending an occupational or industrial therapy unit, the staff of the unit may provide useful information. More able chronic patients may be able to act as self-assessors, in the same way as acute patients. Self-assessment of hallucinations, for example, can even be used as one of the main components of a therapeutic programme (Baker, 1975).

No one wants a complex assessment system that is methodologically pure, but practically irrelevant. The opposing error is to carry out isolated assessment procedures at irregular intervals which are not closely related to the aims of the ward scheme, and which are insensitive to any change which might occur. Careful assessment before and during rehabilitation is essential so that the progress of patients is not a figment of the imagination, but a demonstrated reality. Demonstrating progress to ward staff continuously over several months is itself a major achievement (Woods and Cullen, 1983).

## Approaches to Rehabilitation Based on Wards

The 'hero-innovators' of psychiatric care in Britain of the last century, notably John Conolly and Samuel Tuke, based their approach on a humanitarian concern for their patients coupled with the abolition of physical restraint. As hospitals grew in size, interest in positive rehabilitation dropped, so that there was relatively little patient turnover (Jones, 1972). This state of affairs remained right up to the time of the Second World War, apart from the 'total push' approach of Myerson (1939) which utilized a principle quite at variance with present notions of the defects of chronic schizophrenia. Following the end of the war there was a spate of publications on rehabilitating patients, and on hospital sociology, from both sides of the Atlantic (for example, Stanton and Schwarz, 1954; Freeman *et al.*, 1958). Apart from a number of idiosyncratic treatment approaches, two major trends of development can be discerned. One trend is the milieu therapy approach, exemplified by the therapeutic community type of ward programe. The other trend is the behaviour modification approach, exemplified by the token economy type of ward programme. These two approaches have proceeded independently, with little cross-fertilization between them, and will be described separately.

### The Milieu Therapy Approach

All wards necessarily have some sort of 'milieu', or atmosphere, but it may not be specifically recognized as a major tool in rehabilitation. The milieu therapy approach explictly recognizes the potential therapeutic effect of the ward environment. Van Putten and May (1976) state that milieu therapy includes

varying degrees and combinations of occupational therapy, group activity, vocational rehabilitation, educational therapy, industrial therapy, resocialisation, remotivation, total push, therapeutic community, patient government, recreational activities, formal individual and/or group psychotherapy, and so forth.

This type of definition is so all-embracing as to be of little value, so it is useful further to categorize the approach using the three-fold classification of Rossi and Filstead (1973). *Milieu Therapy* (more usually called 'social therapy' in Britain) is the general concept of the milieu as a mode of treatment. The phrase thus includes theory, practice, and evaluation. A *therapeutic milieu* is a setting positively designed for the practice of social therapy, to produce desired change in those who enter it. It thus refers to a range of possible settings — hostels, workshops — with a range of differing social structures. A *therapeutic community* is a specific type of therapeutic milieu, following the original plans of Maxwell Jones. The therapeutic community concept has been further subdivided by Clark (1964) into the general therapeutic community approach, and the therapeutic community 'proper'. This essentially hierarchical classification means that it is difficult to provide a simple description of milieu therapy at each level, so the main guiding principles will be outlined.

Van Putten and May (1976) have outlined the common factors in all milieu therapy units. Some of these, such as 'improved physical surroundings', should be found in rehabilitation schemes of any type, so are not factors unique to the milieu approach. The distinctive factors appear to be 'a zeitgeist of staff consensus and diffusion of authority, an emphasis on dynamic understanding and discussion of the patients' difficulties and personal problems . . . and an emphasis on social and group interaction'.

A fundamental feature of the milieu approach is its treatment of authority. Early formulations of the milieu approach (Cumming and Cumming, 1962) were explicitly seen as counteracting the authoritarian and custodial organization of hospitals. The patient's submission to authority was seen as forcing him into dependency and as depriving him of a sense of responsibility. Recent studies of severely handicapped schizophrenics cared for at home (Creer and Wing, 1974) have shown the very real responsibility involved in caring for such people; within caring families there may be a high degree of protective supervision. In fact, some of the relatives who coped best were those who laid down a structured framework of expectations for the schizophrenic family member, which might be interpreted as an authoritarian response to the family member. It is thus possible that removing all authority over patients may be justifiable theoretically, but in practice it is not therapeutic for chronic patients.

Where authority is intended to be diffused, a common technique to achieve this goal is a community meeting, and regular staff meetings. Meetings of the whole ward may be held daily. All members of the ward are informed of impending events, and group discussion and decision making on any major events are encouraged. As far as possible, staff members try to encourage patients to participate, rather than the discussion being led by the staff. Morgan (1979) has noted the main topics covered in such a group meeting.

Meetings of the whole ward may be supplemented by regular meetings of small groups. Williams *et al.* (1962), for example, grouped their patients into closed groups of six to eight patients each, who then participated in a structured programme which included social and educational activities, group recreation, intensive group psychotherapy, cooperative group work projects, and psychodrama. An important element of group work may be reality confrontation. This involves regular feedback to ward members of the consequences of their actions. There may be a detailed analysis of events to see how they arose, in the hope that those involved will cope better later on. This element of the milieu approach also discourages keeping secrets, since everything that happens is the property of the group, and may be used by them. Confrontation may occur at formal ward meetings, but also at a crisis meeting close in time to the event being analysed.

An example of the way in which these distinctive features of the milieu approach are translated into a ward programme is given by Boettcher and Schie (1975). They described a milieu therapy programme carried out in a 2,000-bed American state hospital. Ten per cent of the female patients involved were in the advanced stages of getting ready to leave hospital, and 20 per cent were in the early stages of getting ready to go out. The remaining 70 per cent were classified as 'chronic', and most of these 'were poorly motivated for leaving the hospital'.

The small-group programme which was adopted called

for placing patients in autonomous, problem-solving, task oriented small groups whose main business is to help members complete tasks necessary for beginning discharge planning, make recommendations to staff on patients' progress . . . the goals of the programme were these: 1) to maximise the expectation of discharge, 2) to maximise patients' involvement in solving their own problems and organising their living situations, 3) to minimise direct problem-solving by attendants.

All patients were assigned to a group, varying in size between 10 and 13. The groups met twice a week, without staff members present, to evaluate and discuss progress. If a patient wanted to advance to a higher step in the six steps, or levels, of the regime, she had to prepare a written statement for her group, including an assessment of her work ability. Staff met weekly to act on the recommendations of patient groups. Formal votes were taken at staff meetings, with each staff member, irrespective of profession, having one vote.

Each patient group elected a chairperson and secretary to serve for 8 weeks: when their term expired, new ones were elected. Each secretary kept a record of her group's daily activities, and these were evaluated by staff, and suggestions were made about how to improve group functioning and meetings. The patients themselves organized a 'General Domestic Agency' providing a general house-cleaning service to the neighbouring community, and the agency was run by seven patients elected as its board of directors. This illustrates the way in which 'living' rehabilitation programmes tend to develop over time, so that new elements are included in programmes which are born out of local initiative or opportunity rather than from theoretical deduction.

### The Behaviour Modification Approach

The behavioural approach to the rehabilitation of chronic patients is conventionally thought to stem from the classic study of Ayllon and Azrin (1965), which was later republished as an appendix to the same authors' book (1968) *The Token Economy*. Rehabilitation techniques remarkably similar to these had been described by Charles Mercier in 1879, without benefit of modern learning theory, and experimental studies of operant behaviour in chronic patients had been carried out by a number of investigators, notably Lindsley (1956). Matson (1980) has carried out a broad review of behaviour modification procedures with chronic patients, covering token economy, social skills, overcorrections, and other specific types of procedure.

The behavioural approach stresses the necessity of carrying out a functional analysis of the patients' behaviour, to examine the relationship between specific target events and the antecedent setting conditions and the consequent contingencies or environmental responses. This analysis is carried out in the expectation that certain behaviour on the part of the patients, such as nagging nurses for a cigarette, will be found to be associated with certain consequences for the patient, such as receiving a cigarette from the nurses. A defining characteristic of the behavioural approach is, thus, that it tends to emphasize relatively specific target areas of behaviour and the consequences for the patient of attaining those targets. The main skill in designing a behaviour modification programme would then be seen as linking the performance of specified 'target' behaviour to the receipt by the patient of certain specified 'reinforcers', or desirable events or goods such as cigarettes.

A behaviour modification programme is thus one where the main ingredient of the ward programme is a specified set of targets, the performance of which by individual patients is followed by receipt of a reinforcer. The targets may cover the whole ward for the whole day, such as the attainment of reasonable levels of communication between patients, or they may cover the whole ward for part of the day, such as the series of activities forming the early morning routine of the ward, or they may cover only a proportion of the patients, perhaps those performing high-level, community-oriented skills such as purchasing clothing at an ordinary shop outside the hospital. These ward-wide or group targets may be supplemented by programmes to correct individual behavioural problems, such as enuresis (see Baker, 1975, for an account of the various techniques).

The best-known form of a ward behaviour modification programme is the token economy. This type of regime assumes that most, but not necessarily all, reinforcement is delivered in the form of a token, which may be any sort of durable object which can have a definite numerical value attached to it. In practice, tokens are often coloured plastic discs, or token money. The patient receives a token immediately the target behaviour has been performed, and then after a delay of possibly up to a week he trades in the tokens for the goods or events he desires. In this way a complete miniature economy is created, and all the conventional fiscal operations such as taxation, inflation, and even international exchange regulations (with the 'real' cash economy) can be introduced. Indeed, token economy programmes have attracted attention as economic systems in their own right (Winkler, 1971).

One of the defining characteristics of behaviour modification programmes is the attention paid to a regular review of targets, so that the progress of individual patients is monitored. Depending upon progress, new higher-level targets are set, and levels of reinforcement, such as the number of tokens paid for attaining the target, are also re-set. This can only be done by the regular collection of data on patient performance, so complex rating and checking systems may be necessary (see Wallace, 1976).

To ensure that the reinforcers included in a behavioural programme are effective, it may be thought necessary to remove the 'contamination', as it were, of reinforcers freely available to the patient. For example, if a patient were known to respond positively to reinforcement by sweets, then the patient might not respond to a behavioural programme if a relative was regularly bringing in packets of sweets. This implies that a degree of 'environmental control' may be necessary, which may in turn impose some level of restriction on a patient. These issues of control have considerable ethical implications, and in Britain guidance on these topics has recently become available (Joint Working Party on Ethics of Behaviour Modification, 1980).

A token economy ward project has been reported by Presly et al. (1976), who introduced a token scheme into a 600-bed Scottish National Health Service psychiatric hospital. The patients were mostly schizophrenic and 'undoubtedly contained the large majority of the hospital's most disadvantaged male patients'. All the patients were rated initially by ward staff, and a range of particular behaviours was selected for immediate token reinforcement. These included specific self-care activities such as dressing and general tidiness, and constructive efforts within the programme of occupational activities which was supervised by the ward staff. A ward shop was established where tokens could be exchanged for a variety of items, or the patients could save tokens for some future purchases.

An event sampling form was prepared, which allowed the behaviour of the patient at any one time to be recorded by the ward psychologists. Ratings of the patients' abilities were also made by the ward staff. One of the major difficulties noted was the problem of maintaining a consistent level of staffing on the ward, so that the ward Charge Nurse could not plan more than a day at a time. The amount of time required to train each nurse who came on to the ward also meant that it was very difficult to maintain staff training after the initial stages of the project. It was noted that over the duration of the project an increased range of social activities was introduced, and many patients participated in these for the first time.

## Mixed Approaches

Although the milieu approach and the behaviour modification approach have developed separately, and although the major review articles treat each approach separately (see Clark, 1977; Gripp and Magaro, 1974), it is apparent that ward practice in the two approaches shows considerable overlap. An important part of Boettcher and Schie's (1975) programme was a six-fold step system, involving carefully graded and specific targets linked with contingent privileges. Hall *et al.* (1977) included in their experimental token economy programme a weekly patients' meeting, with a patient chairman and secretary. Paul and Lentz (1977) compared milieu therapy, in a therapeutic community structure, with social-learning treatment, in a token economy structure. Yet in this carefully designed study the two treatment units being compared showed certain common procedures and policies. These included emphasizing 'resident' rather than 'patient' status, the necessity for clarity of communication, instrumental skills training, and detailed schedules of activities shared by both groups such as arithmetic and arts and crafts. Heap *et al.* (1970) carried out 'behaviour–milieu' therapy on a chronic ward, the main characteristics of the ward programme being (a) a token economy system, (b) development of patient self-government, and (c) 'attitude therapy', so it is impossible to categorize it as exclusively a token economy or a therapeutic community. One useful way of classifying ward programmes may be to examine them to see what 'therapeutic factors' are present and to what degree, rather than classifying in terms of theoretical concepts which bear no relationship to the reality.

## Effectiveness of Ward Rehabilitation Programmes

As with any treatment method, effectiveness can only be assessed if outcome studies are designed adequately. A number of common experimental design faults have meant that rehabilitation studies have been enthusiastically carried out over the years, yet have added little to scientific knowledge regarding the effectiveness of particular treatments.

Among the most common faults have been a failure to recognize the interaction between drug and environmental therapy effects. Paul *et al.* carried out a well-designed study with 52 'hard-core' patients, testing the effects of continuing drug treatment versus placebo, and therapeutic community versus token economy treatment. Some patients who were on drugs showed a slower response to treatment than those on placebo. This study and others (e.g. Hamilton *et al.*, 1960) have clearly demonstrated the complex relationship between response to drugs and a range of activities, thus emphasizing the necessity to maintain drugs at a standard level during the evaluation of a rehabilitation programme.

Chronic patients respond to even simple environmental changes, and the effects of such changes may take several months to stabilize (Zlotowski and Cohen, 1968). The concept of institutionalization assumes the continued exposure of the individual patient to the institutional environment over a period of months or years: logically one might therefore expect the effects of exposure to a positive regime to be maximal only after a long period. Hall *et al.* (1977) found continuing improvement in a token economy over a period of 2½ years, yet the whole study by Marks *et al.* (1968) only lasted 13 weeks. An adequate length of time should therefore elapse—at least 6 months, and preferably 1 or 2 years—before attempting to assess the final effectiveness of a ward programme.

The effectiveness of a type of treatment will appear to vary depending on the degree of active treatment delivered to any control group, or in a control phase of a study. If a milieu therapy or behaviour modification programme is compared with minimal custodial care, it will appear more effective than if a comparison is made with, for example, an occupational therapy programme. Careful matching of a number of factors, such as the amount of attention received by the control and the experimental groups, and the quality of the physical ward environment, must be made, so matching on simple 'key' variables alone is inadequate (Rappaport *et al.*, 1972).

These examples indicate some of the main design faults in research on the effectiveness of ward rehabilitation programmes. One other pervasive problem is the popularity of discharge as an outcome measure. On one hand, discharge is inappropriate for some patients, and fails to take account of the substantial improvement in independence and functioning which may occur with the most handicapped patients (Hall *et al.*, 1977). On the other hand, a patient may indeed be ready for discharge, yet the lack of suitable accommodation at the right time may mean he cannot be discharged. It must also be acknowledged that a patient may indeed be ready for discharge as far as the hospital is concerned, yet fail miserably on return to the community. Any ward-based programme which includes discharge as one of the main targets must be designed to fit closely with non-ward programmes providing a graded link with the post-hospital community environment (Shedletsky and Voineskos, 1976). Some of the major methodological problems in this area are discussed by Paul (1969) and Cash (1973).

A number of direct comparisons between milieu therapy and behaviour modification programmes have been made. Stoffelmayr *et al.* (1973) compared the effectiveness of a token economy with two different social therapy techniques, and found their token regime superior to social therapy, but since 'nurses in a token economy interact more frequently with patients' there was a failure to control for the effects of attention. By far the most rigorous and detailed investigation of the comparative effectiveness of 'milieu' and 'social-learning' approaches has been reported by Paul and Lentz (1977). Their conclusion is important:

The overall comparative results on the relative effectiveness of the programs in the current project could not be clearer. The social-learning program was significantly more effective than either the milieu program or the traditional hospital programs. Its greater effectiveness was consistent across all classes of functioning in the intramural setting.

If behavioural programmes are, in general, more effective than other forms of programme, other questions remain to be answered. Of the patients in a behavioural programme, what characteristics identify those who respond best? (Kowalski *et al.*, 1976) What is the relative contribution of contingent token reinforcement compared to the associated contingent social reinforcement and informational feedback? (Elliott *et al.*, 1976)

## Conclusion

The realization that not all chronic patients will leave hospital has profound implications. There is, then, a positive place for ward rehabilitation programmes, not only as a means of identifying patients who *can* leave hospital, but as a means of improving the 'quality of life' for patients who are never likely to leave. Undoubtedly these patients should have homely surroundings, good food, adequate creature comforts, and hopefully someone who takes a personal and individual interest in them. But many of the long-stay patients who are unlikely to leave hospital are severely handicapped, and display a range of problem behaviour that is a real burden to the nurses who care for them, as well as the other patients, and which can benefit considerably from an organized ward regime. Even when a 'ward' is placed in the community, so that it may be called a 'hostel-ward' the same issues of management arise (Wykes, 1982).

Despite the historical separation of the two main streams of development in ward-based rehabilitation, the practices of the two systems are not incompatible. With an understanding of the main problems posed by a group of patients, and with a clear specification of the aims of the ward, treatment techniques can be selected to fit the need. In general it appears that a behavioural approach is, for more disabled chronic patients, the most appropriate general framework within which to fit these techniques.

No ward-based rehabilitation scheme will be successful without the active cooperation of the ward staff, most of whom will be nurses. Nurses are not likely to put their efforts into a ward programme unless it fits their idea of what is both desirable and attainable with the patients. Perhaps the most difficult part of guiding and advising ward staff is to communicate an expectation of change in the patients that is positive yet at the same time realistic.

Lastly, successful ward-based rehabilitation depends on time. An innovative psychiatrist or psychologist must be prepared to invest a substantial proportion of his or her time in preparing the programme. The programme must last long enough for treatment effects to reach their highest level. But not only has change to be achieved, it has then to be maintained. Wing and Brown's (1970) account of the changes in level of performance in three separate psychiatric hospitals shows that positive change can be achieved, and then reversed. Constant vigilance is needed to ensure that the reality, and not just the impression, of change in ward behaviour is maintained.

## References

Ayllon, T., and Azrin, N. H. (1965) The measurement and reinforcement of behaviour of psychotics. *Journal of the Experimental Analysis Behaviour*, **8**, 357–383.

Ayllon, T., and Azrin, N. (1968) *The Token Economy*. Appleton Century Crofts, New York.

Baker, R. D. (1975) Behavioural techniques in the treatment of schizophrenia. In A.D. Forrest and J. W. Affleck, eds, *Handbook of Schizophrenia*. Churchill Livingstone, Edinburgh.

Barton, R. (1966) *Institutional Neurosis*. John Wright, Bristol.

Boettcher, R. E., and Schie, R. W. (1975) Milieu therapy with chronic mental patients. *Social Work*, **20**, 130–134.

Brown, G. W. (1973) The mental hospital as an institution. *Social Science and Medicine*, **7**, 407–424.

Butler, R. J., and Rosenthall, G. (1976) Behaviour and rehabilitation: development of an in-service training course. *Nursing Times*, 5 February, 191–193.

Cash, T. F. (1973) Methodological problems and progress in schizophrenia research: a survey. *Journal of Consulting and Clinical Psychology*, **40**, 278–286.

Christie Brown, J. R. W., Ebringer, L., and Freedman, L. S. (1977) A survey of a long-stay psychiatric population: implications for community service. *Psychological Medicine*, **7**, 113–126.

Clark, D. H. (1964) *Administrative Therapy*. Tavistock, London.

Clark, D. H. (1977) The therapeutic community. *British Journal of Psychiatry*, **131**, 553–564.

Creer, C., and Wing, J. K. (1974) *Schizophrenia at Home*. National Schizophrenia Fellowship, London.

Cumming, J., and Cumming, E. (1962) *Ego and Milieu*. Atherton Press, New York.

Department of Health and Social Security (1972) *Rehabilitation Report of a Sub-committee of the Standing Medical Advisory Committee* (Tunbridge Report). HMSO, London.

Department of Health and Social Security (1974) *Health and Personal Social Services Statistics for England 1973*. HMSO, London.

Department of Health and Social Security (1975) *Censuses of: Patients in Mental Illness Hospitals and Units in England and Wales at the End of 1971*. Statistical and Research Report Series No. 10, HMSO. London.

Department of Health and Social Security (1976) *Facilities and Services of Mental Illness and Mental Handicap Hospitals in England 1974*. Statistical and Research Report Series No. 15. HMSO, London.

Elliott, P. A., Barwell, F., Hooper, A., and Kingerlee, P. E. (1976) The token economy package: social vs. token reinforcement. Paper presented at BABP Conference, Exeter.

Freeman, T., Camerson, J. L., and McGhie, A. (1958) *Chronic Schizophrenia*. Tavistock, London.

Georgiades, N. J., and Phillimore, L. (1975) The myth of the hero-innovator and alternative strategies for organisational change. In C. C. Kiernan and F. D. Woodford, eds, *Behaviour Modification with the Severely Retarded*. Associated Scientific Publishers, Amsterdam.

Gripp, R. F., and Magaro, P. A. (1974) The token economy program in the psychiatric hospital: a review and analysis. *Behaviour Research and Therapy*, **12**, 205–228.

Hall, J. N. (1979a) Maintaining change in long-stay wards. *Apex*, **6**, 4–6.

Hall, J. N. (1979b) Assessment procedures used in studies on long-stay patients: a survey of papers published in the British Journal of Psychiatry. *British Journal of Psychiatry*, **135**, 330–335.

Hall, J. N., Baker, R. D., and Hutchinson, K. (1977) A controlled evaluation of token economy procedures with chronic schizophrenic patients. *Behaviour Research and Therapy*, **15**, 261–283.

Hamilton, M., Smith, A. L. G., Lapidus, H. E., and Cadogan, E. P. (1960) A controlled study of thioproprazate dihydrochloride, chlorpromazine and occupational therapy in chronic schizophrenics. *Journal of Mental Science*, **106**, 40–55.

Haynes, S. N. (1978) *Principles of Behavioural Assessment*. Gardner Press, New York.

Heap, R. F., Boblitt, W. E., Moore, C. H., and Hord, J. E. (1970) Behaviour-milieu therapy with chronic neuropsychiatric patients. *Journal of Abnormal Psychology*, **76**, 349–354.

Honigfeld, G., and Klett, C. J. (1965) The nurses observation scale for in-patient evaluation. *Journal of Clinical Psychology*, **21**, 65–71.

Joint Working Party of Royal College of Psychiatrists, Royal College of Nursing, and British Psychological Society (1980) *Report of the Joint Working Party to Formulate Ethical Guidelines for the Conduct of Programmes of Behaviour Modification*. HMSO, London.

Jones, K. (1972) *A History of the Mental Health Services*. Routledge & Kegan Paul, London.

Klett, C. J. (1968) Assessing change in hospitalised psychiatric patients. In M. McReynolds, ed., *Advances in Psychological Assessment*. Science and Behaviour Books, Palo Alto, California.

Kowalski, P. A., Daley, G. D., and Gripp, R. F. (1976) Token economy: who responds how? *Behaviour Research and Therapy*, **14**, 372–374.

Kushlick, A., Felce, D., Palmer, J., and Smith, J. (1976) *Evidence to the Committee of Enquiry into Mental Handicap Nursing and Care*. Health Care Evaluation Research Project, Winchester.

Lindsley, O. R. (1956) Operant conditioning methods applied to research in chronic schizophrenia. *Psychiatric Research Reports*, **5**, 118–153.

Ludwig, A. M., Marx, J. A., Hill, P. A., *et al.* (1967) Forced small group responsibility in the treatment of chronic schizophrenics. *Psychiatry Quarterly Supplement*, **41**, 262–280.

Marks, J., Sonada, B., and Schalock, R. (1968) Reinforcement vs. relationship therapy for schizophrenics. *Journal of Abnormal Psychology*, **73**, 397–402.

Martin, D. V. (1965) A graded rehabilitation scheme for long-stay patients. In H. L. Freeman, ed., *Psychiatric Hospital Care*. Bailliere, Tindall, & Cassell, London.

Matson, J. L. (1980) Behaviour modification procedures for training chronically institutionalised schizophrenics. In M. Hersen, R. M. Eisler, and P. M. Miller, eds, *Progress in Behaviour Modification*. Academic Press, London.

MIND (1974) Coordination or chaos? The run-down of psychiatric hospitals. Quotation from *British Medical Journal* 4 March 1972. MIND Report No. 13, London.

Moos, R. H. (1970) Differential effects of psychiatric ward settings on patient change. *Journal of Nervous and Mental Disease*, **151**, 316–322.

Morgan, R. (1979) Conversations with chronic schizophrenic patients. *British Journal of Psychiatry*, **134**, 187–194.

Murray, J. (1977) *Better Prospects: Rehabilitation in Mental Illness Hospitals*. MIND, London.

Myerson, A. (1939) Theory and principles of the 'total push' method in the treatment of chronic schizophrenia. *American Journal of Psychiatry*, **95**, 1197–1204.

Paul, G. L. (1969) Chronic mental patient: current status — future directions. *Psychological Bulletin*, **71**, 81–94.

Paul, G. L., and Lentz (1977) *Psychosocial Treatment of Chronic Mental Patients*. Harvard University Press, Cambridge, Mass.

Paul, G. L., Tobias, L. L., and Holly, B. L. (1972) Maintenance psychotropic drugs in the presence of active treatment programmes. *Archives of General Psychiatry*, **27**, 106–115.

Phillips, D. L., and Segal, B. E. (1969) Sexual status and psychiatric symptoms. *American Sociological Review*, **34**, 58–76.

Presly, A. S., Black, D., Gray, A., Hartie, A., and Seymour, E. (1976) The token economy in the National Health Service: possibilities and limitations. *Acta Psychiatrica Scandinavica*, **53**, 258–270.

Rappaport, J., Chinsky, J. M., and Mace, D. (1972) Matching of chronic hospitalised patient groups. *Journal of Consulting and Clinical Psychology*, **38**, 462.

Romanczyk, R. G., Kent, R. N., Diament, C., and O'Leary, K. D. (1973) Measuring the reliability of observational data: a reactive process. *Journal of Applied Behaviour Analysis*, **6**, 175–184.

Rossi, J. J., and Filstead, W. J. (1973) *The Therapeutic Community*. Behavioural Publications Inc., New York.

Shedletsky, R., and Voineskos, G. (1976) The rehabilitation of the chronic psychiatric patients: beyond the hospital-based token economy system. *Social Psychiatry*, **11**, 145–150.

Silverman, J. (1968) Towards a more complex formulation of rod-and-frame performance in the schizophrenias. *Perceptual and Motor Skills*, **27**, 1111–1114.

Stannard, D. L. (1973) Ideological conflict on a psychiatric ward. *Psychiatry*, **36**, 143–156.

Stanton, A. H., and Schwartz, M. S. (1954) *The Mental Hospital*. Basic Books, New York.

Stoffelmayr, B. E., Faulkner, G. E., and Mitchell, W. S. (1973) The rehabilitation of chronic hospitalised patients — a comparative study of operant conditioning methods and social therapy techniques. Final report to Scottish Home and Health Department.

Van Putten, T., and May, P. R. A. (1976) Milieu therapy of the schizophrenias. In L. J. West, and D. E. Flinn, eds, *Treatment of Schizophrenia: Progress and Prospects*. Grune & Stratton, New York.

Wallace, C. J. (1976) Assessment of psychotic behaviour. In M. Hersen and A. S. Bellack, eds, *Behavioural Assessment: A Practical Handbook*. Pergamon, Oxford.

Williams, M., McGee, T., Kittleson, S., *et al.* (1962) An evaluation of an intensive group living program with schizophrenic patients. *Psychological Monographs*, **76**, 543.

Wing, J. K. (1961) A simple and reliable subclassification of chronic schizophrenia. *Journal of Mental Science*, **107**, 862–875.

Wing, J. K. (1975) Impairments on schizophrenia: a rational basis for social treatment. In R. D. Wirt, G. Winokur, and G. Roft, eds, *Life History Research in Psychopathology*. Vol. 4. University of Minnesota Press, Minneapolis.

Wing, J. K., and Brown, G. W. (1970) *Institutionalism and Schizophrenia*. Cambridge University Press, Cambridge.

Wing, J. K., and Hailey, A. M. (1972) *Evaluating a Community Psychiatric Service*. Oxford University Press, London.

Winkler, R. C. (1971) The relevance of economic theory and technology to token reinforcement systems. *Behaviour Research and Therapy*, **9**, 81–88.

Woods, P. A. and Cullen, C. (1983). Determinants of staff behaviour in long-term care. *Behavioural Psychotherapy* **11**, 4–17.

Wykes, T. (1982). A hostel-ward for 'new' long-stay patients: an evaluative study of 'a ward in a house'. In J. K. Wing, ed, Long-term community care: experience in a London borough. *Psychological Medicine*, Monograph Supplement 2, Cambridge University Press, Cambridge.

Zlotowski, M., and Cohen, D. (1968) Effects of environmental change upon behaviour of hospitalised schizophrenic patients. *Journal of Clinical Psychology*, **24**, 470–475.

Theory and Practice of Psychiatric Rehabilitation
Edited by F. N. Watts and D. H. Bennett
© 1983, John Wiley & Sons, Ltd.

# 8

# Industrial Therapy in the Mental Hospital

ROGER MORGAN

Work is an essential ingredient of normal, healthy life in our culture. People suffer if they are deprived of it (Hewitt, 1949). During illness it is accepted that people are temporarily excused by society from the obligation to work. This element of the 'sick role' is entirely appropriate to a patient's needs during short-term, recoverable illness but not so appropriate in chronic illness or permanent disability, if what began as a humane and sensible exemption turns later into a demoralizing deprivation.

The health-giving properties of work have been recognized since as long ago as Hippocrates and Galen, but the idea of using work as a treatment for the chronically ill conflicts so violently with the deeply held notions of staff and patients about the sick role, that it has tended to fall repeatedly into disrepute and disuse (Bennett, 1970). Its value has had to be rediscovered again and again by pioneers like Varrier-Jones and Woodhead (1918) in the case of the physically ill and John Conolly (1847) and Simon (1927) of Gutersloh in the case of the mentally ill.

An important development in Britain was the decision of the Medical Research Council's Social Psychiatry Unit to set up an experimental workshop in Banstead Hospital (Carstairs *et al.*, 1956). The Piercy Report (1956) on the rehabilitation training and resettlement of disabled persons took note of this development and recommended hospitals to provide 'simple factory work for deteriorated mental patients and low-grade defectives'. The Ministry of Health (1958) in turn took note of the Piercy Report and repeated several principles:

1.  Rehabilitation must be a single, continuous process from onset of illness to final resettlement. At the beginning of the process the emphasis is on the medical aspects, at the end it is on the work aspects.

2.  Treatment needs to be planned from the outset, intensive, planned for the individual patient, and to have a background of discipline.
3.  Simple factory work has been found valuable.
4.  Hours, pay, and working conditions should be as similar as possible to those in outside industry.
5.  The responsibility for organizing a continuous industrial scheme in any hospital should be given to a specially designated officer.

By 1967, 100 of the 122 hospitals circularized by Wansbrough and Miles (1968) had their own industrial therapy unit. Not only had the idea of using work as a form and a part of treatment come to be widely accepted, but a practicable way had been found of obtaining the necessary volume of work to employ the large numbers of patients who were now seen to need it. To put it at its lowest, simple repetitive work had begun to replace 'simple repetitive sitting' (Collins *et al.*, 1959).

## Rationale of Using Work as Treatment

Intelligently used, work can do more than just provide occupation instead of idleness. Aring (1974) reminds us that Goethe said, 'Employment is nature's physician and is essential to human happiness' and Freud said that 'work has a greater effect than any other technique of living in the direction of binding the individual more closely to reality'. Hewitt (1949) identified the attitude of mind of the disabled man as the largest single factor in determining his prospects of future employment. The Piercy Report (1956) said that the aim of rehabilitation is to restore full function and to reorientate the patient's outlook from that of an invalid to that of a responsible worker.

'Work by satisfying a sick person's need for a status does not, like the patient status, reinforce ideas of weakness and incompetence', said Bennett (1979). He quoted Jaques's (1967) definition of work as the exercise of judgement or discretion within prescribed limits in order to reach a goal or an objective. He goes on to discuss the difference between the prescribed limits and the discretionary content of work and recommends further study and sensitive use of the latter as particularly relevant to rehabilitation.

After listing its 'many uses in the treatment, rehabilitation and care of psychiatric patients' Bennett concludes that:

work can provide the psychiatrically ill with an opportunity for socially productive behaviour, it fosters social interaction and by recognising a sick person's capacity reduces the sense of social incompetence which he may experience as a patient. It helps him to structure his time usefully. By developing skills it prevents the development of secondary disabilities and prepares him to return to an acceptable position and function in society.

Quoting Jaques (1967), he says that work confronts a person with the actuality of his personal capacity to exercise judgement, to carry responsibility, and to achieve concrete and specific results. It gives him a continuous account of the correspondence between outside reality and the inner perception of that reality, as well as an account of the accuracy of his appraisal of himself. In short, a man's work does not satisfy his material needs alone. In a very deep sense it gives him a measure of his sanity.

## Functions

Bennett and Wing (1963) have listed 'at least five different functions' for a 'workshop for chronically disabled persons (whether the handicap is primarily physical or mental)'.

1. Occupation. 'The reasons for making industrial work available to occupy patients are humanitarian and economic. If they can earn a wage, no matter how small, and contribute to their own upkeep, they are helping to preserve their own freedom. They should as a matter of right be allowed to develop their personal independence.'
2. Education. 'The important point is that an external standard of quality is set by the manufacturer and that therefore the standard of work matters. The industrial workshop also makes possible other training procedures under realistic and sensible conditions. Timekeeping, workshop behaviour and routines, and inter-action with workmates and supervisors are matters in which psychiatric patients require considerable practice and polish. Secondary deterioration of habits and attitudes in more recently admitted patients can be prevented.'
3. Treatment. 'The constant and detailed supervision which is necessary for industrial work provides the activation needed by severely handicapped chronic schizo-phrenic patients.'
4. Assessment. 'The information that can be gained by observing a patient's behaviour, performance, and progress in a hospital workshop can be invaluable to the physician.'
5. Research. '. . .primary and secondary handicaps can be defined, their causes investigated, and their treatment or management assessed.'

Too many people make the mistake of regarding work as relevant only to the patient's occupational disabilities. It is well to remember that 'fundamentally economic work is a social activity' (Bennett, 1970) and to recognize the existence and value of the large social element in the work situation in an industrial unit.

The functions noted above by Bennett and Wing in 1963 relate only to work as a means of rehabilitation for the mentally ill. With time it has come to be realized that work also has another set of functions simply as an end in itself. A person who has a job and goes to work and earns his living is a first-class citizen. There is a sense in which this puts him in the *well* category by definition. Work confers on him membership of the working population, keeps him busy, and is one passport to social participation. This has been called the ego-preservative function of work.

**Principles and Policy**

In principle, life inside hospital should be made as much like life outside as possible for long-stay patients. Total likeness is neither practicable nor desirable, but any differences should require to be justified as necessary and therapeutic before adoption. This is because the greater the difference the more the artificial regime will tend to make the patient progressively less fit to take his place once again in the outside world. An ideal regime ought instead to make him progressively more fit to do so by providing practice and preparation under controlled conditions for the very kind of problems and stresses that he will encounter when discharged. 'Going to work regularly is one of the unavoidable pressures of daily life', and if one is aiming 'to reproduce real-life pressures by being no more, and little less, permissive than real life itself', work has to be 'The one really compulsory thing' (Shoenberg and Morgan, 1958).

There is no justification for separating men and women at work. There is no point in providing separate rehabilitation facilities for the mentally ill, the mentally retarded, and the physically disabled. Bennett and Wing (1963) have referred to the advantages of having mentally and physically disabled people working together and Early (1963) has noted that inclusion of mentally retarded subjects causes no administrative difficulties. The Department of Employment (1973) out of its vast experience of rehabilitation recommends more integration of different forms of disability.

Any industrial unit's clientele will have a wide range of disability and will need a correspondingly wide range of graded work experiences. A hospital should aim to develop a number of workplaces with different conditions (length of working day, complexity of jobs, amount of supervision, level of expectation, and system of pay) in each. For the most severely disabled patients conditions need to be very sheltered. For the most accomplished patients, soon to be discharged, conditions should be as similar to life in industry as possible (Ministry of Health, 1958). Intermediate grades of disability require intermediate conditions. Bennett (1975) writes,

Work alone is not enough. It must be paid work. Employment should not only be full; it should be varied and abundant. The . . . patient can then be moved as his capacity increases by gradual steps through a series of more complex and demanding tasks . . . Progress is slow and it may be almost imperceptible. Rehabilitation often takes years.'

This movement, whether up or down through the system, in response to a patient's proficiency, converts a static and stagnant situation into a dynamic flowing one with benefit to patients and staff. It demands some kind of 'central employment bureau so that work placements and work transfers can be instituted without delay' (Freudenberg, 1959). 'Psychiatric rehabilitation consists of a series of small steps, the outcome of each one of which is difficult to predict, but the result at each step determines whether it is possible to move on to the next' (Wing *et al.*, 1964, p. 22). Early (1968) offers us the model of a ladder and sees patients taking their steps up its rungs.

If progress up the rehabilitation ladder usually occurs in some accepted order, this enables a patient to perceive the total system concretely through his view of the progress made by others, and helps to get round the cognitive defects that often prevent him from grasping notions such as progress and the future in purely abstract terms.

This perception allied to his own current place in the system provides him with valuable orientation. Given some idea of where he stands and the possible directions in which he can move, it is easier for him gradually to readjust his attitudes and behaviour to serve his own interests. Motivation is impossible without information. Motivation is the key to the problem. Information may often need to be provided in non-verbal form. (Morgan, 1974)

It is highly desirable to provide a hierarchy of work experiences and to encourage and train rehabilitees to get to the top, but it would be foolish to expect that all will succeed. Most if not all are left with various degrees of residual disability at the end of the process, and it is equally desirable therefore to provide outlets at every level of the system to prevent the flow becoming blocked (Goldberg, 1974). It is not always obvious how a variety of different hospital jobs should be rated for their degree of difficulty and hence how each should be assigned to its correct place in the hierarchy; Philip and Moore (1976) give a useful account of how they did this.

Few patients are without previous experience of work. At the start of rehabilitation most bring to the situation some background of occupational and interpersonal skills, together with abilities and handicaps, likes and dislikes, faulty attitudes and unfortunate prejudices and occasionally an ambition for the future. At the start of rehabilitation the first requirement is to identify these factors by means of the most thorough and detailed assessment that can be devised and carried out. The assessment should consist of a formal interview and a number of tests of ability to carry out as many authentic jobs as may be available and relevant to the individual. The results of this assessment will indicate which available job is most suitable for that patient to do first. The first job need have no direct relevance to the patient's ultimate future. If he is anything more than mildly disabled, it will need to be simple and to offer reeducation and retraining in good work habits. Simple repetitive factory-type work, commonly called industrial therapy, can be admirable for this purpose. It can provide optimal conditions for staff to teach and patients to learn how to keep good time, grasp instructions, accept workshop discipline, get on with their workmates, not waste too much time smoking or in the toilet, and produce a reasonable standard of finished product.

Retraining in good work habits represents the first stage in a more or less long process of *preparation* for subsequent stages that lie ahead. Assessment determines the level at which preparation needs to begin. Repeated reassessment serves to monitor progress gained from previous preparation and to prescribe the nature and requirements of subsequent preparation. Through this process one is aiming tactically to engineer for each patient a success situation. We owe this valuable notion to Wadsworth *et al.* (1962d) who first documented the benefit to a patient of a taste of success, however small, after months or years of experiencing little or nothing but failure. To achieve this success situation, the job needs to be just within the patient's present capacity (Simon, 1927). That capacity does not remain a fixed quantity but increases with practice. The rate of increase, however, particularly in chronic schizophrenic patients, is very slow (O'Connor *et al.*, 1956). Their output on a new job is initially low and rises only very slowly, but it does go on rising long after a healthy person's output would have levelled out. Any estimate of a schizophrenic's work performance that is made in the course of his learning curve's long, slow climb is therefore bound to be an underestimate of his final capacity. For this reason it is justifiable and indeed desirable to leave a schizophrenic patient on the same job for longer than would be right for people with other diagnoses. If such a patient's job is changed too frequently he will never learn any job thoroughly, never reach his peak efficiency, never get the full benefit from feedback, and always be underestimated.

One mentally ill patient can be expected to produce on average about a quarter to a third as much as a healthy worker (Wadsworth *et al.*, 1962a). Slowness and lack of initiative make patients very poor producers and many are consequently unemployable. Without close attention to individual productivity the handicap cannot be overcome (Wadsworth *et al.*, 1962d).

The number of patients to be employed, the range of their needs, and the wish to provide periodical change dictate that a unit should provide patients with varied and abundant employment. Ideally there should always be slightly more work than staff and patients think they can manage (Simon, 1927). The usual way to obtain the necessary volume and variety of work is to approach local firms, some of which will be prepared to subcontract jobs to the industrial unit. This is a popular arrangement because the unit's responsibility is limited to supplying the labour and delivering the completed goods. Some units, because they lack subcontract work or out of unusual enterprise, manufacture and market their own products. A useful list of these units is given by Wansbrough and Miles (1968, pp. 75–80).

Valuable guidance on the many problems met in setting up an industrial unit is offered by Wadsworth *et al.* (1962d). In another paper (Wadsworth *et al.*, 1962c) they stress the need to simplify jobs before presenting them to schizophrenic patients.

The most suitable tasks for chronic schizophrenics are those in which the choices of reaction are kept to a bare minimum. There are obvious decrements in some aspects of attention and memory and with this in mind it follows that tasks should be deskilled as far as possible and the number of elements in any cycle should be kept down; this of course implies short cycle times. Short-cycle operations have the added advantage of keeping training and retraining times within the capabilities of the staff.

Failure to control these factors will result in increased wastage and overheads, and the need to repair incorrect work and reduce earnings. 'On the other hand simplifying and deskilling tasks helps the patient to attain a success situation.'

The deskilling that Wadsworth and colleagues recommend is precisely the strategy adopted in mass-production methods. It is interesting that their careful researches should have led them to the opinion that these methods, which it is fashionable to condemn as soul-destroying, are indeed suited to the clinical needs and limitations of disabled schizophrenics. It is also interesting to note their use of industrial jargon which clearly indicates their view that a high level of industrial expertise is as necessary to an industrial unit as to a factory.

This expertise is required in part to enable a unit to meet the normal commercial obligations of subcontract work. The three main requirements are that quality of workmanship should be satisfactory, agreed delivery dates should be met, and wastage should not be excessive. Unless a unit can meet these obligations, no firm will go on providing it with well-paid good-quality work. A firm's requirements are often seen as hostile to the interests of patients, but this is an illusion. In truth 'for patients to have to live up to standards of work set by people outside the hospital is of great benefit to them' (Bennett and Wing, 1963). Patients' interests may suffer only if in order to meet its industrial targets a unit resorts to retaining its most proficient workers instead of promoting them. Given suitable safeguards against this happening 'there is no law that states that the provision of work for patients cannot go hand in glove with truly therapeutic programmes' (Moores, 1973).

In reaching decisions about what a patient can or cannot do 'it should be a cardinal principle that no opinion should be expressed that does not depend on a practical trial of the patient's capacity' (Bennett and Wing, 1963). No rehabilitation programme is complete unless the occupational part of it is supported by appropriate attention to all the other rehabilitation needs of the patients (Bennett, 1975; Wing and Brown, 1970; Ekdawi, 1972). Medical supervision of a hospital rehabilitation programme including its industrial unit should be the responsibility of one designated consultant psychiatrist with a special interest in the subject (Ministry of Health, 1958; Bennett and Wing, 1963; Wing, 1963; Tunbridge Report, 1972).

## Practice

Attractive premises, attractive jobs, and a good imitation of authentic working conditions all help. Some patients benefit from doing more complicated jobs (often involving machinery) than are usually available (Wansbrough and Miles, 1968). Some patients need retraining in clerical work (Ekdawi *et al.*, 1968). Many patients need to be given predischarge practice in doing service-type jobs if these rather than production-line jobs are what are going to be obtainable for them on resettlement (Morgan, 1974). A valuable survey of existing conditions with detailed discussion of aims, pay systems, types of job, staffing, and other matters of policy and practice is provided by Wansbrough and Miles (1968).

Ultimately the service which a unit gives its patients hinges on the quantity and, more importantly, the quality of staff obtainable. The manager has a heavy burden and is likely to have all his time occupied in seeking contracts, negotiating with firms, instructing in job methods, ensuring quality control, selling the unit's own products, and other responsibilities. Ideally he needs previous industrial experience. Lack of time or lack of knowledge on the manager's part often leaves the personnel function of management partly or completely neglected. Yet it is of equal or even greater importance and includes such essential functions as pay, vocational needs, assessment and training, and monitoring the performance of rehabilitees. These functions can be exercised by another person who can be either a nursing officer or an occupational therapist with suitable training and outlook.

Supervision on the shop floor by people in closest contact with patients is also crucial. One asks that supervisors should combine some knowledge of psychiatric illness and disability with some knowledge of industrial methods, some teaching ability, healthy attitudes, a high level of expectation, and plenty of enthusiasm. 'Supervision must if anything, be of a higher standard than in open industry' (Bennett and Wing, 1963, quoting R. F. Scott, industrial psychologist). 'The occupational therapist must raise her level of expectation from the patients and diminish her protective role' (Bennett and Wing, 1963).

'A nurse's duty lies where the patient is and . . . if patients are being cared for in a factory that is where the nurse should be' (Early, 1968). A redeployment of all ward nurses to provide supervision of workshops as well as wards has been found to work well and offer many advantages (Morgan, 1976a).

It is commonly agreed that the fair price to charge a firm for subcontract work is the cost it would incur for direct labour if the job were done in its own premises (Moores, 1973). Wadsworth *et al.* (1962d) recommend charging an additional amount (up to 50 per cent) for overheads. The firm pays the negotiated and agreed amount to the industrial unit which then has the problem of dividing it up between the patients who did the work.

Freudenberg (1966) recommended four criteria for the payment of patients.

1. Patients must be paid the full industrial rate for the job, with basic pay during the preliminary training period.
2. They should receive graduated supplements.
3. Payment for work done in service departments should equal that in the industrial workshop.
4. There should always be a financial incentive for patients to seek employment outside the hospital.

Bennett (1970, p. 228) writes:

Judgments of capacity are often based on dubious and fallible assessments of a patient's clinical state while rewards are determined by biased moral evaluations of his behaviour worthiness or effort outside the work situation. Such judgments are unreliable and unfair. If, on the other hand, work is paid at rates which have been decided outside the hospital by industrial negotiation, expectation and rewards are balanced in a fair and normal manner. The sick patient who accepts paid work ceases to be a 'patient' and enters a productive social situation. Rates of pay must never be decided by the hospital staff. The patient worker is usually best paid on a piecework basis. . . . Rehabilitees must feel that . . . they are being fairly used. Practical experience shows that patients are never unaware of nor indifferent to the financial rewards of their work.

Methods of pay are considered in more detail by Wansbrough and Miles (1968) and Morgan (1974).

## Clinical Matters

Many doctors underestimate the value of work for the disabled. This is very understandable if their experience is of work purveyed on terms and conditions that are all wrong.

To take an extreme example no patient benefits from being banished month after month to some attic or some dungeon to dismantle telephones under the eye of some disillusioned supervisor for a flat rate of 30/- a week no matter how well or how badly the patient does. On the other hand patients stand to gain considerably if the premises are tolerable, the job methods are good, the pay system fosters motivation and the senior doctors and the senior nurses set an example by showing some sort of vested interest in seeing that the place does patients good. (Morgan, 1976b)

'If industrial work . . . becomes an end in itself the patient will ultimately benefit little if at all' (Early and Magnus, 1968). 'Work must be organized in a way which provides the maximum of social interaction and sense of group membership' (Bennett, 1970). 'A patient in a badly run industrial therapy unit performing the same routine job day in day out is little better off than in his previous ward-bound existence' (Moores, 1973).

In hospitals it is traditionally the doctor who is responsible for the standard of patient care. The doctor is likely to be highly trained in the technique of managing the care of people with short-term illness. It is a mistake to assume that this automatically equips him to manage the care of long-term illness. In rehabilitation it is necessary to adapt to a bigger case load, a larger number of more autonomous colleagues, and a time-scale of months and years instead of days or weeks. The ward-round in its traditional form is no longer the appropriate clinical management tool. It has even been submitted that the ward itself is not as appropriate a focus of clinical attention and nurse deployment (Morgan, 1976a) as the workplace.

A number of principles have been suggested which go some way to raise standards and to put rehabilitation in a valued position within the tradition of clinical work. Rehabilitation should start with assessment. A number of rating scales for the assessment of work performance have been published and the better known ones are reviewed by Van Allen and Loeber (1972) and by Wycherley and Ingham (1973), who recommend the scale described by Cheadle and Morgan (1972) as 'the most useful available'. This 16-item scale has since been extended by the addition of 9 further items by Griffiths (1973) whose further work will be mentioned below.

In Britain the Piercy (1956) and Tunbridge (1972) Reports have recommended a comprehensive system of case conferences in the management of rehabilitation programmes. All relevant staff and the rehabilitee should attend and contribute to such conferences. These should lead to the formulation of and commitment to individual treatment programmes which require regular updating in the light of repeated reassessment and progress. The presence of the work supervisor at the conference, together with his colleagues from other disciplines, symbolizes the place of work as an essential ingredient among others in a rehabilitation regime which depends for its efficiency on cooperation and coordination between the parties concerned. 'The consultant psychiatrist normally has responsibility for ensuring that the needs and progress of each patient are regularly reviewed' (Department of Health and Social Security, 1975).

The patient's progress is made easier and may only be possible if there is a variety of facilities in the hospital (Wing, 1963) arranged in a series of graded steps.

The last step should include a work situation which in its organisation, conditions of work, type of work and payment, approximates as closely as possible to a normal work situation outside hospital. Under such conditions it is not the supervisory staff alone who assess a patient's performance and ability. The patient himself assesses his own performance . . . anxiety and depression are overcome and confidence, which is the key to resettlement, is developed. (Bennett, 1970)

To serve the needs of the patient who is nearing discharge, a rehabilitation unit needs to have developed good working relationships with several key individuals and agencies outside hospital who provide further services for disabled persons. Open employment may be found through state services, newspaper advertisements, the social worker, or the community nurse. Anyone who knows which employers are sympathetic can usefully contribute. In Britain the disablement resettlement officer (DRO), an official of the Department of Employment charged with the resettlement of the disabled, is the key person who can provide access to further industrial rehabilitation, to vocational guidance and training, and to such sheltered employment as is yet available. The local DRO is usually very willing to attend the case conferences of patients being considered for discharge. The early results of experimental full-time appointments of DROs to a number of major hospitals appear promising, as are those from the development of sheltered working groups in open industry (Department of Employment, 1973; Early, 1975). Such arrangements provide initial support when the disabled person returns to normal employment.

## Results

Many pioneers of psychiatric rehabilitation were based in hospital (Department of Health and Social Security, 1975) and all used work as an essential, though never the only, ingredient of the regimes they founded. The general results of the Netherne resettlement unit were described by Bennett *et al.* (1961) and by Ekdawi (1972). Bristol's achievements have been described by Early and Magnus (1968) and by Early (1973). Wing *et al.* (1964) have given a detailed account of what is probably the utmost that can be achieved in the industrial rehabilitation of a sample of chronic schizophrenic patients given outstanding professional skill and uncommon access to special facilities. By comparing the regimes in hospitals A and B they showed that graded social and work preparation in hospital A enabled significantly more patients to avoid breaking down on discharge and to become successfully resettled in open employment. Goldberg (1967) warned that 'industrial therapy work does not do what its earlier proponents never claimed for it. Little or no improvement occurs in the primary handicaps of illness.' Yet Wing and Brown (1970), using patients as their own controls, noted clear evidence of improvement in primary handicaps when patients were given industrial work instead of nothing to do. Wadsworth *et al.* (1962b), investigating the slow pace and low output of schizophrenic patients and, comparing them with non-psychotic depressives, could find no evidence of abnormal fatiguability. Accordingly, they recommend a full day's work which has replaced in most hospitals the former regime of a little work and a little play, once thought to be all that patients could manage.

Esser and Chamberlain (1965) represent the experience of many who found that the introduction of work improved patients' interaction, cleanliness, and tidiness and also raised ward morale. Wing and Freudenberg (1961) were the first to describe the reemergence of florid symptoms of illness in patients receiving too much stimulation for their individual requirements. Miles (1971, 1972) studied 50 schizophrenic patients divided into two groups matched for age, length of stay, and severity of illness. She found that patients' willingness and ability to work improved more in a hospital's industrial unit than in its OT department. The industrial unit patients increased their stock of names and friendships. They had more reciprocal friendships and fewer of them were friendless. Friendships were made more often at work than elsewhere in the hospital. Cooperation between patients was a vital part of the work process, and so it was necessary for them to speak to each other. The staff encouraged them to rely on themselves and each other by regarding them as workers. Patients tended to take pride in helping newcomers and showing them what to do. These effects were not found in the OT department.

Hamilton (1963, 1964) studied three groups of male schizophrenics equated for age and length of illness and doing either OT or industrial work or nothing. He found that patients who were engaged in real or quasi-industrial work showed an improvement in intellectual performance. He noted their increased output and wages, their improved dexterity, faster reaction times, and improved social skills and regarded these as evidence of a learning or relearning process. Since the changes that he found in 'the availability of rational intellectual processes in male chronic schizophrenics were most pronounced in association with industrial therapeutic activities' he felt there was 'a strong case for linking them with factors which characterise industrial life: socially relevant useful and accepted work, male production-centred supervision, time-keeping and payment by results'. However, it should be noted that Hamilton's work has been criticized by Phillips (1964) because of the unsatisfactory nature of the measures used and the discrepancies between the initial performances of the two groups.

Walker et al. (1973), studying 13 mentally ill day patients who served as their own controls, confirmed previous reports (Wing and Freudenberg, 1961) that social reinforcement temporarily improves work performance, but found that those patients whose performance improves most become 'more impoverished and less acceptable to their relatives'. This finding has not been replicated. Harper and Chacon (1976), by contrast, used work performance as one of three indices of mental condition in evaluating the effects of different drugs on 34 male chronic schizophrenics and found it to be more sensitive than the two clinical ratings they employed.

Much early preoccupation with the differential response to work by paranoid and non-paranoid schizophrenic patients is summarized by O'Connor and Rawnsley (1959). 'A programme of treatment, interviews, social encouragement and incentives, designed to overcome the negativism of paranoid patients, served only to uncover it and hence to offset the non-specific therapeutic effect of the work situation.' They therefore recommended that 'chronic paranoid patients will respond better to a regimen in which socially rewarding experiences are made available but not thrust upon them, than to one in which they are immediately involved in person-to-person relationships'.

The motivation of the rehabilitee is of such central importance in determining how he does that it is surprising how little explicit attention it has received. Walker (1979) reviews the subject and 'wonders how seriously the application of effective incentives contingent on improved work performance has been taken in many units', even though 'it is well-known that the majority of psychiatric patients do respond to work related incentive systems'. He proceeded to allocate 32 patients between five different experimental incentive conditions and compared them with 9 patients under a control condition. Payment for merely attending work, regardless of performance standard, was singularly ineffective, yet it is 'a common industrial therapy practice'. Providing the subjects with a written statement of their output was equally ineffective. Social reinforcement by itself increased output but not significantly. Piece rate by itself increased output significantly to about the same extent as a flat rate pay increase plus social reinforcement. The biggest and most significant increase in productivity was obtained with a combination of piece rate and social reinforcement. Walker finally showed that a piece rate system is not difficult or time consuming to administer. His otherwise valuable study may be criticized for using small numbers of patients in unmatched subgroups differing in age, diagnosis, and initial performance level.

Morgan *et al.* (1974) studied 157 patients receiving piece rates before and after the level of permitted earnings in Britain rose from £2.00 to £4.50 per week and, surprisingly, found no connection between individual productivity and degree of clinical handicap. Individual productivity and earnings appeared to be influenced only by the total amount of work available, by the national and local regulations governing permitted earnings, and by the morale and organization of the workplace.

Bennett (1970) has remarked that the patient's attitude to work and his capacity for getting on with workmates and supervisors depend more upon personality factors than upon diagnostic or symptom categories. Simmons (1965) lists the personality characteristics that seem necessary if a worker is to maintain steady employment; they are a realistic perception of his own assets and liabilities, a capacity to overcome failure and perform under stress, some modicum of interpersonal competence, autonomy, independence, and an ability to make stable decisions and implement them effectively.

If comparatively little attention has been given to the effects of motivation and incentives on work performance, more attention has been paid to the bearing that work performance in hospital has on outcome after discharge. Several writers have analysed their results with different groups of patients in attempts to improve accuracy of prediction. Watts and Bennett (1977) studied the pre-illness work histories of 39 patients and came to two conclusions. The patient's ability to make a successful return to work is best indicated by his work record in the 2 years preceding admission; a tendency to seek work at that time will carry over and enable him to get a job after rehabilitation. Having got himself into a job, there is then a separate question about his ability to hold it; this depends upon deeper personality factors which are much better indicated by study of his early work history.

Esser and Chamberlain (1965) found 'no way of telling in advance which patients will become good workers on particular jobs' and noted that 'in most cases the capacity to work seems to be independent of intelligence and clinical picture'. Wing et al. (1964) paid particular attention to patients' attitudes to discharge and to work; before and during rehabilitation these attitudes had no predictive value, but once the process was complete they became significant predictors. Almost all authorities including the above have found that older patients do better than younger ones but no one has explained why.

Morgan and Cheadle (1974) analysed the records of 200 chronically ill patients and found that three variables gave the best prediction of long-term outcome. Work performance was the most sensitive. They combined this with ratings of clinical condition and social withdrawal (Wing, 1961) to derive an index which served to denote degree of disability and hence prognosis. Griffiths (1977) used his 26-item rating scale to analyse the predictive capacity of hospital work performance in greater detail. He studied 30 patients, divided the 26 items into five groups, and compared these with subsequent short-term work success in the community. Of the five groups, relationships with other patients and response to supervision had weak predictive value. Task-competence (8 items), motivation-enthusiasm (7 items) and confidence-initiative (only 3 items) correlated well with outcome. Age, intelligence, personality, or chronicity showed no correlation.

Most writers have studied only one diagnostic category, usually schizophrenia, or have found diagnosis to have no bearing on outcome. Early, however, consistently reports (Early, 1963; Early and Magnus, 1968; Early, 1973) that his paranoid schizophrenics do best, that affective disorders, other schizophrenics, the mentally retarded, and psychopaths are intermediate (in that order) and that idiopathic epileptics do worst.

## References

Aring, C. D. (1974) Work. *American Journal of Psychiatry*, **131**, 901–902.
Bennett, D. H. (1970) The value of work in psychiatric rehabilitation. *Social Psychiatry*, **5**, 224–230.

Bennett, D. H. (1975) The management of schizophrenia. In T. Silverstone and B. Barraclough, eds, *Contemporary Psychiatry*. Headley Bros, Ashford.

Bennett, D. H., Folkard, S., and Nicholson, A. (1961) A resettlement unit in a mental hospital. *Lancet*, **ii**, 539–542.

Bennett, D. H., and Wing, J. K. (1963) Sheltered workshops for the psychiatrically handicapped. In H. Freeman and J. Farndale, eds, *Current Trends in the Mental Health Services*. Macmillan, New York.

Carstairs, G. M., O'Connor, N., and Rawnsley, K. (1956) Organisation of a hospital workshop for chronic psychotic patients. *British Journal of Preventive and Social Medicine*, **10**, 136–140.

Cheadle, A. J., and Morgan, R. (1972) The measurement of work performance of psychiatric patients: a reappraisal. *British Journal of Psychiatry*, **120**, 437–441.

Collins, S. D., Fynn, S. J., Manners, F., and Morgan, R. (1959) Factory in a ward. *Lancet*, **ii**, 609–611.

Conolly, J. (1847, republished 1968) *The Construction and Government of Lunatic Asylums and Hospitals for the Insane*. Dawsons of Pall Mall, London.

Department of Employment (1973) *Sheltered Employment for Disabled People: A Consultative Document*. Department of Employment, London.

Department of Health and Social Security (1975) *Better Services for the Mentally Ill*. Cmnd 6233. HMSO, London.

Early, D. F. (1960) The Industrial Therapy Organisation (Bristol). *Lancet*, **ii**, 754–757.

Early, D. F. (1963) The Industrial Therapy Organisation (Bristol): The first two years. *Lancet*, **i**, 435–436.

Early, D. F. (1968) The role of industry in rehabilitation. In G. R. Daniel and H. L. Freeman, eds, *The Treatment of Mental Disorders in the Community*. Bailliere, Tindall, & Cassell, London.

Early, D. F. (1973) Industrial Therapy Organisation, 1966–1970. *Social Psychiatry*, **8**, 109–116.

Early, D. F. (1975) Sheltered groups in open industry. *Lancet*, **i**, 1370–1373.

Early, D. F., and Magnus, R. V. (1968) The Industrial Therapy Organisation (Bristol) 1960–65. *British Journal of Psychiatry*, **114**, 335–336.

Ekdawi, M. Y. (1972) The Netherne Resettlement Unit: results of ten years. *British Journal of Psychiatry*, **121**, 417–424.

Ekdawi, M. Y., Rogers, W., Slaughter, R. S., and Bennett, D. H. (1968) A patients record office in a mental hospital occupational programme. *British Journal of Psychiatry*, **114**, 1305–1306.

Esser, A. H., and Chamberlain, A. S. (1965) Productivitiy of chronic schizophrenics in a sheltered workshop. *Comprehensive Psychiatry*, **6**, 41–50.

Freudenberg, R. K. (1959) The sheltered workshop within the mental hospital. *Proceedings of the Second Annual Congress of the Association of Occupational Therapists*.

Freudenberg, R. K. (1966) Work therapy in psychiatric hospitals. Maudsley Bequest Lecture, 7 February 1966.

Goldberg, D. (1967) Rehabilitation of the chronically mentally ill in England. *Social Psychiatry*, **2**, 1–13.

Goldberg, D. (1974) Principles of rehabilitation. *Comprehensive Psychiatry*, **15**, 237–248.

Griffiths, R. D. P. (1973) A standardised assessment of the work behaviour of psychiatric patients. *British Journal of Psychiatry*, **123**, 403–408.

Griffiths, R. D. P. (1977) The prediction of psychiatric patients' work adjustment in the community. *British Journal of Social and Clinical Psychology*, **16**, 165–173.

Hamilton, V. (1963) IQ changes in chronic schizophrenia. *British Journal of Psychiatry*, **109**, 642–648.

Hamilton, V. (1964) Psychological changes in chronic schizophrenia. *British Journal of Psychiatry*, **110**, 283–286.

Harper, P., and Chacon, C. (1976) Work performance versus clinical assessment in the evaluation of phenothiazine therapy. *British Journal of Clinical Pharmacology*, **3**, 50–55.

Hewitt, M. (1949) The unemployed disabled man. *Lancet*, **ii**, 523.

Jacques, E. (1967) *Equitable Payment*. Penguin, London.

Miles, A. (1971) Long-stay schizophrenic patients in hospital workshops. *British Journal of Psychiatry*, **119**, 611–620.

Miles, A. (1972) The development of interpersonal relationships among long-stay patients in two hospital workshops. *British Journal of Medical Psychology*, **45**, 105–114.

Ministry of Health (1958) Rehabilitation in the hospital service and its relation to other services. HM (58) 57. Ministry of Health, London.

Moores, B. (1973) Work therapy. *Health and Social Services Journal*, **83**, 791–792.

Morgan, R. (1974) Industrial therapy. *British Journal of Hospital Medicine*, **11**, 231–242.

Morgan, R. (1976a) Patients have been let out of wards: why not nurses too? *British Journal of Psychiatry*, **129**, 82–85.

Morgan, R. (1976b) Rehabilitation. *National Schizophrenic Fellowship Newsletter*, July 1976, 28–32.

Morgan, R., and Cheadle, J. (1974) A scale of disability and prognosis in long-term mental illness. *British Journal of Psychiatry*, **125**, 475–478.

Morgan, R., Cheadle, J., and Staples, P. W. J. (1974) Cash in hand. *British Journal of Psychiatry*, **124**, 487–493.

O'Connor, N., Heron, A., and Carstairs, G. M. (1956) Work performance of chronic schizophrenics. *Occupational Psychology*, **30**, 153–164.

O'Connor, N., and Rawnsley, K. (1959) Incentives in paranoid and non-paranoid schizophrenics in a workshop. *British Journal of Medical Psychology*, **32**, 133–143.

Philip, A. E., and Moore, J. W. (1976) A job rating scale for use in psychiatric rehabilitation. *British Journal of Psychiatry*, **128**, 462–466.

Phillips, J. P. N. (1964) Activity programmes and chronic schizophrenics. *British Journal of Psychiatry*, **110**, 574–575.

Piercy Report (1956) *Report of the Committee of Enquiry on the Rehabilitation Training and Resettlement of Disabled Persons.* Cmnd 9883. HMSO, London.

Royal College of Psychiatrists (1980) *Psychiatric Rehabilitation in the 1980s: Report of Rehabilitation Working Party.* Royal College of Psychiatrists, London.

Shoenberg, E., and Morgan, R. (1958) Starting a schizophrenic unit. *Lancet*, **ii**, 412–415.

Simmons, O. G. (1965) *Work and Mental Illness.* John Wiley, New York.

Simon, H. (1927) Aktivers Krankenbehandlung in der Irrenanstalt. I. *Allgemeine Zeitschrift für Psychiatrie*, **87**, 97.

Tunbridge Report (1972) *Rehabilitation: Report of a Sub-committee of the Standing Medical Advisory Committee.* HMSO, London.

Van Allen, R., and Loeber, R. (1972) Work assessment of psychiatric patients: a critical review of published scales. *Canadian Journal of Behavioural Science*, **4**, 101–117.

Varrier-Jones, P. C., and Woodhead, G. S. (1918) Further experiences in colony treatment and aftercare. *Lancet*, **ii**, 133.

Wadsworth, W. V., Scott, R. F., and Wells, B. W. P. (1962a) The employability of chronic schizophrenics. *Journal of Mental Science*, **108**, 300–303.

Wadsworth, W. V., Wells, B. W. P., and Scott, R. F. (1962b) A comparative study of the fatiguability of a group of chronic schizophrenics and a group of hospitalised non-psychotic depressives. *Journal of Mental Science*, **108**, 304–308.

Wadsworth, W. V., Wells, B. W. P., and Scott, R. F. (1962c) A comparative study of chronic schizophrenics and normal subjects on a work task involving sequential operations. *Journal of Mental Science*, **108**, 309–316.

Wadsworth, W. V., Wells, B. W. P., and Scott, R. F. (1962d) The organisation of a sheltered workshop. *Journal of Mental Science*, **108**, 780–785.

Walker, L. G. (1979) The effect of some incentives on the work performance of psychiatric patients at a rehabilitation workshop. *British Journal of Psychiatry*, **134**, 427–435.

Walker, L. G., Adamson, F. A., Alexander, D. A., and Stoffelmayr, B. E. (1973) A negative correlation between improved production in psychiatric rehabilitation and social behaviour outside. *British Journal of Psychiatry*, **123**, 409–412.

Wansbrough, N., and Miles, A. (1968) *Industrial Therapy in Psychiatric Hospitals*. King's Fund, London.

Watts, F. N., and Bennett, D. H. (1977) Previous occupational stability as a predictor of employment after psychiatric rehabilitation. *Psychological Medicine*, **7**, 709–712.

Wing, J. K. (1961) A simple and reliable sub-classification of chronic schizophrenia. *Journal of Mental Science*, **107**, 862–875.

Wing, J. K. (1963) Rehabilitation of psychiatric patients. *British Journal of Psychiatry*, **109**, 635–641.

Wing, J. K., Bennett, D. H., and Denham, J. (1964) *The Industrial Rehabilitation of Long Stay Schizophrenic Patients*. Medical Research Council Memorandum No. 42, HMSO, London.

Wing, J. K., and Brown, G. W. (1970) *Institutionalism and Schizophrenia*. Cambridge University Press, London.

Wing, J. K., and Freudenberg, R. K. (1961) The response of severely ill chronic schizophrenic patients to social stimulation. *American Journal of Psychiatry*, **118**, 311–322.

Wycherley, R. J., and Ingham, J. (1973) Survey of rating scales in psychiatric hospitals. *Occupational Therapy*, **36**, 327–329.

# PART IV

*Community Rehabilitation*

Theory and Practice of Psychiatric Rehabilitation
Edited by F. N. Watts and D. H. Bennett
© 1983, John Wiley & Sons, Ltd.

# 9

# The Family, the Social Network, and Rehabilitation

JAMES BIRLEY and BARBARA L. HUDSON

## The Family

Each person entering any rehabilitation service has grown from a family which has profoundly influenced his past and will influence his future. In many instances, the family will still be closely involved, often in a very intimate way. In others, the family may be physically remote or even non-existent, but its past activities, and its current absence, still affect the person's present condition. Mr A, who has suffered from chronic schizophrenia for many years, lives in a hostel for 'down and out' men. His family have long since disowned and avoided him. He remains preoccupied with the idea of visiting the grave of his father, with whom he was on very bad terms and of whose death he was informed some time after the event. He has no idea how to find out where his father was buried, and has not followed up any practical suggestions for doing so. Approaches by his doctor to his family indicate clearly that they are equally preoccupied with the threat of his reappearance or of his visiting anywhere near their home.

The general importance of the family is traditionally recognized by psychiatrists and by most other experienced psychological healers. The systematic study of this phenomenon, along lines recognized as scientific, is still in its infancy. Families exert a gravitational pull, but the present laws of family gravity are decidedly pre-Newtonian. Much research has been done in this field, by workers with very varied theoretical viewpoints (Mishler and Waxler, 1968; Nye and Berardo, 1973; Minuchin, 1974; Jacob, 1975; Skynner, 1976; Beavers, 1977; Doane, 1978).

For the purposes of this review, we need to consider, first, family influences on certain important factors which affect the outcome of rehabilitation, and, secondly, attempts which need to be made to promote or control these influences to the patient's best advantage.

## Family Influence on Clinical State

An assumption underlying our approach is that, in psychiatric rehabilitation, there is no real distinction between 'treatment' and 'rehabilitation'. Psychiatric conditions are frequently unstable and, for this reason, require treatment. They differ, in this respect, from the comparatively stable handicaps of some physical illnesses or injuries, or mental handicap. The fluctuation of a person's mental state must be seen as the result of a dynamic process in which several interacting factors are involved, one of which is the actual rehabilitation programme itself. Indeed, total stability can sometimes be seen as the effect of the absence of some important provoking factors. There is no such thing as 'burnt-out' schizophrenia—only 'burnt-out' psychiatric staff and rehabilitation programmes. Findings concerning family influence on clinical state are, therefore, of importance to the study of rehabilitation.

While there have been many—and inconclusive—studies of family influences on the aetiology of schizophrenia, the work of Brown and Wing and their colleagues (1972) has provided some systematic evidence of family influence on the course of the illness. Beginning with the observation that patients did worse on returning to their own families than to non-family settings—an unfashionable observation at a time when families were the 'good objects' of psychosocial folklore—the studies were extended on the basis of sound empirical methodology for rating certain aspects of family interaction (Rutter and Brown, 1966; Brown and Rutter, 1966). Interviews with 'key relatives' soon after the admission of the patient, and soon after discharge, gave a wide variety of measures. Those influencing outcome were the numbers of critical comments and the degree of hostility expressed as judged not only by the content of the comments but also by the tone of voice and manner of expression. The combined measures gave an overall score of 'expressed emotion' (EE). The relapse rate, over a period of 9 months, of those patients with a high family EE score was very much higher (58 per cent) than of those with a lower score (16 per cent). Two 'protective factors' were identified for those patients living in 'high EE' families. The first was a physical separation or reduction of face-to-face contact to a total of less than 35 hours per week. The second was regular phenothiazine medication. These two factors operated independently of each other. When combined, the relapse rate of the patients in 'high EE' families was the same as for those in 'low EE' homes. These findings were subsequently replicated by Vaughn and Leff (1976), and the

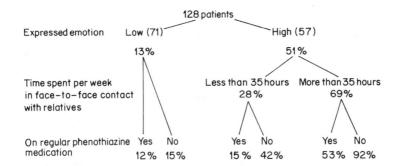

Figure 9.1   Nine-month relapse rate of a group of 128 schizophrenic patients. The percentages indicate the relapse rates for each sub-group of patients (adapted from Vaughn and Leff, 1976; reproduced by permission of the Royal College of Psychiatrists)

results of both studies are shown in Figure 9.1, adapted from their paper. They included in their study a small number of patients suffering from depressive states. These patients had a high relapse rate (53 per cent) and seemed to be highly sensitive to family criticism. Depressive relapse was related to a 'critical comments' score of 2 or more, compared to a score of 7 or more for families of patients suffering from schizophrenia. These findings would agree with suggestions that depressive states are associated with low self-esteem.

For both groups of patients, previous behaviour did not, of itself, predict relapse, but only through its effect on the family's attitudes. There was a significant correlation between the patients' previous behaviour disturbance and the relatives' critical comments, more marked for depressive patients (0.49) than for those suffering from schizophrenia (0.34).

These investigations indicate that family attitudes and feelings have a very considerable influence on the clinical course of patients suffering from schizophrenia or depressive states. Because of the numbers involved, the results on families of schizophrenic patients (total: 128) must be regarded as more definitive than those on families of depressed patients (total: 30). The subsequent studies of Brown and Harris (1978), although in a somewhat different context, suggest that a woman's relationship to her 'key relative' — her 'confidant' (usually her spouse) — may have an important role in the aetiology and course of a depressive state.

It is important to emphasize that, in these studies, the course of the patient's illness was measured by 'clinical relapse', not by 'readmission'. These events are often correlated, especially in psychotic states, but by no means completely. Furthermore, the social and family processes associated with relapse are probably somewhat different to those associated with readmission. In the latter case, concepts of 'family tolerance' have been investigated.

Freeman and Simmons (1963) in their classic study defined tolerance as 'the continued acceptance of the former patient by his family members, even when he fails to perform instrumental roles'. They found that 'tolerance', defined in this way, was not associated with readmission. Greenley (1979a) has recently reviewed this field and reported a study which related readmission to the family's anxieties, in particular their fear of the patient's symptomatic behaviour, and their doubts of their own ability to control the patient. These anxieties were found to be significantly associated with the patient's early readmission. Previous alarming behaviour was not of itself related to readmission but was significantly associated with family fears about the patient's future behaviour. Thus 'tolerance' as defined by Greenley has some features in common with 'expressed emotion' as defined by Brown and his colleagues.

## Family Influence on Patients' Attitudes

The influence of a person's attitude on the outcome of rehabilitation was shown clearly by Wing (1966) in a study of men attending an industrial rehabilitation unit. Those who started with an 'initially realistic and constructive' attitude did well, whereas those with an 'unconstructive attitude' did poorly. This effect applied to all groups whatever the diagnosis, physical or psychiatric. Those with constructive attitudes were able to perceive their circumstances as alterable and were determined to attain some independence in the future. They were more confident in themselves and realistic in their aims. During the course of their rehabilitation, they acquired increased confidence, responding to the social pressures of the unit itself.

Any psychiatric patient, and particularly someone with a chronic and disabling illness, requires to go through some realistic reappraisal of his situation, and this process may well be a painful one. Amongst other things, it will involve some awareness that he has been, and perhaps still is, 'ill', and his improvement depends upon continuing contact with a medical service; that he needs a period of organized activity; that progress may be slow and persistence will be needed; and that independence may be a possibility, but that this may involve some alteration and perhaps lowering of original expectations for a job and an income. In the process of this reappraisal and in the development of 'constructive attitudes', the 'social pressures' from the family are presumably very important.

Two studies (Freeman and Simmons, 1963; Greenley, 1979b) have reported significant positive associations between a family's expectations concerning a patient's future employment and the actual employment performance during the follow-up period. In contrast, they found no such association concerning a patient's symptomatic state at follow-up and the family's expectations of symptoms. These findings could be taken to mean merely that families are better at predicting their sick relative's role performance than his psychiatric state.

It seems more likely that the family actually exerts an influence on the patient's own attitudes and performance at work. Certainly, this is our own impression, derived from clinical experience.

### Sick Role

A family can affect the patient's view of himself as 'sick' either by denial of any such notion, or by an overemphasis on illness. A status quo may have been reached at home, with the patient doing little or nothing, but with all parties anxious that any change may make things worse rather than better. Thus, the patient may feel that he has 'no need' for treatment or that he is 'too ill' to do any work. The family may also have perfectly understandable anxieties about the process of rehabilitation itself. The other people attending the service may be 'much worse' than the patient, and seem to be frightening. Or the actual style of the programme may be very demanding. Many patients have considerable social anxieties, and limited vocabularies, and are somewhat retarded. For such people, group meetings may pose a considerable threat. Their families may feel the same anxieties and reinforce the patients' own. Miss B, a young girl with an IQ of 70 developed schizophrenia in her late teens. She was seen by her family as very naive and easily 'led astray'. She was extremely shy, and sexually provocative in a childish fashion. After her initial admission, she was referred to a day hospital very near her home. After the first day, Miss B told her family that an old man had touched her skirt and that she did not want to go any more. The family strongly supported her decision and Miss B then stayed at home for 15 years, with occasional brief admissions to hospital. Her most recent admission was a longer one, partly because her parents' tolerance was wearing thin and they were keen for her to attend a day centre, and partly because she seemed to be wanting to be more independent. Her sexually provocative behaviour was rather more obvious, and she was quite pleased with having attracted some boyfriends in the protected environment of the hospital. Very soon, however, she complained of undesirable attentions from an older man. Her parents immediately agreed to her staying at home.

### Lowered Expectations

For many patients, the lowering of expectations presents problems both for themselves and for their families. This is particularly obvious with intelligent or middle-class patients. The work offered, at least at the initial stages of most rehabilitation programmes, is often repetitive and boring, but the problem of lowered expectations is not confined to any particular situation, and, in many cases, it is a greater problem for the family than for the patient. Mr C, the son of professional parents, developed schizophrenia soon after leaving university. He had obtained a place there partly through parental influence, and his undergraduate career had been disheartening, both academically and socially. Although not clinically disabled, he could not find work which was 'suitable', in the sense of being approved by his family. His doctor suggested that he should take an unskilled portering job, which he readily accepted. His parents, however, were distressed by this move, and the doctor had to reassure them that it was in their son's best interests and that there were good medical grounds for recommending this course of action as an important first step. The patient found the work congenial, became much more confident, and went on to train successfully as a librarian.

### Effect of Family Attitudes on the Staff of the Rehabilitation Programme

So far, we have considered family attitudes as they might influence the patient directly. However, we need also to consider the effect of family attitudes on the staff involved in rehabilitation. To some extent, the patient becomes involved in 'two families', one being his 'real' family, and the other his 'foster family' in the rehabilitation programme. His own family may be unduly anxious about a potential separation, or, and this is just as common, may look forward to sharing the burden and be unduly optimistic about the prospects of their own relief. The staff, on the other hand, may be ready to take on the 'patient', but reluctant to take on 'the family'. The situation has potential for creating misunderstandings and rivalries. Both groups may feel that the other does not 'really understand' the patient or the difficulties which he creates, and their consequent burden. Sometimes, this makes it difficult for staff and family to work together.

Miss D is aged 18 and has not worked since leaving school 2 years ago. Her IQ is around 70 and her attendance at school was very poor for some years. Her intelligent younger sister is also not attending school. Mr D, her father, suffers from schizophrenia, and attended the day hospital for a long period before returning home, clinically improved but unemployed. Mrs D sees herself as an embittered, struggling, sexually frustrated, unappreciated woman with 3 'patients' on her hands. She finds her husband lazy, irritable, and physically repulsive. Their sex life ceased 5 years ago. A psychiatrist feels that Miss D could benefit from attending the day hospital. Mrs D is convinced that it will do her daughter no more good than it did her husband. The day hospital staff are somewhat inclined to agree with Mrs D whom they regard as an angry woman who undermines all their efforts and regards them as rivals for control of the family. Their tolerance of Miss D and their decision as to whether she should be taken on for a long spell of rehabilitation is influenced by whether they feel they can tolerate another long spell of her mother, who will be a convenient scapegoat if their efforts are unsuccessful.

## Effect of Family Influence on Patients' Financial Rewards

It should not be forgotten that one of the most important rewards in the rehabilitation procedures is a financial one. Patients respond to financial rewards in workshop situations (Walker, 1979), and, conversely, the outcome of rehabilitation is affected by the prospect of earning, in real terms, no more or even less money than that obtainable through social security or sickness benefits (Lamb and Rogawski, 1978). There are several ways in which a family 'reward' the progress of the patient in the rehabilitation programme and finance is one of the most important. There may be conflict as to how the patient should spend his money, and this is seen most obviously when the money is 'taken away' to go to another 'unrewarding' member of the family. This is what may happen to persons who are divorced or separated. Many men bitterly resent their earnings being 'taken away' to contribute towards maintenance of their wife and/or children, when these contributions have, during their unemployment, been paid by social security payments.

## The Involvement of the Family

From the point of view of our presentation, work with families can be conceptualized as having two broad aims, the prevention of relapse, and the encouragement of behaviour which promotes successful rehabilitation and the discouragement of behaviour which prevents this process.

## Prevention of Relapse

The origins of a 'high EE' are not known, but a genetic theory can be discounted. The phenomenon and its consequences can be found regardless of whether the key relative is a spouse or a first-degree relative. It is reasonable to suppose that 'EE' may derive from the many conflicting and painful emotions consequent upon having a relative with a mental illness. The classic studies of Clausen and Yarrow and their colleagues (Clausen and Yarrow, 1955; Yarrow et al., 1955a, 1955b) have given us a vivid description of the impact of a husband's 'developing' mental illness on the spouse.

The equally important research of Creer and Wing (1974) has documented the very considerable burden borne by a family, usually without complaint, which contains a relative suffering from schizophrenia. Very often, amidst the confusion, relatives come to blame themselves and compensate for this by sacrificing their own lives, and those of other family members, to the 'over-care' of their sick relative. Sometimes, indeed, mental health professionals reinforce this sense of guilt among relatives. The family may become controlled by its sickest member. This leads to bitter feelings of unfairness and lack of appreciation. The resentment then turns back into the family and on to the patient, and a vicious circle builds up of 'over-concern' and 'over-criticism'.

Potentially helpful approaches, therefore, depend upon trying to help the family to understand what is going on, and how it is affecting the patient, and attempting, where appropriate, to alter things. In the first place, clarification and explanation are important, about the nature of the patient's illness, the sort of behaviour which can be expected, the aims and limitations of treatment, and the function, where relevant, of medication.

There have been several reports of groups of relatives with a special emphasis on problem solving (Dincin, 1975; Attwood and Williams, 1978; Priestley, 1979). These authors all emphasize the important function of information: about the services, welfare benefits, emergency help, accommodation, and other practical matters. In addition, they emphasize the building up of mutual trust and confidence so that feelings of anger, shame, and self-recrimination can be expressed and shared: anger with doctors and nurses as well as with the patient; shame at having an ill family member and at their own intolerance, and ventilation of 'what went wrong', 'will it affect other children and grandchildren', and 'how will he manage when we die'. Dincin also emphasizes the importance of allowing and encouraging relatives to lead a life of their own, independent of their sick family member, and thus reducing their burden of guilty over-solicitude.

Another important effect of continuing contact between professionals and the family is that it allows for the anticipation of crises, or at least a more rapid response to them when these do occur. One of the most damaging and disheartening experiences for a family is to feel abandoned at a time of crisis — which often occurs at inconvenient hours. Prompt assistance in a crisis, whatever its nature, or knowledge that such is available, should be regarded as an essential component of the family treatment, and an important means of reducing a family's anxieties.

'Family therapy' is another possible approach, of which there are a number of enthusiastic proponents. Recent reviews have given a 'not proven' verdict (Wells *et al.*, 1972; Gurman and Kniskern, 1977) but lean towards a favourable judgement. Gurman (1973) had previously been less sure, and at least one reviewer dissents from the more usual optimistic view (De Witt, 1978). Certainly, caution is required when one member of the family is mentally ill. Such a situation, according to Crowe (1978), makes for a 'poor prognosis'. Many patients may not be sufficiently robust to cope with the tough, active style of most contemporary family therapy with its emphasis on confrontation, role play, and paradoxical injunctions.

Both the 'self-help, problem-solving and sharing groups' and 'family therapy' can be said to have two broad aims in preventing relapse. The first is to have some general effect on family 'attitudes and atmosphere'. The second is to alter specific attitudes or 'bits of behaviour'. The two functions are clearly related and it is possible that the enthusiasm for newer forms of family therapy derives from their permitting goals which are more focused and relate more to current behaviour than are those prescribed by traditional dynamic psychotherapy. Priestley, writing from the 'self-help group' viewpoint, emphasizes this issue.

A survey of the problems experienced by relatives showed that one of the principal complaints was that little advice was given on specific difficulties of 'management'. Questions on such subjects were ignored by professional advisers or answered unhelpfully. If there are no immediate rules on how to cope with psychotic or withdrawn behaviour, the professional adviser may feel helpless and may, as a result, appear abrupt, even aggressive. The relatives may then withdraw from any further questions about very real and distressing problems. The relationships need to be changed to one of mutual learning and contribution to possible solutions.

Two specific 'bits of behaviour' which emerge as important from the studies of relapse in schizophrenia are withdrawal and medication. It is clear from the revealing studies of Creer and Wing that some relatives find a patient's 'negative behaviour' very difficult to tolerate, and this includes withdrawal. At the same time, it clearly has a 'protective' function. Therefore, one aim for the family may be to increase their own tolerance of withdrawal, and in particular they should be helped to see that it does not necessarily imply hostility to or lack of interest in the family—many withdrawn patients are extremely, and even embarrassingly, observant. The patient may need to be encouraged to withdraw more from the family.

The importance of continued medication sets particular problems for the family. There is a delicate balance between intensive and active scrutiny, confirming the patient's sick role, and failing to observe or detect whether the patient is taking his or her pills, or showing early warning signs of relapse. One of the factors contributing to 'non-compliance' is that neither relatives nor patients understand the importance of drugs, nor are they warned adequately about minor or major side-effects. It is well known that only a very small proportion of any form of medical advice is accurately retained by patients or relatives. Therefore, a once-and-for-all consultation about medication is likely to be far less effective than continued contact and clarification with the family. In some cases, this is essential as the important observations of regular medication and of signs of relapse or of drug toxicity are much more likely to be made in the home than in an outpatient consultation.

The Encouragement of Behaviour which Promotes Successful Rehabilitation and the Discouragement of Behaviour which Prevents this Process.

Many of the authors already mentioned have stressed the need to keep continued communication between the patient's family and their social network. In this way, some of the problems related to changing attitudes, to tolerance of greater autonomy of the patient, to possible rivalries between the therapeutic team and the family, and other such general difficulties, can be reduced in intensity, if not actually overcome. In addition, a more focused attempt can be made to alter certain specific 'attitudes' or 'behaviour' by involving the family in a more structured programme.

Traditionally, these programmes have been aimed at the 'patient', but they have often involved a considerable alteration in the family's usual responses to the patient's behaviour. They can thus be regarded as a form of family therapy. The emphasis is on the careful analysis of antecedents and consequences of target behaviours, and on monitoring the effects of altering these. Such programmes have the advantage over hospital intervention in that they offer the possibility of behaviour change that is more enduring and more likely to generalize. Further, the home-based assessment, which includes consultation with the family and the patient as to what their priorities are, ensures that the behaviours encouraged are the ones that are important for successful functioning in a particular person's particular social milieu.

The main thrust of this approach has been in relation to child behaviour problems (see, for example, McAuley and McAuley, 1977; Herbert, 1978; Patterson, 1973), but there are also reports of successful work with a variety of adult problems. These include alcoholism (Hunt and Azrin, 1973; Miller, 1972; Cheek et al., 1971a), neurodermatitis (Walton, 1960), depression (Liberman and Raskin, 1971; McLean et al., 1973). Catts and McConaghy (1975) taught the relatives of obsessional patients to continue the behavioural treatment begun in hospital. Mathews and colleagues (1977) developed a training programme for the spouses of agoraphobics, including an instruction manual, and their results showed significant gains over individual and clinic-based treatment.

Several workers have begun to explore this approach with schizophrenic patients in the home setting. The first such experiment was by Cheek et al., (1971b) who trained parents to use behavioural procedures with 'young ambulant schizophrenics'. However, it seems likely that this American study involved patients who were considerably less handicapped than those in the two British studies by Hudson (1975) and Atkinson (1977). The earlier of these was undertaken mainly to assess feasibility and to identify likely problems, and in fact setting up a behavioural programme for this patient group proved even more difficult than had been foreseen. Obstacles included disagreement about suitable goals, refusal to cooperate, and ill-health in family members. Some problems were largely connected with the patients' illness: their lack of insight, and the families' experience of unpredictable behaviour and relapse, and their adaptation over time to the problems of living with schizophrenia. However, some of the difficulties were to do with working in the home setting: lack of authority to persuade patients and relatives to take part, and the handicapping effects of poor educational background, domestic crises, and low motivation to seek change. All of these latter obstacles are well documented in the literature on behavioural family work (see, for example, Thomas and Walter, 1973; Tharp and Wetzel, 1969; McAuley and McAuley, 1980). Where programmes were put into effect—and the numbers are too small for valid conclusions—it appeared that simple behavioural change goals could be achieved; length of illness and amount of handicap seemed less relevant than the presence of florid symptoms. Atkinson (1977) compared the effectiveness of behavioural programmes with individuals as against those in which families also took part. Preliminary results show that family involvement is indeed of considerable value. However, both Hudson and Atkinson emphasize that this approach is not a panacea where the rehabilitation of chronic psychotic patients is concerned.

## Mentally Ill Relatives

Some relatives need psychiatric treatment for themselves. On the bases of genetics, the strains of having a mentally ill relative, associative mating, and the propinquity of sharing the same psychiatric facilities, the risk of mental illness for a patient's close relative is considerably higher than normal. It is not surprising, therefore, that 'involvement of the family' involves psychiatric treatment of more than one member. It is often difficult to decide whether all members of the family are best treated by one service or should be 'distributed' to different ones. Often there is very little choice in this matter. Most facilities have experience of looking after 'pairs' or spouses who both have chronic psychotic illness. In many cases, these marriages seem to be remarkably supportive, but they are presumably 'survivors' amongst many other pairs which have been far less successful. In Hudson's series of twelve families, there were three key relatives who were severely disturbed. Although families with many mentally ill members clearly meet particular problems, our impression is that many of the problems arise as much from the personalities involved, and their interaction, as from the disturbances resulting from mental illness.

## The Social Network: Friends, Neighbours, and Volunteers

In Western society, the interpersonal context is the network rather than the community or the group and, especially in urban areas where the network is loose knit, it is difficult to locate key figures whose influence in helping the patient can be exploited. The family is not contained within a larger kin group, rather it is connected to a number of other groups and institutions and, according to Bott (1971), 'when a family lives in a network, its members put all their emotional eggs in the family basket'. Contacts change and may diminish if families move from one area to another (Bott, 1957). Isolation is intensified for families with a sick member, who may adapt to real or imagined stigma by 'disassociation' (Lomas, 1967; Davis, 1963; National Schizophrenia Fellowship, 1974).

Nevertheless, friends are the people with whom most people pursue interests and make new contacts. For the single person, especially, friends provide emotional support. Truly successful reintegration into the community ('normalization') must include entry into a friendship group. The psychiatric and sociological literature has little to say on the subject. Horwitz (1978) comments on the lack of research into the wider social network in dealing with illness. He found that people with emotional difficulties — even the married — were more likely to turn to friends than to relatives.

Research in several fields has pointed to the potential contribution of non-professionals and family members to the wellbeing of the psychiatric patient. Malan et al., (1975) report on the 'therapeutic relationships of everyday life' and their contribution to positive change; and Brown and Harris (1978) have shown the value of a close confiding relationship in protecting against the onset of psychiatric disorder in the face of severe difficulties or life events. Although the latter group found that most 'confidants' were spouses, they could also be friends.

Research in the field of counselling and psychotherapy has shown that, for a large proportion of clients, successful outcome bears a close relationship to the levels of certain 'core conditions' of interpersonal behaviour on the part of the therapist. These conditions, which account for some 50 per cent of the variance in outcome (Fischer, 1978), are the expression of empathy (conveying accurately and sensitively the feelings of the other person), non-possessive warmth, and facilitative genuiness (self-congruence, the opposite of 'phoney') (Truax and Mitchell, 1971; Carkhuff, 1969). Several workers have observed that there are many people outside the helping professions who are 'naturally therapeutic' (Carkhuff, 1969). Bergin (1971) noted that neighbours often unwittingly applied effective therapeutic approaches and could be as helpful or more so than some therapists. Collins and Pancoast (1976) found that, besides providing help themselves, these unofficial therapists seem to bring their 'clients' into 'natural helping networks', and these authors suggest that such people should be identified and supported since they are already involved with people at risk. Such advice is not easy to put into practice, but some impression can be gained if patients are encouraged to talk about their associates, and social workers and community nurses may meet them in the patient's home setting. Unfortunately, just as prolonged hospitalization may mean losing one's place in the family, so too it can mean becoming detached from the network of friends and acquaintances. It should be added that a large proportion of psychiatric patients appear to lack the skills required for initiating and sustaining social relationships (Trower et al., 1978). For these reasons, as well as the stigma of mental illness, the patient leaving hospital is likely to lack friends. Two thirds of residents in long-stay hostels investigated by Ryan and Hewett (1976) had no friends, and only one quarter had visited a friend in the month before the survey. Henderson (1977) found that depressed patients, in comparison with controls, had fewer attachment figures, fewer contacts with people outside their own household, and fewer good friends, and the study by McCowan and Wilder (1975) paints a similarly bleak picture.

Can an isolated person be helped to make friends? There is some evidence that he can be helped to recover or learn basic social skills (Marzillier, 1978; Shepherd, 1978), but the social skills training approach has not yet been shown to be effective in terms of social contacts beyond the superficial level, and indeed the problem of generalizing the gains in these programmes to the person's natural environment has still to be overcome. Much depends, therefore, on motivating other people in the community to offer their time and concern. Volunteers may provide this. Research into their actual and potential contribution has barely begun, though their work with the mentally ill is mentioned enthusiastically in several reports (Rahmer, 1973; Ball, 1976; Bruce et al., 1976). The results of evaluative research to date are promising (Dartington, 1978; Gay and Mitkeathley, 1979; Karlsruher, 1974). One attempt to encourage volunteering in a deprived neighbourhood (Holland, 1979) was only moderately successful: a key problem was that it was not acceptable in the culture—giving one's time without being paid was seen as a luxury. Also, Holland points to one important reservation in the use of volunteers: 'Good neighbourliness should not be an excuse for the unprivileged to look after themselves on the cheap.'

Most volunteer schemes are administered by paid organizers. Problems abound in recruitment, role differentiation, and selection. Most workers agree that it is important to 'counsel out' people with unrealistic expectations or who might be likely because of personal difficulties to place stress on those they are seeking to help. Tasks must be designed which not only fulfil client needs but also offer some satisfaction to the volunteer. Though a brief 'induction' period would seem necessary for volunteers dealing with people who suffer from mental illnesses, formal training is not usually recommended since it could create a cadre of semi-professionals no longer able to offer the kind of 'befriending' that is envisaged by most schemes. It would seem that the contrived friendship with a volunteer can become hard to distinguish from a 'natural' friendship if volunteer and client are well matched and the introduction has been well handled (Davies, 1977).

Segal and Aviram (1978) have identified key factors in the successful integration into the community of residents in sheltered accommodation. For our present discussion, the most interesting findings concern the patients' access to and participation in social contacts outside their hostel, as well as 'going out'. Of particular importance for integration were a variety of neighbourhood features, but the most influential of all was the response of neighbours. The hypothesis that positive neighbour response simply reflected the neighbours' tolerance of deviance was not supported, however; the key factor was whether the neighbours made contact with the residents as single individuals rather than as a group. This confirms in the community the notion of the harmfulness of 'batch' treatment, whereby the possessor of deviant attributes is seen primarily in terms of those attributes rather than of the many others which he possesses as a person (Goffman, 1962; King *et al.*, 1971).

## Conclusions

We would like to end with three general points.

First, it cannot be stressed too often that rehabilitation begins while the patient is still on the ward. O'Brien and Azrin (1973) have demonstrated how much can be achieved even in cases where the patient and his family have become estranged. Relatives received definite, individual requests to visit the hospital and to invite the patient for trial visits. The visits were arranged so as to allow the relatives to curtail the meeting when they wished, and the patients were assisted in developing behaviours that would help to make the occasion a pleasant one for both parties. Goldstein and Baer (1976) applied similar principles in a successful drive to increase the patients' contacts by correspondence. Hollingsworth and Sokol (1978) propose pre-discharge conferences to include both relatives and close friends in order to discuss plans and encourage understanding and cooperation in rehabilitation.

Secondly, rather than focusing on the ways in which the patient's associates can be 'psychonoxious', let us turn the thing upside-down and concentrate on those special qualities of the people who help to prevent relapse and who ease the patient out of the sick role. Ultimately, it is upon these people that truly successful community rehabilitation depends, and professional workers have much to learn from them.

Finally, while not claiming in any way to have reviewed or to be aware of all the literature, we have been impressed by the varied and heterogeneous approaches which have been used both to influence and to measure family interaction. It is a subject which is as familiar to social anthropologists as to psychiatrists, psychologists, and sociologists. The 'importance of the family and social network' is in danger of becoming a slogan in psychiatry. It needs to be demystified through systematic research, and there are ample opportunities for both observational and experimental studies.

## References

Atkinson, J. M. (1977) Indications for family involvement in a home-based behavioural programme with chronic schizophrenic patients. Paper delivered at the Annual

Conference of the British Association for Behavioural Psychotherapy, Keele University, 23 July.

Attwood, N., and Williams, M. E. D. (1978) Group support for the families of the mentally ill. *Schizophrenia Bulletin*, **4**, 415–425.

Ball, M. (1976) *Young People as Volunteers*. The Volunteer Centre, London.

Beavers, W. R. (1977) *Psychotherapy and Growth: A Family Systems Perspective*. Brunner Mazel, New York.

Bergin, A. E. (1971) The evaluation of therapeutic outcome. In A. E. Bergin and S. L. Garfield, eds, *Handbook of Psychotherapy and Behaviour Change*. John Wiley, New York.

Bott, E. (1957) *Family and Social Network*. Tavistock, London.

Bott, E. (1971) Family and crisis. In J. D. Sutherland, ed., *Towards Community Mental Health*. Tavistock, London.

Brown, G. W., Birley, J. L. T., and Wing, J. K. (1972) Influence of family life on the course of schizophrenic disorders: a replication. *British Journal of Psychiatry*, **121**, 241–258.

Brown, G. W., and Harris, T. (1978) *The Social Origins of Depression*. Tavistock, London.

Brown, G. W., and Rutter, M. (1966) The measurement of family activities and relationships: a methodological study. *Human Relations*, **19**, 241–263.

Bruce, M., Darville, G., Duncan, S., Rankin, M., and Thompson, M. (1976) *Creative Partnerships: A Study in Leicestershire of Voluntary Community Involvement*. The Volunteer Centre, London.

Carkhuff, R. R. (1969) *Helping and Human Relations*, Vol. 1. Hall, New York.

Catts, S., and McConaghy, N. (1975) Ritual prevention in the treatment of obsessive compulsive neurosis. *Australian and New Zealand Journal of Psychiatry*, **9**, 37–41.

Cheek, F. E., Franks, C. M., Laucius, J., and Birtle, W. (1971a) Behaviour modification training for wives of alcoholics. *Quarterly Journal of Studies in Alcohol*, **32**, 456–461.

Cheek, F. E., Laucius, J., Mahncke, M., and Beck, R. (1971b) A behaviour modification training program for parents of convalescent schizophrenics. In R. Rubin, H. Fensterheim, A. Layanais, and C. Franks, eds, *Advances in Behaviour Therapy*. Academic Press, New York.

Clausen, J. A., and Yarrow, M. R. (1955) Paths to the mental hospital. *Journal of Social Issues*, **11**, 25–32.

Collins, A. M., and Pancoast, D. L. (1976) *Natural Helping Networks: A Strategy for Prevention*. NASW, New York.

Creer, C., and Wing, J. K. (1974) *Schizophrenia at Home*. National Schizophrenia Fellowship, London.

Crowe, M. J. (1978) Behavioural approaches to marital and family therapy. In R. Gaind and B. L. Hudson, eds, *Current Themes in Psychiatry*, Vol. 1. Macmillan, London.

Dartington, T. (1978) *Volunteers and Psychiatric Aftercare*. The Volunteer Centre and MIND, London.

Davies, M. (1977) *Support Systems for Social Work*. Routledge & Kegan Paul, London.

Davis, F. (1963) *Passage through Crisis: Polio Victims and their Families*. Bobbs-Merrill, New York.

De Witt, K. L. (1978). The effectiveness of family therapy: a review of outcome research. *Archives of General Psychiatry*, **35**, 549–561.

Dincin, J. (1975) Psychiatric rehabilitation. *Schizophrenia Bulletin*, **13**, 131–148.

Doane, J. A. (1978) Family interaction and communication deviance in disturbed and normal families: a review of research. *Family Process*, **17**, 357–376.

Fischer, J. (1978) *Effective Casework Practice*. McGraw-Hill, New York.

Freeman, H. E., and Simmons, O. G. (1963) *The Mental Patient Comes Home*. John Wiley, New York.

Gay, P., and Mitkeathley, J. (1979) *When I Went Home: A Study of Patients Discharged from Hospital*. King Edward's Fund, London.

Goffman, E. (1962) *Asylums*, Doubleday, New York.

Goldstein, R. S., and Baer, D. M. (1976) RSVP: a procedure to increase the personal mail and number of correspondents for nursing home residents. *Behaviour Therapy*, **7**, 348–354.

Greenley, J. R. (1979a) Family symptom tolerance and rehospitalisation experiences of psychiatric patients. In R. G. Simmons, ed., *Research in Community and Mental Health*. JAI Press, Greenwick, Conn.

Greenley, J. R. (1979b) Familial expectations, posthospital adjustments and the society reaction perspective on mental illness. *Journal of Health and Social Behaviour*, **20**, 217–227.

Gurman, A. S. (1973) The effects and effectiveness of marital therapy: a review of outcome research. *Family Process*, **12**, 145–170.

Gurman, A. S., and Kniskern, D. P. (1977) Research on marital and family therapy: progress, perspective and prospect. In S. Garfield and A. E. Bergin, eds, *Handbook of Psychotherapy and Behaviour Change*, 2nd edn. John Wiley, New York.

Hagnell, O., and Kreitman, N. (1974) Mental illness in married pairs in a total population. *British Journal of Psychiatry*, **125**, 293–302.

Henderson, A. S. (1977) The social network, support and neurosis. *British Journal of Psychiatry*, **131**, 185–191.

Herbert, M. (1978) *Behaviour Disorders of Childhood and Adolescence*. John Wiley, London.

Holland, S. (1979) The development of an action and counselling service in a deprived urban area. In M. Meacher, ed., *New Methods of Mental Health Care*. Pergamon, Oxford.

Hollingsworth, C. E., and Sokol, B. (1978) Predischarge family conferences. *Journal American Medical Association*, **239**, 740–741.

Horwitz, A. (1978) Family, kin and friend networks in psychiatric help-seeking. *Social Science and Medicine*, **12**, 297–304.

Hudson, B. L. (1975) A behaviour modification project with chronic schizophrenics in the community. *Behaviour Research and Therapy*, **13**, 339–341.

Hunt, G. M., and Azrin, N. H. (1973) A community reinforcement approach to alcoholism. *Behaviour Research and Therapy*, **2**, 91–104.

Jacob, T. (1975) Family interaction in disturbed and normal families: a methodological and substantive review. *Psychological Bulletin*, **82**, 33–65.

Karlsruher, A. E. (1974) The nonprofessional as a psychotherapeutic agent. *American Journal of Community Psychology*, **2**, 61–77.

King, R. D., Raynes, N. V., and Tizard, J. (1971) *Patterns of Residential Care: Sociological Studies in Institutions for Handicapped Children*. Routledge & Kegan Paul, London.

Lamb, H. R., and Rogawski, A. S. (1978) Supplemental security income and the sick role. *American Journal of Psychiatry*, **135**, 1221–1224.

Liberman, R. P., and Raskin, D. E. (1971) Depression: a behavioural formulation. *Archives of General Psychiatry*, **24**, 515–523.

Lomas, P. (1967) The study of family relationships in contemporary society. In P. Lomas, ed., *The Predicament of the Family*. Hogarth Press, London.

McAuley, R., and McAuley, P. (1977) *Child Behaviour Problems*. Macmillan, London.

McAuley, R., and McAuley, P. (1980) The effectiveness of behaviour modification with families. *British Journal of Social Work*, **10**, 43–54.

McCowen, P., and Wilder, J. (1975) *Lifestyle of 100 Psychiatric Patients*. Psychiatric Rehabilitation Association, London.

McLean, P. D., Ogston, K., and Graner, L. (1973) A behavioural approach to the treatment of depression. *Journal of Behaviour Therapy and Experimental Psychiatry*, **4**, 323–330.

Malan, D. H., Heath, E. S., Bacal, H. A., and Balfour, F. M. G. (1975) Psychodynamic changes in untreated neurotic patients. *Archives of General Psychiatry*, **32**, 110–126.

Marzillier, J. (1978) Outcome studies of skills training. In P. Trower, B. Bryant, and M. Argyle, eds, *Social Skills and Mental Health*. Methuen, London.

Mathews, A. M., Teasdale, J., Munby, M., Johnston, D. W., and Shaw, P. M. (1977) A home based treatment programme for agoraphobia. *Behaviour Therapy*, **8**, 9 915–924.

Miller, P. M. (1972) The use of behavioural contracting in the treatment of alcoholism: a case report. *Behaviour Therapy*, **3**, 593–596.

Minuchin, S. (1974) *Families and Family Therapy*. Tavistock, London.

Mishler, E. G., and Waxler, H. E. (1968) *Interaction in Families: An Experimental Study of Family Processes and Schizophrenia*. John Wiley, New York.

National Schizophrenia Fellowship (1974) *Living with Schizophrenia by the Relatives*. National Schizophrenia Fellowship, London.

Nye, F. I., and Berardo, F. M. (1973) *The Family: Its Structure and Interaction*. Macmillan, New York.

O'Brien, F., and Azrin, N. H. (1973) Interaction-priming: a method of reinstating patient–family relationships. *Behaviour Research and Therapy*, **11**, 133–136.

Patterson, G. R. (1973) Reprogramming the families of aggressive boys. In C. R. Thorenson, ed., *Behaviour Modification in Education*. University of Chicago Press, Chicago.

Priestley, D. (1979) Helping a self-help group in schizophrenia and the family. In J. W. Wing and R. Olsen, eds, *Community Care for the Mental Disabled*. Oxford University Press, London.

Rahmer, M. (1973) A home that can work. *New Society*, **26**, No. 585, 722–723.

Rutter, M., and Brown, G. W. (1966) The reliability of family life and relationships in families containing a psychiatric patient. *Social Psychiatry*, **1**, 38–53.

Ryan, P., and Hewett, S. H. (1976) A pilot study of hostels for the mentally ill. *Social Work Today*, **6**, 774–778.

Segal, S. P., and Aviram, U. (1978) *The Mentally Ill in Community-based Sheltered Care*. John Wiley, New York.

Shepherd, G. (1978) Social skills training: the generalisation problem, some further data. *Behaviour Research and Therapy*, **16**, 287–288.

Skynner, A. C. R. (1976) *One Flesh, Separate Persons: Principles of Family and Marital Psychotherapy*. Constable, London.

Tharp, R., and Wetzel, R. J. (1969) *Behaviour Modification in the Natural Environment*. Academic Press, New York.

Thomas, E. J., and Walter, C. L. (1973) Guidelines for behavioural practice in the open community agency: procedure and evaluation. *Behaviour Research and Therapy*, **11**, 193–205.

Trower, P., Bryant, B., and Argyle, M. (1978) *Social Skills and Mental Health*. Methuen, London.

Truax, C. B.., and Mitchell, K. N. (1971) Research on certain therapist interpersonal skills in relation to process and outcome. In A. E. Bergin and S. C. Garfield, eds, *Handbook of Psychotherapy and Behaviour Change*. John Wiley, New York.

Vaughn, C. E., and Leff, J. P. (1976) The influence of family and social factors on the course of psychiatric illness: a comparison of schizophrenic and depressed neurotic patients. *British Journal of Psychiatry*, **129**, 125–137.

Walker, L. G. (1979) The effect of some incentives on the work performance of psychiatric patients at a rehabilitation workshop. *Journal of Psychiatry*, **134**, 427–435.

Walton, D. (1960) The application of learning theory to the treatment of a case of neuro-dermatitis. In H. J. Eysenck, ed., *Behaviour Therapy and the Neuroses*. Macmillan, New York.

Wells, R. A., Dilkes, T. C., and Trivelli, N. (1972) The results of family therapy: a critical review of the literature. *Family Process*, **11**, 189–207.

Wing, J. K. (1966) Social and psychological changes in a rehabilitation unit. *Social Psychiatry*, **1**, 21–28.

Yarrow, M. R., Clausen, J. A., and Robbins, P. A. (1955a) The social meaning of mental illness. *Journal of Social Issues*, **11**, 33–48.

Yarrow, M. R., Schwartz, C. G., Murphy, M. S., and Deasy, L. C. (1955b) The psychological meaning of mental illness in the family. *Journal of Social Issues*, **11**, 12–24.

*Footnote:* Recent work on educational, supportive and therapeutic interventions designed to help the families of schizophrenic patients (Leff *et al.*, 1982; Falloon *et al.*, 1982) together with earlier work by Goldstein *et al.* (1978) has produced encouraging results.

Falloon, J. R. H., Boyd, J. L., McGill, C. W., Razoni, J., Moss, H. B. and Gilderman, A. M. (1982) Family management in the prevention of exacerbation of schizophrenia: A controlled study. *New England Journal of Medicine*, **306**, 1437–1440.

Goldstein, M. J., Rodnick, E. H., Evans, J. R., May, P. R. A. and Steinberg, M. R. (1978) Drug and family therapy in the aftercase of acute schizophrenics. *Archives of General Psychiatry*, **35**, 1169–1177.

Leff, J., Kuipers, L., Berkowitz, R., Eberlein-Vries, R. and Sturgeon, D. (1982) A controlled trial of social interventions in the families of schizophrenic patients. *British Journal of Psychiatry*, **141**, 121–134.

Theory and Practice of Psychiatric Rehabilitation
Edited by F. N. Watts and D. H. Bennett
© 1983, John Wiley & Sons, Ltd.

# 10

# Support and Rehabilitation

DOUGLAS BENNETT and ISOBEL MORRIS

It has been suggested that 'the study of social adaptation is most typically pursued without seriously considering the pervasive influence of social structural variables on personal and social adaptation' (Mechanic, 1974). Yet people, not least the psychiatrically disabled, are dependent on group solutions and the support of others. We all look to our social networks for 'support'. While the concept of support is still poorly conceptualized it usually embraces support for instrumental needs as well as for more intimate and emotional needs. Such support is seen as emanating from the community, its organizations and its institutions or from personal attachments which confirm the feeling that one is appreciated, accepted, valued, and useful. Thus, the social network helps a person to cope with life's stresses. It provides reliable supportive feedback regarding his behaviour and offers a framework for validating his social roles. It sets appropriate expectations of performance and offers the opportunity to satisfy them and feel loved and valued. It can provide the necessities of life and create alternative, and achievable, definitions of social functioning and social relationships (Cobb, 1976).

While the social network plays an important part in meeting human needs and supporting the individual's coping ability, we still know very little about which aspects of that support are the most important. At present we know about those factors which, in patients with schizophrenia, or women with depression, induce relapse or enhance the individual's vulnerability to stress (Brown *et al.*, 1972; Brown and Harris, 1978; Vaughn and Leff, 1976). These findings, however, also suggest that vulnerability to social stress may be reduced and social adaptation improved when support is available. The need for social support and the part that it plays in rehabilitation has only been fully appreciated as rehabilitation has moved from the mental hospital to the community setting. As long as psychiatric rehabilitation was confined to mental hospitals, the effect of life events and social stress could be overlooked until such time as the patient was discharged and forced to readjust to life outside the hospital. There was little discussion of the disabled person's need for support. It was assumed that, because institutional life impaired the adaptation of the psychiatrically disabled, release from hospital would automatically restore that adaptation. The supports of institutional life were overlooked and rejected with the institution itself (Bachrach, 1978).

The aim of rehabilitation is that the disabled person should make the best use of his remaining abilities in as normal a social context as possible. For some the social context is everyday life in society, although this will not be possible for the most severely handicapped. Even so, it has long been accepted that a number of the more severely disabled could function outside hospital if sheltered work or suitable residential environments could be provided. In the provision of these more or less sheltered facilities for the disabled, 'the ladder model' (Barton, 1966) has shaped our thinking. Transitional residential care in the form of halfway houses was to be a part of a step-by-step process of graded community resettlement. It was assumed that at the end of the process the psychiatric patient would emerge as an independent individual able to cope with instrumental tasks and adult roles.

For many disabled persons the ladder concept of rehabilitation is inadequate and this is demonstrated, not only by the limitations of resettlement for mental hospital patients, but also by the failure of transitional hostels. Hewett *et al.* (1975) report that in 24 hostels they studied, 23 stated that they had a policy of transitional and short-term care, although in only 5 was this policy strictly adhered to. Usually 40 to 50 per cent of the residents made up a hard core of long-stay individuals. Similarly, staff in the day centres believe that their aim is to resettle patients in work, although Richards (1971) showed that of the first 100 patients admitted to one day centre in South London, only 11 were known to be in regular employment after leaving the centre. Other studies of day centre populations have shown similar findings in spite of the provision of training in work skills (Carter and Edwards, 1975; Gath *et al.*, 1973).

Carter and Edwards draw attention to the confusion in the use of the word 'rehabilitation' in these centres. They felt that the word was used as a synonym for the care of chronic patients, that it could be coextensive with treatment, or that it could be used as a metaphor for discharge. Ryan (1979), discussing his hostel survey in 1973, pointed out that, in many hostels, staff equated work with rehabilitation. This usage had been less evident in his 1976 study, in part because it was proving more difficult to find employment for residents that year; 80 per cent of the residents were employed in the 1973 survey and only 14 per cent in the 1976 survey.

## Support and Psychiatric Disability

As psychiatric treatment and rehabilitation have moved out of the mental hospitals to other settings, and as social psychiatric formulations have begun to make an impact, there is a more realistic understanding that many disabilities will not be changed and that the possibility of improvements in social functioning is often limited. In certain instances the disabled person can be helped to develop compensatory skills, greater confidence, or more motivation. In some cases, changes in the mutual adjustment of the family and its disabled member, in terms of expectations and the nature of the support provided, can improve the disabled person's adaptation. In either case changes in the family environment are as important as changes in the disabled person himself. Creer and Wing (1974), in a study of patients with schizophrenia, note that 'in many cases relatives and patients had discovered for themselves how best to limit handicaps, promote assets and achieve a mode of life which had its pleasures and rewards as well as its disappointments'. In the family, opportunities for change and thus for mutual adjustment are probably greater than in the monolithic, relatively static, environment of the mental hospital. For any psychiatrically disabled person, whatever the nature or extent of his handicap, whether or not he uses family, hospital, or other supports, there is no possibility of 'once for all' rehabilitation. Not only may step-by-step advances be limited — a step-by-step retreat or sudden collapse of adaptation is quite possible. For such handicapped persons, rehabilitation is not just the process of enabling the handicapped person to make the best use of his abilities to ensure better adaptation. For many, rehabilitation is the maintenance of optimal social adaptation over a long period of time; perhaps the duration of life itself. Since those who are disabled by psychiatric disorders often have a natural tendency to desocialize, it is necessary to provide support to help them maintain the performance of those social roles that remain to them.

Shelter is a roof over one's head. Asylum comprises support and shelter and in past times most patients received it in the mental hospital. The nature of the disability did not matter nor did its extent. The psychiatrically disabled might need a little or a lot of support. This did not determine the amount which they received. They might have only needed shelter, but support was also provided. In giving this routine package of institutional shelter and support the hospital often extinguished what skills or individuality its disabled inmates still possessed. Test and Stein (1976) suggest that while social support systems should meet the needs which the psychiatric patient cannot meet himself and which cannot be met by those in his social network, the provision of shelter or support should not meet needs in those areas in which the patient can function adequately and independently. They emphasize that 'if a support system insists on providing things a person can already do for him or herself it restricts his or her choices and his or her freedom'. This principle is similar to that of the 'minimum therapeutic dose' proposed by Birley who, describing a housing association, suggests that the provision of residential shelter may have its dangers. 'Firstly it may make our patients hammock dependent with a consequent atrophy of their own supportive system. Secondly it may control them and can seriously damage them by limiting or denying opportunities and restricting their individual development' (Birley, 1974). It may have been the recognition of these risks which led the Royal College of Nursing to define rehabilitation as 'the planned withdrawal of support usually in conjunction with or following other active measures for the patients' relief or cure. . .' (Royal College of Nursing, 1963). The disabled need support and shelter as does everyone; but that support must be provided in a flexible way, in amounts and in a form appropriate to the differing and changing needs of the individual.

### The Concept of Support

Support may seem a simple and commonly accepted idea, but closer examination reveals unanticipated complexities and ambiguities. 'If social support does have positive effects, we need to know its most critical and potent ingredients, the social conditions under which positive effects are facilitated, and the types of persons for whom social support would be beneficial or contra-indicated' (Heller, 1979). Hammer (1981) has criticized the emphasis on support which she points out is only one dimension of a social network, while Garrison and Podell (1981) suggest that support can be negative as well as positive from a mental health perspective. They point to the overinvolved families of schizophrenics and drinking companions of alcoholics who may be supportive but in a manner likely to exacerbate the problems of those who are thus supported. Analysing the concept further, Cobb distinguishes between support in the form of goods and services and social support which he defines as information which leads the patient to believe that he is cared for, loved, esteemed, and valued, and that he belongs to a network of communication and mutual obligation. He stressed this distinction, 'for goods and services may foster dependency while the classes of information listed above do not. In fact they tend to encourage independent behaviour' (Cobb, 1976). Thus social support can be seen as an interpersonal transaction consisting of the expression of such positive affects as liking, admiration, and respect; the affirmation of the individual's beliefs and actions; or the provision of aid in terms of material information, and time (Kahn and Quinn, 1977). Caplan (1974) also suggests that support is not just propping up someone who is in danger of falling down, but also the augmentation of strength which facilitates his mastery of the environment. Heller (1979), too, suggests that support which focuses on disabilities and pathology is more likely to promote dependency than that directed towards the encouragement of skills, autonomy, and self-reliance.

The beneficial effects of social support may seem self-evident but Heller (1979) points out that, because of the correlational nature of much of the research data, it is impossible to say whether people are ill because they lack support or because illness impairs their ability to establish and maintain mutual personal relationships. Even so, it seems that support or the lack of it influences the possibilities of hospital admission for the elderly demented (Bergmann *et al.*, 1978). Similarly, Lowenthal and Haven (1968) thought that a single intimate relationship buffered the aged against the threat of social disengagement and the associated depression and poor morale which they might experience.

Lowenthal and Haven also showed that a confidant, while reducing the likelihood of depression, did not buffer the effects of physical illness on depression, and suggested that the support of others may be powerless to deal with fear about the increasing imminence of death. Paykel *et al.* (1980) found that women were more likely to develop a mild clinical depression in the puerperium in the presence of recent stressful life events, or a history of certain factors in their previous experience. This could be exacerbated by certain personality traits and genetic inheritance, together with a poor marital relationship and a lack of social support. Pearlin and Johnson (1977), investigating a greater disposition of unmarried people to psychological disturbance, found that this resulted from the greater exposure of single people to hardship or strain. They expected that single and married individuals contending with life's strains would be similarly inclined to depression. In fact, they found that the effects of stress were more penetrating among the unmarried. A high proportion of chronic psychiatric patients are unmarried. Mann and Cree (1976) found 46 per cent of their sample of long-stay hospital patients had never been married and 32 per cent had been married but were no longer in contact with their spouse. Many therefore lack this social buffer against life's stresses. This tends to support Pearlin and Johnson's contention that marriage can 'function as a protective barrier against the stressful consequences of external threats'. Beiser (1976) found that the ability to use others in the environment for emotional support was one of the factors associated with the spontaneous remission of neurotic symptoms. Other studies have suggested that the absence of social support acts as an independent stressor rather than mediating the effects of life events (Andrews and Tennant, 1978; Miller *et al.*, 1976; Bebbington and Tennant, 1978).

It seems that support can also be more or less effective according to the individual's psychological and coping responses in particular situations. Thus Pearlin and Schooler (1978) elicited 17 coping responses in relation to the persisting everyday life strains to which people are exposed in their roles as parents, workers, spouses, and householders. They subdivided these responses into those which change the situation, those which control the meaning of the threatening experience, and those which function more for the control of the stress itself after it has emerged. One of Pearlin and Schooler's most interesting and most important findings was that these psychological responses and coping resources are not equally effective in all areas of role performance. Certain coping responses reduce strain in marriage, while in work these same responses seem to make little difference. Pearlin and Schooler found that self-reliance is more useful in mitigating the stresses of marriage and parenthood than is a seeking of help and advice from others. Thus outside support in those situations is less likely to be effective than when the individual is dealing with other forms of stress.

There are further complexities. There are most probably differences in the nature of interpersonal support. While studying a Parents Without Partners organization in Boston, Weiss (1968) found that the loss of the marriage partner resulted in a sense of emotional isolation for women who stay at home. On the other hand, the absence of friends was associated with a sense of social isolation. Friends could not make up for the lost marriage; marriage did not make up for lost friends. As an outcome of this study, Weiss went on to suggest that individual wellbeing required five types of interaction. Emotional interaction in marriage or with a very close relative and social interaction in friendships have already been mentioned. Some people need the opportunity for the nurturance of children or others. There are also those relationships which give reassurance of worth by attesting to the individual's worth in role performance as assessed, for example, by colleagues at work. Finally, when there is urgent need, there is assistance, limited in time and extent, from neighbours. Weiss conjectures that deficits in these relationships result in differing forms of stress. He sees an absence of emotional integration leading to loneliness and a lack of social integration producing boredom. The absence of opportunities for nurturance gives a sense of emptiness and pointlessness; the absence of work relationships leads to a sense of worthlessness; while a lack of assistance generates feelings of vulnerability and of having been abandoned. Lack of some or all of these forms of support can diminish a person's sense of self-esteem and mastery or impair coping repertoires in the presence of threatening events. These views are supported by findings about the lack of a confiding intimate relationship resulting in vulnerability to, and the recurrence of, mental illness (Brown and Harris, 1978; Leff and Vaughn, 1980; Miller and Ingham, 1976).

Liem and Liem (1976) found that emotional support and material aid had independent effects on the levels of reported stress in college students. Emotional support and encouragement provided by friends were inversely related to reported depression and inadequacy; the greater the emotional support the less the feelings of distress. On the other hand, the provision of tangible financial support led to greater psychological distress, presumably because it reminded the student of his strained financial position. The Liems also showed that support from family members was associated with physical wellbeing, while availability of friends in a support network was related to psychological wellbeing.

## Social Networks and Support

Many studies of support like those of Brown and Harris have been concerned with individiual supportive figures. Bart (1974) noted that women who were overinvolved in their children's lives were prone to depression when the children left home. A man's sense of worth may be threatened by retirement and a woman's by criticisms of her adult children (Deykin et al., 1966). Jacobson and Klerman (1966) showed that in such conflicts an improvement in the patient's clinical state was associated with increasing agreement between the patient and her family as to role expectations. In all relationships the parties engaged may stress and support each other at the same time. Sometimes the patient provides the support. Stevens (1972) reported that relatives found that the companionship of chronic patients at home was supportive and some valued the contributions patients could make to the household chores. Relationships are not entirely supportive or entirely stressful; there is always some sort of balance. Thus stress exceeds support or vice versa. It is a complicated situation and the reciprocal nature of social support is expressed in the term 'network'. Social networks can be described in terms of their density, range, reciprocity, frequency of contact, context, and so on (Bott, 1957; Mitchell, 1969; Lipton et al., 1981). Most network research has been concerned either with families or with single supportive figures. As research has moved away from a 'social category' approach (as in studies of social class) towards an understanding of social processes (Hammer, 1981), the relevance of the concept of social network to rehabilitation has become increasingly evident. Freeman and Simmons (1963) and Brown et al. (1972) have shown that there is a relationship between the nature of the network and the patient's chances of remaining in the community or having to be readmitted to hospital.

Sokolovsky et al. (1978) found a relationship between the size of the network and the chances of hospital readmission among the residents of single-room occupancy hotels in Manhattan. Hammer (1963) found that patients whose close relatives were not in touch with each other were more likely to have these relationships severed following hospitalisation. In a study of mental illness in East London families, Enid Mills discussed kinship and mental illness. She stated that the patient often 'becomes a focus for family conflict in which some relatives seek to protect or make allowances for the patient while others complain of favouritism'. While some patients came to hospital after the loss of a particular relative who had cared for them, other patients seemed better able to avoid hospital because they were less closely involved with a possessive relative and were outside the range of family quarrels (Mills, 1962). Patients may have different methods of coping with stress in their social network. Tolsdorf (1976) found that psychiatric patients coped with social stress by complete social withdrawal, in contrast to medical patients who could withdraw selectively from some of their network members.

The concept of 'network' may be unfamiliar but it can be explained by comparing and contrasting it with the idea of a group. In an organized group the individuals who compose it make up a larger social whole with common aims, interdependent roles, and a distinctive subculture. In a network some, but not all, of the component individuals have social relationships with one another (Bott, 1957). The degree to which these individuals are connected varies. Thus there are densely connected networks where people whom you and your family know also know each other independently of you. The connectedness of networks differs in rural and urban areas as do the roles of the inhabitants of those areas (Frankenberg, 1966). Generally speaking, as one moves from a rural to an urban environment there is an increasing differentiation of roles. In towns and in conurbations there is a specialization of roles and a separation of parts of a role to form new roles. Greater differentiation of roles in society is accompanied by less differentiation of roles in the home. In rural areas people have to play many roles in front of the same audience; community roles and services are less specialized, while home roles are more differentiated. Social networks seem to react to those whose role performances are impaired by mental disorder in differing ways. The mentally ill who are isolated, having no network and no one to care for them, may enter hospital more frequently. Bott (1976) has argued that the increasing admission of patients to mental hospitals is a result of the decreased density of family networks since the war. On the one hand the close-knit supportive network may be an alternative to other services. Yet, in such a network, role impairments are more public and are known to a wider audience. 'Situations in which mutual avoidance is impossible and mutual disagreement inevitable are especially likely to occur in small scale rural society' (Frankenberg, 1966). It may well be that in these circumstances the only possible solution will be for the patient to withdraw or move out of the community. Other authors have also found that while close networks may be supportive, they also involve demands and constraints which may be stressful (Hammer, 1981). Brown et al. (1977), in a study of a remote rural area, found that women in more closely integrated social networks were less vulnerable to depression but more likely to suffer from anxiety. Doubtless rural communities produce stresses and supports for the mentally ill which are quite different from those which are generated in an urban society.

In the past psychiatrists and other professional workers have been strangely neglectful of the patient's social network as a natural rehabilitation resource, presumably because they were based in the mental hospital. They had little physical or visual contact with the patient's family and his social network. They did not think about it, assess it, or try to use it, and this natural support system was allowed to atrophy, or worse, was regarded as an irrelevant nuisance. The social network, then, is the individual's primary support system, made up of relatives, friends, and acquaintances giving and receiving those services and those social and emotional supports which the giver and the receiver feel are necessary or helpful in maintaining a style of life (Cohen and Sokolovsky, 1979).

## The Secondary Support System

This primary support system can be distinguished from the secondary support system made up of formal and less personal relationships with medical facilities, institutions, social agencies, and the like. This division between the intimate supports of domestic life and the relatively impersonal help of social agencies is somewhat unreal for most people. People normally look to their community for work, housing, and interpersonal relationships and for the feeling of support in their daily activities. Those who are not disabled are thus mutually dependent in that they need community support; at the same time they are independent in that they achieve adequate support, often by virtue of their own efforts. When it becomes impossible to meet personal needs by one's own efforts, for instance in a time of high unemployment, or because of illness or disability, then the balance of interdependency becomes distorted and this is reflected in difficulties of adjustment. It is easier for the disabled patient to contribute and to reciprocate support in the primary support group than in the more one-sided relationship with professional helpers. Severely disabled psychiatric patients, however, are often poorly placed to achieve adequate support through their own efforts. Their disabilities often impair their functioning in normal social roles and thus they often can call on less support. Such chronic patients are most disadvantaged in that they not only have difficulty in making close relationships with others; their behaviour has often alienated them from their friends and families. They may not be able to make new relationships easily or to use the available supportive services effectively. Ebringer and Christie-Brown (1980), studying 74 patients from a London borough, found that 40 per cent of them were homeless and 36 per cent had no visitors. These patients had lost their community supports by the time they had reached the hospital's admission ward. The authors go on to say that once such a patient had been admitted 'landladies, families and employers experience such relief that they often go to great lengths to ensure that there is no possibility of his return . . .'

Patients with stressful family relationships are the most likely to become estranged from their families. Scott and Alwyn (1978) describe the 'closure' which takes place in families following the admission of a patient to hospital. For those chronic patients living at home, the achievement of adequate levels of social support is not only a problem for the patient but may be a problem for the family as a whole. Family members may find that their own social networks are reduced because of the embarrassing or difficult behaviour of the patient (Creer and Wing, 1974). Families with whom the patient has had untenable relationships may even, after the first admission, be unwilling to accept the patient ever again into their social circle. Also many chronic patients are dependent on elderly relatives (Stevens, 1972): a group who themselves have to make adjustments to decreasing social networks. Although much attention has been given in the past to the stress caused by the psychiatrically disabled to their supportive families (Grad and Sainsbury, 1968; Hoenig and Hamilton, 1969), it should be recognized that in many cases the family can be a burden to the patient (Brown *et al.*, 1972). Good rehabilitation practice requires that professionals should not take the side of the individual patient or family member but that they should try to comprehend the behaviour of both in the context of the wider network situation. Thus the supporters need support as well as the handicapped individual. Professionals therefore need to pay special attention to the family member most affected by the disturbance and most important in supporting the disabled patient.

Doctors would not talk so much about the doctor/patient relationship and so little about the mutual rights of doctors and lay persons if doctors did not learn their medicine in hospitals, where, alone, this second relationship is always less obvious and usually less important. (Vickers, 1967)

In the presence of disability, the person's adaptation or readaptation will depend on change in the social environment and, in particular, in the social network. So not only do we seek to improve the disabled person's role performance, we have also to adjust the family's expectations. This cannot be done by simple instruction or exhortation. It is a complex business. Family overinvolvement or criticism may increase disability in such disorders as schizophrenia. Family guilt and anxiety may lead to the lowering of expectations in other situations. Expectations then may vary, being either too high or too low; alternatively they may be quite inappropriate. Bennett *et al.* (1976) have described a family approach to the care of the psychiatrically disabled in a day hospital. They observed that families often compensated for their lack of information with unrealistic fantasies and expectations; these often went unexpressed until the time of the patient's discharge. Then some families would manifest hostility as a means of expressing anxiety about resuming full responsibility for the patient member. These authors felt that the family helped to support the patient and that the staff should try to meet the family's own need for support, particularly at the time of the patient's discharge.

It is not easy to help the family to play a constructive part in the rehabilitation process. For both family and staff it is difficult to maintain a balance between accepting dependent behaviour while at the same time attempting to minimize it. Yet this is a key principle in good rehabilitation practice. The failure to accept some dependence is to deny disability; a denial which may result in the inadequate provision of services. Such a denial of chronic psychiatric disability has been commonplace in recent years. It may be seen in the so-called 'deinstitutionalization' movement in the United States where the abolition of the mental hospital was thought to be synonymous with the abolition of intrinsic psychiatric or extrinsic social handicaps. Even when sheltered accommodation was provided it was thought to be a transitional facility, bridging the gap between illness and full health. Either way the reality of long-term handicap was denied. It was not appreciated that rehabilitation is a process whereby one is constantly seeking to achieve that fine balance between enabling the patient to attain and maintain as high a level of functioning as possible and, at the same time, accepting varying levels of intrinsic and extrinsic disability with a consequent need to alter working, living, and leisure environments. For the disabled patient, support is an aspect of a rehabilitation approach which, at best, aims to improve adaptation and, at worst, to prevent deterioration. Shelter is found in 'protective' environments which provide those needs which the disabled patient is unable to secure by his own efforts in a competitive society. It is equally important that disability should not be regarded as an excuse for not trying.

Just as the disabled psychiatric patient has difficulty in meeting his psychosocial needs through his own efforts so he will have difficulties in securing his material needs. Such people require support for material as well as emotional needs. To suggest, as Cobb (1976) does, that this kind of material support may foster dependency is a matter for concern when one seeks to avoid the excessive dependency fostered by the old mental institutions. Yet the disabled need a network of volunteers or professionals who are committed to giving them the social or medical aid they require if they are to cope without being unnecessarily isolated, or excluded from the community. The disabilities of those who need this extra supportive service have already been described in earlier chapters of this book. By and large, such persons have already had considerable contact with the psychiatric services and cannot be helped by short-term treatment. They have difficulties in employment and in the basic roles of daily life. They are unable to seek out and enjoy leisure activities or to engage and use the help of social and medical agencies. They lack self-confidence, cannot form relaxed relationships with others, and are particularly vulnerable to stress. The community support system should provide (in addition to the personal supports needed by everyone) clothing, housing, medical and dental care, education, and money. Money is provided from pensions as well as from medical and social benefit. Not every area of every service provides rapidly available support throughout the 24 hours; but for some patients this is necessary.

Many disabled patients with long-term disabilities need support of indefinite duration. As Bachrach (1978) has argued, this was one of the functions of the old mental hospitals which cannot be neglected in new systems of community care. A care service is therefore needed to provide continuing support which seeks to maintain, and if possible improve, social adaptation on a long-term basis. Rehabilitation services which assess abilities and disabilities, and seek to develop the adaptive capacities of the disabled by improving their skills or their employability, sometimes have limited success because they fail to consider the problem of long-term maintenance and support. Some have suggested that this requires a continuing commitment from a person or a team who will keep in touch with the disabled individual. Since practices differ from country to country, it is impossible to generalize about the provision of financial support, about social work, or about emergency psychiatric services. However, these are provisions which are essential to most services providing long-term supportive rehabilitation.

## Long-term Supportive Rehabilitation

We can begin with the residential services. Sheltered residential accommodation may vary from bedsitting rooms for those who, while they cannot compete in the open housing market, are quite capable of independent life in a domestic setting, to the hospital care needed by the 'hard core' of chronically disabled psychiatric patients. The need to make use of such hospital facilities should not be viewed either as an alternative to community care or as a failure of community care. Residential services should be part of a network of integrated services which seek to meet different needs and different levels of independence in a flexible manner. It must be emphasized that the provision of material shelter does not preclude the need for other forms of social support.

When we speak of supportive environments we are assuming that they are designed to improve the functioning of the disabled person. It is possible that certain environments will do this. It is equally possible that some settings will not only fail to reinforce the person's adaptation but may actually undermine it. Traditionally, the villain of the piece has been the large old mental hospital. Such hospitals should have helped the disabled by developing their social competence and their capacity to cope with stress. In practice they often increased disability by subordinating the needs of the individual to the requirements of the institution (Goffman, 1961). Mental hospital practices were often determined by an overriding concern for social regulation. There are many ways of looking at social regulation, but Cumming (1968) has suggested that it may be exercised either by control with the implicit threat of punishment or by support which in this sense implies the encouragement of acceptable behaviour. In former times, and to some extent still today, supervision and control were more in evidence than was support. Controlling practices were well suited to the management of large numbers of people by small numbers of staff. Such practices determined the institutional architecture, the attitudes of staff, and the activities pursued, as well as what the patient could and could not do. They led not only to a restriction of patient activities but also of independence and responsibility. It has been easy to produce the numerous critiques of the institutional practices of the traditional mental hospitals (Belknap, 1956; Goffman, 1961) but it has been much less easy to correct these defects. Some approaches have been anti-institutional in purpose. Thus therapeutic communities sought to provide a setting which was not overcontrolling and allowed not only shared decision making but the sharing of activities by patients and staff. At the same time the individual was encouraged to face his problems squarely by so-called 'reality confrontation'. This approach did something to clarify the emotional obstacles to the patient's coping, in terms of his interpersonal relationships. It also did something to ameliorate the harmful effects of loss of independence and responsibility. But the ideology was confused by talk about democracy and by a failure to distinguish between treatment and rehabilitation (Cumming 1969; Rapoport, 1960). While social adaptation was the aim, the practice was to try to change the patient's personality. The whole package of activities was assumed to be 'therapeutic' although it was not clear which activities were effective, or for which individuals. Lamb (1967) questioned the relevance of this approach to the needs of the chronic patients; he considered that

it is frequently the feeling, especially among individuals inbred in the principles of the therapeutic community, that if any group of patints is given a democratic process they will establish the goals of progression towards health, assuming responsibility, and early return to the community. . . .

Instead what is needed is structure, which the disabled patient cannot provide himself. This together with staff directiveness has been shown to be of therapeutic value in hostels for chronic alcoholics (Otto and Orford, 1978). The use of token economies has also emphasized structure in terms of clear instructions, explicit expectations and contingent feedback (Hall *et al.*, 1977).

Wing and Brown (1970) approached the problem of the effect of the social milieu on patients' functioning in a different way. They studied selected ward practices in three mental hospitals and then measured the changes taking place over the subsequent 8 years. They then tried to discover how these alterations paralleled changes in the disabilities of chronic patients with schizophrenia. It was found that the most important single factor associated with an improvement in the patients' intrinsic handicaps was a reduction in the amount of time which they spent doing nothing. A restrictive ward setting seemed to play an independent part in maintaining 'negative' symptoms.

Increased contact with the outside world, a more optimistic mood among the nursing staff, and an increased supply of personal belongings were less important influences on intrinsic disability, but they were of major importance in reducing secondary or extrinsic handicaps.

But knowing what is wrong and what changes are needed are not enough. It is important to modify the methods of social regulation in institutions and to prevent institutionalizing practices. But positive rehabilitation needs something more. In particular, it is necessary to understand the underlying principles of rehabilitation which lead to enhanced functioning, and which promote community integration and foster effective social support. It has often been assumed that these aims may best be achieved by moving support and shelter out of the institution. However, Carter and Edwards (1975) concluded from their survey of day care settings that 'overall, many of the day units visited contained features of the traditional institution, although staff did not seem to be aware of this'. The authors surveyed features of day care which they considered to be potentially institutionalizing. They defined these in terms of the degree of segregation of the unit, the amount of separation between staff and users, and the number of restrictions on users. They found that 'although many of the grossly depriving aspects of the total institution had been eliminated it appeared that some day care units still contained a number of features that day care had been set up to eliminate'. In an examination of four Local Authority day centres, Shepherd and Richardson (1979) also studied the processes underlying the different styles of organization and the different patterns of care. They found varying degrees of institutional practice and emphasized that the environmental features which are likely to lead to institutionalization can be present in settings other than mental hospitals: for example, in hostels, workshops, day centres, and even families. 'The effectiveness of long-term care is therefore ultimately dependent on the exact nature of the service and not on its location, and discharge from hospital is no guarantee that deterioration will not take place' (Shepherd and Richardson, 1979). It is only too clear that the old and harmful features of the total institution can quite easily become a feature of alternative community supportive services.

A number of studies have attempted to clarify the dimensions of care which prevent the development of institutional practices. In their studies of residential settings for mentally retarded children, King et al. (1971) attempted to define more clearly those management practices which are institutionalizing rather than supportive and enabling. Institutional practices were characterized by block treatment, where children were treated as homogeneous groups rather than as individuals; rigidity of routine when activities were tightly scheduled in an inflexible way unrelated to individual need; social distance when the staff increased the distance between themselves and their patients, by wearing uniforms and not eating together; and depersonalization when the children had few personal possessions, made few personal decisions, and had little personal space. The institutionally orientated practices were essentially designed to accommodate the smooth running of the institution, whereas the child-centred practices were geared to the needs of the individual child and would be more likely to result in an enabling, supportive environment. Raynes *et al.* (1979), in a study of the organizational variables which influence quality of care, found that the degree of autonomy which staff had in determining unit policy was important. In those units in which staff roles were not rigidly defined and all staff were involved in decision making, more resident-orientated care was provided.

## Supportive Community Rehabilitation

Increasing numbers of the disabled are no longer hospital patients, but long-term community patients (Bennett, 1978). For them social support is organized on an aftercare basis. This is not a single process of restoring their adaptive capacity but rather an ongoing attempt to enable them to achieve and maintain a reasonable level of social adaptation in the face of the stressful challenges of everyday life. The disabled cannot do without support, but in the community it is important that support should enable them to improve their role performance. Brim and Wheeler (1966) suggest that before a person is able to perform satisfactorily in a role he must know the behaviour and values expected of him, must be able to meet role requirements, and must desire to practise the behaviour and pursue the appropriate ends. This means that the rehabilitation setting must provide clear and unambiguous norms for the patient, opportunities for learning and practising the required role performance, and the selective reward of adaptive behaviour. It must also provide support if the disabled person is to have the confidence to cope with and master the stresses involved in rehabilitation.

The maintenance or development of role performance and coping ability affects both the need for support and the type of support needed. Of this we know little although attention has been drawn to a preliminary finding by Pearlin and Schooler (1978) which suggested that, since a person's coping responses are not equally effective in all areas of role performance, the effectiveness of particular forms of support, too, may vary correspondingly. There is, for example, a difference between role and status socialization. Role socialization, according to Bidwell (1962), is the training and preparation required for the performance of a specific task. Status socialization, on the other hand, refers to a broader pattern of training which prepares the rehabilitee to resume a more generalized status in life. Vocational education and training are examples of role socialization, while participation in treatment groups, receiving advice from doctors or social workers, or participating in the daily life of the ward are examples of status socialization.

While it may be clear to professional staff that patients receive support in status socialization they tend to overlook the support available through role socialization. Thus professional workers often tend to 'downgrade the importance of occupational and recreational therapy and to see individual and group psychotherapy as the cornerstone of treatment' (Lamb, 1967). The successful performance of roles, whether in the family, in employment, or in social life, itself generates support, because the disabled person then engages in the give and take of life and avoids passive dependence. The performance of adult social roles, whether in work or elsewhere, enables the disabled person to contribute, to give something back to society which in turn leads him to believe that he is esteemed and valued, and also belongs to a network of communication and mutual obligation. If he cannot perform adult roles he will only achieve that support given to the very sick or very young, which fosters dependency. Not all disabled people can be employed, nor can they achieve the same status in the outside world as those who are not disabled. They can, however, engage in work settings which are more or less sheltered and which provide differing levels of expectation and types of supervision. It should not be forgotten that earnings are an important form of support, for money does allow person to take on other roles and engage in other activities.

What is needed is a variety of services so that the individual can be placed in a work setting which makes the best use of his capacities. Outside the hospital it is possible to provide widely varying forms of support or shelter in open or sheltered employment, in day centres and various forms of residential accommodation, in clubs and self-help groups, in addition to support from the individual's family and social network. The reversal of institutionalizing practices does not necessarily foster adaptation, but whether rehabilitation is being undertaken in the community or in hospital it is important that work, living, and leisure roles should be carried on in different places under different authorities. For, as Goffman (1961) says, 'it is a basic social arrangement in modern society . . . that the individual tends to sleep, play and work in different places, with different co-participants, under different authorities and without an overall rational plan'. While this is the basic social arrangement in life, the disabled often need some modification of both the physical and social environment if they are to function effectively. The normal community offers a very wide range of natural supports which can be combined in various ways to provide for very individual needs. While the disabled can and should use as many of the general community facilities as possible, they often need special medical and social supports. It has to be recognized that the community outside the hospital is no more 'therapeutic' than the hospital itself. General social facilities are no substitute for specific social treatment aimed at each individual and based upon a detailed knowledge of that person's handicap (Wing and Brown, 1970). 'By keeping the patient out of hospital, it was assumed that he would be kept in the community and that his tenure in the community, if it did not immediately cure him, would at least avoid the dehumanising process of institutionalization' (Kirk and Therrien, 1975). Merely resettling patients in the community does not in itself constitute rehabilitation and it is only the starting point from which supportive rehabilitation begins. Yet it is not unrealistic to undertake rehabilitation in the community. Nor is it unrealistic to support the disabled psychiatric patient in the community rather than in an institution. One must, however, recognize the disadvantages as well as the advantages of the community situation. While the community can provide a most extensive and varied social network and supportive system, it is not organized in accordance with any overall rational therapeutic plan. Though it is possible to arrange highly individualized help, that help may not have a rehabilitation goal and thus will be ineffective.

Most people organize their own supportive system in accordance with their needs and inclinations. It is certainly possible for the less disabled individuals to do this. But disabilities vary in extent and severity. Those individuals with lesser degrees of disability can adapt in the sense that adaptation requires not only that they should be independent and able to meet society's expectations, but that they should be able to impose their own direction on events and take some responsibility for other people. Such people can usually organize the support they need and use it to their advantage. Those who are more disabled will only be able to adjust to life in the community in the sense that they will be able to meet society's expectations without being able to shape events or take responsibility for others. They may need some help from professionals and others in organizing support. Finally, there are those who are so disabled that they need 'asylum' within the framework of the district service, in the sense that they can accommodate to community life if they are provided with shelter and support; they cannot organize this for themselves or do much to help others. Supports have to be provided for them. Even so, they may also use some of those services used by the wider community as will the most adapted patients. Those 'asylum' patients use the semi-segregated services provided for other disadvantaged groups and the segregated services used by the psychiatrically disabled alone. It should not be assumed that even the most disabled are totally incapable of organizing their own supports. There should be no sharp distinction and between those who can manage full adaptation and integration in society and those who are only able to 'adjust' or need asylum and will become isolated in group homes (Ryan, 1979) or in the hospital ward.

Disabled psychiatric patients living at home will spend the majority of their time in desegregated normal environments, but they may attend a Remploy factory which is a semi-segregated work environment. Alternatively, they may be attending a club which is provided solely for psychiatric patients. Those who lack families, or are estranged from them, may need more help in the integration of their social resources. However, the need for support, the ability to integrate support, and the ability to integrate and adapt in society are not all or nothing matters. They can be arranged along a graduated scale on which the individual's place is determined not only by his or her intrinsic disabilities but also by personality characteristics, social disadvantage, or choice. Thus the need or demand for support does not imply that an individual qualifies for psychiatric services, in the absence of a primary or intrinsic handicap. Mann and Cree in their study of new, long-stay patients in a number of mental hospitals identified a group of 'asylum seekers' who preferred life in a mental hospital to a community existence. 'These patients knew that they no longer had symptoms necessitating in-patient care but could put forward good reasons for not wishing to be discharged' (Mann and Cree, 1976).

Many of the severely disabled have unstable disabilities which vary from time to time, and such patients need continuing medical support in terms of the supervision and management of their condition as well as the integration of a number of other supports. Watson et al. (1970) described a flexible support system offered by a hospital psychiatric unit to severely disabled patients living in the community. Support was provided largely by the nursing staff. Patients would come to the hospital in the evening of any day of the week, including weekends. When visiting the hospital they sat and talked, had a bath or an occasional meal, met other patients or friends, played a game with them or watched television. Preliminary findings from the study of this service (Mitchell and Birley, 1982) show that 104 patients used it during 6 months in 1978. Of these 57 patients were selected for detailed study; 22 were attending four different day facilities in the area, 32 were attending as outpatients, 11 were admitted as inpatients once, 1 on two occasions during the 6 months. A number were living in special residential facilities provided by voluntary organizations. Thus the hospital not only provided medical and social support for very disabled patients, it also provided a central focus for the integration of other services. If such community support is to be effective, those operating the statutory and voluntary facilities must be aware of the social influences affecting the disabled not only in, but also outside, their own particular setting. Failure to do this makes it difficult for organizations to relate their own efforts to the supportive or therapeutic activities going on outside their own boundary (Astrachan et al., 1970). If there is an uneasy relationship between the medical and social services or between the professional workers and the family, those who provide support will feel unsupported themselves; they will not feel themselves to be part of a network of communication and mutual obligation.

Different types of support must be equally valued. Kushlick et al., (1976) describes the considerable differences in the amount of time which different grades of staff spend in direct contact with patients. Increase in status is usually related to a decrease in time spent in direct contact, which can serve to devalue this level of direct support. Rigid professional boundaries will result in fragmented, poorly integrated support. Caplan (1974) thought that new models of working will require professional workers to accept that many problems have to be handled by members of different professions. The importance of team support must not be forgotten. Individual staff members may become sick, get promotion, or leave for another appointment. They are also unable to be on call 24 hours a day, 7 days a week. A team can provide more continuous support, and mutual support and the influence of different disciplines are more likely to provide a broadly based service.

The potential importance of self-help services for psychiatrically disabled people is not commonly recognized. Certainly they do not seem to set up formal organizations, but there has been a tendency to overlook the informal relationships between patients which are a considerable source of mutual support. Even when patients draw attention to their mutual dependence, staff tend to underrate this and distrust or refuse the relationship. There are few recent studies of this to compare with that of Rowland (1938).

In the study by Mitchell and Birley (1982) it was found that the social contact which patients had with each other was considered important both by the patients themselves and the nursing staff. The degree of support varied. For female patients, in particular, other patients were often part of a coherent network of acquaintances and friends. For many of the male patients just being in the company of others was valued. In some instances patients reported that they found other patients supportive because they were in the same situation and had a shared understanding of the experience of being a chronic psychiatric patient.

Some rehabilitation programmes have utilized the mutual support between patients. Fairweather (1964) describes a programme which was designed to enable small groups of patients to meet increasing expectations and responsibilities by encouraging mutual support and obligations. The method of resettlement by developing 'group homes' also depends upon the ability of the rehoused patients to relate to each other supportively in a domestic setting.

The importance of the relationships of the psychiatrically disabled with each other is described in investigations of the social networks of ex-mental patients living in single-room occupancy hotels in Manhattan. It was often assumed that such people were isolated and loners. Cohen and Sokolovsky (1979), having described a way of analysing such networks, suggest that professional staff can be taught to understand their client's behaviour within this support system. They found that patients with schizophrenia with minimal residual psychopathology, who had hotel networks averaging 11 or more persons, never experience rehospitalization. This correlation with hotel networks did not hold for schizophrenics with more severe psychopathology. They also suggested that it might be possible to solve the problems of some clients by the reorganization and readjustment of the informal support system. One should not forget the marriage of patients in terms of mutual support. There are few studies, but one study of mentally retarded patients who married (Mattinson,

1970) was 'particularly impressed by the mutual help these husbands and wives gave to each other and by the complementary nature of the partnership'.

Huessy (1981), summarizing one of the mistaken premises of the community health movement in the USA, states that 'chronic patients in hospitals have no social networks. This is due to their having been in hospital. Therefore we will take care of patients in the community—they will not lose their social networks, and they will not become chronic patients.' Subsequent experience has indicated that desocialization is as likely to take place in the community as in hospital unless adequate professional and social support is available to ensure that the patient is able to maintain existing social networks, or when necessary to supplement existing but inadequate networks with relevant services. Support is therefore a key process in rehabilitation, but conceptual and empirical anlayses are only beginning to be elaborated. Beels (1981) comments that we do not really know which patients have supportive networks which are helping them and should be left alone; which patients have no access to support and need to have it constructed for them by professionals; which patients have potential supports to which they have not become connected; and which patients will continue to require lengthy periods of hospitalization in spite of available personal and professional support. Despite such limitations in understanding, the experience of community care has served to emphasize the principle that social adaptation cannot be assessed and improved in isolation from other aspects of the social context. The literature on support and social networks provides a conceptual framework in which to understand the interaction between the disabled person and his community and those processes which lead through mutual modification to adaptation.

## References

Andrews, G., and Tennant, C. (1978) Life events, stress and psychiatric illness. *Psychological Medicine*, **8**, 545–549.

Astrachan, B. M., Flynn, H. R., Geller, J. D., and Harvey, H. H. (1970) Systems approach to day hospitalisation. *Archives of General Psychiatry*, **22**, 550–559.

Bachrach, L. L. (1978) A conceptual approach to deinstitutionalization. *Hospital and Community Psychiatry*, **29**, 573–578.

Bart, P. E. (1974) The sociology of depression. In P. Roman and H. M. Trice, eds, *Explorations in Psychiatric Sociology*. Davis, Philadelphia.

Barton, R. (1966) *Institutional Neurosis*. John Wright, Bristol.

Bebbington, P., and Tennant, C. (1978). Social causation of depression: an evaluation of the work of Brown and his colleagues. *Psychological Medicine*, **8**, 565–575.

Beels, C. C. (1981) Social support and schizophrenia. *Schizophrenia Bulletin*, **7**, 58–72.

Beiser, M. (1976) Personal and social factors associated with the remission of psychiatric symptoms. *Archives of General Psychiatry*, **33**, 941–945.

Belknap, I. (1956) *Human Problems of a State Mental Hospital*. McGraw-Hill, New York.

Bennett, D. (1978) Community psychiatry. *British Journal of Psychiatry*, **132**, 209–220.

Bennett, D., Fox, C., Jowell, T., and Skynner, A. C. R. (1976) Towards a family approach in a psychiatric day hospital. *British Journal of Psychiatry*, **129**, 73–81.

Bergmann, K., Foster, E. M., Justice, A. W., and Matthews, V. (1978) Management of the demented elderly patient in the community. *British Journal of Psychiatry*, **132**, 441–449.

Bidwell, C. E. (1962) Pre-adult socialisation. A paper presented at the Social Science Research Council Conference on Socialisation and Social Structure.

Birley, J. L. T. (1974) A housing association for psychiatric patients. *Psychiatric Quarterly*, **48**, 568–571.

Bott, E. (1957) *Family and Social Network*. Tavistock, London.

Bott, E. (1976) Hospital and society. *British Journal of Medical Psychology*, **49**, 97–140.

Brim, O. G., and Wheeler, S. (1966) *Socialisation after Childhood: Two Essays*, John Wiley, New York.

Brown, G. W., Birley, J. L. T., and Wing, J. K. (1972) The influence of family life on the course of schizophrenic illness: a replication. *British Journal of Psychiatry*, **121**, 241–258.

Brown, G. W., Davidson, S., Harris, T., MacLean, U., Pollack, S., and Prudo, E. (1977) Psychiatric disorder in London and North Uist. *Social Science and Medicine*, **11**, 367–377.

Brown, G. W., and Harris, T. (1978) *Social Origins of Depression: A Study of Psychiatric Disorder in Women*. Tavistock, London.

Caplan, G. (1974) *Support Systems in Community Mental Health*. Behavioural Publications, New York.

Carter, J., and Edwards, C. (1975) *National Day Care Study: Pilot Report*. National Institute for Social Work, London.

Cobb, S. (1976) Social support as a moderator of life stress. *Psychosomatic Medicine*, **38**, 300–314.

Cohen, C. I., and Sokolovsky, J. (1979) Clinical use of network analysis for psychiatric and aged populations. *Community Mental Health Journal*, **15**, 203–213.

Creer, C., and Wing, J. K. (1974) *Schizophrenia at Home*. National Schizophrenia Fellowship, Surbiton.

Cumming, E. (1968) *Systems of Social Regulation*. Atherton Press, New York.

Cumming, E. (1969) 'Therapeutic community' and 'milieu therapy' strategies can be distinguished. *International Journal of Psychiatry*, **7**, 204–208.

Deykin, E. Y., Jackson, S., Klerman, G. L., and Soloman, M. (1966) The empty nest: psychological aspects of conflict between depressed women and their grown children. *American Journal of Psychiatry*, **122**, 1422–1426.

Ebringer, L., and Christie-Brown, J. W. R. (1980) Social deprivation among short-stay psychiatric patients. *British Journal of Psychiatry*, **136**, 46–52.

Fairweather, G. W. (1964) *Social Psychology in Treatment of Mental Illness*. John Wiley, New York.

Frankenberg, R. (1966) *Communities in Britain*. Penguin, Harmondsworth, Middx.

Freeman, H. E., and Simmons, O. G. (1963) *The Mental Patient Comes Home*. John Wiley, New York.

Garrison, V., and Podell, J. (1981) 'Community Support Systems Assessment' for use in clinical interviews. *Schizophrenia Bulletin*, **7**, 101–108.

Gath, D. H., Hassall, C., and Cross, K. W. (1973) Whither psychiatric day care? A study of day patients in Birmingham. *British Medical Journal*, **1**, 94–98.

Goffman, E. (1961) *Asylums: Essays on the Social Situation of Mental Patients and Other Inmates*. Anchor Books, New York.

Grad, J., and Sainsbury, P. (1968) The effects that patients have on their families in a community care and a control psychiatric service: a two-year follow-up. *British Journal of Psychiatry*, **114**, 265–268.

Hall, J. N., Baker, R. D., and Hutchinson, K. (1977) A controlled evaluation of token economy procedures with chronic schizophrenic patients. *Behaviour Research and Therapy*, **15**, 261–283.

Hammer, M. (1963) Influence of small social networks as factors on mental hospital admission. *Human Organization*, **22**, 243–251.

Hammer, M. (1981) Social supports, social networks and schizophrenia. *Schizophrenia Bulletin*, **7**, 45–57.

Heller, K. (1979) The effects of social support: prevention and treatment implications. In A. P. Goldstein and F. J. Kanfer, eds, *Maximising Treatment Gains: Transfer Enhancement in Psychotherapy*. Academic Press, New York.

Hewett, S., Ryan, P., and Wing, J. K. (1975) Living without mental hospitals. *Journal of Social Policy*, **4**, 391–404.

Hoenig, H., and Hamilton, M. W. (1969) *The Desegregation of the Mentally Ill*. Routledge & Kegan Paul, London.

Huessy, H. R. (1981) Discussion. *Schizophrenia Bulletin*, **7**, 178–180.

Jacobson, S., and Klerman, G. L. (1966) Interpersonal dynamics of hospitalised depressed patients' home visits. *Journal of Marriage and the Family*, **28**, 94–102.

Kahn, R. L., and Quinn, R. P. (1977) Mental Health, Social Support and Metropolitan Problems. Research Proposal. University of Michigan.

King, R., Raynes, N., and Tizard, J. (1971) *Patterns of Residential Care*. Routledge & Kegan Paul, London.

Kirk, S. A., and Therrien, M. E. (1975) Community mental health myths and the fate of former hospitalised patients. *Psychiatry*, **38**, 209–217.

Kushlick, A., Felce, D., Palmer, J., and Smith, J. (1976) *Evidence to the Committee of Enquiry into Mental Handicap Nursing and Care*. Health Care Evaluation Research Project, Winchester.

Lamb, H. R. (1967) Chronic psychiatric patients in the day hospital. *Archives of General Psychiatry*, **17**, 615–621.

Leff, J. P., and Vaughn, C. E. (1980) The influence of life events and relatives' expressed emotion in schizophrenia and depressive neurosis. *British Journal of Psychiatry*, **136**, 146–153.

Liem, J. H., and Liem, R. (1976) Life events, social supports and physical and psychological well-being. Paper presented at the meeting of the American Psychological Association.

Lipton, F. R., Cohen, C. I., Fischer, E., and Katz, S. E. (1981) Schizophrenia: a network crisis. *Schizophrenia Bulletin*, **7**, 144–151.

Lowenthal, M. F., and Haven, C. (1968) Interaction and adaptation: Intimacy as a critical variable. *American Sociology Review*, **33**, 20–30.

Mann, S. A., and Cree, W. (1976) 'New' long-stay psychiatric patients: a national sample survey of fifteen mental hospitals in England and Wales 1972/3. *Psychological Medicine*, **6**, 603–616.

Mattinson, J. (1970). *Marriage and Mental Handicap*. Duckworth, London.

Mechanic, D. (1974) Social, structural and personal adaptation: some neglected dimensions. In G. V. Coelho, D. A. Hamburg, and J. E. Adams, eds, *Coping and Adaptation*. Basic Books, New York.

Miller, P. McC., and Ingham, J. G. (1976) Friends, confidants and symptoms. *Social Psychiatry*, **11**, 51–58.

Miller, P. McC., Ingham, J. G., and Davidson, S. (1976) Life events, symptoms and social support. *Journal of Psychosomatic Research*, **20**, 515–522.

Mills, E. (1962) *Living with Mental Illness*. Routledge & Kegan Paul, London.

Mitchell, J. C. (1969) *Social Networks in Urban Situations*. Manchester University Press, Manchester.

Mitchell, S. F., and Birley, J. L. T. (1982) The use of ward support by psychiatric patients in the community. *British Journal of Psychiatry*, **142**, 9–15.

Otto, S., and Orford, J. (1978) *Not Quite Like Home — Small Hostels for Alcoholics and Others*. John Wiley, Chichester.

Paykel, E., Emms, E. M., Fletcher, J., and Rassaby, E. S. (1980). Life events and social support in puerperal depression. *British Journal of Psychiatry*, **136**, 339–346.

Pearlin, L. I., and Johnson, J. S. (1977) Marital status, life-strains and depression. *American Sociological Review*, **42**, 704–715.

Pearlin, L. I., and Schooler, C. (1978) The structure of coping. *Journal of Health and Social Behaviour*, **19**, 2–21.

Rapoport, R. N. (1960) *Community as Doctor: New Perspectives on the Therapeutic Community*. Thomas, Springfield, Ill.

Raynes, N. V., Pratt, M. W., and Roses, S. (1979) *Organisational Structure and Care of the Mentally Retarded*. Croom Helm, London.

Richards, H. (1971) Local authority day centre for the mentally ill. *Lancet*, **i**, 793–795.

Rowland, H. (1938) Interaction processes in the state mental hospital. *Psychiatry*, **1**, 323–327.

Royal College of Nursing and National Council of Nurses of the United Kingdom (1963) *The Role of Psychiatric Ward Sisters and Charge Nurses in the Rehabilitation of Patients*. Royal College of Nurses, London.

Ryan, P. (1979) Residential care for the mentally disabled. In J. K. Wing and R. Olsen, *Community Care for the Mentally Disabled*. Oxford University Press, London.

Scott, R. D., and Alwyn, S. (1978) Patient–parent relationships and the course and outcome of schizophrenia. *British Journal of Medical Psychology*, **51**, 343–355.

Shepherd, G., and Richardson, A. (1979) Organisation and interaction in psychiatric day centres. *Psychological Medicine*, **8**, 573–579.

Sokolovsky, J., Cohen, C., Berger, D., and Geiger, J. (1978) Personal networks of ex-mental patients in a Manhattan S R O Hotel. *Human Organisation*, **37**, 5–18.

Stevens, B. C. (1972) Dependence of schizophrenia patients on elderly relatives. *Psychological Medicine*, **2**, 17–32.

Test, M. A., and Stein, L. I. (1976) Use of special living arrangements: a model for decision making. Paper presented at NIHM sponsored conference. Community Living Arrangements for the Mentally Ill and Disabled, Rosslyn, Virginia.

Tolsdorf, C. C. (1976) Social networks, support and coping: an explanatory study. *Family Processes*, **15**, 407–418.

Vaughn, C., and Leff, J. P. (1976). The influence of family and social factors on the course of psychiatric illness. *British Journal of Psychiatry*, **129**, 125–137.

Vickers, G. (1967). Community medicine, *Lancet*, **i**, 944–947.

Watson, J. P., Bennett, D. H., and Isaacs, A. D. (1970) Psychiatric units in general hospitals. *Lancet*, **i**, 511–514.

Weiss, R. S. (1968) Materials for a theory of social relationships. In W. G. Bennis, E. H. Schein, F. I. Steale, and D. E. Berlew, eds, *Interpersonal Dynamics*. Dorsey Press, Homewood, Ill.

Wing, J. K., and Brown, G. W. (1970) *Institutionalisation and Schizophrenia*. Cambridge University Press, London.

# PART V

*Social Roles*

Theory and Practice of Psychiatric Rehabilitation
Edited by F. N. Watts and D. H. Bennett
© 1983, John Wiley & Sons, Ltd.

# 11

---

# Employment

---

FRASER WATTS

There is no denying that psychiatric patients often have difficulty with employment. Anthony *et al.* (1972) have reviewed some of the evidence on how many patients return to work after being discharged from a psychiatric hospital. The proportion of patients in work in the 6 months after discharge ranges from 30 to 50 per cent, but a year after discharge it is only 20 to 30 per cent. Clearly, these patients have difficulties not only with finding but also with keeping employment. Studies that have compared employment rates before and after admission have also found a substantial reduction in the numbers employed. For example, Cole *et al* (1964) found that 62 per cent of the patients they surveyed were employed before admission, but only 43 per cent afterwards.

However, it must be noted that these figures relate entirely to psychiatric inpatients, who can be presumed to have relatively serious psychiatric problems as well as to be suffering from some of the secondary handicaps that can accrue from an admission to a psychiatric hospital. The figures also relate to samples composed entirely or substantially of psychotic patients. We do not appear to have adequate data on the extent to which being a psychiatric outpatient is associated with unemployment, or much data on the extent to which non-psychotic psychiatric conditions are associated with employment (though see Chapter 4). It is likely that there is an association, though a less strong one than exists for psychotic patients who have been admitted to hospital. However, the size of the association can only be a matter for speculation at present. It really is not sensible to try to reach any general estimate of the employment rate in such a diverse group as psychiatric patients. Different estimates are needed for various subgroups.

The main focus of this chapter will be, not on whether psychiatric patients have difficulty with employment, but on why many do so and on what can be done to help them overcome these difficulties. Rehabilitation needs to be based on a clear analysis of each patient's handicap, and in as far as these handicaps vary from person to person, rehabilitation programmes will need to be planned for each individual patient. Unless patients' employment difficulties are understood, rehabilitation effort may be directed at aspects of work functioning that will make only a marginal difference to their employability.

Further, the assessment of individual patients' employment handicaps needs to be set within a general conceptualization of employment problems. Unfortunately, as Tiffany *et al.* (1970) have pointed out, occupational psychology has taken very little interest in this question of the distinguishing characteristics of employable and unemployable people. The unemployed have been outside the normal work settings, and so have tended to be ignored. Occupational psychology has been concerned with such matters as how people choose jobs, how much satisfaction they get out of them, how well they perform in them, etc. These are all questions that arise among employed people. Scientific work on the problems of the marginally employable has so far been very limited, and has arisen almost entirely within the context of particular problem groups, whether it is the disadvantaged, the unemployed black, the psychiatric patient, or whatever. So far, we have only a fragmentary conceptual and scientific understanding of employability as a general issue.

Employability can be analysed under three headings. Two of these can be found in several previous theories of vocational adjustment. They are highlighted, for example, in the title of a paper written some years ago by Heron (1954): 'Satisfaction and satisfactoriness: complementary aspects of occupational adjustment'. By satisfaction is meant the extent to which the job meets the requirements of the worker. By satisfactoriness is meant whether the worker meets the requirements of the job. The third component of employability is the ability to find a suitable job. There is now some scientific understanding of the difficulties psychiatric patients have in finding work, and what can be done to overcome these.

A theory that has provided a formal statement of the contribution of satisfaction and satisfactoriness to vocational adjustment has been provided by Lofquist and Dawis (1969). It is proposed that good work adjustment depends on the combination of satisfaction and satisfacortiness. One consequence of this is that satisfaction will predict work adjustment best among those who are also satisfactory, and satisfactoriness will predict best among those who are also satisfied. They have brought forward evidence for the latter claim but not for the former. These propositions suggest an explanation of a common finding in the rehabilitation literature that single measures of vocational functioning pick out the unemployable better than the employable among psychiatric patients. This is true, for example, for work performance (Watts, 1978) for motivation (Griffiths, 1974), and for work history (Watts and Bennett, 1977).

The theory also proposes that voluntary terminations are likely to arise from a lack of satisfaction, dismissals from a lack of satisfactoriness. Voluntary terminations are relatively more common than dismissals (Caplow, 1954) and it is probably quite common for people to resign voluntarily in order to avoid possible dismissal. So the connection of satisfaction and satisfactoriness with these two kinds of termination of employment is probably far from an exact one.

Another proposition of the Lofquist and Dawis theory is that job tenure is a function of vocational adjustment. No limit is put on the range of job lengths over which this relationship is supposed to hold. However, empirical work on the theory does not seem to have considered job lengths of more than 3 years. In some cases, very long job tenures might reflect a lack of capacity for normal career development, and so represent a poor capacity for vocational adjustment. Nevertheless, it is reasonable to regard the ability, not only to get, but to keep a job as one of the criteria by which successful rehabilitation can be judged. The particular issues involved in keeping jobs will be discussed later in this chapter.

### Satisfactoriness

It is widely assumed that there is a significant relationship between intelligence and employability, that patients who are intelligent are more likely to make satisfactory workers and so be able to find employment. The evidence on this point is mixed. Though there has been some supporting evidence (e.g. Tseng, 1972a) most studies (e.g. Sandler, 1952; Lowe, 1967; Griffiths, 1974) have failed to find any significant relationship between intelligence and return to work. However, the data are generally too briefly reported for critical analysis. The range of intelligence covered by the data is probably relevant. Among the mentally handicapped, intelligence is probably of greater importance, though even here work attitudes may be more important than IQ (Stephens et al., 1968). The link between low intelligence and not returning to work is probably stronger than that between high intelligence and return to work.

In addition, as the Lofquist and Dawis theory would predict, intelligence may be a better predictor of return to work when attention is confined to patients who have the other necessary qualities of motivation, interpersonal skills, etc. Also, intelligence may be more important if the criterion is simply return to work rather than a stable resettlement at work. Eber (1967) found that intelligence predicts employment status immediately after rehabilitation but not at follow-up. This is probably partly because of the greater importance of intelligence in learning a new job than in continuing to perform it once it has been learned (Ghiselli, 1966).

Finally, it should be noted that intelligence is less likely to be related to employability than to the level of job a person obtains. Occupational level can be predicted from intelligence better than can most other criterion measures, certainly better than occupational success (Matarazzo, 1972). Though the more intelligent will tend to get higher level jobs, most people will find that there is some job or other they can do, whatever their intelligence, provided they are employable in other ways. Among those doing any particular job, success will probably be related less closely to intelligence than to other relevant factors.

Another related approach to the prediction of employment status is to use tests of specific aptitudes rather than of general intelligence. Of such tests the General Aptitude Test Battery is generally regarded as the most satisfactory. Unfortunately, the test has a number of weaknesses, and does not stand up to critical examination. It contains 12 different subtests, which are combined in various ways to yield measures of eight specific aptitudes and a measure of general ability. Unfortunately, as Watts and Everitt (1980) have shown, this cannot be justified by the correlational structure of the subtests, and no more than three adequately determined factors can be extracted. The validity of the GATB is also suspect. Though a considerable number of validity studies have been carried out, correlations of more than about 0.3 have been rare (Ghiselli, 1966; Bemis, 1968). Predictive power of this low order is not likely to be of much value in clinical work with individual patients. The prediction of relative occupational success among the employed is, in any case, quite different from predicting which rehabilitation patients will succeed in obtaining work. Taylor (1963) found that GATB scores did not predict employment status after rehabilitation. However, Burstein et al. (1968) were able to predict return to work on other tests of psychomotor ability.

Another approach to the prediction of employment status is the 'work sample' method in which patients are assessed on carefully devised tasks typical of those found in work situations. However, the results of this approach are also disappointing. Reviewing the evidence, Overs (1970) has concluded that performance on work samples is highly correlated with performance on standard tests of ability and does no better in predicting employment status. Clearly, the work sample method has so far failed to tap the critical determinants of employability, though tasks which assess employability more adequately may eventually be devised (Neff, 1966).

A more promising approach has been to use a simulated work environment, such as a rehabilitation workshop. To provide a good setting for assessments, such a unit needs to be run as closely as possible to the way in which a small factory would be run. There is an accumulation of evidence that assessments of work behaviour in such an environment, made by experienced supervisors, are a very good predictor of vocational resettlement. Van Allen and Loeber (1972) review a number of studies of this kind. The point at which such studies become most interesting for an understanding of employability is where they provide assessments of various aspects of work behaviour, and compare their usefulness in predicting vocational resettlement.

There are two workshop scales that deserve particular comment. One is the scale developed by the Chicago Jewish Vocational Service (Gellman et al., 1963; Soloff and Bolton, 1969) which has a number of good methodological features including explicit criteria for observation and ratings. It also has a well-replicated factor structure as data from three different workshops yielded the same five factors: (a) attitudinal conformity to the work role; (b) maintenance of quality; (c) acceptance of work demands; (d) interpersonal security and (e) speed of production. The ability of the CJVS workshop scale to predict subsequent employment has been demonstrated in some ten studies using a variety of different populations (Bolton, 1974).

Also of particular interest are a series of British studies carried out first at Malvern (Cheadle et al., 1967; Cheadle and Morgan, 1972) and later at the Maudsley Hospital, London, using a revised version of the same rating scale (Griffiths, 1973, 1977; Watts, 1978). Griffiths carried out a principal component analysis of the scale showing that it measures five aspects of work behaviour: (a) task competence; (b) response to supervision; (c) social relationships; (d) enthusiasm, and (e) confidence/initiative. However, as Watts (1978) pointed out, the last component is weak and should be regarded cautiously. The important question is which of these areas of work behaviour are most closely related to subsequent employment.

Examining the data of Cheadle and Morgan (1972) in the light of Griffiths's principal component analysis, it can be seen that none of the task competence items is significantly related to resettlement at work, but five of the eight remaining items covering response to supervision, social relationships, and enthusiasm are significantly correlated with return to work. Watts (1978) obtained similar results, though the results were slightly different for psychotic and non-psychotic patients. Social relationships were closely correlated with subsequent employment in both groups of patients. In contrast, response to supervision and enthusiasm were associated with subsequent employment only in psychotic patients. Also, social relationships assessed at an early stage of rehabilitation predicted return to work, though only later ratings of response to supervision and enthusiasm did so. Task competence ratings failed to predict return to work. Against these results must be set those of Griffiths (1977) who found that all groups of items, including task competence, predicted return to work, but it seems that a retrospective method of completing the ratings was used in this study which would be liable to increase halo effects. This is the most likely explanation of his discrepant results.

Two studies (Tseng, 1972b; Griffiths, 1975) have examined work ratings completed by the patients themselves. Neither has examined the value of these ratings in predicting subsequent employment, though they have established that there are often large discrepancies between the ratings of supervisors and patients.

These findings provide the basis for understanding the employment satisfactoriness of psychiatric patients. The next step is to explore in more detail the performance characteristics of the unsatisfactory worker in the three critical areas of enthusiasm, response to supervision, and social relationships.

Several of the aspects of performance covered by the heading 'enthusiasm' (e.g. 'works continuously', 'eager to work', 'looks for more work') proved to be better predictors of subsequent employment in the inpatient rehabilitation unit at Malvern than the community-based unit at the Maudsley (Bennett, 1972). In addition, 'enthusiasm' only seems to be an important determinant of employment in psychotic patients (Watts, 1978). It seems a reasonable hypothesis that it is the chronic, institutionalized schizophrenic who is most disadvantaged in obtaining employment by his performance in this area. Studies of the work performance of chronic schizophrenics at the Cheadle Royal Hospital (Wadsworth *et al.*, 1962, 1963) describe the nature of the deficit. In one of these studies (Wadsworth *et al.*, 1962) the fatiguability of workers was examined. Though schizophrenics proved no worse than other workers in this respect when they were being monitored regularly, they were more 'fatiguable' when not closely supervised. Apparently they were dependent on external supervision to maintain continuity of work. Their ability to pace their own work was inadequate. In the second study, Wadsworth *et al.* (1963) looked at the ability of schizophrenics to organize a simple psychomotor task, and found that they were often unable to devise an efficient way of doing it. Even when they had been shown how to do a job, they often deviated from this by inserting unnecessary steps (putting tools down and taking them up again, fiddling with the materials). These are examples of the difficulties schizophrenic workers have in organizing themselves and showing sustained and efficient effort. Such characteristics would have resulted in lower ratings on 'enthusiasm' (perhaps not a wholly appropriate label for this group of items). Another item in this 'enthusiasm' group which has regularly proved a good predictor of employment is good time-keeping. This may depend on the same kind of organizing abilities as the other items which are concerned with continuous performance, etc.

The 'response to supervision' items also proved to be a significant predictor of employment only in schizophrenic workers (Watts, 1978). Some of the items in this group are rather general (e.g. 'welcomes supervision'), but two of the more specific ones ('willing to change jobs' and 'accepts criticism and correction of work readily') invite some comment. Both of these seem to involve sensitivity to failure, either to the risk of failure or to its consequences.

The laboratory research on 'fear of failure' motivation (Birney *et al.*, 1969) has confirmed that it has a distorting effect on people's willingness to engage in tasks and to take risks. Fear of failure would almost certainly affect a worker's willingness to try an unfamiliar task. So far there have been no direct investigations of the effects of fear of failure on job changing in a rehabilitation workshop, nor apparently of the strength of fear of failure in schizophrenic as opposed to other psychiatric patients. However, it is generally accepted that schizophrenics are hypersensitive to censure. Indeed it has been proposed that this may account for their performance deficits (Rodnick and Garmezy, 1957) though the evidence for this is not wholly convincing (Buss and Lang, 1965). In psychotic workers, response to supervision is more satisfactory in those who feel relatively confident and well supported by others (Watts and Yu, 1976). This is consistent with an interpretation of this aspect of work performance as reflecting anxiety about failure. However, even if this idea is on the right lines, much more work is clearly needed to elucidate how anxiety affects work performance.

Social relationships, unlike response to supervision and enthusiasm, are a good predictor of employment in both psychotic and non-psychotic workers. However, it is possible that the critical social disabilities are different in different categories of patients. The study reported by Neff and Koltov (1967) goes some way towards clarifying the nature of the social performance deficit involved. Ratings were made on seven aspects of behaviour 2 weeks after admission to a rehabilitation unit (fearful, dependent, impulsive, socially naïve, withdrawn, self-deprecatory, and hostile). Most of these were concerned with social behaviour. The criterion was whether patients completed the rehabilitation programme, or dropped out or were terminated prematurely. Those who completed the programme had significantly less social naïvety (i.e. not realizing what effect one's behaviour has on other people or what is appropriate) and hostility (i.e. anger, contradicting and arguing with others, irritating, insulting, criticizing them, etc.) than those who did not. There were no differences in fearful, dependent, or withdrawn behaviour. (The 'completers' were also more impulsive and less self-deprecatory, but the differences are not directly relevant to social behaviour.) It is interesting that withdrawn behaviour was less detrimental to rehabilitation than more 'active' forms of deviant social behaviour. Most (81 per cent) of the patients in this study were schizophrenic. Whether similar conclusions would emerge in a study of other groups is an open question. It is also not certain that the same types of social behaviour would predict subsequent employment as predicted completion of the rehabilitation programme.

Some useful clinical information about areas of poor work performance can be obtained from a thorough work history. Many patients are, of course, reluctant to admit that their performance in jobs was unsatisfactory, but there are ways of phrasing questions (e.g. If your supervisor could have changed one thing in your performance on the job, what would he have chosen?) that enable patients to provide this information without condemning themselves. Such information is clinically very helpful in specifying a patient's critical employment handicaps.

Another approach to the examination of the importance of personality functioning in rehabilitation is through standard personality questionnaires. The results here have been somewhat mixed. Claims have been made for the predictive value of the Edwards Personal Preference Schedule in rehabilitation programmes, but initial results have not been replicated (Distefano and Pryer, 1970). Claims have also been made for Rotter's Locus of Control Scale (Tseng, 1970). However, because of the considerable degree of situational specificity in social behaviour (Mischel, 1968) it cannot be expected that general measures of personality will be as relevant as direct measures of personality functioning in the work situation.

The emphasis on 'work personality' rather than task competence as a critical aspect of the employability of psychiatric patients converges with work in other areas. For example, Wynne (1974) has reached a similar conclusion in his studies of college dropouts, emphasizing the lack of what he calls 'affective skills' (i.e. the ability to interpret the attitudes of others, to foresee the effects of immediate actions on long-range personal relationships, etc.). The analysis of employability of psychiatric patients developed here can be taken as a contribution to the growing understanding of personalogical and social psychological factors contributing to unemployment (Tiffany et al., 1970).

## Improving Satisfactoriness

Traditionally, much rehabilitation has proceeded by offering a standard rehabilitation programme through which each patient moves at his own pace. There have not been many direct attempts to modify the particular employment handicaps presented by individual patients. But now, with an increasing conceptual understanding of the components of employability, and with the development of assessment tools for identifying the handicaps of individual patients, it has become possible to develop a style of rehabilitation that takes specific steps to modify discreet employment handicaps.

Much of this work will need to be done at a relatively early stage of rehabilitation. In the final stage it is usually desirable to provide a patient with a fairly realistic work environment (in terms of hours of work, styles of supervision, etc.) so that the gap between the culmination of the rehabilitation programme and the open employment that it is hoped will follow it is as small as possible. A realistic work setting of this kind also makes it easier to assess when a patient is ready for open employment. On the other hand, it is very difficult to do much in the way of specific remedial work with individual patients without undermining the realism of the work atmosphere. It is desirable, therefore, that such remedial work should be largely undertaken before patients reach this final stage of the rehabilitation programme.

Watts (1976) has suggested that the principles of behaviour modification have an important place in remedial work on employment handicaps. Most important here, perhaps, is simply the methodological style that is characteristic of behaviour modification, a style that seeks to specify as exactly as possible the target for the modification programme, finds a way of measuring this target variable so that the progress of the programme can be monitored, and devises a specific strategy for modifying the target variable based on a detailed functional analysis of the problem as it is presented by the individual patient and also on what is known generally about the methods by which psychological change can be brought about. It is a secondary matter whether any of the standard techniques of behaviour modification can be applied directly to employment problems.

Dallos and Winfield (1975) have provided a valuable general approach to giving work instructions. They bring together guidelines for the style to be used by instructors who are dealing with various kinds of workers. With anxious people, for example, the initial stimuli to be distinguished should be clearly discernible, there should be considerable feedback in the early stages, and ego-involving instructions should be avoided. Often one of the main problems for the patient will be adapting to stresses introduced by the supervisor, such as grasping instructions that the supervisor does not expect to have to repeat, or working under time-pressure. It may be helpful to provide patients with explicit practice at coping with these stresses, following a carefully graded hierarchy.

Where attempts have been made to improve specific aspects of patients' performance in rehabilitation the focus has usually been on productivity. Industrial workshops often operate a system of piecework payment, which has been shown to improve productivity in at least some patients. The evidence relating to the effects of financial incentives on productivity is reviewed by Morgan in Chapter 8. In addition, social stimulation and encouragement can have considerable effects on productivity. Taylor and Persons (1970) describe a programme in which the amount of time a patient spent working was recorded on a wall chart, and the staff commented approvingly on this whenever the amount of work done showed an increase. Wing and Freudenberg (1961) have reported a classic experiment in which they showed that patients receiving increased 'social stimulation' from supervisors in the workshop increased their productivity. One of the ingredients of this was encouragement for improved performance. Unfortunately, the effects of the programme were short-lived and did not survive the withdrawal of extra stimulation. This is a common problem with 'reinforcement' methods but one that there are ways of combatting (see Kazdin, 1977).

However, in view of the argument that has been made for the critical importance of work personality in determining employability, it is essential that rehabilitation programmes should include, where appropriate, specific measures to improve these more general aspects of work functioning. Social behaviour is often a critical matter. Available methods of training people in the skills of social interaction (see Shepherd, Chapter 13) can be applied to problems of social behaviour in the workshops. For example, Sanders and Walters (1972) report encouraging results from a programme that made part of the piecework rate contingent on appropriate verbal behaviour in the workshop. The social interaction problems presented are very varied, ranging from an excess of inappropriate talk to a severe deficit in appropriate talk. Programmes will therefore need to be geared to the problems presented by each individual.

Further, behavioural methods of desensitization (e.g. Rachman, 1978) may be useful in modifying excessive emotional reactions that interfere with work performance. This can be applied to excessive anxiety about making mistakes, switching from one task to another, and working under pressure of time. There is some evidence that desensitization can also modify reactions of excessive anger at such irritants as being given orders or being criticized (Evans and Hearn, 1973) but the usefulness of this in rehabilitation needs further evaluation.

### Satisfaction

We turn now from the factors responsible for someone's satisfactoriness in a job to an examination of the satisfaction derived from work. In vocational psychology the main emphasis has normally been on the relative degree of satisfaction that people can obtain from different kinds of work, and the implications of this for their selection of a job. The emphasis here will need to be a different one. The critical question regarding job satisfaction as far as rehabilitation is concerned is whether any jobs at all of those that a patient might be able to undertake would provide him or her with at least the minimum degree of satisfaction necessary to seek employment and remain in it. The crucial comparison is between the satisfaction that would be provided by whatever work is available and the satisfaction provided by unemployment; the relative satisfactions afforded by different jobs is a secondary matter. In many cases there will not need to be a great deal of positive satisfaction in employment for it to be preferable to unemployment.

It has been mainly in periods of high unemployment that research has been carried out on the general effects of employment and unemployment. Some of the classic research was carried out during the 1930s. With the increase in unemployment in the 1970s research interest in this question has revived (e.g. Marsden and Duff, 1975). The impact of long-term unemployment has been broadly similar in these two periods (Jahoda, 1979), showing the same features of boredom, declining self-respect, and apathetic resignation. The fact that the absolute poverty of the unemployed in the 1970s was not as great as in the 1930s does not appear to alter the psychological impact. The available data, though less systematic than one could wish, are sufficient to establish the important psychological effects of unemployment in our society, functions that do not depend on the content or particular characteristics of individual jobs. Rather, they flow, as Jahoda has argued, from the function of employment in structuring time, enforcing activity, providing shared experiences, linking the individual to external goals, and conferring personal status and identity.

It is important to emphasize at the outset that work satisfaction is by no means a unitary variable. Indeed, there may be very little connection between the degree of satisfaction felt with different aspects of a job. The question of the 'structure' of job satisfaction has been tackled in a series of factor analytic studies. It is not possible to review these here. However, the conclusion reached by Smith *et al.* (1969, p.30) still stands, that the factors that have emerged repeatedly, besides a general factor, cover satisfaction with pay and material rewards, supervision, other workers, and the skills demanded by the work itself. Herzberg *et al.* (1959) have designated such things as pay, supervision, and co-workers as sources of 'extrinsic' satisfaction, contrasted with the 'intrinsic' satisfaction provided by the work itself.

An approach to satisfaction with employment that is suggested by this component analysis of job satisfaction is to estimate the degree of satisfaction or dissatisfaction created by these various aspects of work, and to examine whether the balance of satisfactions and dissatisfaction is a valid indicator of net employment satisfaction, hence a predictor of whether patients will be willing to seek and retain work.

Before proceeding with this it is necessary to consider a hypothesis put forward by Herzberg *et al.*, which has generated a vast amount of research in occupational psychology, that these various aspects of work do not each contribute in the same way to overall job satisfaction, but rather that there are two separate and independent feeling states created by work, one of satisfaction and one of dissatisfaction. It is further hypothesized that the 'extrinsic' factors such as pay, supervision, and other workers determine how dissatisfied a person feels whereas the 'intrinsic' factors determine how satisfied a person feels. It has been accepted by most reviewers of the literature (e.g. Bockman, 1971) that studies using the 'critical incident' method devised by Herzberg, in which people are asked to identify events that led to marked increases or decreases in satisfaction, have tended to support these propositions, though studies using other methods have generally failed to do so. In defence of Herzberg's theory it can be argued (Grigaliunas and Weiner, 1974) that the studies that claim to have refuted it are not strictly relevant, because they have not attempted to measure two separate emotional reactions to work. This is really the central question. In retrospect one can say that the research on Herzberg's theory should have tackled first the question of whether job satisfaction and dissatisfaction are indeed independent of each other, before going on to the question of which aspects of work are relevant to them. In fact, no consensus on whether or not satisfaction and dissatisfaction are separate, independent reactions to work has been reached. Even if there were a clear distinction between these two work reactions, it seems very unlikely that there would be any universally applicable correspondence between them on the one hand and intrinsic and extrinsic aspects of work on the other. At best there would be a tendency for there to be some correspondence, but with many individuals in whom it did not apply.

In approaching the assessment of job satisfaction and dissatisfaction in individual rehabilitation clients, it therefore seems unwise to have any firm preconceptions about which aspects of work are relevant to each. Nevertheless, one can easily advance some hypotheses about sources of work dissatisfaction that are likely to recur among psychiatric patients. Dissatisfaction with supervision will be common. This can take various forms. There will be patients with paranoid attitudes who will interpret the criticism of work that is a necessary part of supervision as personal hostility. There will be anxious patients who will find it very stressful to be moved on to a new job that they are not confident they can cope with. It seems unlikely that supervision will often be a source of positive satisfaction and a motive for seeking employment.

The effects of co-workers on satisfaction and dissatisfaction will be more varied. For some people, despite what Herzberg says, co-workers are a very important aspect of work satisfaction, especially for women (Centers and Bugenthal, 1966). There are certainly some patients who seek employment because they value the companionship it offers. On the other hand, there will be patients who are easily made anxious and annoyed by other people, for whom co-workers will be an important source of dissatisfaction with employment. For many rehabilitation patients, pay is a marginal consideration, as their income is only slightly increased by being in employment. Most do not seem to mind this, though some regard it as unacceptable and a reason for not working. MacLean (1977) has argued that the small financial benefits that many patients derive from employment tend to reinforce their dependence on welfare benefits. Employment will frequently offer little in the way of reinforcements, whereas acceptance of unemployment benefit may well have some anxiety-reducing function.

It is thus not difficult to identify some of the common causes of dissatisfaction with employment that will operate in rehabilitation. What is more puzzling is what sources of satisfaction can offset these potential dissatisfactions, and apparently do so for a surprising number of patients. One can speculate that employment is an important source of self-respect for some people. Similarly, being in work may bring increased status in the family and social network. This is one of the functions of work within the mental hospitals. Goldberg (1967) showed that patients assigned to work programmes felt that their needs for belongingness and esteem are met more than those not in such programmes. Tiffany *et al.* (1970, pp. 62–64) report similar findings for ex-psychiatric patients. Patients in full-time work were more likely to rate themselves, for example, as 'having the ability to do what is expected of them' and generally seemed to have higher self-evaluation.

Particularly interesting was the fact that these patients were also more likely to feel that in the home they influenced what went on and were satisfied with how things were. Of course, such correlational studies do not imply causation, but it seems likely that employment contributed to the self-respect and social influence of these patients.

It ought to be possible along these lines to identify the various satisfactions and dissatisfactions that people associate with employment and unemployment. A decision-making analysis could then be applied in which, through summing each of these and comparing them, a prediction could be made as to whether a particular patient would be willing to seek employment. Such an approach would, however, present considerable problems of calibration. One of the interesting issues that would arise is how far satisfactions and dissatisfactions can offset each other, or whether there are some reasons for seeking or for not seeking work that have an absolute and overriding importance.

A second conceptual approach to the analysis of employment satisfaction could be developed on the basis of patients' work needs and how far these would in fact be met by employment. Useful tools in such an approach would be the Minnesota Job Importance Questionnaire, designed to assess vocational needs, and the Minnesota Satisfaction Questionnaire, designed to assess how far these needs are met by jobs (Lofquist and Dawis, 1975). In a rehabilitation setting it would again be more important to assess how far employment would meet work needs, rather than to compare the relative satisfaction provided by different jobs. It should also be noted that people will differ in how they cope with non-correspondences between needs and satisfactions (Davis and Lofquist, 1976). Purvis (1969) has provided data regarding the work needs of a sample of 77 psychiatric patients using the Minnesota Job Importance Questionnaire. The main point of interest was that the work needs of the patients assessed in this way were not significantly different from those of the sample of matched controls who were tested. However, in the patients' group there was more likely to be a discrepancy between their work needs and abilities than in the matched control group.

The Minnesota theory of work adjustment predicts that work adjustment and job tenure will be a function of the correspondence between the individual work needs and the pattern of 'work reinforcers' provided by the job (Lofquist and Dawis 1975). This has received empirical support. For example,

Betz (1969) found that satisfaction was correlated with a correspondence between work needs and work reinforcers and that job satisfaction predicted job tenure.

Following this line of argument and evidence, it can be predicted that (a) whether a patient seeks employment will be a function of the correspondence between work needs and the anticipated rewards provided by employment; (b) whether a patient remains in work will be a function of the correspondence between work needs and the work reinforcers actually experienced. In many cases the anticipated work reinforcers will be crucial, and a very important question that deserves investigation is whether patients anticipate work reinforcers correctly. It seems very likely that patients who have been out of work for a long period will not be able to do this at all well. This misperception of the available work reinforcers will have important implications for work motivation. Another matter that needs attention is which areas of job satisfaction are most crucial as far as overall satisfaction with employment is concerned. It is likely that discrepancies between needs and satisfactions in some areas will have a bigger effect than in others on willingness to seek work.

As with satisfactoriness, a thorough work history can provide important information about the satisfactions and dissatisfactions patients have experienced with their jobs so far. Questions about what they liked and disliked about their various jobs, and about events that led to increases and decreases in their work satisfaction will indicate the critical areas of satisfaction for the patient concerned. Similar questions need to be asked about satisfactions and dissatisfactions with unemployment.

So far this discussion has been largely restricted to 'extrinsic' sources of satisfaction, and little attention has been given to the actual content of the work. This has been deliberate. The working population as a whole, apart from people in managerial and professional jobs, rate the content of work as less important than extrinsic factors (Centers and Bugenthal, 1966), and this is no doubt also true of most psychiatric patients. However, there is a tendency for psychiatric patients to report high levels of interest in artistic and in social service jobs which are perhaps intrinsically rewarding, but for most people an unrealistic vocational aspiration (Patterson, 1957).

On the face of things it might be assumed that largely unattainable vocational interests would represent an obstacle to employment, but this is not necessarily so. It seems that many people have a variety of vocational interests that span the range from the realistic to the ideal. This emerged in a study of the aspirations of disturbed adolescents (Small, 1953). Whereas well-adjusted adolescents gave a realistic vocational choice first and an unrealistic one second, this order was reversed in the disturbed adolescents. The interesting point was that both kinds of aspiration could be elicited in both groups. The fact that some patients may put forward an apparently unrealistic vocational aspiration does not mean that they do not also have a realistic choice which will influence their behaviour.

Most of the empirical studies relevant to the work satisfaction in rehabilitation have not attempted the detailed assessment of different aspects of satisfaction that is really necessary in this field, but instead have used general measures of work motivation, work values, and so on. Such measures have been shown to be effective in predicting return to work, but they are of no use in indicating the detailed factors that are relevant in particular patients. For example, Griffiths (1974) showed that ratings of work motivation based on a structured interview significantly predicted return to work. Similarly, Hartmann (1972) developed a good questionnaire measure of keenness to work and found that it was a highly significant predictor of return to work in a mixed sample of physically and psychiatrically disabled patients, though Watts and Yu (1976), using a much shorter questionnaire composed of similar items with a purely psychiatric sample, were not able to demonstrate such predictive validity. It is encouraging that it is possible to develop valid measures of motivation based on self-report. It might have been thought that the 'social desirability' response set would have been so powerful as to render such questionnaires useless. Fortunately, this is not the case. In addition there are a number of other questionnaires such as the Adult Vocational Maturity Inventory (Shepherd, 1971), the Survey of Work Values (Goodale, 1973), and the Employment Readiness Scale (Alfano, 1973), that have been developed for the assessment of the unemployed generally, that may well have predictive value to psychiatric patients in rehabilitation. One that has been shown to be of some relevance is the Orientation Inventory that assesses task, self, and interaction orientations in work situations. High task orientation has been shown to be related to motivated performance in a rehabilitation workshop (Distefano and Pryer, 1964) and to successful resettlement (Distefano et al., 1966). Questionnaires of this kind that seek to measure commitment to the work role are probably very relevant to the relative net satisfaction provided by employment and unemployment.

## Improving Satisfaction

There is little that can be said about the modification of work satisfaction. Perhaps the most important effect a rehabilitation programme can have in this area is to reduce dissatisfactions with work. Improvements in job performance will tend to reduce dissatisfactions. People whose quality of work is relatively good will receive less criticism from supervisors. People who are skilful at getting on with new work colleagues will find starting at a new job less stressful. Also improved job performance will tend to bring generally increased self-confidence (a proposition that will be discussed more fully in Chapter 14).

Various job dissatisfactions, especially those arising from interaction with colleagues and supervisors, will be reduced as confidence increases. It is consistent with this view that measures of confidence in rehabilitation patients are significant predictors of return to work (Wing, 1966; Griffiths, 1974) though this has not always been found (Hartmann, 1972; Watts and Yu, 1976).

This raises the general question of the relationship between job performance and job satisfaction. Though it is now recognized that there is by no means always a close relationship between performance and satisfaction, there is some connection between them. Locke (1970) has suggested that the effect of performance on satisfaction is stronger than the reverse effect, though the extent to which performance affects satisfaction will be dependent on the extent to which it exemplifies work values. However, in rehabilitation the central value is often simply for the patient to demonstrate his employability both to himself and to other people. Successful performance in the context of rehabilitation will normally contribute to this, and so tend to create satisfaction.

Motivation to work seems to be related to contact with the work role. When people first become unemployed their attitude to employment shows little change, though it begins to fall after about 6 months and continues to fall over the following year (Alfano, 1973). There is evidence that this process tends to be reversed during rehabilitation. Positive attitudes to employment increase over the course of a rehabilitation programme (Brewer *et al.*, 1975). The reasons for this are not entirely clear. However, at least some changes in work motivation are likely to be mediated though changes in the attitude of the patients' families. If the family believes that it is feasible for a patient to return to work they will probably encourage him to do so.

### Resettlement in Employment

Finally, even if a patient is potentially both satisfactory and satisfied as a worker, there is the problem of actually finding a job. The number of job vacancies fluctuates markedly with changes in the economic situation, and this influences the prospects for patients being successfully resettled. It seems ikely that unemployment will continue to show a generally increasing trend over the coming years with the proliferation of labour-saving industrial technology, though service industries may not be affected by this (Williams, 1980). What chance, then, have marginally employable psychiatric patients got of competing for a dwindling number of job vacancies and obtaining employment?

This raises many complicated questions to which only incomplete answers can be given. The theory of differential employment presented by Hodge (1973) is a useful starting point. He suggests that the labour market can be conceptualized as a queue. In principle the relative employability of the members of the job queue could be quantified, perhaps in terms of such factors as training and previous experience. The simplest possible model would then predict that the available vacancies would go to the most employable people in the queue. However, there would clearly be a variety of factors mitigating against the operation of the system in this simple way. For one thing there would be some selection error, either because employers are not aware of the most employable candidates for their jobs or because they assess the employability of candidates for the job incorrectly. There might also be a tendency systematically to discriminate for or against whole sets of potential workers. The prospects of psychiatric patients obtaining work depends largely on whether these factors operate for or against them in the job queue.

What is known about the attitudes of employers to hiring psychiatric patients? This is no easy matter to assess. The answers of employers to questions about their willingness to employ ex-psychiatric patients have produced very discrepant results depending on how the questions have been worded. This is clear in the study reported by Whatley (1964). Some 79 per cent of employers gave a questionnaire reply indicating that ex-patients do about as well on a job as everyone else with the same qualifications. However, only 38 per cent said they would just as soon hire a patient who had been in a mental hospital as anyone else. In any case, it cannot be assumed that there is much connection between the answers given to such questions and the actions of employers when it comes to selecting workers. There is an inevitable tendency for people to give what they regard as the expected answer to such questions. It is a common finding (e.g. Olshansky et al., 1958) that though many employers claim that they would be willing to employ ex-patients, very few have knowingly done so.

The recent work of Farina and Felner (1973) has been more sophisticated methodologically than many earlier studies (see Blum and Kujoth, 1972) in assessing the prejudices of employers. The interviewees were non-patients acting as confederates in the experiment. Some indicated that they had spent the last 9 months travelling, others that they had been in a mental hospital for this period. Employers who were led to believe they were interviewing ex-patients were less favourable in their attitudes. They were less friendly, were less likely to offer a job, and gave a lower estimate of the prospect of work being obtained. Similar findings were obtained in an experiment involving workers on jobs similar to those being applied for. Those who believed they were meeting psychiatric patients rated the applicants as having a variety of liabilities and as being less likely to get on with other workers. They were more likely to say that they should not be hired.

It is clear what employers are most worried about in employing psychiatric patients (Hartlage, 1965). They fear sudden outbursts of violence, believe that the ex-patients will not be able to stand up under pressure, that they will not be able to adjust to new situations, that they will need more supervision, and so on. The fear of violence is perhaps the least realistic of these worries. However, there are many areas such as dishonesty and absenteeism in which they apparently do not anticipate any particular problems.

How can psychiatric patients seeking work overcome these prejudices against them? Patients seeking to return to their old jobs after a psychiatric admission are in an unusually strong position. Between 50 and 70 per cent of such patients are reemployed afterwards (Olshansky *et al.*, 1958; Cole *et al.*, 1964). Comparatively few are refused. It seems that prejudices operate less strongly against patients who have established a work record with a particular firm. Union membership increases such patients' chances of being reemployed (Cole *et al.*, 1964).

The other commonly used method is simply to conceal the psychiatric history from the prospective employers. This is the course taken by most patients (Cole *et al.*, 1964). Quite apart from increasing their chances of employment, there is evidence (Farina *et al.*, 1971) that patients perform better if they believe people do not know about their psychiatric history.


Job Interviews

How patients present themselves at interview is probably a critical determinant of whether or not they obtain work. Searls *et al.* (1971), found that inappropriate behaviour (seeming to lack physical vitality, difficulty in making oneself understood, and not seeming able to handle responsibilities) were all associated with failure to obtain work. Barbee and Kiel (1973) approached a similar question by asking personnel interviewers to rank aspects of interviewee behaviour in order of importance. The following five items emerged as the most significant: honesty and openness, level of information regarding present job skills, personal adaptability, level of information regarding past job experiences, and ability to respond to interviewer's questions. It is significant that most of these items relate directly to the provision of information rather than to general impressions. Psychiatric patients will often find it difficult to know how best to respond to questions about their personal circumstances and recent past, but clearly it is not a good strategy to respond to questions evasively. It seems to be important to respond fully to questions and to relate previous experience and personal circumstances to the job.

Many patients can benefit from training in interview skills. Kiel and Barbee (1973) evaluated the effects of videotape feedback and behaviour modification, comparing it with control conditions (feedback only, and no treatment). The effects were assessed on a rating scale that was shown to yield reliable ratings of interview behaviour. The patients in the experimental group improved significantly more than the controls, especially on assertiveness, initiative, and ability to ask questions about the job, though there was no direct assessment of whether this method improved the chances of being offered a job. Venardos and Harris (1973) reported a similar study showing that either videotape feedback or role playing produced more improvement in interview behaviour as rated by judges than did an attention-control condition.

Two recent studies have used multiple baseline methodology to evaluate the effects of job interview training for patients. Furman *et al.* (1979) were able to demonstrate improvements in various specific interview skills such as gesturing or asking questions as efforts were made to modify them. Kelly *et al.* (1979) reported a similar study showing effects on number of questions asked, amount of information provided, and expressions of enthusiasm as efforts were made to modify them in turn. The subjects were rated as having better interview performance after training and five of the six patients successfully obtained employment.

Also important is how patients seek out information about possible jobs and follow up job leads when they hear of them. Jones and Azrin (1973) carried out a survey of how job vacancies are filled. Over half of the jobs that are filled are not advertised or notified in any way. Clearly, then, if patients limit themselves to jobs that are notified to official job counsellors or resettlement officers they narrow the range of jobs open to them. Two thirds of jobs are filled through an informal network, i.e. from information from friends or relatives working at the place where the vacancy has occurred. This presents a difficulty for many psychiatric patients who may have lost touch with this informal job network. To compound the problem many patients are poor at following up information about jobs. Resistance to accepting job referrals, procrastination in following them up, and missing appointments are all significantly associated with failure to obtain work (Searls *et al.*, 1971).

Azrin *et al.* (1975) have described an energetic and apparently effective approach to overcoming this problem. They formed a 'Job Finding Club' which people were encouraged to attend each day until they found a job. It provided a comprehensive structuring of the job-seeking process, which the clients were expected to regard as a full-time activity. To obtain information about jobs they were encouraged to make full and systematic use of friends, relatives, and previous employers as sources of information about vacancies, to place attractively worded 'situation wanted' advertisements, and to explore every reasonable lead obtained through advertisements of vacancies. Full use was made of the telephone both in arranging interviews and obtaining employers' decisions. Advice was given on dress and general presentation at interviews, and rehearsal of interview skills was provided. Clients were advised to take letters of recommendation with them to all interviews. The results were encouraging. Clients assigned to the club obtained jobs significantly more quickly than comparable subjects assigned to a control condition (a median of

14 as opposed to 53 days). Also clients in the club tended to obtain higher level jobs than the control subjects.

In addition to encouragement to pursue job leads energetically, patients may also need advice about what sort of job they are suitable for. Vocational guidance is one of the traditional facilities that has been made available to patients seeking work. Characteristically such vocational guidance makes an assessment of people's abilities and interests, and helps them to find an available job for which both their abilities and interests are relevant. This style of vocational guidance is out of key with the view of employability that has been argued here. It is quite possible, for example, that patients will be unemployable in any job at all because of their poor interpersonal skills, and this can easily go undetected in a traditional assessment of work aptitudes. Equally, traditional assessments of work interests focus on interests in different types of work and ignore the general motivation for employment. Because of these inadequcies of assessment, it is possible to make quite unrealistic recommendations about suitability for particular jobs.

However, it is possible to give vocational guidance that is based on more relevant data. One critical topic is very often the style of supervision. The counsellor would need to know how well the patient functions with different degrees and styles of supervision. He would also need to know the patient's emotional reactions to different types of supervision. With this, and a knowledge of the different supervisory styles in different jobs, a start could be made on giving more realistic advice about which sorts of jobs patients would be suitable for. Similar data would be needed on regularity of attendance, interaction with co-workers, and other structural aspects of jobs.

## Job Tenure

Even after patients have found suitable jobs there are issues related to their ability to stay in them. There are some patients who always seem to be able to get a job, but who never stay in one for more than a month or two. This can be predicted to some extent from patients' occupational history. Watts and Bennett (1977) found that the amount of employment in the 2 years before admission predicted return to work, but was not related to a stable (at least 6 months) resettlement in employment. On the other hand, occupational stability, early on in the work history, though unrelated to return to work, successfully predicted stable resettlement. Anthony and Buell (1974) also found that occupational stability predicted a stable return to work, whereas Lorei and Gurel (1973) found that both recent employment and job stability were about equally effective predictors of a stable return to work. Other relevant predictive data summarized by Buell and Anthony (1975). It is a plausible view that the capacity for a stable work record is a personality trait that will manifest itself equally before and after a psychiatric admission.

The assessment of previous occupational stability raises a number of methodological problems. These relate chiefly to comparing the occupational stability of people at different stages of their careers, and of people in different kinds of occupation. It is common for people to change jobs more frequently in the first few years of their working life than later on. Unless this is taken into account it will give the misleading impression that people early in their careers are unusually unstable workers. To deal with this it is necessary to select a particular period of the working career and to compare the same period in all subjects. Watts and Bennett (1977) in a study of this kind chose the first 10 years of the working life. The other problem relates to the comparability of occupational stability in different professions. There are two points here. One is that there are some occupations such as the construction industry where frequent job changing is standard and almost inevitable so that people in this industry may get misleadingly inflated assessments of occupational instability. The other point is that a more relevant aspect of occupational stability may be pursuing an orderly career within a certain occupation than staying a long time in a particular job. Both of these points can be met by considering changes of type of work rather than changes of job. Watts and Bennett (1977) found that the mean length of time in each kind of work was a better predictor of stable resettlement in employment than was the mean time in each job. Also, the longest time in a single type of work was a better predictor than the length of the longest job. What is important is to have had stable jobs. It is irrelevant to the prediction of stable resettlement in employment whether or not someone has also had a lot of short-term casual jobs.

Though the tendency of some patients to leave jobs after only a short period maybe a long-standing pattern of behaviour, there are other current reasons for the short duration of jobs that are more directly related to psychiatric problems. Cole et al. (1968, 1970), in their follow-up study of former patients in employment, found that significantly more of the patient sample than of the matched controls they were compared with left their jobs within the 4-year follow-up period. Many of these were medical retirements. The patients concerned tended to be in the older age group, though not yet at the official retiring age.

The attitudes of employers to the behaviour of ex-psychiatric patients on the job may also be a factor that makes it more difficult for them to keep their jobs, even if they concealed their psychiatric status in order to obtain employment. Whatley (1964) carried out a survey of 100 employers who had employed patients, about half of them unknowingly. Employers who had kept patients in jobs for less than 9 months on average responded to questions about the employment of patients in a way that indicated greater prejudice against them than those who kept them for longer than 9 months on average.

However, this must be interpreted with some caution as these employers also had a greater tendency to dismiss workers generally.

One of the difficulties with resettlement is that the gap between the rehabilitation workshop and open employment can be too great for some patients, perhaps especially schizophrenic patients, to take in their stride. This remains true however much care is taken to make the rehabilitation workshop as realistic as possible. The gap between the conditions of the workshop and those of open employment probably reduces the number of patients obtaining employment and also their chances of staying in their jobs. Wansborough (1975) presents evidence that patients who go to open employment straight from psychiatric hospitals show significantly less stability in their jobs than those coming from other sources.

One possible solution to this problem is to use sheltered work outside the hospital as a final bridging stage to open employment. Sheltered factories could be used in this way to a greater extent. But, more importantly, special positions for sheltered workers can be established in the normal employment network with this purpose in mind. It would be hoped that a period as a sheltered worker would enable the ex-patient to adapt more gradually to the stresses of open employment, and also that he would be able in time to demonstrate his competence as a worker to his employers and so overcome the prejudice that might operate against him at an initial interview. If all went well he would eventually be taken onto the ordinary pay-roll, and his 'sheltered' place could go to someone else. More data are needed about the effectiveness of this kind of integration of sheltered work with the rehabilitation service.

### References

Alfano, A. M. (1973) A scale to measure attitudes towards working. *Journal of Vocational Behaviour*, 3, 329–333.

Anthony, W. A., and Buell, G. J. (1974) Predict psychiatric rehabilitation outcome using demographic characteristics: a replication. *Journal of Counselling Psychology*, 21, 421–422.

Anthony, W. A., Buell, G. J., Sharratt, S., and Althoff, M. E. (1972) Efficacy of psychiatric rehabilitation. *Psychological Bulletin*, 78, 447–456.

Azrin, N. H., Flores, T., and Kaplan, S. J. (1975) Job Finding Club: a group assisted program for obtaining employment. *Behaviour Research and Therapy*, 13, 17–27.

Barbee, J. R., and Kiel, E. c. (1973) Experimental techniques of job interview training for the disadvantaged: videotape feedback, behaviour modification and micro-counselling. *Journal of Applied Psychology*, 58, 209–213.

Bemis, S. E. (1968) Occupational validity of the General Aptitude Test Battery. *Journal of Applied Psychology*, 52, 240–244.

Bennett, D. H. (1972) Principles underlying a new rehabilitation workshop. In J. K. Wing and A. M. Hailey, eds, *Evaluating a Community Psychiatric Service*. Oxford University Press, London.

Betz, E. (1969) Need-reinforcer correspondence as a predictor of job satisfaction. *Personnel and Guidance Journal*, 47, 878–883.

Birney, R. C., Burdick, H., and Teevan, R. C. (1969) *Fear of Failure*. Van Nostrand, New York.

Blum, L. P., and Kujoth, R. K. (1972) *Job Placement of the Emotionally Disturbed*. Scarecrow Press, Metuchen, NJ.

Bockman, V. M. (1971) The Herzberg controversy. *Personnel Psychology*, **24**, 155–189.

Bolton, B. (1974) *Introduction to Rehabilitation Research*. C. C. Thomas, Springfield, Ill.

Brewer, E. W., Miller, J. H., and Ray, J. R. (1975) The effect of vocational evaluation and work adjustment on clients' attitude towards work. *Vocational Evaluation and Work Adjustment Bulletin*, **8**, 19–25.

Buell, G. J., and Anthony, A. A. (1975) The relationship between patient demographic characteristics and psychiatric rehabilitation outcome. *Community Mental Health Journal*, **11**, 208–214.

Burstein, A. G., Soloff, A., and Mitchell, J. (1968) Psychomotor performance and the prognosis of chronic mental patients. *Perceptual and Motor Skills*, **26**, 491–498.

Buss, A. H., and Lang, P. J. (1965) Psychological deficit in schizophrenia: I. Affect, reinforcement and concept attainment. *Journal of Abnormal Psychology*, **70**, 2–24.

Caplow, T. (1954) *The Sociology of Work*. University of Minnesota Press, Minneapolis.

Centers, R., and Bugenthal, D. E. (1966) Intrinsic and extrinsic job motivation among different segments of the working population. *Journal of Applied Psychology*, **50**, 193–197.

Cheadle, A. J., Cushing, D., Drew, C. D. A., and Morgan, R. (1967) The measurement of the work performance of psychiatric patients. *British Journal of Psychiatry*, **113**, 841–846.

Cheadle, A. J., and Morgan, R. (1972) The measurement of work performance of psychiatric patients: a reappraisal. *British Journal of Psychiatry*, **120**, 437–441.

Cole, N. J., Blair, W., McDonald, B. W., and Branch, C. H. H. (1968) A two-year follow-up study of the work performance of former psychiatric patients. *American Journal of Psychiatry*. **124**, 1070–1075.

Cole, N. J., Brewer, D. L., Allison, R. B., and Branch, C. H. H. (1964) Employment characteristics of discharged schizophrenics. *Archives of General Psychiatry*, **10**, 314–319.

Cole, N. J., and Shupe, D. R. (1970) A four-year follow-up of former psychiatric patients in industry. *Archives of General Psychiatry*, **22**, 222–229.

Dallos, R., and Winfield, I. (1975) Industrial strategies in industrial training and rehabilitation. *Journal of Occupational Psychology*, **48**, 241–252.

Dawis, R. V., and Lofquist, L. H. (1976) Personality style and the process of work adjustment. *Journal of Counselling Psychology*, **23**, 55–59.

Distefano, M. K., and Pryer, M. W. (1964) Task orientation, persistence and anxiety of mental patients with high and low motivation. *Psychological Reports*, **14**, 18.

Distefano, M. K., and Pryer, M. W. (1970) Predicting vocational outcome of psychiatric patients with the Edwards Personal Preference Schedule. *Journal of Applied Psychology*, **54**, 552–554.

Distefano, M. K., Pryer, M. W., and Rice, D. P. (1966) Orientation and job success of mental hospital patients. *Psychological Reports*, **19**, 113–114.

Eber, H. W. (1967) The multivariate analysis of a rehabilitation system: cross validation and extension. *Multivariate Behavioural Research*, **2**, 477–484.

Evans, D. R., and Hearn, M. T. (1973) Anger and systematic densensitization: a follow-up. *Psychological Reports*, **32**, 569–570.

Farina, A., and Felner, R. D. (1973) Employment interveiwer reactions to former mental patients. *Journal of abnormal Psychology*, **82**, 268–272.

Farina, A., Gliha, D., Boudreau, L. A., Allen, J. G., and Sherman, M. (1971) Mental illness and the impact of believing others know about it. *Journal of Abnormal Psychology*, **77**, 1–5.

Furman, W., Geller, M., Simon, S. J., and Kelly, J. A. (1979) The use of a behaviour rehearsal procedure for teaching job-interviewing skills to psychiatric patients. *Behaviour Therapy*, **10**, 157–167.

Gellman, W., Stern, D. J., and Soloff, A. (1963) *A Scale of Employability for Handicapped Persons*. Jewis Vocational Service, Chicago.

Ghiselli, E. E. (1966) *The Validity of Occupational Aptitude Tests*. John Wiley, New York.

Goldberg, R. T. (1967) Need satisfaction and rehabilitation progress of psychotic patients. *Journal of Counselling Psychology*, **14**, 253–257.

Goodale, J. G. (1973) Effects of personal background and training on work values of the hard-core unemployed. *Journal of Applied Psychology*, **57**, 1–9.

Griffiths, R. D. P. (1973) A standardised assessment of the work behaviour of psychiatric patients. *British Journal of Psychiatry*, **123**, 403–408.

Griffiths, R. D. P. (1974) Rehabilitation of chronic psychotic patients: an assessment of their psychological handicaps, an evaluation of the effectiveness of rehabilitation and observations of the factors which predict outcome. *Psychological Medicine*, **4**, 316–325.

Griffiths, R. D. P. (1975) The accuracy and correlates of psychiatric patients' self assessment of their work. *British Journal of Social and Clinical Psychology*, **14**, 181–189.

Griffiths, R. D. P. (1977) The prediction of psychiatric patients' work adjustment in the community. *British Journal of Social and Clinical Psychology*, **16**, 165–173.

Grigaliunas, B., and Weiner, Y. (1974) Has the research challenge to motivation-hygiene theory been conclusive? An analysis of critical studies. *Human Relations*, **27**, 839–871.

Hartlage, L. C. (1965) Expanding comprehensiveness of psychiatric rehabilitation. *Mental Hygiene*, **49**, 238–243.

Hartmann, P. (1972) A study of attitudes in industrial rehabilitation. *Occupational Psychology*, **46**, 87–97.

Heron, A. (1954) Satisfaction and satisfactoriness: complementary aspects of occupational adjustment. *Occupational Psychology*, **28**, 140–153.

Herzberg, F., Mausner, B., and Snyderman, B. (1959) *The Motivation to Work*. John Wiley, New York.

Hodge, R. W. (1973) Toward a theory of racial differences in employment. *Social Forces*, **52**, 16–31.

Jahoda, M. (1979) The impact of unemployment in the 1930s and the 1970s. *Bulletin of the British Psychological Society*, **32**, 309–314.

Jones, R. J., and Azrin, N. H. (1973) An experimental application of a social reinforcement approach to the problem of job-finding. *Journal of Applied Behaviour Analysis*, **6**, 345–353.

Kazdin, A. E. (1977) *The Token Economy*. Plenum, New York.

Kelly, J. A., Laughlin, C., Clairborne, M., and Patterson, J. (1979) A group procedure for teaching job interviewing skills to formerly hospitalised psychiatric patients. *Behaviour Therapy*, **10**, 299–310.

Kiel, E. C., and Barbee, J. R. (1973) Training the disadvantaged job interviewee. *Vocational Guidance Quarterly*, **22**, 50–56.

Locke, E. A. (1970) Job satisfaction and job performance: a theoretical analysis. *Organizational Behaviour and Human Performance*, **5**, 484–500.

Lofquist, L. H., and Dawis, R. V. (1969) *Adjustment to Work: A Psychological*

*View of Man's Problems in a Work-Oriented Society.* Appleton-Century-Crofts, New York.

Lofquist, L. H., and Dawis, R. V. (1975) Vocational needs, work reinforcers and job satisfaction. *Vocational Guidance Quarterly*, **24**, 132–139.

Lorei, T. W., and Gurel, L. (1973) Demographic characteristics as predictors of post-hospital employment and readmission. *Journal of Consulting and Clinical Psychology*, **40**, 426–430.

Lowe, C. M. (1967) Prediction of posthospital adjustment by psychological tests. *Journal of Counselling Psychology*, **14**, 248–252.

MacLean, M. E. (1977) Learning theory and chronic welfare dependency: a hypothesis of etiological and contingency relationships. *Journal of Behaviour Therapy and Experimental Psychiatry*, **8**, 255–259.

Marsden, D., and Duff, E. (1975) *Workless*. Penguin, Harmondsworth, Middx.

Matarazzo, J. D. (1972) *Wechsler's Measurement and Appraisal of Adult Intelligence*, 5th edn. Williams & Wilkins, Baltimore, Md.

Mischel, W. (1968) *Personality and Assessment*. John Wiley, New York.

Neff, W. S. (1966) Problems of work evaluation. *Personnel and Guidance Journal*, **44**, 682–688.

Neff, W. S., and Koltov, M. (1967) Toleration for psychiatric rehabilitation as a function of coping style. *Journal of Consulting Psychology*, **31**, 364–370.

Olshansky, S., Grob, S., and Malamud, I. T. (1958) Employers' attitudes and practices in the hiring of ex-mental patients. *Mental Hygiene*, **42**, 391–401.

Overs, R. P. (1970) Vocational evaluation: research and implications. *Journal of Rehabilitation*, **36**, 18–21.

Patterson, C. H. (1957) Interest tests and the emotionally disturbed client. *Educational and Psychological Measurement*, **17**, 264–280.

Purvis, S. A. (1969) Congruence of work-related needs and abilities: traditional psychiatric patients and normals. *Journal of Employment Counselling*, **6**, 64–71.

Rachman, S. J. (1978) *Fear and Courage*. W. H. Freeman, San Francisco.

Rodnick, E. H., and Garmezy, N. (1957) An experimental approach to the study of motivation in schizophrenia. In *Nebraska Symposium on Motivation*. University of Nebraska Press, Lincoln.

Sanders, R. M., and Walters, G. M. (1972) Behaviour modification on the assembly line: collateral behaviour training. *Rehabilitation Psychology*, **19**, 153–158.

Sandler, J. (1952) Follow-up inquiry: II. Statistical analysis and the concept of general adjustment. In M. Jones, ed., *Social Psychiatry: A Study of Therapeutic Communities*. Tavistock, London.

Searls, D. J., Wilson, L. T., and Miskimins, R. W. (1971) Development of a measure of unemployability among restored psychiatric patients. *Journal of Applied Psychology*, **55**, 223–225.

Shepherd, D. I. (1971) The measurement of vocational maturity in adults. *Journal of Vocational Behaviour*, **1**, 399–406.

Small, L. (1953) Personality determinants of vocational choice. *Psychological Monographs*, **67** (351).

Smith, P. C., Kendall, L. M., and Hulin, C. L. (1969) *The Measurement of Satisfaction in Work and Retirement*. Rand McNally, Chicago.

Soloff, A., and Bolton, B. F. (1969) The validity of the CJVS scale of employability for older clients in a vocational adjustment workshop. *Educational and Psychological Measurement*, **29**, 993–998.

Stephens, W. B., Peck, J. R., and Veldman, D. J. (1968) Personality and success profiles characteristic of young male retardates. *American Journal of Mental Deficiency*, **73**, 405–413.

Taylor, F. R. (1963) The GATB as a predictor of vocational readjustment by psychiatric patients. *Journal of Clinical Psychology*, **19**, 130–131.

Taylor, G. P., and Persons, R. W. (1970) Behaviour modification techniques in a physical medicine and rehabilitation setting. *Journal of Psychology*, **74**, 117–124.

Tiffany, D. W., Cowan, J. R., and Tiffany, P. M. (1970) *The Unemployed: A Social Psychological Portrait*. Spectrum, Englewood Cliffs, NJ.

Tseng, M. S. (1970) Locus of control as a determinant of job proficiency, employability, and training satisfaction of vocational rehabilitation clients. *Journal of Counselling Psychology*, **17**, 487–491.

Tseng, M. S. (1972a) Predicting vocational rehabilitation dropouts from psychometric attributes and work behaviours. *Rehabilitation Counselling Bulletin*, **15**, 154–159.

Tseng, M. S. (1972b) Self-perception and employability: a vocational rehabilitation problem. *Journal of Counselling Psychology*, **19**, 314–317.

Van Allen, R., and Loeber, R. (1972) Work assessment of psychiatric patients: a critical review of published scales. *Canadian Journal of Behavioural Science*, **4**, 101–117.

Venardos, M. G., and Harris, M. B. (1973) Job interview training with rehabilitation clients: a comparison of videotape and role-playing procedures. *Journal of Applied Psychology*, **58**, 365–367.

Wadsworth, W. V., Wells, B. W. P., and Scott, R. F. (1962) A comparative study of the fatiguability of a group of chronic schizophrenics and a group of hospitalised non-psychotic depressives. *Journal of Mental Science*, **108**, 304–308.

Wadsworth, W. V., Wells, B. W. P., and Scott, R. F. (1963) An experimental investigation of the qualitative differences between the work performance of normals and chronic schizophrenics. *Psychiatric Quarterly Supplement*, **37**, 325–335.

Wansborough, N. (1975) Up the enclaves. *New Society*, 27 February.

Watts, F. N. (1976) Modification of the employment handicaps of psychiatric patients by behavioural methods. *American Journal of Occupational Therapy*, **30**, 487–491.

Watts, F. N. (1978) A study of work behaviour in a psychiatric rehabilitation unit. *British Journal of Social and Clinical Psychology*, **17**, 85–92.

Watts, F. N., and Bennett, D. H. (1977) Previous occupational stability as a predictor of employment after psychiatric rehabilitation. *Psychological Medicine*, **7**, 709–712.

Watts, F. N., and Everitt, B. S. (1980) The factorial structure of the General Aptitude Test Battery. *Journal of Clinical Psychology*, **36**, 763–767.

Watts, F. N., and Yu, P. Q. (1976) The structure of attitudes in psychiatric rehabilitation. *Journal of Occupational Psychology*, **49**, 39–44.

Whatley, C. D. (1964) Employer attitudes, discharged patients and job disability. *Mental Hygiene*, **48**, 121–131.

Williams, S. (1980) *Jobs in the 1980s: What Alternatives to the Dole Queue?* Policy Studies Institute, London.

Wing, J. K. (1966) Social and psychological changes in a rehabilitation unit. *Social Psychiatry*, **1**, 21–28.

Wing, J. K., and Freudenberg, R. K. (1961) The response of severely ill chronic schizophrenic patients to social stimulation. *American Journal of Psychiatry*, **118**, 311–322.

Wynne, E. (1974) Socialization to adulthood: different concepts, different policies. *Interchange*, **5**, 23–35.

Theory and Practice of Psychiatric Rehabilitation
Edited by F. N. Watts and D. H. Bennett
© 1983, John Wiley & Sons, Ltd.

# 12

# Domestic Roles

GLENYS PARRY

## Introduction

Despite its pervasive importance in everyday life, the domestic world has received scant attention in the literature or practice of psychiatric rehabilitation. Many writers in the field seem to conceptualize rehabilitation in a way which disregards the family as an arena of social performance. In practice, the emphasis on occupational roles is overwhelming, and much rehabilitative effort involves job surrogates such as sheltered employment and industrial and occupational therapy. Generally, patients' performance as mothers, fathers, wives, and husbands has not yet been seen as an appropriate concern. Some studies, however, have considered the role that domestic factors play in post-hospital outcome, and these will be reviewed.

The disproportionate emphasis on relevant occupational factors within psychiatric rehabilitation should be placed in a broader context. It can be seen as one aspect of the fundamental dichotomy between the public and the private spheres so characteristic of modern technological societies. This dichotomy separates the home from the workplace, reproduction from production, and women's experience from men's. Within the field of mental health, aetiology is generally associated with the private, domestic sphere and rehabilitation with the public, employment worlds. For example, the role of family processes in causing mental ill-health has often been explored, but not the possible role of organizational structures. Similarly, the rehabilitative potential of domestic roles has been almost entirely neglected, and when beginning research for this chapter, it was indeed dismaying to find how little published work is available. There exists no systematic method of exploration of the ways in which the rehabilitation specialist can facilitate the stable and independent performance of domestic roles by psychiatric patients. For these reasons, what follows can only be an exploratory essay, rather than a review of a field of systematic research.

The private nature of domestic roles tends to blind us to the conceptual distinction between 'work' and 'employment'. As Hartley (1980) points out, the way that the words are used interchangeably is in itself informative of our values. Bennett (1970), drawing on Jaques's definition of work, carried this conceptual confusion into the rehabilitation field. Employment is concerned with economic reward for labour, the performance of activities which have a market value, and it places constraints on the behaviour of the employee. Employment is the relationship between employer and employee, and it is a relationship based on exchange. Work, on the other hand, is an activity. Work can be performed either inside or outside the employment relationship. For example, housework, child care, voluntary work, educational study, and do-it-yourself tasks are all work outside the employment context. Employment gives a relationship which has socially recognized meaning and value, quite apart from what is involved in the activity of the work itself. Watts (1976, 1978) is drawing on this distinction in his view that employability is more a function of what is referred to as work personality, than it is of task competence. In the following discussion of rehabilitation and domestic roles, the distinction becomes crucial and must be clearly kept in mind.

A further general point must be made. Patterns of family life have altered considerably over the past 50 years. In particular, the 'traditional' segregation of sex-appropriate domestic roles may be less marked (Young and Willmott, 1973, pp. 93–96). Similarly, other authors have noted that within marriage there has been a shift away from 'closed, defined' interaction patterns towards an 'open, emergent' structure (Rausch et al., 1963). The traditional marriage, where the husband takes responsibility for the family's relation to the public world, the wife concerning herself with internal family matters, is no longer the norm (Blood and Wolfe, 1960). Although there is evidence that these trends may not have fundamentally disrupted the balance of conjugal power or domestic work-sharing (Laws, 1971; Working Family Project, 1978; Perrucci et al., 1978), they do point to the importance of eschewing narrow, stereotyped assumptions about what constitutes the domestic role. Gowler and Legge (1982), for example, make the point that in statistical terms the normal family in present society is dual-worker. This relates to the Rapports' (1977) argument that there is a wide diversity of family life-styles, sex role definitions, child care arrangements, and methods of domestic and occupational role integration. It is important that the rehabilitation worker is aware of this pluralism before considering specific aspects of domestic role functioning.

The present chapter will first examine the structure of the maternal role, giving an account of its instrumental, interlocutionary, and affective aspects. The role of the father will then be discussed leading to a general consideration of issues relating to parenting. Rehabilitation and marital relationships will then be examined, and work on reinstating patient–family relationships referred to. Finally, research on family structure and post-hospital outcome will be summarized.

## Mothers' Work

The most striking absence within rehabilitation concerns the central and essential tasks of child care and home management. These are roles which have traditionally been, and largely remain, the responsibility of women. Bringing up young children is the single most common cause of women's withdrawal from the labour market, and is clearly work, but outside an employment context. It may at first seem puzzling that there have been no widespread attempts to find effective ways of helping patients regain or achieve maternal competence. Women patients outnumber men and few would deny that a good proportion of psychiatric patients have difficulty in coping with the demands of the role. However, this is consistent with the finding of Tudor *et al.* (1977) that women psychiatric patients tend to be treated later than their male counterparts and for shorter periods. There may, therefore, be a relative lack of effort in their rehabilitation, despite their preponderance in the psychiatric population. Furthermore, the concept of 'maternal competence' is itself problematic. Unlike many occupational role titles (e.g. bus driver, schoolteacher, hairdresser), the word 'mother' is used to describe what a person is, not what she does. For example, a man who had full-time and sole responsibility for nurturing his baby would not be described as a mother. The belief dies hard that 'mothering' is an intrinsic part of being a woman, that it 'comes naturally' and requires no special preparation or training. A number of influential writers in the child care and mental health fields seem to reinforce this belief (e.g. Winnicott, 1964). Whilst their benign intention is to give women confidence that they are able to trust their hunches about what is best for their babies, there are dangers in this approach. It is not helpful for a psychiatric patient to over-identify with her maternal role to the point where the belief 'I am an inadequate mother' immediately implies 'I am a bad person', rather than 'I have a lot to learn about being a mother'. A first step in rehabilitation is to make a systematic analysis of the specific skills and tasks involved in the role, and to describe the structure of the role. It is unlikely that even this first step will be taken if 'mothering' is defined as merely the 'natural' responses of a woman to her children.

Related to this point is the importance of being aware of the cultural relativism of the maternal role. All of the 'maternal' functions to be described here have been, in different cultures or in different ages, performed by people other than the biological mother. Such people might include nannies, wet-nurses, fathers, grandparents, childminders, neighbours, and older siblings. This is also true in contemporary life. For this reason, the content and structure of the role of mothers described here should not be seen as prescriptive. The general question of the delegation of maternal tasks will be discussed further under 'General Issues in Parenting'.

The structure of the maternal role can be explored by comparing it with occupational roles. There are a number of ways in which mothering is not like having a job. There is no employer–employee relationship based on exchange of labour for money. The work is not rewarded with wages, and no explicit contract exists stating terms and conditions of employment to which both parties agree. There are no selection criteria, and no formal training procedures. There is no explicit job description; there are no criteria of successful performance. There is no promotion into roles of higher status. On the other hand, the mother cannot be sacked or made redundant. There is no externally imposed time structure according to which the mother is expected to have completed different parts of her tasks or after which her commitment to her work ceases. Central to the role is a total loyalty and, in the early years, a round-the-clock vigilance. Few employers demand this level of commitment and those jobs involving it are of very high status within politics or industry (see for example, Dean 1977).

It is useful to extend this comparison by examining the maternal role in terms of Jahoda's (1979) five 'latent functions' of employment: that it imposes a time structure on the working day, it provides shared experiences and contacts outside the nuclear family, it links an individual to goals and purposes which transcend his own, it defines aspects of personal status and identity, and it enforces activity. (As is usual in discussions of unemployment, Jahoda makes no specific reference to the work of mothers and the terms 'work' and 'employment' are used interchangeably.) Jahoda sees the latent function of employment as central to its role in psychological wellbeing. It is clear that full-time mothering, when not combined with an employment role, does not necessarily fulfil these latent functions, with the exception of defining aspects of personal identity and status and perhaps also providing external goals and purposes. The value of these functions of employment in rehabilitation must be acknowledged (Bennett, 1970) and their absence in the maternal role presents a special challenge. However, such evidence as exists about the effect of employment on psychological wellbeing in women suggests that if the woman's social and psychological needs are already being met, paid employment exerts little extra beneficial effect (Warr and Parry, 1982). It is where the mother is socially disadvantaged that the problems of a unitary role arise.

The nature of the maternal role does provide a certain flexibility which could be used to advantage. It is possible that fairly disabled patients who would not necessarily be employable can continue their work as mothers, if an accurate assessment is made of what the patient can and cannot cope with and adequate support is given. The resources of hospital staff, the day hospital, relatives, local playgroup leaders and teachers can be utilized in providing such support. This can be seen as analogous to sheltered employment, and preliminary to more independent role performance.

It would seem that unemployment has different meanings for women and men, and social expectations of woman can work to their advantage in psychiatric rehabilitation. Keskiner *et al.* (1973) demonstrate this point, although in a different context. In their study of chronic psychiatric patients entering a fostering programme in the New Haven community, it was found that female patients had a better chance of successful placement. This was not due to differences in age, length of hospitalization, or diagnosis. The authors conclude that

it is more acceptable for female patients to assume relatively dependent social roles in the foster community, providing they will maintain an acceptable level of self-care, housekeeping and social contacts. For men, employment seems to be an additional prerequisite of moving to the foster community.

Compared with occupational roles, the maternal role has a surprising lack of 'job requirements', that is 'those rules and procedures that may be defined as the non-discretionary element in the occupational "role"' (Gowler and Legge, 1972). Of course, *in extremis*, the limits of maternal incompetence are defined by law, and children may in these circumstances be removed from the care of the mother by the Local Authority. However, the absence of defined rules and procedures for carrying out the work is the most striking difference between domestic child care and most work carried out within an employment context. This has two main implications. First, it provides the mother with a degree of autonomy. Oakley (1974) found that the majority of women in her housewife sample felt that this was the best aspect of the work. However, the second implication of the absence of explicit role demands is that mothers feel the need to specify for themselves certain standards of role performance. Oakley says, 'Women enter into a form of covert contract with themselves to be their own bosses, judges and reward givers.' She found that as standards continued to be specified and routines to be elaborated, so self-imposed rules tended to be externalized, and consequently the autonomous aspects of housework and child care became more of an ideal than a reality.

Moving from general considerations of role structure to a description of specific role components, it is possible to attempt an account of what the mother actually does in the 'space and time defined by the role', to use Gowler and Legge's description of 'job performance'. The problem here is that most mothers are not exclusively responsible for child care, but also for housework. We must define the role of the mother in terms of providing the optimal environment for the growth, physical and emotional, of her children. This does not logically include many of the tasks of housework, and indeed in practice there is quite often a conflict of interest between child care and housework, as anyone who has attempted to complete a pile of ironing in the presence of a bored 2-year-old can attest. So although conceptually separate, housework and child care are often not distinguished in practice either by mothers or by rehabilitation workers. Thus the mother becomes responsible for a great variety of household tasks, some more relevant than others to the needs of her children. The list includes dusting, vacuum cleaning, tidying, making beds, cooking meals, washing dishes, washing clothes, ironing clothes, mending clothes, shopping, budgeting, washing children, and changing nappies.

This aspect of the role is less skilled, consisting of a variety of repetitive, short-cycle tasks. The work is paced when there are young infants who need to be fed on a regular and frequent schedule. It is this aspect of the role that mothers report as the least satisfying. Oakley's findings have been replicated in this regard by a number of other researchers. Avery and Begalla (1975) analysed the housework role using the Position Analysis Questionnaire (PAQ) and found it to be as demanding as Oakley suggests. Avery and Gross (1977), in a survey of both housewives and part-time workers, found that both groups reported dissatisfaction with the tasks involved.

The extent to which the husband participates in household tasks has been found to influence the degree of mothers' reported satisfaction with housework (Gross and Richard, 1977). The availability of 'labour-saving' domestic appliances does not seem to have affected the time spent on these tasks, however, and over the last 50 years there seems to have been a continually rising standard for these instrumental tasks (Vanck, 1974).

Paul (1969) lists 'improvement of instrumental role performance' as one of four key elements for successful post-hospital rehabilitation, and the issue of standards of performance of these tasks is relevant here. Seidel (1978), in a small-scale investigation of housework standards in depressed patients and non-psychiatric controls, did not find significant differences between the two groups on either ideal standards or housework performance when they were interviewed approximately 9 months after the onset of treatment. She felt this result may be due to the recovery of housework performance during this time, which would be consistent with Weissman and Paykel's (1974) finding that employment performance recovered more quickly than impaired performance in other areas, such as interpersonal functioning. Seidel did find, however, that the depressed group had a lower degree of routinization of household tasks. Her data support the hypothesis that routine is generally protective against depression, although they do not falsify the alternative hypothesis of depression leading to loss of routine. The implication for rehabilitation is that improved standards of instrumental housework task performance may, in some cases, not be as crucial as routinization skills. Routinization, however, is a different order of skill from instrumental task adequacy.

Within the field of home management research, Nichols and her colleagues (1971) make it clear that home management skills are exercised within a context of expressive relationships within the family. The mother-homemaker is assumed to occupy both instrumental and expressive roles, but these have traditionally been analysed separately. The authors emphasize the mediating role of the mother within a family, and show, for example, that organizational style is related to affective, situational, and personality variables. It would seem likely that instrumental performance can be improved within a hospital setting, either in a home management unit within an occupational therapy department, or in a day hospital setting for outpatients. However, in order to set up a programme to improve an individual patient's managerial and organizational performance, the rehabilitation worker must be prepared to work within the patient's home. Not only this, but the worker needs to understand failures of task standardization, assignment, regularization, and arrangement (to use Mumaw's (1967) index of organisational activity) in terms of a total pattern of family interaction.

The distinction between task performance and the ability to plan, schedule, and organize one's working day is an important one which will be discussed further, following consideration of the other components of the maternal role.

The job of a mother does not only, or even centrally, involve meeting the physical needs of her children, but it also consists of providing an optimal environment for the social and psychological development of the growing children. The mother is an important mediator between the child and the adult social world, particularly when the mother is caring for a small baby. This can be termed the interlocutionary aspect of the role. Studies in mother–infant interaction show that the mother is constantly creating varied opportunities for her child to participate in social interactions (Schaffer, 1971, 1977a). In Schaffer's terms, the infant must develop the concept of a dialogue. At first this is one-sided and the mother must sustain the interaction. Later the infant learns reciprocity and intentionality. However, he or she cannot do so unless the mother provides structured experiences leading to turntaking and communication. Ideally, then, this early relationship is a reciprocal one, where one can observe that the baby imitates the mother, but the mother also imitates the child (Bell, 1968). Schaffer described 'maternal interactive strategies' of phasing, adaptation, facilitation, elaboration, initiation, and control.

The importance of playing with young children is emphasized by Schaffer's work, as it is by Winnicott (1971). Playing is one maternal task that other adults, in particular fathers, seem willing to share (Kotelchuck, 1976). However, many psychiatric patients are not able to play with their young children, despite the fact that this is potentially a most rewarding aspect of the role. Lindsey et al. (1978) found that this formed a major focus of their work with mothers and their preschool children in a cooperative playgroup within a psychiatric setting. They used participant modelling to help their patients learn the important functions of play: imaginatively entering into the child's view of the world, using symbols and fantasy, expressing approval at a child's self-expression, sharing a dialogue with the child.

The mothering role clearly has an expressive component, although it is extremely difficult to specify the nature of maternal love. Bowlby (1977) has placed the affectional bond at the centre of healthy child development. Schaffer (1977b, p.86) reminds us that this emotionally charged relationship heightens all emotions, not only positive ones; hence the Tizards' (1971) finding that mothers, when compared with nurses who were employed to provide child care, not only gave their children more physical contact of an affectionate nature, but were also more frequently angered or upset by their children's behaviour. The affectional bond gives the mother an increased sensitivity to the child's signals and communications and, as Ainsworth (1974) points out, this requires that the competent mother has the ability to see things from the infant's point of view.

Heath (1977) relates maternal competence to developmental maturity, believing that adequate mothers have moved from egocentricity to allocentricity, have an ability to symbolize, are consistent, self-confident, and autonomous. These qualities are rare enough anyway, and are even more rare among a psychiatric population. Within rehabilitation, therefore, modest and realistic goals must be formulated. As far as the affectional component of the maternal role is concerned, this may mean mitigating the worst effects of maternal failure rather than developing the 'ideal' maternal environment. Winnicott's (1960) concept of the 'good enough' mother is useful here.

An example of this might be the ability of the mother to 'contain' the child's anxieties. The concept of containment has become central to child psychotherapists' discussion of emotional and cognitive development, and originates with Bion (1962). Although a metaphoric concept, it is made very concrete if one observes the competent or experienced mother handling an anxiously crying baby. She seems unperturbed by the infant's screams, and accepts the baby's communication without becoming anxious herself, and therefore the affective message she gives to the child is more or less benign. For a psychiatric patient the primitive anxiety and range in a baby's screams can be desperately stressful. She may not be able to accept and 'contain' these feelings, merely reflecting them. It is not uncommon for the mother to return the child's anxieties amplified by her own fear or anger. In this situation, a positive feedback loop can become established, and the feeding relationship seriously disrupted. The baby may come to be seen as a persecutory object by the mother whose best efforts to comfort it have failed. Child abuse is a real possibility, and even if the baby escapes physical injury, psychological damage is a risk. The rehabilitation workers should make a systematic assessment of those aspects of the mothering role which the patient, because of her own psychiatric problem, finds particularly difficult. Special efforts must then be made to support her. Local resources should be exploited fully, including the health visitor, any neighbour who is an experienced mother, and groups of volunteers who operate telephone support systems or home visiting schemes. The work of Robertson (1976) and of Garbarino and Stocking (1980), developing effective support systems for families where children are at risk of abuse and neglect, should be consulted.

Unfortunately, good empirical work on the concept of containment is not yet available, although there have been recent attempts to integrate the empirical work of the developmental psychologists with psychodynamic theory (Boston, 1975; Bentovim, 1979).

The instrumental, interlocutory, and affective aspects of the mother's role may conflict with each other; most commonly, instrumental tasks take precedence over social interaction with the children. For this and other similar reasons it is an important aim of the rehabilitation worker to improve the patient's capacity for exercising independent discretionary choice. Put simply, it is not enough to know how to cook a meal or wash clothes. It is just as important to know when to, or even whether to do that rather than something else, such as spending an hour playing with a toddler or a baby.

These 'discretionary skills' are all but impossible to impart in a conventional hospital setting. Lindsey, Pound, and Radford's valuable work in a playgroup attached to a day hospital has already been mentioned, as has the importance of becoming familiar with working in the patient's home. Elizabeth Karn (1972) gives a full account of another approach: residential training for mothers with behaviourally disturbed children. The advantage of organizing a residential setting, for a short period, lay in the mothers' learning through peer interaction as well as the trainers' participant modelling and led group discussions. A flexible combination of all three approaches (day hospital playgroups, training in the mother's home with community support, and residential training workshops) probably gives the best opportunity for adult socialization and for helping mothers to acquire discretionary as well as instrumental competence.

An example of what is possible when these issues are approached conscientiously is provided by the work of PACE, a unit attached to the Bronx psychiatric clinic in New York, specializing in treatment and education for women patients, their children, and their families (Goodman, 1980). The centre was started in 1968 to provide a support network of therapeutic and educational services to young mothers with psychiatric or drug use problems. The programme is run from a day hospital and patients' participation is for 4 days per week, in an intensive schedule of psychotherapy, mother and child groups, and parent education seminars.

### The Role of the Father

It should not be thought that the neglect of domestic life in rehabilitation only concerns female patients. It springs from a distorted picture of the totality of men's lives no less than women's. As the Rapoports' point out (1977, p.87), for over 30 years there has been an idealized conception of the nuclear family with a standard composition, division of labour, and life-cycle timetable. This model of the family defines the role of the 'normal mature woman' as a housewife and mother, the man's being to provide economically for 'his' family. This view of the family is often referred to as traditional, although the term is a misnomer. It was only in the nineteenth century that this pattern emerged (Richards, 1974), with a renewed emphasis after the Second World War, although the nature of the mother–child relationship had altered (Helterline, 1981). During the 1950s this model of family life was supported by psychiatry, medicine, sociology, and professionals in law, education, and social work. It has been vastly influential within rehabilitation, where the aim of restoring the married male patient to some semblance of the 'normal male' role of economic provider was cherished, perhaps at the expense of a critical examination of other aspects of men's social role with regard to the family. It can be argued that an overemphasis on the Parsonian model of the father's role as provider and authority figure may strain the capacity of the patient to meet the demands of the role. Alternative paradigms should be explored, to provide the flexibility that is so necessary in the rehabilitation of the particular patient. This section attempts to redress the balance and show that there are many dimensions to the father's role that can be used to advantage. The aspects of the role that will be discussed here include sharing the care of the children, performance of household tasks, expressive involvement with children, and acting as confidant to the mother.

There has been a revival of research interest in the role of the father in the care of young children. As mothers are almost always the primary caretakers, child development research during the 1950s and 1960s all but ignored the relationship of the father to the young child. At that time it was assumed that the feeding relationship was crucial, due to the dominance of secondary drive theory. Drive reduction as the primary mechanism of socialization had been replaced by an ethological analysis, when Harlow (1958) demonstrated that feeding is not the critical factor for early social development and that social and sensory stimulation are also important. Schaffer and Emerson (1964) showed that infants become 'attached' to individuals, such as fathers, who were never involved in routine caretaking. These studies set the scene for greater awareness of the father–child relationship. There is now a considerable body of work outlining the way in which the father's influence on the child is mediated both directly and indirectly through his participation in the family system (see for example Lamb, 1976; Parke, 1979). These studies suggest the complexity of the father's relationship with the child, and it is only fair to acknowledge that much is still unknown.

A number of authors agree that there are limits to what can be learned about parental and marital roles through anticipatory socialization (Hill and Aldous,

1969; Rapoport *et al.*, 1977; Perkins and Morris, 1979). Hill and Aldous point out that the process by which a son learns about paternal and marital role behaviours from his father is more incidental and less formal than the similar process in the mother–daughter relationship. They predict greater discontinuity between the generations in paternal role performance. It can also be argued that this will lead to a greater variability in what fathers actually do.

There is research which suggests that if there is a failure to establish the bond between mother and baby in the early weeks of life, the risk of child abuse is increased (Lynch, 1975; Garbarino, 1977). However, there has not been a parallel interest in the way fathers become attached to their children, and the consequences of failures of attachment. Greenberg and Morris (1974) tried to remedy what they describe as this 'glaring' scarcity of research. In their study of the newborn baby's impact on the father, they interviewed 30 first-time fathers whose wives had had normal pregnancies, vaginal deliveries, and healthy babies. They found a common response of absorption, preoccupation, and interest in the baby, which they termed 'engrossment'. They hypothesize that this father–baby attachment, beginning to develop by the third day, is a basic, innate potential among all fathers. However, the response is shaped by cultural influences. They go on to suggest that this has important implications for adequate performance of the father's role in the family, which are perhaps unrecognized by hospital procedures. This study suggests that the father's expressive involvement with the child may be more important than previously recognized.

Heath (1976) interviewed 49 fathers as part of a longitudinal study, asking questions about parenting behaviours. The subjects' wives and closest male friends were also interviewed and rated the subjects' closeness to their children. Neither the subjects nor their parents related paternal competence to routine involvement in specific socialization decisions. Being 'a good father' was first and foremost associated with expressive involvement; a good father was seen as loving his children, caring about them. This study, however, only interviewed fathers in professional and managerial socio-economic groups, and therefore these results may not be generalizable. Interestingly, although these fathers did not feel they were making inadequate material provision for their children, they did feel guilt over the limited time they had available for them. Cohen (1977) also emphasizes 'father absence' in ordinary settings when ambitious, occupationally orientated men are not putting much energy into fathering.

It is not necessarily the case, however, that time availability is the determining factor in male family role performance. Perrucci *et al.* (1978) examined the determinants of husbands' participation in twelve selected household and child care activities, using a stratified probability sample of 98 couples. Using regression analysis they found that the items relating to socialization and ideology were the best predictors of task performance, with the 'less available time' hypothesis doing relatively badly. It does seem as if the man's beliefs about what is appropriate in the role, and his expectations of it, are crucial.

There is certainly a wide variation in the amount of time that fathers spend with their young children. Pedersen and Robson (1969) reported an average of 8 hours contact per week, but the range was from 45 minutes to 26 hours per week. Kotelchuck (1976) obtained a similar pattern of results, with only 7.5 per cent of fathers taking joint responsibility for child care. Of the middle-class fathers in this study, 75 per cent took no responsibility for infant care. These studies are American, and Gavron (1966) and the Newsons (1963, 1968) showed that English fathers are more accessible to their young children. The Newsons, for example, rated 25 per cent of their sample 'highly participant', although the term is relative, not absolute. What all these studies note, as confirmed by Richards et al. (1975) in another British study, is that fathers' involvement with their children tends to be through play, whereas nappy changing and bathing children are the least common paternal behaviours.

There is a substantial amount of evidence to show that an absent or indifferent father is associated with ill-effects in the children. The temptation to make a direct casual inference must be resisted. The mechanism could be indirect, for example through the effect of the father's absence on the mother, or it may be confounded with other critical variables such as social disadvantage. That having been said, a number of studies implicate deficiencies of fathering in juvenile delinquency, and in anxiety and emotional disturbance in children (Andry, 1960; Anderson, 1968; Holman, 1959; see also Lamb, 1976). Scott (1975) suggests an intergenerational tendency to violence in men, and Hyman and Mitchell (1975) confirm that those who are violent towards their children suffered during their own childhood from the absence of an accessible, involved father.

Another component of the father's role is highlighted by research on psychiatric disorder in mothers, namely that of providing emotional support and acting as confidant to the mother. In situations where the mother is the primary caretaker of preschool children, the quality of her social supports may be of considerable importance in enabling her to do the job properly. There is evidence that women who have an intimate, confiding relationship with their husbands are far less likely to develop psychiatric disorder, following a threatening life event, than those without such a relationship (Brown and Harris, 1978).

This selection from the available literature on the role of the father serves to illustrate the importance of the expressive aspects of the role. The way in which this research becomes relevant to the rehabilitation worker will vary from patient to patient. In a time of high unemployment, the chances of the psychiatric patient's rehabilitation into a job are less favourable, and it is especially important to have a broad and flexible conception of the appropriate behaviours in the father's role. It is worth giving thought to methods of providing the male patient with the opportunity to acquire skills of active parenting. The patient may only feel able to discuss problems he has with his role as a parent if the rehabilitation worker takes the initiative in raising the matter as an appropriate focus of a rehabilitation programme. Many men find it difficult to confide in others about domestic problems. There is some evidence that active coping strategies are more effective in the domestic sphere than in the occupational one (Pearlin and Schooler, 1978). It is possible that much can be achieved through discussion of specific problems, role-play of situations that habitually cause problems, planning a programme to change specific behaviours, with the cooperation of the wife, and working in men's groups focusing on domestic issues. The types of interventions outlined in the following sections will also be found useful.

### General Issues in Parenting

It will have been seen from the previous sections that the roles of parents are complex, but that they can be analysed in terms of simpler elements. Further general considerations concerning parents and their children which merit attention on the part of rehabilitation workers include a realistic awareness of the demands of the parent role (for both women and men), problems with the disciplinary aspects of the role, and the added burden of disturbed behaviours in the children.

From an anthropological perspective, five parental functions can be identified (Goody, 1974): nurturance, teaching role skills, sponsorship, status placement, and adult role modelling. In modern society, three of these functions are shared with the State (teaching skills, giving children a start in life, and establishing a career), parents retaining responsibility for nurturant child care and providing adult role models. Rehabilitation workers wishing to help their parents to return to full parental responsibility should not assume that the parental role is, compared to occupational ones unproblematic. There is now considerable awareness of the financial, psychological, and physical strains of parenthood, and evidence that becoming a parent is a stressful life crisis (Le Masters, 1957; Feldman, 1971; Rossi, 1974). Marital satisfaction decreases more sharply in the years following the birth of children than at any other time over the life-cycle (Rollins and Feldman, 1970).

The needs of children can be listed quite simply although the appropriate way of meeting these needs alters as the child grows older. Children need love which is child-centred and unconditional security and discipline, new experiences through play and language, praise and recognition, responsibility and personal independence (Kelmer Pringle, 1975). A fundamental aspect of the parents' role is to provide for these needs, so that their children have optimal opportunities for mental and emotional growth. The demands of children to have those needs met are constant and unremitting, and there are countless opportunities for failing to meet them. Adverse social and economic circumstances can exacerbate the strains of parenthood.

Given the demanding nature of the parental role even for those without psychiatric problems, it is important to make a systematic assessment of the capacity of the patient to take on the full range of parental duties. Hospitalization, in particular, can mean that a patient has 'all or nothing' of his or her parental role. On discharge from hospital, the patient with young children may not immediately be able to cope, and the rehabilitation worker should take time to plan a systematic phased return to the full parental role. Parental tasks can be delegated within the family, and the support of others in the community should be enlisted. Health visitors, home helps, social workers, and community psychiatric nurses can often work together in 'parenting' a family during the rehabilitation period. During this time the parents themselves can learn new skills.

Discipline is one parental responsibility which commonly causes problems and which, where there are two parents, needs to be tackled by both. This parental skill is extremely difficult to teach in a hospital, and post-hospital work is called for. There are large social class differences in responding to aggression and tantrums in children. Middle-class parents use verbal reasoning and a democratic approach to disciplining children, backed up with withholding rewards. Working-class parents are on the whole authoritarian and non-verbal, responding to aggression with counter-aggression and using words to threaten, not to reason (Klein, 1970, p.476; Newson and Newson, 1977). There is no evidence to suggest that one of these approaches is 'right' and the other 'wrong'. Rather it seems that both extreme permissiveness and either harsh or inconsistent punishment increase tantrums and aggression in children (Mussen *et al.*, 1969).

There is evidence that psychological and emotional disturbance in the parents significantly increases the risk of their children having a typical or 'problem' behaviour and poor cognitive development (Hall and Pawlby, 1981). (This finding seems obvious, but it is not, since surprisingly few continuities in the behaviour of parents and children have been discovered in longitudinal studies.) The psychiatric patient is therefore likely to have an even more demanding parental role than is normal. Part of the rehabilitation workers' role is to arrange support and teaching for parents whose children are themselves disturbed, and this may of course imply collaboration with child specialists. Teaching parental skills is not unproblematic because, as Perkins and Morris (1979) point out, although many people assume that 'good' parenting is a skill which can be taught, they forget that we have only a limited understanding of the process by which disadvantage is transmitted. We literally do not know the 'best' way to parent, although research does offer some relevant evidence. It is as well, therefore, to have a broad conception of alternative parental styles, and to aim to help patients remedy obvious deficits and problems.

Parental groups can be organized to teach behaviour management skills and to discuss the problems of the role (see Patterson, 1974; Kolko-Phillips *et al.*, 1980; Miller and Ellis, 1980). A potential danger is that groups such as these are more often attended by women than by men, and special efforts should be made both to involve fathers and to run fathers' groups, for example by meeting in the evening rather than during the day.

A plethora of books giving parents guidance about their role is now available, and the rehabilitation specialist should be familiar with a selection of these so that an appropriate book can be recommended to the parents (see, for example, Gribben, 1979; Rakowitz and Rubin, 1980).

## Roles Within Marriage

The benefits of being involved in an intimate relationship with another adult are widely recognized, although the advantages of marriage may be more marked for men than for women in contemporary society (Gove, 1972; Rapoport *et al.*, 1977; Bebbington *et al.*, 1981). However, the marriage relationship, in all its diverse forms (included here are unmarried cohabitees and homosexual partnerships), makes demands on the two participants as well as conferring benefits. Looked at from this perspective each partner has a role in maintaining a marital system that is mutually supportive, collaborative, and can handle problems without breaking down in crisis. It is the rehabilitation of the psychiatric patient into the successful performance of this role which is the focus of this section. However, the individualist formulation is perhaps least appropriate when discussing such relationships. There is a widespread preference amongst marital and family theorists and therapists to see the dyad as a system with its own dynamics. In this way the focus for intervention is not the individual but rather the mutual patterns of marital interaction. In understanding the requirements of adequate role performance, and in planning improvement of marital role performance, the boundaries between rehabilitation and treatment become blurred.

The field of marital interaction and therapy is a large and complex one, and only a selection of studies from this literature can be cited in order to illustrate relevant points. In particular, studies will be summarized for what they contribute to a broad consensus, and attention will not be paid to the numerous points of detail where different authors enter into controversy. There is a wide range of differing theoretical perspectives within the field of marital and family relationships, including an ethological approach (Hinde, 1978); straightforward behavioural formulations (Jacobson and Martin, 1976); systems-behavioural theories (Alexander, 1973); family therapies of diverse kinds, including problem-solving approaches (Haley, 1976);

psychoanalytic perspectives (Pincus and Dare, 1978); humanistic approaches (Satir, 1964); together with the work of other practitioners not so easily labelled (e.g. Minuchin, 1974). This list of examples is by no means complete, but it does give the rehabilitation worker some sources when beginning to explore this interesting field, as well as emphasizing the problem of summarizing in a short essay the work being done.

Despite the range of theoretical approaches to marital interaction and role structure, a surprisingly coherent picture emerges of the ways in which disturbed or distressed marriages differ from functioning, happy ones. Interaction in dysfunctional marriages is characterized by higher levels of defensive communication and lower levels of supportive communication (Alexander, 1973; Birchler et al., 1975). Defensive communications may invite a reciprocal response, and lead to a climate where it is progressively more difficult to solve problems or resolve crises. Such communications tend to be evaluative, controlling, to use strategies, to be indifferent, superior, dominating, and intended to impress others (Gibb, 1961). Partners attempt to control each other's behaviour by means of coercion, using aversive behaviour, both verbal and non-verbal, to achieve control (Patterson and Hops, 1972). In this situation there is a breakdown of the mutually rewarding interactions typical of good relationships (Stuart, 1969). Problem solving is inhibited by lack of positive feedback between couples (Vincent et al., 1975). Supportive behaviours, such as asking for and giving genuine information, showing emphatic understanding, or assuming equality between partners, are not demonstrated (Alexander, 1973). What is more, a partner tends to perceive the other's communications are more hostile than were actually intended, at least on a conscious level (Gottman et al., 1976). These results tend to confirm the hypothesis that distressed couples have deficits in communication skills. Communications may also be inconsistent or ambiguous, leading to more mistrust between partners (Friedman, 1972). The lack of open and direct communication amongst distressed couples has been mentioned by Fensterheim (1972) and Knox (1971) amongst others. Furthermore, when negative feelings are expressed, they tend to be stated in global terms, and attributed to the partner's conscious intention, i.e. malice (Weiss et al., 1973). An example of this would be to say, 'You're always trying to humiliate me in public', rather than, 'It hurt me this morning when you told me to shut up in front of your friends.'

This picture has been built up from studies using a range of samples, including patients, parents of delinquent children, and marriages in the general population. Different settings for the studies are also represented, including laboratory studies, videotaping conflict resolution tasks or using more intrusive technology, and more naturalistic environments.

In general, methods of intervention can be described under two headings, those using prescriptive techniques and those emphasizing exploratory, interpersonal interventions. Amongst the former are the use of such techniques as assertiveness training (Eisler *et al.*, 1974), developing communication skills and problem-solving ability using modelling, behavioural rehearsal and monitored progress (Patterson and Hops, 1972), and contracting, a form of negotiation where partners produce written agreements about behaviour change. Contracting may be on a *quid pro quo* basis (Rappaport and Harrell, 1972), or may involve a commitment to change independently of the partner's behaviour (Weiss *et al.*, 1973, p. 328). The latter form is more difficult to operate, but may be necessary where there is entrenched hostility and no marital alliance is possible.

The behavioural literature provides techniques that are easily summarized, and relatively easy to learn. However, there is evidence that good outcome in changing destructive interaction is linked to the therapists' general skills in relationships, such as the ability to relate expressed emotion to behaviour, and a tendency to display warmth and humour. Structuring skills were also found to be important to good outcome, in interaction with enabling skills (Alexander *et al.*, 1976). What seems likely is that experienced therapists have both types of general skill at their disposal, and are less reliant on specific techniques, being prepared to act swiftly and intervene decisively when they see a specific pattern of interaction that is habitual for the particular couple (Haley, 1976).

It is almost impossible to evlauate the relative merits of the plethora of approaches briefly described here. There is a dearth of reliable outcome literature for marital and family interventions. For the present, the worker should become familiar with the experience of working with the patient in the context of his or her marriage, which may in itself be a new development for some rehabilitation specialists. A cautionary note: the patterns of interaction described here may be extremely subtle and resistant to change. It is worth remembering that although marriage enrichment is a laudable aim (e.g. Margolin and Weiss, 1978), realistic goals must be set and worked towards. In many settings, the most that can be expected is to identify the most glaring deficiency in role functioning, and to put into effect a simple systematic intervention aimed at providing a modest but significant improvement.

To complete the present review of issues in rehabilitation into marital roles, it is necessary to turn from communication and interaction, central though they are, and briefly consider the pattern of role allocation within the marriage. In addition to the task of maintaining a functioning relationship, there are other, more concrete tasks to be considered, such as housework, child care, decisions about leisure, money, and housing. There is evidence that certain patterns of task allocation and decision making predominated in the marriages of male psychiatric patients compared to those of non-patient controls (Collins *et al.*, 1971). These patient–spouse pairs made fewer joint decisions, were more segregated in task performance, and were husband dominated rather than egalitarian. The patient group showed the greatest problems compared to the non-patient group in the areas of childrearing and social contacts outside the home. The male patients participated significantly less than the control men in housework and child care, even though they spent more time at home (also bearing in mind the modest amounts of time ordinary husbands spend in child care). These results suggest that the rehabilitation worker may be involved in an intervention where quite specific behaviours are targets for change, in addition to improvement of the interpersonal relationship (see Shepherd, Chapter 13).

### Reinstating Patient–Family Relationships

The foregoing discussion of the parental and marital roles has assumed that the patient is still actively involved with family life. In many cases, however, the patient loses contact with his or her family, especially in chronic conditions where the patient has been in hospital for a number of years. It is worth mentioning briefly that a number of accounts have appeared demonstrating the possibility of reinstating patient–family relationships. O'Brien and Azrin (1973) took a behavioural approach to restoring long-term patients' social relationships. Referring to their previous work on 'response priming' and 'reinforcer sampling', they established the value of sending the patient's relatives individual letters, requesting them to visit the hospital and to invite the patient home for trial visits. The hospital provided transport to the home, and a member of the rehabilitation team was present, allowing the relatives to curtail the visit when they wished. Furthermore, the three chronic patients described in this study (all women, aged 36, 54, and 64) were helped between visits to develop those skills that the rehabilitation worker had noticed would be useful or required in the patient's home. In practice these were instrumental performance skills of household tasks. In two of the patients, significant improvement was achieved, and one of the patients was discharged to live with her husband. Goldstein and Baer (1976) applied similar principles in a successful programme designed to increase the patients' contact by correspondence. Hollingsworth and Sokol (1978) propose predischarge conferences to include both relatives and close friends in order to establish understanding and cooperation in rehabilitation. Jacobson and Klerman (1966) give an account of the interpersonal dynamics of the home visits of hospitalized depressed patients. They began with the hypothesis that where there is compatibility of role expectations and role performance between partners, the family system will be stable. Disturbances in role complementarity will result in disequilibrium and emotional conflict. They used Spiegel's (1957) descriptions of role induction and modification to plan a programme for four middle-aged female depressed patients. Their claim that role complementarity could only be reestablished through the gradual change family members' expectations was partially supported by their results. Their study is of interest for the detailed way in which the interpersonal dynamics of the visits were studied, which, if used in a procedure similar to Azrin and O'Brien's, could complement their observation of instrumental behaviour.

It seems from these few reports that the theoretical stance underlying the intervention may not be as important as the non-specific effect of the care and attention given to individual patients and their families as a result of any systematic and planned approach to reinstating their relationships.

## Family Structure and Post-hospital Outcome

In planning the rehabilitation of a particular patient, it is useful to have in mind a broader picture of which domestic factors are likely to influence the outcome. Within this framework, the rehabilitation specialist is, so to speak, fore-armed in knowing which patients returning to which social contexts are likely to have problems, and what intervention or extra support is appropriate to prevent further breakdown. Some knowledge of the relevant research on family structure and post-hospital outcome is therefore a necessary first step.

Freeman and Simmons (1963), in their study of 649 patients and their families, point out that their data do not support the view of rehabilitation as a unitary process where patients are first resettled into the community and then attain levels of occupational and social performance comparable to those of their peers. Rather, they found the level of instrumental performance and the likelihood of readmission to hospital to be independent of each other. The importance of this distinction was confirmed by Mannino and Shore (1974) in their smaller scale study of 82 patients, half of whom were participating in a hospital aftercare programmed described by Fisher et al. (1973). The study found a clear pattern of results when family variables were used to predict achievement on a broad range of performance measures. However, when rehospitalization (i.e. length of community tenure) was the dependent variable, their results were less clear-cut. A first point to be noted, therefore, is that length of community tenure appears to be a more complex criterion of success in rehabilitation than levels of role performance. Because of this complexity it cannot (at least in research terms) be adequately predicted from domestic factors, such as whether the patient is married or single, living with parents or spouse, occupying a central role or a peripheral one, and so on.

It is also worth noting those variables which *do not* predict either the level of patients' social performance or how likely they are to be rehospitalized. Age and diagnosis are two such factors (Freeman and Simmons, 1963, p.85). Type of treatment also seems immaterial when predicting post-hospital adjustment, although there is evidence that readmission is made more likely if medication is discontinued following discharge (Hogarty and Goldberg, 1973; Mannino and Shore, 1974). Length of hospitalization is a good predictor of how well patients manage on returning to the community. The problem with the studies cited here is that their design does not allow the use of multivariate techniques of statistical analysis. It is therefore not possible to assess the *relative* importance of different variables, or whether variables in *interaction* have a stronger effect than singly. These limitations must be remembered when interpreting their findings.

A number of studies have shown a relationship between family variables and measures of social performance. A consistent finding is that ex-patients occupying central positions in conjugal families perform at higher levels (Dinitz *et al.* 1961; Freeman and Simmons, 1963; Mannino and Shore, 1974). Kowalewski (1972) reported that married patients showed more initiative in tackling problems than single patients living with their parents. Gender effects are more complex, and there may be an interaction between gender and family stage (i.e. parental and conjugal) which has not been fully explored because of the lack of multivariate analysis already referred to. We can infer, however, that women do better than men in parental families (Mannino and Shore, 1974) and in 'foster' families (Keskiner *et al.*, 1973). On the other hand, men in central roles within conjugal families do better than women.

Problems arise when attempting to interpret this pattern of results in terms of underlying processes. Freeman and Simmons did not find direct evidence for their 'differential tolerance of deviance' hypothesis, which states that central family positions are advantageous in that there is a greater tolerance for a needed spouse than for a more peripheral relative or adult child. They revised this formulation, making a more general statement that they key variable is the balance of demands and expectations between family members in different settings.

An alternative explanation of these findings is that the patients occupying these roles are 'pre-selected' according to other criteria (such as the severity of disturbance and the age at onset) and are intrinsically more likely to be socially competent. This interpretation of the evidence places less emphasis on the importance of family structural factors and is a plausible explanation of why, to take an obvious example, single adult men living with their parents are consistently found to have the lowest levels of social performance and the highest rates of rehospitalization. It is likely that pre-existing social performance deficits resulted in both their unmarried status and their greater risk of rehospitalization rather than that the family position influenced rehospitalization directly. It is quite possible that 'pre-selection' and 'effects of role structure' both play their part to varying degrees. In so far as structural factors do have an effect on outcome, it is probably by facilitating the resumption of everyday social performance. Mannino and Shore point out that patients holding high-status positions with clear expectations, in families that demand specific role functioning, seem to do best. It is not clear, however, whether this set of role characteristics has in their study (and in those of other workers) been confounded with the effect of paid employment. This is because employment status has not been analysed separately from the domestic variables in these studies. However, it is clear that, for whatever reasons, women returning to conjugal families tend to be in a disadvantageous position compared with men. Although she occupies a central place in her conjugal family, the mother's role demands may not be adequately structured and 'clear expectations of specific role functioning' may be lacking. Further, where a mother of older children has been hospitalized, she may have been replaced in her role to some extent (for example by a sister-in-law or teenage daughter) and may find that she is more peripheral in the family on her return. Unemployment is still socially more acceptable for women, and this may be an advantage in terms of greater tolerance afforded them; yet it may also involve the problem of lower expectations. In contrast, if a father is not immediately employable on discharge from hospital, he may suffer if his 'breadwinner' status is the only one which defines his relationship to the family. Where he has also been involved expressively with his family, occupying an active domestic role, the deleterious effects of joblessness on his post-hospital adjustment may be mitigated.

In summary, it seems likely that the optimal situation combines flexibility of roles, a tolerance for necessary role changes, but specific and well-defined expectations.

## References

Ainsworth, M. D. S. (1974) The development of infant–mother attachment. In B. M. Caldwell and H. N. Riccuiti, eds, *Review of Child Development Research*, Vol. 3. University of Chicago Press, Chicago.

Alexander, J. F. (1973) Defensive and supportive communications in normal and deviant families. *Journal of Consulting and Clinical Psychology*, **40**, 223–231.

Alexander, J. F., Barton, C., Schiavo, R. S., and Parsons, B. V. (1976) Systems-behavioural intervention with families of delinquents: therapist characteristics, family behaviour and outcome. *Journal of Consulting and Clinical Psychology*, **44**, 656–664.

Anderson, R. E. (1968) Where's dad? Paternal deprivation and delinquency. *Archives of General Psychiatry*, **18**, 641–649.

Andry, R. (1960) *Delinquency and parental pathology*. Methuen, London.

Avery, R., and Begalla, M. (1975) Analysing the homemaker job using the position analysis questionnaire (PAQ). *Journal of Applied Psychology*, **60**, 513–517.

Avery, R., and Gross, R. (1977). Satisfaction levels and correlates of satisfaction with the homemaker job. *Journal of Vocational Behaviour*, **10**, 13–24.

Bebbington, P., Hurry, J., Tennant, C., Sturt, E., and Wing, J. K. (1981) Epidemiology of mental disorders in Camberwell. *Psychological Medicine*, **11**, 561–580.

Bell, R. P. (1968) A reinterpretation of the direction of effects in studies of socialization. *Psychological Review*, **75**, 81–95.

Bennett, D. (1970) The value of work in psychiatric rehabilitation. *Social Psychiatry*, **5**, 224–230.

Bentovim, A. (1979) Child development research findings and psychoanalytic theory: an integrative critique. In D. Shaffer and J. Dunn, eds, *The First Year of Life: Psychological and Medical Implications of Early Experience.* John Wiley, Chichester.

Bion, W. R. (1962) *Learning from Experience.* Heinemann, London.

Birchler, G. R., Weiss, R. L., and Vincent, J. P. (1975) Multimethod analysis of social reinforcement exchange between maritally distressed and non-distressed spouse and stranger dyads. *Journal of Personality and Social Psychology*, **31**, 349–360.

Blood, R. O., and Wolfe, D. M. (1960) *Husbands and Wives: The Dynamics of Married Living.* Free Press, Glencoe, Ill.

Boston, M. (1975) Recent research in developmental psychology. *Journal of Child Psychotherapy*, **4**, 15–34.

Bowlby, J. (1977) The making and breaking of affectional bonds, I, aetiology and psychopathology in the light of attachment theory. *British Journal of Psychiatry*, **130**, 201–210.

Brown, G. W., and Harris, T. O. (1978) *Social Origins of Depression.* Tavistock, London.

Cohen, G. (1977) Absentee husbands in spiralist families: the myth of the symmetrical family. *Journal of Marriage and the Family*, **39**, 595–604.

Collins, J., Kreitman, N., Nelson, B., and Troop, J. (1971) Neurosis and marital interaction III. Family roles and functions. *British Journal of Psychiatry*, **119**, 233–242.

Dean, J. (1977) *Blind Ambition: The White House Years.* W. H. Allen, London.

Dinitz, S., Lefton, M., Angrist, S., and Pasamanick, B. (1961) Psychiatric and social attributes as predictors of case outcome in mental hospitalization. *Social Problems*, **8**, 322–328.

Eisler, R. M., Miller, P. M., Hersen, M., and Alford, H. (1974) Effects of assertive training on marital interaction. *Archives of General Psychiatry*, **30**, 643–649.

Feldman, H. (1971) The effects of children on the family. In A. Michel, ed., *Family Issues of Employed Women in Europe and America.* Brill, Leiden.

Fensterheim, H. (1972) Assertive methods and marital problems. In R. D. Rubin, H. Fensterheim, J. Henderson, and L. P. Ullman, eds, *Advances in Behaviour Therapy.* Academic Press, New York.

Fisher, T., Nackman, N., and Vyas, A. (1973) Aftercare in a family agency. *Social Casework*, **54**, 131–146.

Freeman, H. E., and Simmons, O. G. (1963) *The Mental Patient Comes Home.* John Wiley, New York.

Friedman, P. M. (1972) Personalistic family and marital therapy. In A. A. Lazarus, ed., *Clinical Behaviour Therapy.* Brunner/Mazel, New York.

Garbarino, J. (1977) The human ecology of child maltreatment: a conceptual model for research. *Journal of Marriage and the Family*, **39**, 721–736.

Garbarino, J., and Stocking, S. H. (1980) *Protecting Children from Abuse and Neglect: Developing and Maintaining Effective Support Systems for Families.* Jossey-Bass, San Francisco.

Gavron, H. (1966) *The Captive Wife: Conflicts of Housebound Mothers.* Routledge & Kegan Paul, London.

Gibb, J. R. (1961) Defensive communications. *Journal of Communication*, **3**, 141–148.

Goldstein, R. S., and Baer, D. M. (1976) A procedure to increase the personal mail and number of correspondents for nursing home residents. *Behaviour Therapy*, **7**, 348–354.

Goodman, C. (1980) A treatment and education program for emotionally disturbed women and their young children. *Hospital and Community Psychiatry*, **31**, 687–689.

Goody, E. M. (1974) Parental roles in anthropological perspective. In *The Family and Society, Dimensions of Parenthood.* HMSO, London.

Gottman, J., Notarius, H. M., Bank, S., and Yoppi, B. (1976) Behaviour exchange theory and marital decision making. *Journal of Personality and Social Psychology*, **34**, 14–23.

Gove, W. (1972) The relationship between sex roles, mental illness and marital status. *Social Forces*, **51**, 34–44.

Gowler, D., and Legge, K. (1972) Occupational role development, Part I. *Personnel Review*, **1**, 12–27.

Gowler, D., and Legge, K. (1982) Dual-worker families. In R. Rapoport and R. N. Rapoport, eds, *Families in Britain*. Routledge & Kegan Paul, London.

Greenberg, M., and Morris, N. (1974) Engrossment: the newborn's impact upon the father. *American Journal of Orthopsychiatry*, **44**, 520–531.

Gribben, T. (1979) *Pyjamas Don't Matter*. John Murray, London.

Gross, R., and Richard, D. (1977) Marital satisfaction, job satisfaction and task distribution in the home-maker job. *Journal of Vocational Behaviour*, **11**, 1–13.

Haley, J. (1976) *Problem-solving Therapy*. Harper & Row, New York.

Haley, J. (1980) Family therapy. *International Journal of Psychiatry*, **9**, 233–242.

Hall, F., and Pawlby, S. J. (1981) Continuity and discontinuity in the behaviour of British working-class mothers and their first-born children. *International Journal of Behavioural Development*, **4**, 13–36.

Harlow, H. F. (1958) The nature of love. *American Psychologist*, **13**, 673–685.

Hartley, J. (1980) Psychological approaches to unemployment. *Bulletin of the British Psychological Society*, **33**, 412–414.

Heath, D. H. (1976) Competent fathers: their personalities and marriages. *Human Development*, **19**, 26–39.

Heath, D. M. (1977) *Maturity and Competence*. Gardner Press, New York (distributed UK, Wiley).

Helterline, J. (1981) The emergence of modern motherhood: motherhood in England 1899 to 1959. *International Journal of Women's Studies*, **3**, 590–614.

Hill, R., and Aldous, J. (1969) Socialization for marriage and parenthood. In D. A. Goslin, ed., *Handbook of Socialisation Theory and Research*. Rand McNally, New York.

Hinde, R. A. (1978) Interpersonal relationships: in quest of a science. *Psychological Medicine*, **8**, 373–386.

Hogarty, G., and Goldberg, S. (1973) Drug and sociotherapy in the aftercare of schizophrenic patients. *Archives of General Psychiatry*, **28**, 54–64.

Hollingsworth, C. E., and Sokol, B. (1978) Predischarge family conference. *Journal of American Medical Association*, **239**, 740–741.

Holman, P. (1959) The etiology of maladjustment in children. *Journal of Mental Science*, **99**, 654–688.

Hyman, C. A., and Mitchell, R. (1975) A psychological study of child battering. *Health Visitor*, **48**, 294–296.

Jacobson, N. S., and Martin, B. (1976) Behavioural marriage therapy: current status. *Psychological Bulletin*, **83**, 540–556.

Jacobson, S., and Klerman, G. L. (1966) Interpersonal dynamics of hospitalized depressed patients' home visits. *Journal of Marriage and the Family*, **28**, 94–102.

Jahoda, M. (1979) The impact of unemployment in 1930s and 1970s. *Bulletin of the British Psychological Society*, **32**, 309–314.

Karn, Elizabeth (1972) Residential group project for mothers of children referred to a child guidance clinic. *British Journal of Social Work*, **2**, 175–186.

Kelmer Pringle, M. (1975) *The Needs of Children*. Hutchinson Educational, London.

Keskiner, A., Zalcman, M. J., and Ruppert, E. H. (1973) The advantages of being female in psychiatric rehabilitation. *Archives of General Psychiatry*, **28**, 689–692.

Klein, J. (1970) *Samples from English Cultures*. Routledge & Kegan Paul, London.

Knox, D. (1971) *Marriage Happiness: A Behaviour Approach to Counselling*. Research Press, Champaign, Ill.

Kolko-Phillips, N., Davidson, M., and Auerbach, A. B. (1980) Discussion groups for mothers of high-risk infants and toddlers: an early intervention approach to treatment. *Child Care Quarterly*, **9**, 206–208.

Kotelchuck, M. (1976) The infant's relationship to the father: experimental evidence. In M. E. Lamb, et., *The Role of the Father in Child Development*. John Wiley, New York.

Kowalewski, N. (1972) A follow-up study of patients in a psychiatric day hospital for the purpose of planning a follow-up service. *Social Service Review*, **46**, 457.

Lamb, M. E. (1976) The role of the father: an overview. In M. E. Lamb, ed., *The Role of the Father in Child Development*. John Wiley, New York.

Laws, J. L. (1971) A feminist review of the marital adjustment literature: the rape of the Locke. *Journal of Marriage and the Family*, **33**, 483–516.

Le Masters, E. E. (1957) Parenthood as crisis. *Marriage and Family Living*, **19**, 352–355.

Lindsey, C. R., Pound, A., and Radford, M. (1978) A co-operative playgroup in a psychiatric day hospital. *Group Analysis*, **11**, 289–296.

Lynch, M. A. (1975) Ill-health and child-abuse. *Lancet*, 16 August, No. 7929, pp. 317–319.

Mannino, F. V., and Shore, M. F. (1974) Family structure, aftercare and post-hospital adjustment. *American Journal of Orthopsychiatry*, **44**, 76–85.

Margolin, G., and Weiss, R. L. (1978) Communication training and assessment. 1. A case of behavioural marital enrichment. *Behaviour Therapy*, **9**, 508–520.

Miller, A., and Ellis, J. (1980) A behaviour management course for a group of mothers: the importance of the course setting for effective use of available resources. *Child: Care, Health and Development*, **6**, 147–155.

Minuchin, S. (1974) *Families and Family Therapy*. Tavistock, London.

Mumaw, C. R. (1967) Organisational patterns of homemakers related to selected predispositional and situational characteristics. Unpublished PhD thesis, Pennsylvania State University.

Mussen, P. H., Conger, J. J., and Kagan, J. (1969) *Child Development and Personality*. Harper & Row, New York.

Newson, J., and Newson, E. (1963) *Patterns of Infant Care in an Urban Community*. Allen & Unwin, London.

Newson, J., and Newson, E. (1968) *Four Years Old in an Urban Community*. Allen & Unwin, London.

Newson, J., and Newson, E. (1977) *Seven Years Old in the Home Environment*. Allen & Unwin, London.

Nichols, A., Mumaw, C. R., Paynter, M., Plonk, M. A., and Price, D. Z. (1971) Family management. *Journal of Marriage and the Family*, **33**, 112–118.

Oakley, A. (1974) *The Sociology of Housework*. Pitman Press, Bath.

O'Brien, F., and Azrin, N. H. (1973) Interaction-priming: a method of reinstating patient family relationships. *Behaviour Research and Therapy*, **11**, 133–136.

Parke, R. D. (1979) Perspectives on father–infant interaction. In J. D. Osofsky, ed., *Handbook of Infant Development*. John Wiley, New York.

Patterson, G. R. (1974) Interventions for boys with conduct problems: multiple settings, treatments and criteria. *Journal of Consulting and Clinical Psychology*, **42**, 471–481.

Patterson, G. R., and Hops, H. (1972) Coercion, a game for two: intervention techniques for marital conflict. In R. E. Ulrich and P. Mountjoy, eds, *Experimental Analysis of Social Behaviour*. Appleton-Century-Crofts, New York.

Paul, G. (1969) Chronic mental patient: current status—future directions. *Psychological Bulletin*, **71**, 81–94.

Pearlin, L. I., and Schooler, C. (1978) The structure of coping. *Journal of Health and Social Behaviour*, **19**, 2–21.

Pedersen, F. A., and Robson, K. S. (1969) Father participation in infancy. *American Journal of Orthopsychiatry*, **39**, 466–472.

Perkins, E. R., and Morris, B. (1979) *Preparation for Parenthood: A Critique of the Concept.* Occasional Paper No. 17, Leverhulme Health Education Project, University of Nottingham, Nottingham.

Perrucci, C. C., Potter, H. R., and Rhoads, D. L. (1978) Determinants of male family-role performance. *Psychology of Women Quarterly*, **3**, 53–67.

Pincus, L., and Dare, C. (1978) *Secrets in the Family.* Faber & Faber, London.

Rakowitz, E., and Rubin, G. S. (1980) *Living with Your New Baby: A Survival Guide.* Souvenir Press, London.

Rapoport, R., Rapoport, R. N., and Strelitz, Z. (1977) *Fathers, Mothers and Others: Towards New Alliances.* Routledge & Kegan Paul, London.

Rappaport, A. F., and Harrell, J. A. (1972) A behavioural-exchange model for marital counselling. *Family Coordinator*, **21**, 203–213.

Rausch, H. L., Goodrich, W., and Campbell, J. D. (1963) Adaption to the first years of marriage. *Psychiatry*, **26**, 368–380.

Richards, E. (1974) Women in the British economy since about 1700: an interpretation. *History*, **59**, 337–357.

Richards, M. P. M., Dunn, J. F., and Antonis, B. (1975) Caretaking in the first year of life: the role of fathers' and mothers' social isolation. *Child: Care, Health and Development*, **3**, 23–36.

Robertson, J. M. (1976) The abusive parent: a different perspective. *Canada's Mental Health*, **24**, 18–19.

Rollins, B. C., and Feldman, H. (1970) Marital satisfaction over the family life cycle. *Journal of Marriage and the Family*, **32**, 20–28.

Rossi, A. (1974) Transition to parenthood. In C. Greenblat, ed., *Game.* Random House, New York.

Satir, V. (1964) *Conjoint Family Therapy.* Science and Behaviour Books, Palo Alto.

Schaffer, H. R. (1971) *The Growth of Sociability.* Penguin, Harmondsworth, Middx.

Schaffer, H. R. (1977a) *Studies in Mother–Infant Interaction.* Academic Press, London.

Schaffer, H. R. (1977b) *Mothering.* Open Books/Fontana, London.

Schaffer, H. R., and Emerson, P. E. (1964) The development of social attachments in infancy. *Monographs of the Society for Research in Child Development*, **29**, No. 94.

Scott, P. D. (1975) Battering husbands: a complex of causes. *The Times*, 29 August.

Seidel, H. A. (1978) Housework organisation: marital relationship and the availability of confidants to young housewives. M. Phil. thesis, Institute of Psychiatry, London.

Spiegel, J. P. (1957) The resolution of role conflict within the family. *Psychiatry*, **20**, 1–16.

Stuart, R. B. (1969) Operant interpersonal treatment for marital discord. *Journal of Consulting and Clinical Psychology*, **33**, 675–682.

Tizard, J., and Tizard, B. (1971) The social development of two-year-old children in residential nurseries. In H. R. Schaffer, ed., *The Origins of Human Social Relations.* Academic Press, London.

Tudor, W., Tudor, J. F., and Gove, W. R. (1977) The effect of sex role differences on the social control of mental illness. *Journal of Health and Social Behaviour*, **18**, 98–112.

Vanck, J. (1974) Time spent in housework. *Scientific American*, **23**, 116–120.

Vincent, J. P., Weiss, R. L., and Birchler, G. R. (1975) A behavioural analysis of problem-solving in distressed and non-distressed married and stranger dyads. *Behaviour Therapy*, **6**, 475–487.

Warr, P., and Parry, G. (1982) Paid employment and women's psychological wellbeing. *Psychological Bulletin*, **91**, 498–516.

Watts, F. N. (1976) Social treatments. In H. J. Eysenck and G. D. Wilson, eds, *A Textbook of Human Psychology*. MTP Press, Lancaster.

Watts, F. N. (1978) A study of work behaviour in a psychiatric rehabilitation unit. *British Journal of Social and Clinical Psychology*, **17**, 85–92.

Weiss, R. L., Hops, H., and Patterson, G. R. (1973) A framework for conceptualising marital conflict, a technology for altering it, some data for evaluating it. In L. A. Hamerlynch, L. C. Handy, and E. J. Mash, eds, *Behaviour Change: Methodology, Concepts and Practice*. Research Press, Champaign, Ill.

Weissman, M. M., and Paykel, E. S. (1974) *The Depressed Woman. A Study of Social Relationships*. University of Chicago Press, Chicago.

Winnicott, D. W. (1960) Ego distortion in terms of the true and false self. In *The Maturation Process and the Facilitating Environment* (1965). Hogarth, London.

Winnicott, D. W. (1964) *The Child, the Family and the Outside World*. Penguin, Harmondsworth, Middx.

Winnicott, D. W. (1971) *Playing and Reality*. Tavistock, London.

Working Family Project (1978) Parenting. In R. Rapoport and R. N. Rapoport, eds, *Working Couples*. Routledge & Kegan Paul, London.

Young, M., and Willmott, P. (1973) *The Symmetrical Family*. Routledge & Kegan Paul, London.

Theory and Practice of Psychiatric Rehabilitation
Edited by F. N. Watts and D. H. Bennett
© 1983, John Wiley & Sons, Ltd.

# 13

---

# Interpersonal Relationships

---

GEOFF SHEPHERD

Difficulties in social interaction lie at the heart of the problems faced in rehabilitating psychiatric patients. Social performance is critical in determining a patient's employment prospects (Watts, Chapter 11), and is a key factor in a patient's adjustment at home and in the community (Parry, Chapter 12; Bennett and Morris, Chapter 10). Interpersonal relationships are therefore central to successful role performance and to the ability to maintain social roles, which in turn is one of the primary determinants of social integration and long-term adaptation (Shepherd, 1980; Watts, Chapter 14). It is important, then, that we have an adequate understanding of what is involved in social interaction, how we might go about assessing social difficulties, and to what extent they can be effectively alleviated. These are the issues for discussion in this chapter.

## Social Performance

Social performance, like work performance, depends on both motivation and skills. Patients must be prepared to engage in social interaction and they must be motivated to cope with the difficulties involved. They must also possess certain skills, behavioural, cognitive, and emotional, and be able to use these appropriately. These requirements are complex and perhaps it is not surprising that difficulties frequently arise. Therefore, let us try to examine what is involved.

### Motivation

Motivation is obviously central: but what do we mean when we say that patients are more or less motivated in terms of their social interaction?

Motivation conventionally refers to an apparent willingness to perform certain actions—on what does this willingness depend? This is not an easy question to answer. In the first place, we must acknowledge that the processes underlying motivation are often obscure. We simply do not know why people do certain things and often they cannot tell us. In psychiatry we are familiar with the idea that people may act according to reasons of which they themselves are apparently unaware. However, there is now also good experimental evidence that we may often have little or no direct access to many higher order mental processes such as those involved in evaluation, judgement, problem solving, and the initiation of behaviour (Nisbett and Wilson, 1977). While these motivational processes remain unconcious they can only be the subject of speculation. However, there are ways of formulating motivation at an explicit, conscious level and these can be used to investigate and check out our theories.

Contemporary social psychologists seem to agree that what is important for understanding social motivation is the perceived 'meaning' of events (Harre and Secord, 1972; Gauld and Shotter, 1977). 'Meaning', in this sense, implies a concern with ends or outcomes. It is argued that the perceived meaning of an event is determined by the expectancies that it generates among participants as to the likelihood of particular outcomes. These outcomes are themselves evaluated in the light of some set of personal and subjective goals. If we then assume that people will generally prefer and be led to perform those actions which they expect to be associated with the most favourable consequences (Irwin, 1971), we have a general expectancy or 'decision theory' model of motivation (see Edwards, 1961). This kind of model has yet to be extensively applied to the analysis of social motivation, but there does seem to be good evidence from related areas such as occupational preference (Mitchell and Beach, 1976) that people do behave as if decision theory models are operating.

The importance of goals for understanding social interaction has also been emphasized by Argyle (1969) in his 'social skills' model. He makes an analogy between social interaction and the performance of a simple motor skill and argues that in both cases the effects of one's action are being continuously evaluated according to some set of internal goals. The outcomes of these judgements are then used to adjust behaviour to produce a smooth, 'skilled' performance. The social skills model has made an important contribution and has served to focus attention on the details of skilled social behaviour, but it does not really do justice to the diversity of the goals that may be operating when the behaviour of psychiatric patients is considered. It also fails to acknowledge the extended time period over which such goals may have their influence and minimizes the importance of conflict when understanding social motivation.

Social goals are both personal and varied. Goffman (1959) suggested that the motivation to present oneself in a favourable light to others is important. White (1959), and more recently Bandura (1977), have focused on the value of a subjective feeling of mastery or coping. Berkowitz (1970) discusses the role of altruism in social motivation and Argyle himself presents a long list of possible social goals, e.g. conveying information, changing attitudes, pleasing others, etc. (Argyle, 1969, p.181). The goals influencing the social motivation of psychiatric patients often seem particularly unusual and idiosyncratic. For example, they may have the goal of terminating a social interaction as soon as possible and thereby escaping from the situation; or conversely, of monopolizing an interaction so completely that the other person makes no contribution at all. The differences between psychiatric patients in terms of their social goals can thus be very marked.

Important social goals also tend to be rather stable and to operate over long periods of time. In contrast the social skills model tends to focus on the way in which goals influence moment-to-moment social interaction. For many patients there is actually very little evidence of such careful monitoring, and it is only by looking at the nature of their social relationships at work and in the family over many years that a pattern of stable underlying goals becomes apparent. Many patients also experience conflicts because of the simultaneous presence of contradictory goals: for example, the individual who finds interaction with the opposite sex very difficult and anxiety provoking but at the same time wants very much to have successful relationships and marriage; or the individual who feels that his parents, or wife, are highly critical of him but also feels unable to manage independently and therefore needs to stay with them. These kinds of 'approach–avoidance conflicts' (Miller, 1959) are highly disabling in motivational terms and can only be resolved by either strengthening the approach tendencies or weakening the avoidance tendencies. In practice these may be difficult to achieve.

## Behavioural Skills and Social Adequacy

Motivation is of primary importance in social interaction, but skills are needed, too, if social goals are to be achieved. As already indicated, Argyle's model has generated considerable research aimed at identifying the elements of skilled social performance, yet there is still some doubt as to whether socially inadequate individuals can be distinguished by deficits in their observable social skills. Bryant et al. (1976) found that a group of psychiatric outpatients defined as socially inadequate using multiple criteria (global ratings on interview, psychometric tests, clinical interview, and history) differed from a socially adequate group in terms of patterns of eye contact, speech volume, etc., when placed in a role-played interview with a stranger. However, although there were some significant differences between the groups there was also still a great deal of variation within each (particularly in the inadequate group), and consequently some degree of overlap between them. Bryant et al. also report that the qualities which correlated most highly with social adequacy across all patients were those concerned with taking an interest in others and being able to bring them into the interaction effectively ('rewardingness' and 'control'). These qualities seem to be strongly based on underlying cognitive processes rather than overt behaviour.

American research reported by Arkowitz *et al.* (1975) and Glasgow and Arkowitz (1975) has looked at the social skills of men involved in interaction with women. They found that socially skilled men who had relatively high frequencies of contact with the opposite sex did not differ very much in behavioural terms from unskilled men who had relatively low frequencies of contact. However, they did differ in terms of self-ratings of skills and anxiety. So, although they did not appear to observers as particularly 'unskilled', they felt themselves to be so. Perhaps this is more often the problem with psychiatric patients.

It is really only in the area of assertiveness (being able clearly to express one's needs and feelings) that a clear difference has emerged in behavioural terms between the skilled and the unskilled. Eisler *et al.* (1973, 1975) compared groups of psychiatric inpatients, again globally rated by independent observers in a role-play test, as generally assertive or not, and found some fairly clear differences. For example, the assertive group showed significantly clearer requests for change, they replied more quickly, and spoke longer and louder. There was also evidence that the pattern of assertive responses was influenced by various aspects of the situation itself. It depended, for example, on whether the assertiveness was being expressed to a man or a woman, and on whether it was 'negative' (i.e. criticizing, complaining, demanding) or 'positive' (i.e. expressing pleasure, affection, gratitude).

Taken together these studies suggest that detailed behavioural skills are not the only important factor in determining social effectiveness. Obviously, they do play some part, but a clear difference between behaviourally 'skilled' and 'unskilled' individuals is apparent only at the extremes. If patients make virtually no eye contact, or their speech is completely inaudible, obviously they will have difficulty with social interactions. However, the range and limits of acceptable social behaviour actually appear to be quite broad. There is certainly little evidence for a correlation in the statistical sense, i.e. a direct and continuous relationship between the objective aspects of behavioural performance and its judged adequacy. Thus, it may not be necessary for clinical purposes to focus on the minutiae of social behaviour; in practical terms people can cope socially in an enormous variety of ways, and other social deficits are perhaps more important. Even in the area of assertiveness, where behavioural skills do seem to be relatively important, situational factors exert a strong influence on the behaviour and there is no simple relationship between effective assertiveness and a specific set of skilled responses.

Cognitive Skills

Behavioural skills on their own, therefore, do not provide an adequate guide to what is involved in effective social performance. As indicated earlier, we need to consider cognitive and emotional skills as well. Cognitively, there are two main kinds of processes involved. The first centres around the ability to predict accurately the expectations and reactions of other people, and the second involves the ability to predict accurately the consequences of one's own actions.

Assessing accurately the expectations of others is a complicated task (Watts, Chapter 14). The expectations of individuals in any given role relationship are varied and it is therefore necessary to discover the social demands that are operating in each particular case. No two employers, husbands, or friends have exactly the same expectations of a particular relationship and one must therefore be sensitive to the needs and demands of others. This is a skill akin to 'empathy' and Watts suggests it may be related at a cognitive level to 'decentring'. It would seem that deficiencies in this kind of skill were present in the socially inadequate patients studied by Bryant *et al.* (1976). They were found to be unable to convey an interest in others and to bring them into the interaction effectively. It is also the same kind of dimension referred to by Hinde (1976) as 'meshing' and which he argued from studies of higher primates to be a fundamental starting point for forming social relationships. It is interesting to note in this connection that Fischetti *et al.* (1977) found that subjects who were deficient in their social skills had problems with the *timing* of their responses, not their absolute frequency or quality.

Predicting accurately the reactions of others also often causes problems. We are all susceptible to making generalizations about other people and these are often embodied in pervasive and enduring 'stereotypes'. For psychiatric patients the content of these stereotypes may give rise to particular difficulties. For example, Nichols (1974), in a survey of patients with social problems, notes that they have a strong general tendency to perceive criticism and disapproval from others. This point is reinforced in a study by Eisler *et al.* (1978) who investigated the generalized expectancies of assertive and unassertive psychiatric patients in terms of how they predicted others would react to a standard set of social situations. The unassertive group expected generally less positive or rewarding consequences to follow from the same set of responses as those chosen by the assertive group. They also tended to choose less acceptable and more passive response alternatives. Thus a patient may avoid contact with his employer (or parent) because he expects a very critical or hostile response. In contrast, the supervisor himself, or an independent observer, may not expect or predict the same degree of criticism or hostility in the relationship. However, it is the patient's expectancies that are important because they determine his motivation.

Bower (1978) has recently reviewed some of the evidence on stereotypes and shows how they can lead to misperceptions. People tend to infer from the presence of a single characteristic in an individual that he or she also possesses the traits associated in the perceiver's mind with that characteristic. Further, when we interact with others the information we receive is the result of a process of selective attention, the selection process being actively directed by previously held attitudes and expectations. So, when a patient complains that his parents or employers are *always* criticizing him he may be reporting perfectly accurately on what he experiences. He expects criticism and this is what he notices and remembers. The fact that others do not see the situation in this way is irrelevant as far as the individual's experience is concerned. Stereotypes thus have a built-in bias towards confirmation and a corresponding prejudice against disconfirmation. This makes them durable and very difficult to change. They can even influence the way we behave towards others so that we elicit responses from them which eventually confirm the stereotype. For example, a patient may complain that he is constantly being rejected by others, that he is a failure, that nobody cares, etc., but eventually by his own behaviour he makes it increasingly likely that rejection and failure do occur.

Stereotypes about other people are thus important for understanding social interaction. However, we may also have generalized expectancies about the consequences of our own actions which may be equally distorted. Positive motivation seems to be at least partly dependent on a feeling that one can bring about certain consequences through one's actions. This has been referred to as an attribution of 'internal control' over reinforcement (Rotter, 1966) and it may be contrasted with an attribution of external control, i.e. a general tendency to perceive events as being outside one's own efforts, due to chance, luck, fate, etc. The 'internal–external control' dimension seems to be an important one in rehabilitation and is related conceptually to feelings of self-esteem (Rosenberg, 1965) and 'powerlessness' (Pearlin and Schooler, 1978). Attribution of control thus provides an alternative way of conceptualizing 'confidence'. If an individual is not confident, i.e. he does not believe that his actions are likely to achieve the goals he sets himself, then he is unlikely to be positively motivated. This would apply to social motivation as well as to other kinds of motivation.

There is one final cognitive skill that needs to be mentioned. One must not only know what to do in social situations and have the confidence to do it, one must also be able to select a suitable 'plan' easily when the situation arises. As indicated, the plan consists of a complicated set of responses geared towards a particular end. Given what was said earlier about the ambiguity of social situations, the relationship between the stimulus (the situation) and the selection of the response (the plan) is obviously complex. Recent work on the information processing of schizophrenic patients suggests that they have particular difficulties with tasks in which the stimulus and the required response are not readily compatible (Hemsley, 1977). Thus, they might have difficulties in selecting their 'plans'. Whether the situation can be simplified, and the required stimulus–response connections made more 'compatible', will be discussed later when we consider treatment.

## Emotional Skills

We can turn now to the question of emotional skills. Coping with the emotional side of social interaction is obviously a central part of the process. Interacting with people inevitably leads to a variety of emotional responses and these have to be coped with. The prominence of anxiety and depressive symptoms in patients with social difficulties has been noted by several writers (Lewinsohn, 1974; Hall and Goldberg, 1977), although the precise role of these affective disturbances is not yet clear. Some authors view anxiety as the primary symptom, hence the term social 'phobia' (Marks, 1969), and it is well established that high levels of affective arousal can disrupt skilled performance (Yerkes and Dodson, 1908). Thus there is a case for regarding anxiety as primary and the skills deficits as secondary. However, other writers such as Argyle (1969) take the opposite view and see the behavioural and cognitive deficits as primary and the emotional disturbance as a consequence. Whichever of these views is the more correct (and it is probably safe to assume that both are at least partially true) there is no doubt that emotional disturbances and the anticipation of them are an integral part of the syndrome of social difficulties. We shall consider later whether it may be more profitable to concentrate on the emotional disturbance or the skills deficits when carrying out treatment.

There is one final point that should be added in connection with the question of emotional arousal and social interaction. This is the possibility that for some patients an avoidance of excessive emotional arousal and a consequent withdrawal from some social situations may in fact serve a protective function. Wing and Brown (1970) and Hemsley (1978) have argued strongly that for some schizophrenics there are dangers inherent in overstimulation, particularly of a social nature. Thus, there are some problems of avoidance motivation which should be approached rather cautiously.

To summarize, then, we have noted some of the complexities involved in arriving at an adequate understanding of social interaction. We have emphasized the central importance of motivation and argued that, although motivational processes are often obscure, in some cases we can begin to formulate them in terms of the interaction of various kinds of expectancies. These expectancies are each necessary, but not sufficient, conditions for positive motivation. A patient must have: (a) a reasonably clear goal, (b) without undue conflict, (c) a minimum level of behavioural skills, (d) an ability to be sensitive to the needs of others, (e) confidence that he/she will achieve his/her goal, (f) an ability to select a suitable plan, and (g) a capacity to manage his/her emotional state. If any one of these factors is significantly deficient then positive motivation will be impaired, or at least subject to conflict. Seen in this way, the complexity of social motivation and the difficulties of social interaction are apparent. Let us now turn to the implications of this kind of model for assessment and treatment.

## Assessment

### Behavioural Assessment

Methods for assessing behavioural skills are perhaps the best developed in the social area, and these have been comprehensively reviewed by Hersen and Bellack (1977) and Bellack (1979). The usual procedure is to construct some kind of simulated social interaction (a role-play with a stooge, or audiotaped stimulus) and then rate performance on a number of behavioural items. These tend to be the familiar elements from Argyle's social skills model, e.g. speech volume, latency; duration, content; patterns of eye contact; facial expressions; etc. (For a full description of Argyle's rating scales covering both verbal and non-verbal behaviour, see Trower *et al.*, 1978a, pp. 144–168). This method is relatively quick and convenient for researchers, but it also has some serious disadvantages.

First, as indicated earlier, it is not at all certain that 'behaviour' is the most important variable to assess. However, even if social behaviour is what we want to measure, it still does not follow that role-plays provide the most appropriate method. Situational factors play an important part in determining the nature of the response obtained and this has been noted in the assessment literature for some time (Mischel, 1968). It follows that difficulties in social behaviour cannot be validly assessed without taking the situational context into account. Some patients may show very little 'generality' in their social behaviour; their responses may be very specific to particular situations, even to particular people. As Harré and Secord (1972) comment, there can be a 'multiplicity of social selves' and this simple point is overlooked if we assume that more or less any assessment situation will automatically give a representative sample of behaviour. The extent to which the sample is likely to be representative depends on the extent to which the assessment situation replicates the conditions that occur in the natural environment where the problems arise. Thus, a patient may perceive interacting with other patients in hospital as very different from interacting with colleagues at work. To the extent that he expects different consequences to arise from his behaviour, then he is likely to modify his actions accordingly. For example he/she may become more or less withdrawn, aggressive, or dependent. It may therefore become very difficult to obtain valid assessments of social functioning in a hospital environment.

As an illustration of this problem, Ellsworth *et al.* (1968) showed that those patients who were assessed as having the most problems with social interaction in hospital actually had the *fewest* problems on discharge; conversely, those patients who adjusted 'best' to the hospital had the most difficulties when they left. Thus an attempt should be made to 'normalize' the situation in hospital, so that social interaction occurs in as realistic a context as possible. Normal role relationships can be imported through the provision of paid work (Bennett, 1970). Similarly, units which are 'open' to the outside world, where patients can go into the community unhindered, will allow opportunities for direct observation of social difficulties.

Staff attitudes are also crucial and if staff can avoid creating high levels of 'distance' (Goffman, 1961) between themselves and the patients, then this will further help to create the kind of situation where more valid social assessments can be made. The general point to bear in mind is that the more realistic the assessment situation, the more likely it is to be valid; the more artificial the situation, the less likely it is to be valid.

Viewed in this light, role-play tests and formal interview situations are particularly suspect. They carry strong 'demand characteristics' (Orne, 1962) and as a consequence they may generate quite atypical patterns of social responding. Bellack *et al.* (1978) have demonstrated this in a study where they investigated the correspondence between the social behaviour of female psychiatric patients when placed in a behavioural role-play test and two other assessment situations, a structured interview and a general discussion group. They found that the patients' social performance in the last two situations were highly correlated but bore little relationship to their behaviour in the role-play setting. In our research, we have developed a rating scale for observing the free social behaviour of chronic patients in a day hospital (Shepherd, 1977, 1978). This measure has satisfactory reliability as far as total score is concerned and good validity. There is some degree of unreliability for some of the individual items, depending on the raters used, and this emphasizes the 'trade-off' between reliability and validity discussed by Levy (1973). Measures which are highly reliable tend to have to be taken under very controlled, artificial conditions and therefore they often lack validity. Measures of free, naturally occurring behaviour have much better validity, but may have reduced reliability as a result of the inherent loss of control. Our results also serve as a reminder that the accuracy of assessments depends as much upon the raters as it does upon the instrument and thus the reliability of new raters should always be checked. Nevertheless, the measure does give good results, even with inexperienced raters, and it can be administered 'non-reactively', i.e. without the patients' knowledge that they are being assessed. Similar measures have been reported by other workers, e.g. Gutride *et al.* (1974).

Even with valid behavioural assessments of this kind it is still not clear how such measures relate to social functioning outside the institutional setting. Direct observation of social interactions in the community is often difficult, and so obtaining information about whom patients interact with, and the quality and range of their social contacts, poses some major methodological problems. We usually have to rely on self-reports and it is therefore important to attempt to ensure that the method of self-reporting is as valid and reliable as possible. Studies on interviewing procedures yield a number of useful suggestions as to how the accuracy of such self-report data can be improved (Brown and Rutter, 1966; Shapiro, 1979). For example, it is recommended that specific questions should be asked, of a factual nature, about discrete events which occurred within a recent and clearly specified time period. Social 'diaries', or 'time budgets' of the type described by Marzillier *et al.* (1976) and Krietman *et al.* (1970), would seem to conform to these recommendations. But such measures still lack independent corroboration of their validity and this should always be borne in mind. We have recently reported on some data collected using a 'social network' interview (Shepherd *et al.*, 1982). This instrument seems highly reliable and has revealed the importance of families and workmates in the social networks of chronic patients. Contacts with friends were rather infrequent. Scott Henderson and his colleagues have also developed a similar interview schedule (Henderson, 1980; Duncan-Jones, 1980), and they have used it to investigate social networks, in both community and outpatient samples. They have found a consistent negative relationship between psychological symptoms and the presence of social attachments (Henderson *et al.*, 1978a, 1978b). This work is outstanding for its thoroughness, and their careful approach to the development of the interview schedule and this whole area of assessment deserves further attention.

### Assessment of Cognitions

We have placed considerable emphasis up to now on the cognitive processes underlying social difficulties. How are these to be assessed? The cognitions associated with anxiety have been traditionally measured using various standard questionnaires, e.g. the Social Anxiety and Distress Questionnaire (Watson and Friend, 1969); the Wolpe-Lazarus Assertiveness Scale (Wolpe and Lazarus, 1966); Argyle *et al.'s* Social Anxiety Questionnaire (1974). Similarly, Rotter (1966) has developed a standard questionnaire to measure the internal–external attribution of control dimension, and Eisler *et al.* (1978) illustrate the use of simple rating scales to measure patients' expectancies. Again, all these methods may be quick and convenient for researchers, but they make some doubtful assumptions.

First, they assume that all patients possess generalized expectancies, whereas in fact patients may wish to give specific responses for specific individuals or situations. They may expect some people to be angry with them but not everybody; they may attribute 'externally' for some situations but not others. We have already noted that social behaviour is frequently specific to particular situations and there may be a corresponding specificity in social expectancies. Most personality theorists now agree that both specificity and generality are important and that it is the interaction between the two within any individual that determines, at least statistically, the response (Wiggins, 1973; Endler and Magnusson, 1976). It has even been suggested that the degree of specificity and generality shown in behaviour itself varies from person to person (Alker, 1972). It is therefore necessary to investigate empirically how far an individual's behaviour and expectancies are specific to particular situations and how much they are generalized and not assume that either is the case.

The second assumption of the standard questionnaire approach is that the concepts supplied by the assessor will be understood by the patient in the way that he intends. For example, it is assumed that the patient will understand questions about fear and anxiety in the same way that the researcher does. However, there is evidence, e.g. from work by Leff (1978), that suggests this may not be the case. The patients in this study seemed to have much less differentiated concepts of emotions such as anger and fear than did the professionals. Bem and Allen (1974) have also argued that it is the individualistic nature of conceptual organization that underlies apparent 'inconsistencies' in behaviour assessed across different situations. The 'inconsistencies' arise because we take the observer's, rather than the participant's, view of what constitutes behaviour consistent with a given attitude.

These points cast doubt on the validity of responses to individual items on standard attitude scales or general questionnaires. But in addition to concerns about validity, it is also desirable to have some way of checking the internal reliability (logical consistency) of each response. If a response is unreliable, it is unlikely to be valid. Traditional attitude scales or questionnaires sometimes provide checks on the internal consistency of the total scale but seldom provide such information for individual items. For simple target problem rating scales, e.g. those used in the Eisler et al. (1978) study, there is not guide at all as to the internal reliability of the ratings. Shapiro (1970, 1975) has developed a method which overcomes these problems. Symptom statements are elicited from the patient during the course of a structured interview and these statements are formulated to reflect different degrees of severity. The patient then sorts the statements on a paired comparison forced-choice basis. This method of administration allows a numerical score to be obtained from the pattern of responses to each statement and it is possible to check on the internal consistency of each score. The methodology has been adapted to assess a number of the important cognitive elements in social interaction such as expectancies concerned with predicting the responses of others or predicting the consequences of one's own actions (Shepherd and Bilsbury, 1979). It is preferable to using a standard questionnaire or attitude scale because it makes no assumptions about generality or common linguistic frameworks and it also provides a built-in check on the internal reliability of each response. We have evidence from our preliminary work that such a measure is feasible and can be used to assess expectancies about degrees of coping and emotional distress in chronic patients with social difficulties. The personal questionnaire method has also been extended by Phillips (1977) who has shown that a whole 'family' of personal questionnaires are possible, depending on the underlying scaling of the items. All the variants have in common the use of the patients' own language to describe their problems and a method whereby the internal reliability of individual items can be examined. (For a fuller discussion of the assessment of cognitions related to social difficulties, see Shepherd, in press.)

Thus in general we are advocating an approach to the assessment of social difficulties which attempts to obtain as valid assessments as possible by directly observing natural social behaviour. If interview data have to be used, care should be taken to maximize their accuracy and cognitions (anxiety, expectancies, etc.) should be measured reliably, using the patients' own linguistic and conceptual frameworks to avoid misunderstandings.

The final stage of the assessment process is to set treatment goals and these, too, must be as individualized as possible. Relevant behavioural goals may be derived by asking the patients to supply the targets themselves, as in the excellent study by Goldsmith and McFall (1975), rather than relying on the therapist's preconceptions. Similarly, targets for cognitive change may arise out of careful interviewing or discussion of questionnaire results. It may also be useful to inquire into 'coping-strategies' (Litman et al., 1979) and consider whether these might be changed, or expanded (Pearlin and Schooler, 1978). Given the likelihood of motivational problems, it is important to stress that goals should only be set after careful negotiation with the patient and with his or her cooperation and participation if at all possible. Written 'contracts' can also sometimes be helpful in making the goals fully explicit (Falloon et al., 1977; Priestley et al., 1978).

Having said all this, it must be acknowledged that many of the goals and expectancies underlying the social performance of psychiatric patients may still remain quite baffling to all concerned. The assessment procedures described here (e.g. careful interviewing and negotiation) may serve to uncover motivational processes which would otherwise remain obscure, but there are still certain to be instances where this will not be the case. In these cases, perhaps it is necessary to fall back on clinical intuition in place of objective assessment. Dynamic theories often provide useful clinical insights and they can be used reliably by trained observers (Malan *et al.*, 1975) however their therapeutic usefulness remains debatable.

## Treatment

Improving Behavioural Skills

This brings us finally to the question of treatment. Improving behavioural skills is probably the best known development of the social skills model and the various training packages have been extensively described elsewhere (Liberman *et al.*, 1975; Goldstein *et al.*, 1976; Trower *et al.*, 1978a). Once the targets have been agreed upon (for example to speak louder, to engage in more eye contact, to develop listening skills, to ask more questions) these are demonstrated (modelled) for the patients, using either other members of the group, or prepared audiotapes or videotapes. The patients are then asked to practise the new skills in a short role-play and are given immediate feedback, either verbally from the therapist and the other group members, or from tape recordings. Depending upon their performance, they may then be asked to practise again. An attempt is usually made to ensure that the feedback is as positive as possible, and negative comments are used only sparingly. Considerable use is made of 'shaping' new responses (i.e. building them up gradually) and emphasis is placed on the importance of homework assignments. Since there are often problems with ensuring that treatment effects generalize from one setting to another, it is important for patients to 'overlearn' new responses (practise them beyond the first correct performance). In addition, it has been suggested that if the reinforcement is phased out during the training then this will make for conditions that approximate more closely to those that obtain in everyday life outside the treatment setting, and thus generalization of the new behaviour may be enhanced (Liberman *et al.*, 1976). The evidence regarding the relative effectiveness of different techniques within the treatment package is equivocal, but there is some reason to suppose that modelling is the strongest single component, particularly with chronic patients (Hersen, 1979). We noted earlier how the information-processing difficulties of schizophrenics may adversely affect their ability to learn new and complex 'plans'. This implies that new social skills need to be broken down into very small units and each unit presented very slowly and as distinctively as possible, allowing the patient to 'overlearn' each one before attempting to 'chain' the elements together into new, complex skills.

There are limitations to the skills training approach. The problem of generalization is perhaps the most formidable one and considerable efforts have been made to analyse it and to make recommendations about how it might be tackled (Hersen and Bellack, 1976; Shepherd, 1980; Hersen, 1979).

There are basically two approaches: first, we can attempt to make the treatment situation as much like the outside world as possible; secondly, we can try to replicate some of the conditions that obtain in treatment in certain other settings. The treatment situation can be made more like the outside world by varying the conditions and the therapist so that treatment effects do not become too closely tied to any one place or person (Marholin and Touchette, 1979). Treatment can also be made more real by introducing stooges who are strangers to the group rather than using members who are already familiar and whose behaviour is predictable. Complete sessions may even be carried out '*in vivo*' (Shepherd, 1978), and the importance of homework and real-life practice needs to be strongly emphasized (see Falloon *et al.*, 1977). pairing patients ('buddy systems') may also help to secure cooperation in facing up to new and difficult social situations. Reinforcement (praise, encouragement, etc.) which is given liberally during treatment may be gradually 'thinned' so as to approximate more closely the conditions of everyday social interactions. This is necessary because in the natural environment social behaviour is reinforced neither continuously nor contingently as it is during treatment.

However, these kinds of technical improvements will probably not be sufficient to bridge completely the gap between treatment and real life and therefore we also need to consider how the conditions that prevail in the treatment setting can be extended to influence the rest of the institutional environment. Unless this is achieved there is a danger that social skills training programmes will simply become isolated pockets of therapeutic activity within what are otherwise neglected institutions. We do know how to produce changes in social behaviour, but how to generalize these and to maintain them, even within the institution, requires an additional understanding of how the organization of the setting affects the kind of care that is provided (Shepherd and Richardson, 1979a, 1979b). 'Non-institutional' institutions have high levels of staff–client contact, individual-centred treatment programmes, and flexible routines (King *et al.*, 1971), and these can only be achieved by a shared ideology and high levels of involvement and participation in decision making by all levels of staff (Raynes *et al.*, 1979). Thus, certain organizational conditions are necessary to ensure that the effects of social skills training will generalize and be maintained. Of course, this is still limited to generalization *within* the institution. The problem remains of generalization outside it. This involves working with families and other caretakers, supporting them and enlisting their cooperation in exactly the same way as with staff in institutions (see Chapters 9 and 10).

Treating Cognitions

There is one other possible method by which generalization may be enhanced and that is to focus on the cognitive skills rather than the behavioural ones. In an analogue study with a student population, Glass *et al.* (1976) reported that cognitive treatment for the alleviation of dating problems resulted in more generalized improvements than training in behavioural skills. This kind of cognitive behaviour therapy has received considerable attention in recent years (Mahoney, 1974, 1977) and is based on the idea that social and other difficulties are mediated by cognitive events. There are often negative 'self-statements' of the kind 'I feel a total failure', 'I'm making a mess of this', 'Why are people always critical of me?', etc. Such negative thoughts are held to exert a primary casual influence, leading to emotional distress and to the disruption of skilled behaviour. Treatment is therefore aimed at identifying negative thoughts and supplying rational 'antidotes' (Ellis, 1977) or 'positive self-statements' (Beck *et al.*, 1979). The patient is then given direct practice in 'talking himself through' the difficult situation in a more positive way (Meichenbaum, 1973).

Although, as indicated earlier, there is good evidence that patients with social difficulties often display these kinds of generalized negative expectancies, it is another matter whether they can be easily changed. Reviews of the effectiveness of cognitive therapies suggest that the evidence from controlled trials is not impressive (Ledwidge, 1978). The few studies that have been conducted with psychiatric patients, for example Rush *et al.* (1978) comparing a cognitive therapy with conventional medication for depressed outpatients, have quite serious methodological flaws (Becker and Schuckit, 1978). So, although the cognitive 'self-talk' approach seems promising, as yet it lacks solid empirical support. Direct training in 'meshing' or empathy skills has also received little attention in relation to patients' social difficulties.

There is a considerable literature on the training of empathy as a therapeutic skill for therapists (Carkhuff, 1969; Matarazzo, 1971) and this research sounds a note of caution in that, although levels of empathy can be improved, the differences between subjects in terms of their initial levels is usually greater than any improvement achieved as a result of training. Whether empathy training has anything to offer in the treatment of social difficulties remains to be seen.

Social skills training therefore seems to have some major limitations and, although Trower *et al.* (1978a) may be correct when they assert that 'some forms of psychiatric disturbance are caused or exacerbated by a lack of social competence' (p. 1), whether these can be 'cured or alleviated by means of training in social skills' (*ibid*) remains doubtful. To suggest that since social skills are 'learned', they can therefore be 'taught' to those who lack them (p. 4) is to confuse aetiology with treatment. Social skills may well be learned, but can they be 'taught'? It seems clear that cognitive skills are very much more difficult to 'teach' than motor skills and perhaps different methods of 'teaching' may be required.

In this connection, Brehm (1976) has reviewed possible applications of social psychological theories to these kinds of problems. She suggests that reactance theory and dissonance theory may be used to promote changes in cognitions and behaviour. Reactance theory maintains that it is important to minimize the threat to a client's freedom of action which is inherent in any treatment if his cooperation is to be obtained. Dissonance theory also emphasizes the importance of free choice, and of effort too. It predicts that greater change in patients' attitudes will be obtained where they experience their treatment as demanding considerable effort on their part, but also as being freely chosen. So, when introducing a new treatment, one might say, 'Look, I know this is going to be very difficult for you; no one can force you, so you must really choose for yourself. But, you need only try it for this one occasion; after all it may not produce any permanent change. You can think of it as just an "experiment".' These kinds of manipulations would seem a promising adjunct to the traditional skills training approach.

Attempts have also been made to change the extent to which patients attribute emotional states to themselves by providing them with false feedback that minimizes their physiological responsiveness (Valins and Ray, 1967), but this approach seems limited by the intensity of the subjects' problems (Singerman et al., 1976). Chronic psychiatric patients are unlikely to be persuaded to reattribute the source of their subjective feelings on the basis of brief exposure to false feedback cues. Another use of attribution theory may be to reduce patients' sense of being influenced by external events. Probably the most effective way to do this is simply to expose patients repeatedly to evidence of their own success (positive feedback) and hope that this will eventually increase their confidence in being able to exert personal control over positive changes. Confidence is a factor that does increase on its own, providing there is an opportunity to practise the relevant skills and there is some degree of success and adequate feedback is given. However, it does take time.

We can now turn to the question of treating the emotional distress associated with social difficulties. Obviously, medication has a part to play here, but from a psychological viewpoint it would seem important to examine the possibility that focusing on emotional problems might prove a more effective strategy than concentrating on behavioural performance or cognitive skills. Psychological treatments for anxiety and fear reduction are now very well established and there have been several attempts to use these, especially systematic desensitization, in the treatment of patients with social difficulties (Marzillier et al., 1976; Hall and Goldberg, 1977; Trower et al., 1978b). These studies are not entirely satisfactory due mainly to the measures used and the inadequate demonstration of generalization beyond the treatment situation, but they do suggest that the treatment of social anxiety can sometimes be as effective as behavioural skills training. As yet, there are few studies that have specifically selected subjects with social anxiety as the most prominent component of their social difficulties, and perhaps if this were done then clearer evidence for the superiority of fear-reducing techniques with specific kinds of patients might be forthcoming.

Our discussion of treatment implications seems to suggest generally that no one approach is likely to prove either adequate or of singular effectiveness. In terms of rehabilitation programmes we therefore need to think of broad-based treatment packages with behavioural, cognitive, and emotional components. These different components will have to be selected and combined according to the needs of the individual patients concerned (Shepherd, 1980), and in order to obtain generalization of improvements, staff outside the immediate treatment setting need to be involved. Such an approach places considerable responsibility on the skills of the therapist to select and combine techniques in an intuitive and flexible way and also to be able to work in cooperation with other staff. Currently, we know very little of what it is that effective therapists actually do, although some attempt has been made to define this in the area of working with families (Alexander *et al.*, 1976). Specifying the characteristics of effective therapists will almost certainly entail going beyond the non-directive therapist variables (empathy, warmth, and genuineness) identified by Truax and Carkhuff (1967). We also need individual-centred assessment routines, such as those developed in the work-skills field (Dallos and Winfield, 1975), to enable therapists to identify individual problems and move to formulating appropriate interventions (see also Shepherd and Durham, 1977). Finally, we will need much more information about how individual differences affect treatment outcome. This has to be based on the evaluation of single cases (e.g. Marzillier and Winter, 1978) rather than group designs where random allocation deliberately obscures individual differences.

Conclusions

These are developments for the future. In the meantime it is apparent that our models of social functioning are crude and that our ability to treat social difficulties is limited. Given the magnitude of some of the problems involved it seems likely that these limitations are going to persist. This does not mean that we should give up trying to assess social difficulties as systematically as possible and to treat them as effectively as we can, but simply that we should be prepared to accept chronic disabilities in social functioning just as we are prepared to accept chronic disabilities in other areas of rehabilitation. Chronic disabilities require environments where the patient can still cope given his disabilities. Long-term hostels, workshops, supportive groups in the community, continuing family contact, are all ways in which such environments might be created (see Chapter 10). A good model of social inter-action is an integral part of the effective operation of such settings.

## References

Alexander, J. F., Barton, C., Schiavo, R. S., and Parsons, B. V. (1976) Systems behavioural intervention with families of delinquents: therapy characteristics, family behaviour and outcome. *Journal of Consulting and Clinical Psychology*, 44, 656–664.

Alker, H. A. (1972) Is personality situationally specific or intrapsychically consistent? *Journal of Personality*, 40, 1–17.

Argyle, M. (1969) *Social Interaction*. Methuen, London.

Argyle, M., Bryant, B., and Trower, P. (1974) Social skills training and psychotherapy: a comparative study. *Psychological Medicine*, 4, 435–443.

Arkowitz, H., Lichtenstein, E., McGovern, K., and Hines, P. (1975) A behavioural assessment of social competence in males. *Behaviour Therapy*, 6, 3–13.

Bandura, A. (1977) Self-efficacy: toward a unifying theory of behavioural change. *Psychological Review*, 84, 191–215.

Beck, A. T., Rush, A. J., Shaw, B. F., and Emery, G. (1979) *Cognitive Therapy of Depression*. Guildford Press, New York.

Becker, J., and Schuckit, M. A. (1978) The comparative efficacy of cognitive therapy and pharmacotherapy in the treatment of depression. *Cognitive Therapy and Research*, 2, 193–198.

Bellack, A. S. (1979) Behavioural assessment of social skills. In A. S. Bellack and M. Hersen, eds, *Research and Practice in Social Skills Training*. Plenum Press, New York.

Bellack, A. S., Hersen, M., and Turner, S. M. (1978) Role-play tests for assessing social skills: are they valid? *Behaviour Therapy*, 9, 448–461.

Bem, D. J., and Allen, A. (1974) On predicting some of the people some of the time: the search for cross-situational consistencies in behaviour. *Psychological Review*, 81, 506–520.

Bennett, D. H. (1970) The value of work in psychiatric rehabilitation. *Social Psychiatry*, 5, 224–230.

Berkowitz, L. (1970) The self, selfishness and altruism. In J. McCaulay and L. Berkowitz, eds, *Altruism and Helping Behaviour*. Academic Press, New York.

Bower, G. (1978) Contacts of cognitive psychology with social learning theory. *Cognitive Therapy and Research*, 2, 123–146.

Brehm, S. (1976) *The Application of Social Psychology to Clinical Practice*. Hemisphere Books, New York.

Brown, G. W., and Rutter, M. (1966) The measurement of family activities and relationships. *Human Relations*, 19, 241–263.

Bryant, B., Trower, P., Yardley, K., Urbieta, H., and Letemendia, F. J. J. (1976) A survey of social inadequacy among psychiatric outpatients. *Psychological Medicine*, 6, 101–112.

Carkhuff, R. R. (1969) *Helping and Human Relationships*. Holt, Rinehart, & Winston, New York.

Dallos, R., and Winfield, I. (1975) Instructional strategies in industrial training and rehabilitation. *Journal of Occupational Psychology*, 48, 241–252.

Duncan-Jones, P. (1980) The structure of social relationships: an analysis of a survey instrument. *Social Psychiatry*, 16, 55–61.

Edwards, W. (1961) Behavioural decision theory. *Annual Review of Psychology*, 12, 473–498.

Eisler, R. M., Blanchard, E. B., Fitts, H., and Williams, J. G. (1978) Social skills training with and without modelling for schizophrenic and non-psychotic hospitalized psychiatric patients. *Behaviour Modification*, 2, 147–171.

Eisler, R. M., Hersen, M., and Miller, P. M. (1973) Effects of modelling on components of assertive behaviour. *Journal of Behaviour Therapy and Experimental Psychiatry*, **4**, 1–6.

Eisler, R. M., Hersen, M., Miller, P. M., and Blanchard, E. R. (1975) Situational determinants of assertive behaviour. *Journal of Consulting and Clinical Psychology*, **43**, 330–340.

Ellis, A. (1977) The basic clinical theory of Rational Emotive Therapy. In A. Ellis and R. Grieger, eds, *Handbook of Rational Emotive Therapy*. Springer Publishing Co., New York.

Ellsworth, R. B., Foster, L., Childers, B., Arthur, G., and Kroeker, D. (1968) Hospital and community adjustment as perceived by psychiatric patients, their families and staff. *Journal of Consulting and Clinical Psychology*, **32**, Monog. Suppl., 1–41.

Endler, N., and Magnusson, D. (1976) Toward an interactional psychology of personality. *Psychological Bulletin*, **83**, 956–974.

Falloon, I. R., Lindley, P., McDonald, R., and Marks, I. M. (1977) Social skills training of out-patient groups: a controlled study of rehearsal and homework. *British Journal of Psychiatry*, **131**, 599–609.

Fischetti, M., Curran, J. P., and Weisberg, H. W. (1977) Sense of timing: a skill deficit in heterosexual socially anxious males. *Behaviour Modification*, **1**, 179–194.

Gauld, A., and Shotter, J. (1977) *Human Action and its Psychological Investigation*. Routledge & Kegan Paul, London.

Glasgow, R. E., and Arkowitz, H. (1975) The behavioural assessment of male and female social competence in dyadic heterosexual interactions. *Behaviour Therapy*, **6**, 488–498.

Glass, C. R., Gottman, J. M., and Shmurak, S. H. (1976) Response acquisition and cognitive self-statement modification approaches to dating-skills training. *Journal of Counselling Psychology*, **23**, 520–526.

Goffman, E. (1959) *The Presentation of Self in Everyday Life*. Penguin Books, Harmondsworth, Middx.

Goffman, E. (1961) *Asylums: Essays on the Social situation of Mental Patients and Other Inmates*. Doubleday, New York.

Goldsmith, J. B., and McFall, R. M. (1975) Development and evaluation of an interpersonal skill-training program for psychiatric in-patients. *Journal of Abnormal Psychology*, **84**, 51–58.

Goldstein, A. P., Sprafkin, R. P., and Gershaw, N. J. (1976) *Skills Training for Community Living: Applying Structured Learning Therapy*. Pergamon Press, New York.

Gutride, M. E., Goldstein, A. P., Hunter, G. F., Carol, S., Clark, L., Furia, R. and Lower N. (1974) Structured learning therapy with transfer training for chronic inpatients. *Journal of Clinical Psychology*, **30**, 277–279.

Hall, R., and Goldberg, D. (1977) The role of social anxiety in social interaction difficulties. *British Journal of Psychiatry*, **131**, 610–615.

Harré, R., and Secord, P. F. (1972) *The Explanation of Social Behaviour*. Blackwells, Oxford.

Hemsley, D. R. (1977) What have cognitive deficits to do with schizophrenic symptoms? *British Journal of Psychiatry*, **130**, 167–173.

Hemsley, D. R. (1978) Limitations of operant procedures in the modification of schizophrenic functioning: the possible relevance of studies of cognitive disturbance. *Behaviour Analysis and Modification*, **2**, 165–173.

Henderson, S. (1980) A development in social psychiatry: the systematic study of social bonds. *Journal of Nervous and Mental Diseases*, **168**, 63–69.

Henderson, S., Bryne, D. G., Duncan-Jones, P., Adcock, S., Scott, R., and Steele, G. P. (1978a) Special bonds in the epidemiology of neurosis: a preliminary communication. *British Journal of Psychiatry*, **132**, 463–466.

Henderson, S., Duncan-Jones, P., McAuley, H., and Ritchie, K. (1978b) The patient's primary group. *British Journal of Psychiatry*, **132**, 74–86.

Hersen, M. (1979) Modification of skill deficits in psychiatric patients. In A. S. Bellack and M. Hersen, eds, *Research and Practice in Social Skills Training*. Plenum Press, New York.

Hersen, M., and Bellack, A. S. (1976) Social skills training for chronic psychiatric patients: rationale, research findings and future directions. *Comprehensive Psychiatry*, **17**, 559–580.

Hersen, M., and Bellack, A. S. (1977) Assessment of social skills. In A. R. Ciminero, K. S. Calhoun, and H. E. Adams, eds, *Handbook of Behavioural Assessment*. John Wiley, New York.

Hinde, R. A. (1976) On describing relationships. *Journal of Child Psychology and Psychiatry*, **17**, 1–19.

Irwin, F. W. (1971) *Intentional Behaviour and Motivation*. Lippincott, Philadelphia.

King, R., Raynes, N., and Tizard, J. (1971) *Patterns of Residential Care*. Routledge & Kegan Paul, London.

Kreitman, N., Nelson, B., Collins, J., and Troop, J. (1970) Neurosis and marital interaction II: Time sharing and social activity. *British Journal of Psychiatry*, **117**, 47–58.

Ledwidge, B. (1978) Cognitive behaviour modification: a step in the wrong direction? *Psychological Bulletin*, **85**, 353–375.

Leff, J. P. (1978) Psychiatrists' versus patients' concepts of unpleasant emotions. *British Journal of Psychiatry*, **133**, 306–313.

Levy, P. (1973) On the relation between test theory and psychology. In P. Kline, ed., *New Approaches in Psychological Measurement*. John Wiley, London.

Lewinsohn, P. H. (1974) A behavioural approach to depression. In R. J. Friedman and M. M. Katz, eds, *The Psychology of Depression: Contemporary Theory and Research*. Winston-Wiley, Washington DC.

Liberman, R. P., King, L. W., Derisi, W. J., and McCann, M. (1975) *Personal Effectiveness*. Research Press, Champaign, Ill.

Liberman, R. P., McCann, M. J., and Wallace, C. J. (1976) Generalisation of behaviour therapy with psychotics. *British Journal of psychiatry*, **129**, 490–496.

Litman, G. K., Eiser, J. R., Rawson, N. S. B., and Oppenheim, A. N. (1979) Differences in relapse precipitants and coping behaviour between alcohol relapsers and survivors. *Behaviour Research and Therapy*, **17**, 89–94.

Mahoney, M. J. (1974) *Cognitive and Behaviour Modification*. Ballinger, Cambridge, Mass.

Mahoney, M. J. (1977) Reflections on the cognitive learning trend in psychotherapy. *American Psychologist*, **32**, 5–13.

Malan, D. H., Heath, E. S., and Bacal, H. A. (1975) A study of psychodynamic changes in untreated neurotic patients: II. Apparently genuine improvements. *Archives of General Psychiatry*, **32**, 110–126.

Marholin, D., and Touchette, P. E. (1979) The role of stimulus control and response consequences. In A. P. Goldstein and F. H. Kanfer, eds, *Maximising Treatment Gains*. Academic Press, New York.

Marks, I. M. (1969) *Fears and Phobias*. Heinemann, London.

Marzillier, J. S., Lambert, J. C., and Kellett, J. (1976) A controlled evaluation of systematic desensitisation and social skills training for chronically inadequate psychiatric patients. *Behaviour Research and Therapy*, **14**, 225–239.

Marzillier, J. S., and Winter, K. (1978) Success and failure in social skills training: individual differences. *Behaviour Research and Therapy*, **16**, 67–84.

Matarazzo, R. G. (1971) Research on the teaching and learning of psychotherapeutic skills. In A. E. Bergin and S. L. Garfield, eds, *Handbook of Psychotherapy and Behaviour Change*, 2nd edn. John Wiley, New York.

Meichenbaum, D. H. (1973) Cognitive factors in behaviour modification: modifying what clients say to themselves. In C. M. Franks and G. T. Wilson, eds, *Annual Review of Behaviour Therapy: Theory and Practice*, Vol. I. Brunner/Mazel, New York.

Miller, N. E. (1959) Liberalization of basic S-R concepts: extensions to conflict, behaviour, motivation and social learning. In S. Koch, ed., *Psychology: A Study of a Science*, Vol. I. McGraw-Hill, New York.

Mischel, W. (1968) *Personality and Assessment*. John Wiley, New York.

Mitchell, T. R., and Beach, L. R. (1976) A review of occupational preference and choice research using expectancy theory and decision theory. *Journal of Occupational Psychology*, **49**, 231–248.

Nichols, K. A. (1974) Severe social anxiety. *British Journal of Medical Psychology*, **47**, 301–306.

Nisbett, R. E., and Wilson, T. D. (1977) Telling more than we can know: verbal reports on mental processes. *Psychological Review*, **84**, 231–259.

Orne, M. T. (1962) On the social psychology of the psychological experiment: with particular reference to demand characteristics and their implications. *American Psychologist*, **17**, 776–783.

Pearlin, L. I., and Schooler, C. (1978) The structure of coping. *Journal of Health and Social Behaviour*, **19**, 2–21.

Phillips, J. P. N. (1977) Generalised personal questionnaire techniques. In P. Slater, ed., *The Measurement of Intrapersonal Space by Grid Techniques*, Vol. II. John Wiley, New York.

Priestley, P., McGuire, J., Flegg, D., Hemsley, V., and Welham D. (1978) *Social Skills and Personal Problem Solving. A Handbook of Methods*. Tavistock, London.

Raynes, N., Pratt, M., and Roses, S. (1979) *Organisational Structure and the Care of the Mentally Handicapped*. Croom Helm, London.

Rosenberg, M. (1965) *Society and the Adolescent Self-Image*. Princeton University Press, Princeton, NJ.

Rotter, J. B. (1966) Generalised expectancies for internal vs. external control of reinforcement. *Psychological Monographs*, **80**, No. 609.

Rush, A. J., Hollon, S. D., Beck, A. T., and Kovacs, M. (1978) Depression: must pharmacotherapy fail for cognitive therapy to succeed? *Cognitive Therapy and Research*, **2**, 199–206.

Shapiro, M. B. (1970) Intensive assessment of the single case: an inductive–deductive approach. In P. Mittler, ed., *The psychological Assessment of Mental and Physical Handicaps*. Methuen, London.

Shapiro, M. B. (1975) The assessment of self-reported dysfunctions: a manual with its rationale and applications. Parts I and II. Unpublished manuscript. Department of Psychology, Institute of Psychiatry, London University.

Shapiro, M. B. (1979) Assessment interviewing in clinical psychology. *British Journal of Social and Clinical Psychology*, **18**, 211–218.

Shepherd, G. W. (1977) Social skills training: the generalisation problem. *Behaviour Therapy*, **8**, 100–109.

Shepherd, G. W. (1978) Social skills training: the generalisation problem—some further data. *Behaviour Research and Therapy*, **116**, 287–288.

Shepherd, G. W. (1980) The treatment of social difficulties in special environments. In P. Feldman and J. Orford, eds, *Psychological Problems: The Social Context.* John Wiley, Chichester.

Shepherd, G. W. (in press) Assessment of cognitions in social skills training. To appear in P. Trower, ed., *Cognitive Approaches in Social Skills Training.* Croom Helm, London.

Shepherd, G. W., and Bilsbury, C. (1979) The assessment of social cognitions. Paper presented at the Annual Conference of the British Association for Behavioural Psychotherapy, Bangor, North Wales, July.

Shepherd, G. W., and Durham, R. (1977) The multiple techniques approach to behavioural psychotherapy: a retrospective evaluation of effectiveness and an examination of prognostic indicators. *British Journal of Medical Psychology,* **50,** 45–52.

Shepherd, G. W., McGill, P., and Nairne, K. (1982, in preparation) The assessment of social functioning. III: Social networks.

Shepherd, G. W., and Richardson, A. (1979a) Social skills and beyond: environments for the care of chronic problems. *Behavioural Psychotherapy,* **7,** 31–38.

Shepherd, G. W., and Richardson, A. (1979b) Organisation and interaction in psychiatric day centres. *Psychological Medicine,* **9,** 573–579.

Singerman, K. J., Borkovec, T. D., and Baron, R. S. (1976) Failure of a 'misattribution therapy' manipulation with a clinically relevant target behaviour. *Behaviour Therapy,* **7,** 306–313.

Trower, P., Bryant, B., and Argyle, M. (1978a) *Social Skills and Mental Health.* Methuen, London.

Trower, P., Yardley, K., Bryant, B., and Shaw, P. (1978b) The treatment of social failure. A comparison of anxiety reduction and skills acquisition procedures on two social problems. *Behaviour Modification,* **2,** 41–60.

Truax, C. B., and Carkhuff, R. R. (1967) *Toward Effective Counselling and Psychotherapy.* Aldine, Chicago.

Valins, S., and Ray, A. A. (1967) Effects of cognitive desensitisation of avoidance behaviour. *Journal of Personality and Social Psychology,* **7,** 345–350.

Watson, D., and Friend, R. (1969) Measurement of social-evaluative anxiety. *Journal of Consulting and Clinical Psychology,* **33,** 448–457.

White, R. W. (1959) Motivation reconsidered: the concept of competence. *Psychological Review,* **66,** 297–333.

Wiggins, J. S. (1973) *Personality and Prediction: Principles of Personality Assessment.* Addison Wesley, Reading, Mass.

Wing, J. K., and Brown, G. L. (1970) *Institutionalism and Schizophrenia.* Cambridge University Press, London.

Wolpe, J., and Lazarus, A. A. (1966) *Behaviour Therapy Techniques.* Pergamon Press, Oxford.

Yerkes, R. M., and Dodson, J. D. (1908) The relation of strength of stimulus to rapidity of habit formation. *Journal of Comparative Neurology and Psychology,* **18,** 459–482.

Theory and Practice of Psychiatric Rehabilitation
Edited by F. N. Watts and D. H. Bennett
© 1983, John Wiley & Sons, Ltd.

# 14

## Socialization and Social Integration

Fraser Watts

The last chapter presented an analysis of the requirements of competent social functioning, and examined the implications of this for the assessment and modification of social relationships in rehabilitation. Central to this analysis is the fact that the requirements of social roles are far from straightforward, implying that relatively subtle cognitive skills are involved in meeting them. Others (Jackson, 1966; Kelvin, 1970) have made similar points.

Role expectations are often implicit rather than explicit, i.e. spouses or work supervisors are not always prepared to spell out what expectations they have of their role partners. Expectations are often not fully crystallized, so that it is necessary to select from among a range of behaviours, any of which might meet the requirements of the role. Further, role expectations are often formulated at the level of broad, long-term objectives rather than immediate, detailed requirements, so it is necessary to have the ability to work out a specific strategy for meeting them. Finally, role expectations vary in the degree of force they carry, i.e. in the amount of positive reaction that will come from meeting them or negative reaction from not meeting them. Some sensitivity to this is essential for successful role performance.

Of course, roles vary in the extent to which they require these kinds of perceptiveness and discretion. For example, Jaques (1967) has attempted to measure the varying time-span over which discretion has to be exercised in work roles. Patients whose capacity for discretion is very limited would need to be advised to seek jobs in which the requirements were relatively explicit and the supervision frequent.

So far, relatively little effort has been made in rehabilitation to teach the cognitive skills that seem to be required in social roles, though work in related fields suggests that at least some patients may be able to make useful gains in this area. Operating in a role where expectations are tacit seems to require the skill of seeing things from the point of view of the other person, 'decentering' in the terminology of Piagetian psychology (Feffer, 1967). There is evidence that role-playing methods can be used to improve decentration skills (Chandler, 1973). Because role requirements are often long-term, the capacities to adopt a future-oriented time perspective and to work for long-term rewards are likely to be important. There is some evidence that both time perspective (Ricks *et al.*, 1964) and delay of gratification (Walls and Smith, 1970) are amenable to modification. Problem-solving skills are also likely to be involved in working out a viable approach to meeting broad role requirements and explicit training in these (D'Zurilla and Goldfried, 1971; Janis and Mann, 1977) may therefore contribute to better role performance.

In addition to these capacities for effective role performance, it will be necessary to have ways of coping with the strains created by social roles. Without such effective coping capacities, engagement in social roles may become so stressful that it becomes unrewarding or even intolerable to remain in the role. Pearlin and Schooler (1978) have distinguished three broad categories of coping mechanism: (a) ways of changing the situation producing strain, by negotiation or some kind of constructive action; (b) ways of reconstruing a situation that is causing strain, through ignoring some aspects of the situation, reorganizing values, making favourable comparisons with alternative situations, etc.; (c) responses aimed at coping with stress after it has emerged through accepting it fatalistically, trying not to worry, etc. Pearlin and Schooler assessed the value of these various coping mechanisms in terms of how much their use diminishes the amount of stress that is felt when one is exposed to potential strains. The findings are not easy to summarize, though some general points emerge. Ignoring aspects of a situation seems a relatively poor strategy. Strategies involving self-reliance seem to be better than those based on seeking help from others, and changes of goals and values seem to be relatively good ways of dealing with strain.

However, perhaps the most important conclusion is that the range and variety of coping mechanisms makes a big difference to the amount of stress people feel. Litman *et al.*, (1979) reach a similar conclusion about the importance of a number of different coping strategies in differentiating alcoholics who stayed off drink from those who relapsed. It follows that it will be important to assess the gaps in patients' repertoire of coping skills and to use training methods (e.g. Mahoney, 1974, Chapters 11 and 12) to fill these.

### Rehabilitation as a Socialization Process

As the previous chapter emphasizes, there are limitations in the extent to which patients in rehabilitation programmes can successfully be taught the skills that are crucial both to adequate performance and to an acceptable level of satisfaction in social situations. A programme designed to teach new skills needs to be supplemented with an attempt to provide the conditions needed for patients to use the skills they already possess. The immediate aim is to enable patients to function at their best level in the rehabilitation environment. The secondary aim, more important though more difficult to achieve, is to increase patients' ability to function at their best level elsewhere, when they have left the rehabilitation programme. It will be suggested here that there is a substantial degree of continuity between the conditions needed to elicit optimal social functioning from children and adults and that processes of socialization are involved in both cases.

## Support and Demands

Studies of the basic dimensions influencing social behaviour have repeatedly arrived at two dimensions that can be described as affection and control. These dimensions underly Leary's 'interpersonal behaviour circumplex' (Leary, 1957). Carson (1969) and Foa and Foa (1974) have reviewed a number of other studies leading to the same conclusions. More relevant for the present purpose is the importance these same two dimensions have in the socialization of children and in the leadership of adults in social organizations.

In the socialization of children these two dimensions are usually termed 'nurturance' and 'discipline'. The literature has been summarized by Becker (1964) and Aronfreed (1968) among others. Effective socialization does not occur without a consistent disciplinary policy. But equally, discipline is not effective unless it occurs against a background of a certain minimum level of nurturance. Danziger (1971) sums up the position well.

It must be emphasised that parental firmness and parental warmth and support for the child are quite different dimensions of behaviour, and that any set of parents may well receive a high score on both these scales. Indeed it appears to be precisely such parents that are most likely to have children characterised by high self-esteem. (p. 84)

Personality development can be looked at as the achievement of some balance between the individual need to make demands on others and his ability to recognise the demands which others make on him. The achievement of this balance may be considered to depend on the balance and consistency of demands and support which the individual has been exposed to at various stages of his development. Gross inbalance or inconsistency in the externally presented demand–support structure is unlikely to be conducive to the achievement of a balanced internal structure. (pp. 87–88)

Two very similar dimensions have emerged in the description of the effective leadership of adults in social organizations, known in this context as 'consideration' and 'initiating structure' (see, for example, Kerr et al., 1974). A high score on *initiating structure* indicates a person who plays an active role in directing group activities through planning, communicating information, scheduling, trying out new ideas, etc. (e.g. 'He sees to it that people under him are working up to their limits' and 'He decides in detail what shall be done and how it shall be done'). A high score on *consideration* indicates a climate of good rapport and two-way communication (e.g. 'He makes those under him feel at ease when talking to him' and 'He expresses appreciation when one of us does a good job'). The majority of studies have found that the optimum combination is a high level of consideration and a high level of initiating structure. There have, however, been exceptions. Sometimes high levels of consideration have been found to be associated with dissatisfaction. Of particular interest here is the way in which the effects of initiating structure appear to depend on the prevailing levels of consideration (Fleishman and Harris, 1962). Structure is found to be helpful only when consideration is also high. If consideration is only moderate, then structure tends to result in dissatisfaction.

It is not difficult to discern the operation of these same two basic dimensions of socialization in rehabilitation. It is an essential characteristic of a rehabilitation milieu that it creates expectations for normal social performance. Indeed, this is one of the main things that differentiates rehabilitation from traditional custodial care. The socialization literature suggests that this needs to be combined with understanding and support to achieve the best results.

## Primary and Secondary Socialization

Though there are these substantial similarities in the optimal socializing conditions needed for children and adults, the differences between the two should not be overlooked. In the socialization of children there is an emphasis on the acquisition of basic skills that will subsequently be employed in a great variety of situations. In adult socialization the emphasis is rather more on the synthesis of old skills in a new context. This has not perhaps been fully appreciated in rehabilitation. It has already been argued (Chapter 11) that in occupational rehabilitation there has been more emphasis than is justified on the rehearsal of specific occupational skills. What is more relevant is whether people are able to deploy their skills appropriately in a particular work situation. After a rehabilitation programme has done what it can to improve patients' capacities for socialization, the task remains of enabling them to make the best possible adjustment with the behavioural and cognitive skills that they have.

Related to this is the fact that adult socialization tends to have shorter-term effects than does the socialization of children. Indeed, socializing conditions in adults may do little to affect behaviour after the person concerned has left the particular socializing environment. Consistent with this, there is evidence that there may be relatively little carry-over from a hospital-based programme to subsequent community functioning. Ellsworth *et al.* (1968) reported that patients who are rated as the most unpleasant and hostile in hospital were regarded as having the best friendship skills after discharge. Similarly, Walker and McCourt (1965) found no significant association between those patients who worked in hospital and those patients who gained employment on discharge. This is perhaps not surprising in view of what is known generally about the considerable degree of situational specificity in the structure of social behaviour (Mischel, 1968).

Finally, as Brim (1966) has suggested, adult socialization tends to be concerned merely with behaviour, not with the values underlying behaviour. Values and behaviour are often less closely related than might be assumed, as has been shown, for example, in the sphere of moral behaviour (Pittel and Mendelsohn, 1966). Childhood socialization normally seems to engender a basic commitment to social roles for the contribution they make to self-respect, to the structuring of time, to the range of personal relationships, and to general predictability and control (Jahoda, 1979; Williams and Blackler, 1971). If this predisposition to social roles is not already established through primary socialization, it is difficult to establish it subsequently in rehabilitation.

In preparing patients for specific social roles the emphasis, as in other forms of adult socialization, is on behaviour rather than values. Rosow (1965) has suggested that this is indeed the dominant mode of socialization in our society. It is no obstacle to rehabilitation if patients are not committed to the particular roles they are being prepared for, though it may be an obstacle if they feel it is inappropriate for them to show socialized behaviour without the corresponding values and commitment.

In these various ways the objectives and achievements of adult socialization are less fundamental than those of primary socialization. Nevertheless, there is sometimes scope for providing conditions during rehabilitation that will have a lasting effect on patients' ability to function at their best level. If this happens at all it will most likely be through the modification of what Pearlin and Schooler (1978) call 'general psychological resources': self-esteem, the sense of control, etc.

## Self-confidence

Increasing self-esteem in rehabilitation appears to depend on a judicious use over time of the basic socializing dimensions of support and demands. At first, because patients' self-confidence is low, they normally need to be provided with a high level of support. During this period demands should be increased gradually. If patients respond constructively to these demands, their performance should improve, providing a basis for increased self-confidence. At a later stage support could be reduced somewhat, in as far as the patients' confidence in themselves permits this. The hope would be that increased self-confidence would set in motion a positive cycle in which higher role expectations would be met with better role performance. The latter, in turn, would further enhance confidence, ensuring a continuing constructive response to expectations. Watts and Yu (1976) have designed a set of short attitude scales for testing this model of the rehabilitation process in a longitudinal study.

It is normally best that demands for role performance should be introduced at as early a stage as possible. Patients' treatment and rehabilitation can then proceed concurrently. It will be necessary to have graded rehabilitation facilities, such as a hierarchy of industrial workshops, so that demands can be introduced gradually, beginning at a level the patient is able to meet. How far it will be possible to reduce support is one of the crucial issues in the rehabilitation of an individual patient, and one that calls for good clinical judgement. There are some patients who need moderate levels of support on a fairly long-term basis if they are to function at their best level. On the other hand, it would be potentially disabling for patients to be provided with more support than they actually need.

In trying to provide the right conditions for the development of confidence in rehabilitation patients, there are two problems that cannot be lost sight of. One is that improvements in confidence may not be as permanent as those that take place in childhood. The relatively temporary nature of much adult socialization has already been discussed. The other potential limitation that must be considered is that increases in self-confidence may be relatively specific to particular tasks. Though there is value in improvements in confidence in specific areas, a generalized improvement in confidence is obviously of much greater consequence. In planning the rehabilitation of an individual patient it is important to estimate which areas are particularly salient as far as general self-confidence is concerned. If a patient feels particularly sensitive about poor arithmetic ability, improved functioning in this area may be of great importance in rehabilitation generally. The general principle is that particular efforts should be made to improve performance not only in areas that are of practical importance in their own right, but also in areas that are most salient as far as patients' general self-confidence is concerned.

One of the characteristics of people with low self-esteem is that they do not show the usual positive correlations between the qualities that they rate themselves as possessing and those that are important to them (Cooper, 1972). It is not just that they rate themselves as having fewer positive qualities, but that they have a poor estimate of themselves in the areas that are most important to them.

Another important structural characteristic of self-esteem relates to the difference between people's absolute evaluation of themselves, and their comparison of themselves with other people. It is quite possible, for example, for people to evaluate themselves poorly by their own standards but highly in comparison with other people. A similar distinction has been established in the field of achievement motivation between autonomous and social comparison achievement motivation (Birney *et al.*, 1969). There appears to be no evidence at present on the question of whether 'absolute' or 'comparative' self-evaluation is more important in determining willingness to take on social roles and to remain in them.

### Stress and Anxiety

Care also needs to be taken over the introduction of demands. If demands for role performance are increased too suddenly they can bring about a deterioration in mental state, at least in schizophrenic patients. Wing *et al.* (1964) found that 13 per cent of schizophrenic patients transferred to an industrial rehabilitation unit showed florid psychotic symptoms within the first week after transfer, even though these had been in abeyance for many years. This emphasizes the importance of ensuring that increased demands are made only gradually during the rehabilitation process.

There is another, superficially similar problem in rehabilitation that depends not only on the level of demands that are made but also on patients' estimate of whether they have the resources to meet them. In Lazarus's model of coping processes (Lazarus, 1966; Lazarus *et al.*, 1974) there are two 'appraisal' processes which determine response to stress. The primary appraisal is of the degree of threat posed, such as the stress arising from employment or from family responsibilities. The secondary appraisal is of the resources that are available for meeting the threat. This is based both on patients' perception of their own resources and their estimate of the support available from others (Lazarus, 1966, p. 101). A constructive response depends on patients' estimating that they have the necessary personal resources and support to meet the demands being made on them.

If patients do not feel able to make a constructive response to rehabilitation, this can show itself in increased attention to psychiatric symptoms, and increased efforts to gain recognition of their status as patients. This is one example of the general phenomenon referred to as 'illness behaviour' (Mechanic, 1966). It is by no means confined to psychiatric patients. Mechanic and Volkart (1961), in a naturalistic study, have documented the increased use of medical facilities by some students under the stress of examinations. It was those students who had a general and long-standing propensity to use medical services who reacted to examination stress in this way. Presumably many rehabilitation patients can be expected to react to the stresses of rehabilitation in a similar way.

Increased illness behaviour as a result of efforts to increase patients' level of functioning in normal social roles can be seen as a form of 'psychological reactance' (Brehm, 1976). Attempts to move patients too quickly away from a sick role can produce a reaction in the opposite direction. The task is to apply expectations for normal performance in a way that will meet with a constructive response rather than with resistance of this kind. The reaction obtained will depend to a great extent on the degree of confidence patients have in themselves at the start of the rehabilitation process. Experimental social psychology has produced a body of research (Scotland and Canon, 1972, Chapter 10) substantiating the view that good self-evaluation leads to more constructive social responses. People with high self-esteem are more likely to be helpful (Kazdin and Bryan, 1971) and less likely to be hostile to others (Berkowitz, 1962, p. 278). Presumably patients with high self-esteem will also make a more constructive response, first to the rehabilitation process, and subsequently to the needs and demands of their role partners (spouses, work supervisors, etc.).

Research on fear of failure is helpful in showing how this may operate in rehabilitation. People whose anxiety about failure exceeds their positive motivation for success show a curious pattern of vocational choices. They are unlikely to indicate a preference for jobs at an appropriate occupational level, but instead prefer jobs that are either at a higher or a lower level than would be realistic (Mahone, 1960; Burnstein, 1963). It is understandable that lack of confidence should lead to unrealistically low-level preferences, but unrealistically high-level preferences are most puzzling. However, there may be some esteem-boosting value in proclaiming rather grand aspirations, secure in the knowledge that they are unlikely ever to be put to the test. The important point here, though, is that unrealistic vocational choices (in whichever direction) represent a failure of that appropriate, constructive approach to social roles which is associated with self-confidence and which is central to successful rehabilitation.

### Integration into the Social Network

It has been suggested that a judicious use of demands and support can improve patients' level of functioning in the rehabilitation environment, and may even succeed in bringing about the kind of stable increase in general psychological resources that can ensure that social functioning continues at a good level after the end of the rehabilitation programme. However, it will normally be necessary for patients to continue to be exposed to balanced social demands and supports in their natural social roles if any gains made in rehabilitation are to be maintained. The achievement of a network of stable social roles is in any case a central part of what constitutes 'resettlement', and is the objective of the rehabilitation process.

The social positions that underpin the social integration of most people are located in employment and in the family. People commonly spend a high proportion of their time in meeting the expectations associated with these core social roles. It is generally clear whether or not people have such roles. The only exception is with some domestic roles. For example, in the case of an adult who makes a very marginal contribution to housework, it may be unclear whether or not he or she should be regarded as having this role.

Besides these core roles there are a great number of opportunities for social participation involving associations with friends, neighbours, relatives, and formal organizations. Between them, they can make a considerable contribution to an individual's social integration. Here the problems of assessment are much greater, though several attempts have been made to develop scales to measure community participation. An example is a scale developed by Cumming and Henry (1961) to assess the social disengagement of the elderly. Three separate indices were used. The first was based on the *amount of time* each day spent in situations where others could exercise normative control over the subject's behaviour. The second assessed the *amount of contact* with various groups of associates. Finally, there was a 'role count' based on the total *number of contacts* in various situations (household members, relatives, friends, neighbours, co-workers, people such as shopkeepers contacted for specific purposes, church contacts, and other organizational contacts). These indices of social participation are fairly typical, but others have been used. Wilensky (1961) and Phillips (1966) have tried to measure patterns of friendship in more detail, focusing on the number of close friends, the stability of friendships, and the diversity of social contacts. Various measures of community participation, such as voting in elections, have also been used.

## Social Integration and Psychiatric Prognosis

The assumption is often made that improving patients' social integration will also tend to improve their psychiatric condition and reduce their future dependency on hospital services. Though this is a central assumption of rehabilitation theory, it is not one that is easily tested. There are certainly a number of interventions, such as the 'community lodge' project of Fairweather *et al.* (1969), that have both improved social integration and also reduced dependence on hospital services. But such studies do not show exactly how improved social integration results in reduced risk of rehospitalization. The same point could be made about many other studies. For example, Hunt and Azrin (1973) reported that a special programme of social and vocational counselling resulted not only in a better record of social and work adjustment after discharge compared with that of patients receiving a standard inpatient programme, but also in their spending fewer days drinking and in institutional care. It is a reasonable interpretation of such data that improved social adjustment had a secondary effect on drinking and hospitalization, though other possibilities, such as a direct effect of the social counselling programme on attitudes to drinking, cannot be ruled out.

There is a similar ambiguity in the interpretation of studies that have examined the correlation between social adjustment after discharge and the risk of readmission to hospital (e.g. Kunce and Worley, 1970). It would be a prediction of rehabilitation theory that patients who achieved a better level of social adjustment after discharge would be less likely to need readmission. Though a correlation has been found between employment after discharge and community tenure, the two variables are normally not independent of each other as readmission affects continuation in employment. Those embarking upon further studies of this kind would be well advised to divide the post-discharge period into two and to see whether the amount of employment in the first phase (e.g. 6 months) among those remaining in the community throughout that time predicts hospitalization in a second phase. At present there is no satisfactory evidence that employment after discharge from hospital directly predicts subsequent community tenure.

However, there is a good deal of evidence in related fields that social integration is related to good prognosis in psychiatric patients, though the causal basis of this relationship is seldom beyond dispute. This relationship is of considerable importance for the theory of rehabilitation. One way of examining possible effects of social integration on psychiatric disorder is to examine the effects of naturally occurring changes in social integration on the *onset* of disorders. Such studies involve considerable methodological problems, largely stemming from the necessity of using retrospective accounts of social changes (i.e. reported after the onset of psychiatric disorder) if the numbers involved in the study are not to become too unwieldy. Some have used a 'free recall' kind of interview in which subjects have simply been asked to describe any important or distressing changes in their life in the period concerned. However, this allows the data to be distorted by the subjects operating different criteria regarding what is worth reporting. Those who have conducted more satisfactory studies have decided in advance what changes they are concerned with and asked explicitly about them.

Psychiatric disorders of old age present a particularly interesting opportunity for studying the relationship between social integration and mental health. Many people experience a quite sudden fall in their level of social integration in old age. Rosow (1967) has summarized the data. Of men over 65 about half have no employment at all. Of those who have some, the great majority are either part-time or self-employed (or both). Widowhood also becomes increasingly common, especially in women. Of the 65–69 age group, 13 per cent of men and 44 per cent of women are widowed. In the 85 + age group it is 83 per cent of women. There is also a tendency for contacts with friends and membership of groups to decline in old age. It is also known (e.g. Adelstein *et al.*, 1968) that old age sees an increasing rate of referral to both hospital and community forms of psychiatric care. This suggests the possibility that declining social integration is at least partly responsible for the higher rate of psychiatric disorder. To examine this, it is necessary to look more closely at the relationship between loss of social integration and psychiatric disorder.

One obvious prediction from the hypothesis is that there would be a disproportionately large number of the widowed and retired among those with psychiatric disorders. It is well known (Parkes, 1964) that there is a much higher proportion of *recent* widows in a mental hospital population than would be expected by chance. It seems, however, that this represents an immediate but temporary reaction to bereavement. The evidence suggests that widowhood is not associated with chronic mental disorder (Stein and Susser, 1969). Lowenthal (1965) has suggested that retirement may have a similar relationship to mental illness, in as far as a substantial proportion of people admitted to mental hospital over 60 have recently retired. However, it should be remembered that the majority of general community surveys have failed to find that retirement results in deterioration in health (e.g. Donahue *et al*, 1960). There is a growing understanding of the pattern of role losses that is most likely to precipitate mental illness. Lowenthal (1968, p. 191) claims that it is partly dependent on sex, with men showing more traumatic reactions to widowhood; working women show more traumatic reactions to retirement. Losses of these core roles are probably more important than a reduction in other forms of social participation. Certainly, they are more closely related to general morale (Lowenthal and Boler, 1965).

However, it seems that life-long social integration problems are more closely related to mental health in old age than are recent losses of social roles. The importance of life-long social integration has emerged as a conclusion from a number of studies (e.g. Vispo, 1962; Kay *et al.*, 1964), but the most interesting is perhaps that of Lowenthal (1964). The basic strategy was to compare the socialization patterns of a sample of 534 people over 60 years of age who had recently been admitted to a psychiatric ward, with a random sample of 600 over 60s living in the community in San Francisco. Unfortunately, the study has some serious weaknesses. (The method of obtaining information about subjects' social isolation is not adequately described, and large numbers of the subjects were not classified at all with regard to their social isolation.) The conclusions must, therefore, be treated with caution. Nevertheless, it appeared that the pattern of social integration most heavily overrepresented in the psychiatric group was one of relatively *unsuccessful attempts* at social integration during adulthood. Those who had lived in almost complete social isolation all through their lives, without even attempting to achieve social integration, did not seem more likely to have a psychiatric admission in old age. Thus, though there is some evidence that role losses can have a direct effect on mental illness in old age, it is apparent that to a large extent poor mental health and poor social integration in old age are both predictable from long-standing social integration problems.

The implications of this conclusion for rehabilitation theory are not altogether encouraging. If specific role losses are less important for the mental health of the elderly than their long-standing social adjustment problems, then specific role additions as a result of rehabilitation may do less than some rehabilitation workers would hope for the future prognosis of the patients concerned. Patients with long-standing social adjustment problems may continue to have a bad prognosis, regardless of any specific extensions of social integration that rehabilitation is able to achieve.

A similar conclusion arises when the connection between marital status and schizophrenia is examined. Marital status can be taken as one index of social integration. The fact that married schizophrenics have a better prognosis might therefore support the hypothesis that social integration tends to improve patients' prognosis. However, there could be other explanations. The question is whether marriage serves to select out people who would, for other reasons, need relatively little hospital care, or whether marriage has a direct effect on outcome (by providing an incentive to leave hospital or by providing additional social support). If marriage has a direct effect, then it should be related to outcome whatever other variables are controlled for. On the other hand, if it can be shown that when certain other variables are controlled for the relationship between marriage and outcome disappears, the effect of marriage cannot be a direct causal one.

There are, in fact, suggestions in the literature that the relationship can be reduced to zero by controlling various other variables. This has been suggested for symptom severity, though the data indicate that the predictive value of marital status is not attributable to this (Turner and Zabo, 1968; Turner et al., 1970). Turner et al. (1970) suggested that the effect of marital status can be attributed to social class, though this is not established by the statistical analysis they present nor is it supported by visual inspection of their data, though marital status certainly seems a more powerful prognostic indicator in the lower social classes. However, it is possible that the predictive value of marital status is partly due to confounding with age differences (Rosen et al., 1971). Furthermore, there is good reason to think that the predictive power of marital status disappears when the degree of sociability in early life is controlled for. This was first claimed by Farina et al. (1963), though objections to their statistical analysis were raised by Garfield and Sundland (1966). More satisfactory data were reported by Gittleman-Klein and Klein (1968). Good early sociability was a necessary but not a sufficient condition for both marriage and a good outcome after hospitalization. The sample was divided into eleven groups, each homogeneous for sociability. Each of these groups was then dichotomized according to outcome. There was no significant tendency for the married patients to fall into the good outcome half of each group. Rosen *et al.* (1971) report a different kind of analysis of the data on an overlapping sample of patients, also indicating that within groups that were homogeneous for early sociability there was no significant tendency for marriage to be related to outcome. It is a potential weakness of such studies that the information that is available about early socialization may not be free from bias. One way out of this difficulty is to make use of official records that were made during schooldays, though the prognostic value of such records remains to be investigated. However, on the present evidence it is reasonable to conclude that in as far as marital status is related to prognosis in schizophrenia it is because it refects a preexisting personality trait.

Unfortunately, much fewer data are available on the relationship between employment status and prognosis. Certainly, there has not been any systematic attempt to determine whether employment has any independent predictive power, though it is fairly well-established that schizophrenics with a good employment record tend to have a better outcome. Rawls (1971) found that readmission to hospital could be predicted from questionnaire answers about past occupational performance. Readmitted patients had been late in starting to earn their own money, were more likely to be out of work before their first admission, to have changed jobs more often, and to have spent less time in their last job. Gregory and Downie (1968) and Turner and Zabo (1968) have also reported significant relationships between work record and future hospitalization. It is plausible that, again, a good work record and a good outcome after a psychiatric breakdown both result from the same set of pre-morbid personal qualities.

Though the literature generally lends only modest support to the hypothesis that changes in social integration directly affect mental health, it is of considerable importance that life-long patterns of good social adjustment are relevant. Life-long socialization determines whether role losses in old age precipitate psychiatric illness. Also early socialization (rather than current marital status) determines prognosis in a schizophrenic breakdown. The conclusions are important from both a theoretical and a practical point of view.

On the practical side they indicate that it is important for rehabilitation to concern itself with general capacities for social adjustment and with the general level of social integration a patient achieves. A single major role such as employment may not be sufficient to offset the unfavourable effects of generally weak social integration as far as prognosis is concerned. From a theoretical point of view, these conclusions add weight to the analogy between rehabilitation and basic socialization that has been raised already in this chapter. Presumably similar personal qualities are required both to make a good initial social adjustment and to make a good readjustment after a psychiatric breakdown or to survive a major role loss without the inception of a psychiatric disorder.

The Network of Social Roles

The conclusion that the addition or loss of a single social role makes relatively little difference to the prognosis of psychiatric patients, compared to their long-standing level of social adjustment, raises an important dilemma for rehabilitation. Is it best to attempt to extend patients' social integration on a wide variety of fronts on the grounds that only this will make a substantial difference to their prognosis? Will integration in one area facilitate that in another, thus strengthening the patients' overall level of social integration? Or, alternatively, will it overextend a patient to try to increase his social integration on several fronts so that no single social role will be securely established?

The question, put in its most general form, is whether social roles facilitate or detract from each other. Either possibility seems quite plausible. On the one hand, having too many roles could result in a situation in which not enough time or energy could be given to any one and in which the person would become overstretched and unable to function adequately at all. On the other hand, participation in one area could result in the development of general confidence or skill in social functioning that would be helpful in other areas.

To approach this question, the general literature on the relationship between social roles will be examined, beginning with that between work and family roles. The question of the employed wife has attracted particular attention. Arising out of widespread anxieties that the employment of wives would undermine marital adjustment, there has been a long series of empirical investigations of the relationship between the two. There is some evidence (e.g. Gover, 1963) that marital adjustment is poorer in working than in non-working wives, especially among women in the lower socio-economic classes. However, among working wives there is a positive correlation between commitment to the job and high marital satisfaction (e.g. Odern and Bradburn, 1969).

Though relationships between levels of work and domestic functioning are mostly positive in the general population, this may not be so among people with few social or personal resources. This is presumably why there is more likely to be a negative relationship between marital adjustment and wives' employment in a lower social class group. The more seriously disadvantaged the subjects studied, the more likely will such an effect be to appear. There seems to be a substantial number of people in local authority hostel accommodation who are able to work provided they live in such 'sheltered' accommodation, but do not seem able to combine employment with independent living. In a similar vein, Walker *et al.* (1973), in a study of psychiatric rehabilitees, found a negative association between social behaviour at home (agreeableness, sociability, etc.) and improvement of productivity in the rehabilitation unit. Clearly, it will be important in future research on the relationship between employment and other aspects of social functioning to look more carefully at relatively disadvantaged people before reaching general conclusions on this issue.

There is some evidence that various general indices of community participation are positively intercorrelated (Axelrod, 1956). For example, Schaffer and Schaffer (1968) found that families with a high level of social participation were less likely to need institutional care for children while the mother was confined for childbirth. Wilensky (1961) investigated the relationship between career patterns and social integration. He found a significant association between orderly career patterns (basically the proportion of time in jobs that are functionally related and arranged in a hierarchy of prestige) and various indices of community participation. The number of memberships of formal associations, the amount of time spent in them, correlated with orderly career patterns, as did various indices of relatively informal social participation such as having two or three close friends and the number of long-standing relationships. Finally, orderly career patterns were related to overlapping patterns of contacts (e.g. overlap between work associates and personal friends), and to diversity and heterogeneity of contacts in both informal and formal associations. Wilensky believed 'vitality' of social participation to be a function of employment experiences. Orderly careers were seen as both providing the scope for the exercise of freedom and discretion, and necessitating sustained and wide-ranging contacts. Of course, his assumption about the direction of the casual relationship involved was not validated by his correlational results, though they are consistent with such a view.

There may well be important differences in the function of different kinds of social contacts. Weiss (1968) in a survey of single parents found indications that a spouse protects against emotional isolation and loneliness whereas friends protect against social isolation and boredom. The two cannot easily compensate for each other. Some data presented by Adams (1967) suggest important differences between functions of parents and best friends. People more often reported that obligation was a motive for contact with parents, that they felt close to them and shared mutual aid with them. However, they were more likely to agree in ideas and opinions with their friends and were more likely to engage in social activities with them. Along similar lines, Litwak and Szelenyi (1969) have suggested that different social groups are likely to help with problems on a different time scale. Neighbours tend to help with emergencies, kin with long-term problems, while friends help with problems of intermediate length. There may also be social class differences in patterns of social participation with the middle classes making more use of formal meeting places and visits from friends and neighbours and working-class people having more contact with their kin. However, these differences between social classes are becoming less marked with the passage of time (Bott, 1971).

If it is decided that it would be likely to overstretch a particular rehabilitation patient to try to achieve maximum social integration on all fronts, a rational decision needs to be made about which areas of social integration are to be preferred. There are two questions to be considered here. One concerns which areas of social integration it will be easiest for the patient to achieve. This will need to take account of his social background and personality characteristics as well as his psychiatric disabilities. The other question concerns what sorts of social integration will be most beneficial. It is sometimes too readily assumed that employment will be the most helpful form in all cases. However, there are enough indications in the social integration literature that different kinds of social contact are used in different ways to suggest the value of making an assessment of the particular requirements of a patient as far as social integration is concerned, and which areas best meet these needs. Some people may benefit from a role conferring social status, others from one that involves extensive social contact, and so on. It should also be emphasized that decisions about which areas of social integration to concentrate on should be made in conjunction with the patient, on the basis of an assessment of his needs. The value judgements of the rehabilitation worker should be excluded as far as possible.

Social Disorganization

So far the kind of poor social integration that has been considered is one in which people have *few* social roles. But there is another, that can be termed social disorganization, in which social roles tend to be unstable. Socially disorganized people are more likely to be divorced, to change jobs frequently, etc. There is some evidence that unstable social roles, rather than lack of social roles, are particularly associated with behaviour disorders. For example, Evans and Maloney (1974) found that delinquency was associated with job changing rather than with unemployment.

The different social correlates of behaviour disorder and other psychiatric conditions are also reflected in different types of housing. Galle *et al.* (1972) report that while mental hospital admissions are highest in areas where there is a large number of people living alone, delinquency is highest in areas where there is overcrowding (as measured by people per room). Similarly, Philip and McCulloch (1966) have reported a number of other correlates of overcrowding including self-poisoning and self-injury, number of children in care, absences from school for reasons other than sickness, etc. But interestingly, they found that mental hospital referrals correlated *negatively* with overcrowding.

Differences can also be found in the way marital status relates to outcome. Among psychotic patients single persons have the worst outcome, with those with lapsed marriages coming between the single and the currently married (Norris, 1956). In contrast, among alcoholics (Rosenblatt *et al.*, 1969) and people who make a suicide attempt (Bagley and Greer, 1971) those with broken marriages have a worse prognosis than the single. In fact, a clear distinction between the socially isolated and the socially disorganized can be made among those who attempt suicide (McCulloch et al., 1967; Ovenstone and Kreitman, 1974). It is the socially disorganized group who tend to make repeated attempts. Also, behaviour disorders such as excessively heavy drinking and delinquency, tend to be associated with this group.

Again the question of the causal relationship arises. Why, for example, do alcoholics and attempted suicides who also have lapsed marriages have a worse outcome? One possibility is that separation selects out those who would, in any case and for other reasons, have a bad prognosis. The necessary research to unravel this problem has not been done. It would be valuable to follow the same strategy as has been used for psychotics, i.e. to specify the possible factors which may account for the worst outcome in the separated. If, when these factors are controlled, the relationship between marital status and outcome disappears, it can be taken that there is no direct causal relationship involved.

There also seems to be a relationship between work record and the prognosis of alcoholics (Kissin et al., 1968), of people who attempt suicide (McCulloch and Philip, 1970), and of delinquents (Mannheim and Wilkins, 1955). But the data are very meagre. It is not possible to distinguish the relative contributions of unemployment and job changing, nor to unravel the causal factors involved. Neither are we able to assess whether this represents a direct effect of employment on outcome.

Rehabilitation has traditionally concentrated on schizophrenic patients whose problem is with low levels of social integration. Patients with behaviour disorders present a different problem of disorganized social roles. At the present time we know very little either about whether rehabilitation services are able to help this kind of social adjustment or about what effect improved social stability might have on subsequent behaviour disorder. The study of Massimo and Shore (1963) showing that vocationally oriented counselling can not only improve the subsequent work record but also reduce delinquency indicates the kind of contribution that rehabilitation would hope to be able to make to patients who present with behaviour disorders in the context of social disorganization. However, the kind of rehabilitation services needed to achieve this may well be different from the traditional ones developed for schizophrenic patients.

It is probably the case that with behaviour disordered patients the task is not one of rehabilitation but of enabling patients to make a stable social adjustment for the first time. But it is not so very different from the care of patients presenting with other conditions such as schizophrenia in the context of social isolation. The evidence that has been reviewed suggests that it is patients who have long-standing social adjustment problems who have most difficulty in reestablishing themselves after a psychiatric episode and who stand most in need of rehabilitation.

## Conclusion

This chapter has presented rehabilitation as a socialization process analogous to the primary socialization of childhood, and has tried to make explicit the psychological capacities that are needed for good psychological adjustment, and the features of the social environment that are necessary to produce them. It has become clear that those who most require rehabilitation are those whose primary socialization is most deficient. Regrettably, it must also be emphasized that what adult socialization can do to make good the deficiencies of primary socialization is limited, though the limits have perhaps not yet been fully probed. Very often, therefore, rehabilitation will have to content itself with assessing what degree of permanent shelter or support (see Chapter 10) will be needed if a person is to maintain a good social adjustment, and arranging for this to be provided with the maximum cost-effectiveness and the minimum of institutionalization.

There is no doubt, however, that social adjustment problems are a relevant focus of attention for a large number of patients. Those who continue to make heavy use of the services after a psychiatric breakdown are those whose social adjustment has always been poor. There is also evidence (Godber, 1972) that a large number of people presenting as psychiatric patients have relatively mild psychiatric symptoms in the context of poor social adjustment, and that such patients largely account for the increasing use of psychiatric services. Faced with this situation there is no practical alternative to giving explicit attention to their social adjustment problems, and developing effective ways of dealing with them. This is what the rehabilitation approach to psychiatric problems seeks to do. There is room for doubt about the effectiveness of the methods currently used, but not about the importance of the task.

## References

Adams, B. T. (1967) Interaction theory and the social network. *Sociometry*, **30**, 64–78.
Adelstein, A. M., Downham, D. Y., Stein, Z., and Susser, M. W. (1968) The epidemiology of mental illness in an English city. *Social Psychiatry*, **3**, 47–59.
Aronfreed, J. (1968) *Conduct and Conscience*. Academic Press, New York.
Axelrod, M. (1956) Urban structure and social participation. *American Sociological Review*, **21**, 13–18.
Bagley, C., and Greer, S. (1971) Clinical and social predictors of repeated attempted suicide: a multivariate analysis. *British Journal of Psychiatry*, **119**, 515–521.
Becker, W. C. (1964) Consequences of different kinds of parental disciplines. In M. L. Hoffman and L. W. Hoffman, eds, *Review of Child Development Research*, Vol. 1. Russel Sage Foundation, New York.
Berkowitz, L. (1962) *Aggression: A Social Psychological Analysis*. McGraw-Hill, New York.

Birney, R. C., Burdick, H., and Teevan, R. C. (1969) *Fear of Failure*. Van Nostrand, New York.

Bott, E. (1971) *Family and Social Network: Roles, Norms and External Relationships in Ordinary Urban Families*. 2nd edn. Tavistock, London.

Brehm, S. S. (1976) *The Application of Social Psychology to Clinical Practice*. John Wiley, New York.

Brim, O. G. (1966) Socialisation through the life cycle. In O. G. Brim and S. Wheeler, eds, *Socialization after Childhood: Two Essays*. Wiley, New York.

Burnstein, E. (1963) Fear of failure, achievement motivation, and aspiring to prestigeful occupations. *Journal of Abnormal and Social Psychiatry*, **67**, 189–193.

Carson, R. C. (1969) *Interaction Concepts of Personality*. Allen & Unwin, London.

Chandler, M. J. (1973) Egocentrism and anti-social behaviour: the assessment and training of social perspective taking skills. *Developmental Psychology*, **9**, 322–332.

Cooper, F. J. (1972) An investigation of self-esteem in psychiatric patients. Unpublished MPhil dissertation, University of London.

Cumming, E., and Henry, W. E. (1961) *Growing Old: The Process of Disengagement*. Basic Books, New York.

Danziger, K. (1971) *Socialisation*. Penguin, Harmondsworth, Middx.

Donahue, W., Orbach, H. L., and Pollack, O. (1960) Retirement: the emerging social pattern. In C. Tibbetts, ed., *Handbook of Social Gerontology*. University of Chicago Press, Chicago.

D'Zurilla, T. J., and Goldfried, M. R. (1971) Problem solving and behaviour modification. *Journal of Abnormal Psychology*, **78**, 107–126.

Ellsworth, R. B., Foster, L., Childers, B., Arthur, G., and Kroeker, D. (1968) Hospital and community adjustment as perceived by psychiatric patients, their families and staff. *Journal of Consulting and Clinical Psychology*, **32**, Monograph Supplement, 1–14.

Evans, J., and Maloney, L. (1974) Adolescents and work difficulties. *British Journal of Psychiatry*, **124**, 203–207.

Fairweather, G. W., Saunders, D. H., Cressler, D. L., and Maynard, H. (1969) *Community Life for the Mentally Ill: An alternative to Institutional Care*. Aldine, Chicago.

Farina, A., Garmezy, N., and Barry, H., III (1963) Relationship of marital status to incidence and prognosis of schizophrenia. *Journal of Abnormal and Social Psychology*, **67**, 624–630.

Feffer, M. (1967) Symptom expression as a form of primitive decentering. *Psychological Review*, **74**, 16–28.

Fleishman, E. A., and Harris, E. F. (1962) Patterns of leadership behaviour related to employee grievances and turnover. *Personnel Psychology*, **15**, 43–56.

Foa, U. G., and Foa, E. B. (1974) *Societal Structures of the Mind*. C. C. Thomas, Springfield, Ill.

Galle, O. R., Gove, W. R., and McPherson, J. M. (1972) Population density and pathology: what are the relations for man? *Science*, **176**, 23–30.

Garfield, S. L., and Sundland, D. M. (1966) Prognostic scales in schizophrenia. *Journal of Consulting Psychology*, **30**, 18–24.

Gittleman-Klein, R., and Klein, D. F. (1968) Marital status as a prognostic indicator in schizophrenia. *Journal of Nervous and Mental Diseases*, **147**, 289–296.

Godber, C. (1972) Reasons for increase in admissions. In J. K. Wing and A. M. Hailey, eds, *Evaluating a Community Psychiatric Service*. Oxford University Press, London.

Gover, D. A. (1963) Economic differential in the relationship between marital adjustment and wife's employment status. *Marriage and Family Living*, **25**, 452–456.

Gregory, C. C., and Downie, N. M. (1968) Prognostic study of patients who left, returned and stayed in a psychiatric hospital. *Journal of Counselling Psychology*, **15**, 232–236.

Hunt, G. M., and Azrin, N. H. (1973) A community-reinforcement approach to alcoholism. *Behaviour Research and therapy*, **11**, 91–104.

Jackson, J. (1966) Structural characteristics of norms. In B. J. Biddle and E. J. Thomas, eds, *Role Theory: Concepts and Research*. John Wiley, New York.

Jahoda, M. (1979) The impact of unemployment in the 1930s and the 1970s. *Bulletin of the British Psychological Society*, **32**, 309–314.

Janis, I. L., and Mann, L. (1977) *Decision Making: A Psychological Analysis of Conflict, Choice and Commitment*. Free Press, New York.

Jaques, E. (1967) *Equitable Payment*. Penguin, Harmondsworth, Middx.

Kay, D. W. K., Beamish, P., and Roth, M. (1964) Old age mental disorders in Newcastle-upon-Tyne. Part II: A study of possible social and medical causes. *British Journal of Psychiatry*, **110**, 668–682.

Kazdin, A. E., and Bryan, J. H. (1971) Competence and volunteering. *Journal of Experimental Social Psychology*, **7**, 87–97.

Kelvin, P. (1970) *The Bases of Social Behaviour: An Approach in Terms of Order and Value*. Holt, Rinehart & Winston, London.

Kerr, S., Schreisheim, C. A., Murphy, C. J., and Stodgill, R. M. (1974) Toward a contingency theory of leadership based upon the consideration and initiating structure literature. *Organisational Behaviour and Human Performance*, **12**, 62–82.

Kissin, B., Rosenblatt, S. M., and Machover, S. (1968) Prognostic factors in alcoholism. *Psychiatric Research Reports*, **24**, 22–43.

Kunce, J. T., and Worley, B. (1970) Simplified prediction of occupational adjustment of distressed clients. *Journal of Counselling Psychology*, **17**, 326–330.

Lazarus, R. S. (1966) *Psychological Stress and the Coping Process*. McGraw-Hill, New York.

Lazarus, R. S., Averill, J. R., and Opton, E. M. (1974) The psychology of coping: issues of research and assessment. In G. V. Coelho, D. A. Hamburg, and J. E. Adams, eds, *Coping and Adaptation*. Basic Books, New York.

Leary, T. (1957) *Interpersonal Diagnosis of Personality: A Functional Theory and Methodology for Personality Evaluation*. Ronald, New York.

Litman, G. K., Eiser, J. R., Rawson, N. S. B., and Oppenheim, A. N. (1979) Differences in relapse precipitants and coping behaviour between alcohol relapsers and survivors. *Behaviour Research and Therapy*, **17**, 89–94.

Litwak, E., and Szelenyi, I. (1969) Primary group structures and their functions: kin, neighbours and friends. *American Sociological Review*, **34**, 465–481.

Lowenthal, M. F. (1964) Social isolation and mental illness in old age. *American Sociological Review*, **29**, 54–70.

Lowenthal, M. F. (1965) Antecedents of isolation and mental illness in old age. *Archives of General Psychiatry*, **12**, 245–254.

Lowenthal, M. F. (1968) The relationship between social factors and mental health in the aged. *Psychiatric Research Reports*, **23**, 187–197.

Lowenthal, M. F., and Boler, D. (1965) Voluntary versus involuntary social withdrawal. *Journal of Gerontology*, **20**, 363–371.

McCulloch, J. W., and Philip, A. E. (1970) The social prognosis of persons who attempt suicide. *Social Psychiatry*, **5**, 177–182.

McCulloch, J. W., Philip, A. E., and Carstairs, G. M. (1967) The ecology of suicidal behaviour. *British Journal of Psychiatry*, **113**, 313–319.

Mahone, C. H. (1960) Fear of failure and unrealistic vocational aspirations. *Journal of Abnormal and Social Psychology*, **60**, 253–261.

Mahoney, M. J. (1974) *Cognition and Behaviour Modification*. Ballinger, Cambridge, Mass.

Mannheim, H., and Wilkins, L. T. (1955) *Prediction Methods in Relation to Borstal Training*. HMSO, London.

Massimo, J., and Shore, M. (1963) The effectiveness of a comprehensive vocationally-oriented psychotherapy programme for adolescent delinquent boys. *American Journal of Orthopsychiatry*, **33**, 634–642.

Mechanic, D. (1966) Response factors in illness: the study of illness behaviour. *Social Psychiatry*, **1**, 11–20.

Mechanic, D., and Volkart, E. H. (1961) Stress, illness behaviour and the sick role. *American Sociological Review*, **26**, 51–58.

Mischel, W. (1968) *Personality and Assessment*. John Wiley, New York.

Norris, V. (1956) A statistical study of the influence of marriage on the hospital care of the mentally sick. *Journal of Mental Science*, **102**, 467–486.

Odern, S. R., and Bradburn, N. M. (1969) Working wives and marriage happiness. *American Journal of Sociology*, **74**, 392–407.

Ovenstone, I. M. K., and Kreitman, N. (1974) Two syndromes of suicide. *British Journal of Psychiatry*, **124**, 336–345.

Parkes, C. M. (1964) Recent bereavement as a cause of mental illness. *British Journal of Psychiatry*, **110**, 198–204.

Pearlin, L. I., and Schooler, C. (1978) The structure of coping. *Journal of Health and Social Behaviour*, **19**, 2–21.

Pittel, S. M., and Mendelsohn, G. A. (1966) Measurement of moral values: a review and critique. *Psychological Bulletin*, **66**, 22–35.

Philip, A. E., and McCulloch, J. W. (1966) Use of social indices in psychiatric epidemiology. *British Journal of Preventive and Social Medicine*, **20**, 122–126.

Phillips, L. (1966) *Human Adaptation and its Failures*. Academic Press, New York.

Rawls, J. R. (1971) Toward the identification of readmissions and non-readmissions to mental hospitals, *Social Psychiatry*, **6**, 58–61.

Ricks, D., Umbarger, C., and Mack, R. (1964) A measure of increased temporal perspective in successfully treated adolescent delinquent boys. *Journal of Abnormal and Social Psychology*, **69**, 685–689.

Rosen, B., Klein, D. F., and Gittleman-Klein, R. (1971) The prediction of rehospitalisation: the relationship between age of first psychiatric treatment contact, marital status and pre-morbid social adjustment. *Journal of Nervous and Mental Diseases*, **152**, 17–22.

Rosenblatt, S. M., Gross, M. M., and Chartoff, S. (1969) Marital status and multiple psychiatric admission for alcoholism. *Quarterly Journal of Studies in Alcohol*, **30**, 445–447.

Rosow, I. (1965) Forms and functions of adult socialization. *Social Forces*, **44**, 35–45.

Rosow, I. (1967) *Social Integration of the Aged*. Free Press, New York.

Schaffer, H. R., and Schaffer, E. B. (1968) *Child Care and the Family: A Study of Short-term Admission to Care*. Bell, London.

Stein, Z., and Susser, M. (1969) Widowhood and mental illness. *British Journal of Preventive and Social Medicine*, **23**, 106–110.

Stotland, E., and Canon, L. K. (1972) *Social Psychology: A Cognitive Approach*. Saunders, Philadelphia.

Turner, R. J., Dopkeen, L. S., and Labreche, G. P. (1970) Marital status and schizophrenia: a study of incidence and outcome. *Journal of Abnormal Psychology*, **76**, 110–116.

Turner, R. J., and Zabo, L. J. (1968) Social competence and schizophrenic outcome: an investigation and critique. *Journal of Health and Social Behaviour*, **9**, 41–51.

Vispo, R. H. (1962) Pre-morbid personality in the functional psychoses of the senium. A comparison of ex-patients with healthy controls. *Journal of Mental Science*, **108**, 790–800.

Walker, L. G., Adamson, F. A., Alexander, D. A., and Stoffelmayr, B. E. (1973) A negative correlation between improved production in psychiatric rehabilitation and social behaviour outside. *British Journal of Psychiatry*, **123**, 409–412.

Walker, R., and McCourt, J. (1965) Employment experiences among 200 schizophrenic patients in hospital and after discharge. *American Journal of Psychiatry*, **122**, 316–319.

Walls, R. T., and Smith, T. S. (1970) Voluntary delay of reinforcement as a function of model status. *Journal of Counselling Psychology*, **17**, 123–126.

Watts, F. N., and Yu, P. K. (1976) The structure of attitudes in psychiatric rehabilitation. *Journal of Occupational Psychology*, **49**, 39–44.

Weiss, R. S. (1968) Materials for a theory of social relationships. In W. G. Bennis, E. H. Schein, F. I. Steele, and D. C. Berlew, eds, *Interpersonal Dynamics*. Dorsey Press, Homewood, Ill.

Wilensky, H. L. (1961) Orderly careers and social participation: the impact of work history on social integration in the middle mass. *American Sociological Review*, **26**, 521–539.

Williams, A. R. T., and Blackler, F. H. M. (1971) Motives and behaviour at work. In P. B. Warr, ed., *Psychology at Work*. Penguin, Harmondsworth, Middx.

Wing, J. K., Bennett, D. H., and Denham, J. (1964) *The Industrial Rehabilitation of Long-stay Schizophrenic Patients*. Medical Research Council Memorandum No. 42. HMSO, London.

# PART VI

*Principles into Practice*

Theory and Practice of Psychiatric Rehabilitation
Edited by F. N. Watts and D. H. Bennett
© 1983, John Wiley & Sons, Ltd.

# 15

---

# Management of the Staff Team

---

FRASER WATTS and DOUGLAS BENNETT

A rehabilitation service is no better than the people who provide it. Though it is important to have a good scientific understanding of the process of rehabilitation, little can be achieved unless the rehabilitation staff as a whole are able to provide the right kind of service. One of the most critical tasks for anyone responsible for a rehabilitation service, as for any other similar clinical service, is how he leads the staff team. It may not be possible to recruit 'ideal' staff. Often it is a matter of enabling the available staff to provide the best rehabilitation service of which they are capable.

The leadership of the staff team is thus of critical importance, but it has received surprisingly little explicit attention. Though the importance of the multidisciplinary team is on everyone's lips, the principles of teamwork have seldom been worked out in detail. Our aim here is to provide an exposition of the principles of rehabilitation teamwork that is rooted both in the scientific literature and in a realistic view of clinical practice. We are conscious that we are attempting something which, however important, is very difficult and others have probably been prudent to avoid. Among the scant literature available is a useful discussion of the psychiatric team by Bowen *et al.* (1965).

## The Need for an Integrated Staff Team in Rehabilitation

It may be useful to begin by highlighting some of the problems and inadequacies that will beset a rehabilitation service that makes no explicit attempt to develop staff teamwork. Because successful rehabilitation needs to take a broad and comprehensive view of patients' problems, it is necessary for a number of different professions to share the work that needs to be done with each individual patient. In some areas of psychiatry it is feasible to have a style of teamwork in which one member of the team works with each patient on behalf of the team, the others having only an advisory or consultative role. This type of teamwork is inappropriate in rehabilitation because the range of problems that need to be tackled in each case call for the active involvement of several different professions.

This raises considerable problems of coordination. How can members of several different professions be engaged with a patient without working at cross purposes? It might be thought that the solution would be for the members of each profession to confine themselves to their proper roles, so as not to overlap with what others are doing. Each profession has a number of 'core' functions that can only be performed by that profession (e.g. prescription of medication by doctors, psychological testing by psychologists, arrangement of financial support by social workers). However, the concern of rehabilitation for patients' capacity for social adjustment goes beyond any of these core functions. If the various professions concerned were to restrict themselves to their core functions, much of the most important work would go undone. It would also fail to make the best use of the staff, as most members of psychiatric teams have skills that go beyond their core functions.

But once staff begin to operate outside their core roles, there is a danger of work being duplicated or, worse, of their working at cross purposes. A method of coordination is needed if this is to be avoided. It might be thought that the team leader, normally the doctor, could take the responsibility for deciding what contribution each profession should make to the work with each patient. However, there are two reasons why this is not feasible. Such a pattern of hierarchical control tends to create an inflexible style of working. In addition, it is not possible for any single person to have sufficient information and expertise to control the work of the staff team effectively. These points require development.

Burns and Stalker (1966) argue that hierarchical control can be effective in a team in which the problems that arise are predictable, and where tasks can be distributed in a fixed way. However, where staff are regularly required to find innovative solutions to problems a network of control, in which roles are adjusted through mutual interaction, is more effective. It is consistent with this that Wilkinson (1973) found that resistance to innovations is less strong where there is a high level of interaction among staff. The problems presented in psychiatric rehabilitation are frequently very complicated and apparently intractable, and do not admit of stereotyped solutions. It is therefore necessary for the staff to work out together how each problem should be tackled and what their respective contributions should be. The flexibility and ingenuity that are required by rehabilitation are unlikely to be developed in any other way.

A further argument for having a flexible distribution of tasks within the team is that this makes it easier for staff to deputize for one another. It is not uncommon for the staff of a psychiatric unit to be presented with a problem that requires urgent action. The key worker who is most involved in the case may not be available when this happens. To deal effectively with emergencies it is necessary that there should be a number of staff who know enough about a particular case to be capable of making urgent decisions. Equally important is that junior staff who may have to do this should feel confident enough of the support of the team to be willing to take decisive action when it is required.

No single person, acting as team leader, can hope to be able to decide how the rehabilitation of each patient should be tackled, or what the contribution of the various staff members should be. In medicine it may be feasible for a single clinician to acquaint himself with all the information necessary for a decision about a patient's management. The information is largely of a technical kind that the doctor's training equips him to understand and evaluate. In psychiatric rehabilitation, matters are very different. The contributions of the non-medical professions are crucial. The representatives of these professions need to be involved not only in providing information, but in interpreting their specialist contributions and in considering their implications for the rehabilitation programme. It is unrealistic for a single person to think that he can either know all the relevant information or that, unaided, he can make the best use of it. Leadership styles such as direction or manipulation that are based on the leader having high levels of information (Bass and Valenzi, 1974) are not open to the leader of a rehabilitation team.

There may, however, be merit in having a single member of the team who is designated a 'key worker' for each patient and who has the responsibility, not for decision making, but for coordinating and monitoring the work of the team as a whole with that particular patient. There is often a great deal of such coordinating work to be done, much of it at a very detailed day-to-day level. It is seldom realistic to expect one or two people who occupy positions of leadership in the team to do this for all patients. The task is likely to be done better if each member of staff is a key worker for relatively few patients. The coordinating and monitoring functions involved can be undertaken by members of any profession.

Members of the staff team are valuable not only for their specialist professional contributions, but also for their diferent social backgrounds and life experience. In dealing with problems of social adjustment, the varied social experience and attitudes of the members of the staff team are a considerable asset in planning a realistic and sensible rehabilitation programme. Between them the members of a team often provide a good cross-section of ages, sexes, races, social classes, and educational attainments. Together they are likely to have a better grasp of what pattern of social adjustment it is realistic to aim at with each patient than any person could have individually.

But it is not just that decisions are likely to be based on better information, and more realistic, if they are taken by all the relevant members of the staff.

Equally important is the fact that rehabilitation plans are unlikely to be effectively *implemented* unless those who have the task of doing so have shared in the decision-making process. Research on group processes has established that decisions are more likely to be implemented by the members of a group if they work together in making those decisions (see Secord and Backman, 1964; Cartwright and Zander, 1968). There are no doubt a variety of reasons for this. People are more likely to understand the reasons for decisions if they have been involved in making them. They also identify more closely with the decision, and are influenced by the fact of having made some kind of public commitment to the rehabilitation plan (Janis and Mann, 1977, Chapter 11) through being involved in its formulation.

It is often junior members of staff who are most critical as far as the hour-by-hour implementation of a rehabilitation plan is concerned, and these are the people who can very easily be left out of the decision-making process. It is wise for a staff team to make an explicit policy of including these junior staff in the formulation of the rehabilitation plan. Psychiatric 'aides' tend to have different attitudes to patients, which are probably linked to their own social class background (Band and Brody, 1962), and this will lead to a lack of coordination in the implementation of the rehabilitation policy unless steps are taken to deal with it. It should, however, be emphasized that the evidence is that these aides can be a highly effective therapeutic resource when they are liberated and mobilized (Ellsworth and Ellsworth, 1970).

Close teamwork can also have an effect on staff motivation. Working with the chronic cases that a rehabilitation service is concerned with can be very discouraging for the staff. The members of the staff team can have an important effect in maintaining each other's interest and engagement. This also requires a high degree of interaction, and a feeling among the staff as a whole that they are responsible for the quality of the rehabilitation service. Finally, there are some patients' who have been designated 'special problem patients' (Main, 1957; Burnham, 1966), who seem able to exploit any potential divisions between staff. The well-integrated team will be better able to maintain an integrated policy for such patients, and to resolve whatever conflicts are generated between them. Stanton and Schwartz (1954) presented an interesting empirical demonstration that the excitable behaviour of such patients subsided when the conflicts surrounding them were discussed fully and openly by the staff.

## Problems in Rehabilitation Teamwork

Though close teamwork is, for these reasons, a necessary part of a good rehabilitation service, it should not be imagined that staff will find belonging to such a team an entirely satisfactory experience. The team will frequently become divided in its approach to patients and trying to work in close collaboration with other staff in spite of fundamental differences of approach is inevitably a stressful experience.

One conflict that frequently arises depends on the amount of time spent in the direct care of patients. Kushlick *et al.* (1976) have used the amount of 'direct care time' as an interesting way of classifying staff. Those who have the most intensive care of patients (usually nurses and occupational therapists) can become understandably resentful of other professionals who see less of patients. This can lead to a low level of cooperation between these two groups of staff and create a feeling that interaction with patients is a relatively low-status activity. The consequences of this for effective rehabilitation are obviously very serious.

This kind of split between staff can be overcome to some extent if those staff who normally have least contact with patients show themselves to be willing to share the work of direct care staff when the need arises. In the mental handicap field (King *et al.*, 1971) it has been shown that one of the critical determinants of whether a patient-oriented or a custodial pattern of care develops is whether senior staff 'model' involvement with patients. The same applies on a psychiatric ward (Wallace *et al.*, 1973) or day centre (Shepherd and Richardson, 1979).

On the other hand, staff members with higher academic qualifications can become resentful of working on an equal basis with less well qualified staff. This shows itself particularly in frustration over the way clinical decisions are taken by the team. Meehl (1973) has provided a forceful and well-reasoned statement of these objections in his paper 'Why I do not attend case conferences'. His objections are not just to the level of the contributions of the less qualified staff, but to the way in which the ethos of the clinical conference tends to lower the intellectual contributions of everyone present. Many of his objections are well founded, though it should be noted that they are objections not so much to the quality of the information provided, as to the way in which it is interpreted and used in making clinical decisions. The objective should be to formulate rehabilitation plans that are based on a rigorous and clear-headed analysis of all the relevant information.

There will also be conflicts over policy towards patients. It was argued in Chapter 14 that it is a necessary aspect of the socialization process involved in rehabilitation to present patients with a balance between demands and support. But within the team some will want to emphasize one and some the other. Some will feel that the patient is too ill to be subjected to increasing demands for performance; others that the patient's progress is being held back by excessive concern and sympathy. There is nothing necessarily unhelpful about such disagreements. Indeed, they may be a sign that the team as a whole is taking a broad and balanced view of patients. One of the problems that can afflict an over-cohesive team is a kind of 'groupthink' in which the team ceases to pay attention to information that conflicts with its general assumptions, and strong social pressures are brought to bear on any members who challenge these assumptions (Janis and Mann, 1977, pp. 129–133). To avoid this, a team needs to be able at least to tolerate, even to welcome, divergent views among its members. But this makes yet another potential stressful demand on the rehabilitation team. It takes a mature team indeed to tolerate differences of view and resolve them into a broadly based and coordinated plan.

Rehabilitation work seldom forms a major part of the basic training of the professionals who make up the rehabilitation team. When they come to this field the members of the team will therefore find themselves needing to learn new skills and approaches. This requires flexibility and a capacity for change. Perhaps doctors and nurses are initially the most uncomfortable with rehabilitation work as it is a long way removed from the traditional principles of 'treatment' and 'care' on which their professions are based. The attitudes of the nursing members of the team are especially critical as nurses have such a major impact on the kind of service a hospital offers patients. Nursing attitudes are also the most likely to be conservative and custodial in orientation (see Rabkin, 1972; Foster *et al.*, 1974).

The personalities of individual nurses, especially the extent to which they show authoritarian attitudes, are a major determinant of their approach to patients (Noble, 1971), though there is reason to think that attitudes can be modified by the prevailing orientation of the hospital and clinical team. Hospitals differ enormously in their clinical orientations and staff attitudes (Wing and Brown, 1970; Rice *et al.*, 1966). Particularly relevant are studies of hospitals in transition (Foster *et al.*, 1974) which indicate that staff attitudes are far from immutable. Sometimes substantial changes can be achieved. It is one of the challenges of staff management in rehabilitation teams to provide a climate that will tend to change traditional and custodial staff attitudes in a direction that emphasizes actively trying to increase patients' capacity for social adjustment and independence.

It also has to be recognized that the members of a staff team will often be involved with issues connected with their general professional role and status that may well take priority over their commitment to the rehabilitation team (Etzioni, 1960). Members of the various professions enter the rehabilitation team with preconceived ideas, that may not be shared by the members of other professions, about their respective roles and about how the service should be organized. For example, Davis (1974) has documented the fact that psychiatric nurses have expectations about their involvement in unit decisions that are not shared by either physicians or patients. Probably each profession regards itself as more important in the team than it is thought to be by others. This is an inevitable source of conflict between staff.

In an excellent theoretical paper on problems in multidisciplinary teamwork, Braga (1972) makes use of the notion of role strain. Two aspects of role strain are normally distinguished: role ambiguity and role conflict (Kahn and Quinn, 1970). It has been pointed out that an integrated style of teamwork produces some inevitable *conflict* between the roles a person assigns himself, those which his profession assigns to him, and those which his colleagues in the multidisciplinary team assign to him. Further, there may be some degree of role *ambiguity*. Members of the team may easily be left not knowing how to handle patients. Even when a common approach has been agreed by the staff team, there is a danger that this will not be spelt out in enough detail for the members of the staff who have most contact with patients actually to implement. However, it will be argued in this chapter that role ambiguity to a large extent can and should be avoided. There is no reason why the policies worked out for each individual patient should not be detailed enough to reduce ambiguity to a bare minimum. Role conflict is less easy to avoid though there are indications in the literature (House and Rizzo, 1972) that it is less important than role ambiguity as far as organizational effectiveness is concerned.

Further, it seems that the relative importance of role conflict and ambiguity may depend on the level of an organization at which people work (Schuler, 1975). At low levels there is normally relatively little role ambiguity, and this is not a serious issue as far as satisfaction is concerned. It is much more likely to be felt as an issue by senior people in an organization. On the other hand, when conflict develops at the lower levels of an organization, it is relatively serious because the people concerned normally have little scope for reducing it. More senior people usually have greater freedom to change their responsibilities in a way that can reduce conflict between incompatible demands.

In some therapeutic communities, the policy has been developed of deliberately blurring the roles of team members as much as possible. The results of this policy are by no means always successful (Bowen *et al.*, 1965; Doyle, 1977). Indeed, it seems to be a policy for maximizing the degree of role strain that staff will experience, and this is hardly likely to be helpful. It is perhaps relevant, however, that personality seems to be a major factor in affecting tolerance of role strain (Brief and Aldag, 1976). For example, it produces most dissatisfaction in people with a high need for clarity and independence. However, what is being advocated here is the development of an integrated and cohesive style of teamwork. It is neither necessary nor desirable that this should include a blurring of roles to the point where members of different professions have interchangeable functions.

## Structuring of Tasks

If role ambiguity is to be kept to a minimum, it will be necessary to have a policy for ensuring that the work of the team is organized as clearly as possible. We have argued that it is necessary for the team as a whole to participate in this organization of the work, but this does not mean it can be left to chance.

The first essential is to ensure that tasks are clearly specified. Before this can be attempted it is necessary for the rehabilitation team to decide what their aims should be with a particular patient. However, it is all too easy for the process to stop at this point, without the detailed staff tasks by which these aims are to be achieved ever being specified. Team leaders cannot assume that the members of the team will be able to do this spontaneously.

Mager (1972) has provided a useful, popular manual for goal analysis, setting out how broad aims can be reduced to detailed tasks. He suggests five steps: (a) write down the goal; (b) jot down 'performances' (i.e. detailed behavioural tasks) relevant to the goal; (c) sort out these jottings by removing any remaining fuzziness or abstraction; (d) write down an exact specification of each performance; (e) test the relevance of the performances by asking whether they could amount to achievement of the required goal. This programme makes a good agenda for a team meeting.

Once the performances have been listed the final stage is to make sure that it is quite clear which members of the staff team have the responsibility for carrying each of them out. It is essential that the staff who are to carry out individual tasks should leave a planning meeting in no doubt about what their colleagues expect of them. Staff who have publicly accepted responsibility for particular tasks can later be held accountable by their colleagues for carrying them out.

A team leader must also be sure that individual staff members know how to carry out the peformances that have been specified in this way. It is no use for staff members to know what is required of them if they do not have the necessary skills in their repertoire. This issue has been investigated most extensively in connection with training staff to participate in token economy programmes (Kazdin, 1977, Chapter 6). The results of research carried out in this field are salutary. Merely telling staff what behaviours to reinforce has relatively little effect, even if written reminders are provided, though Stoffelmayr et al. (1979) were able to demonstrate the value of regular, daily telephone calls. Formal didactic instruction also has little practical effect. It conveys the principles on which the programme is based, but does not alter the behaviour of the staff charged with carrying out the programme. Instruction about what is required often needs to be followed up with practical training during which staff are supervised while carrying out the required performances in the actual clinical situation (Gardner, 1972).

Kazdin (1977, pp. 143–145) reports a number of studies which have shown that staff carry out programmes more effectively if they monitor their own performance or are given feedback on their performance by others. However, the evidence on this is by no means consistent. One important point is that objective feedback is more effective if it is accompanied by praise

(Cossiart *et al.*, 1973). However, feedback alone is not sufficient to produce an improvement in staff effectiveness. Ellsworth (1973) reports a study in which feedback was to be supplied to the staff of psychiatric wards on patients' post-hospital adjustment. The results were mixed. He suggests that feedback is only likely to be helpful if staff have identified a strategy capable of improving their effectiveness, are willing to adopt and persist with this new approach, and receive the necessary institutional support. One can add to this that feedback will be more effective if it shows whether the necessary staff 'performances' have been carried out rather than whether patients have been successfully rehabilitated, and if it relates to the work of individuals rather than the work of the staff as a whole. Of course, it is important that the effectiveness of the unit in rehabilitating patients should be known and the methods of the unit reconsidered in the light of this information, but feedback of this kind is not what is needed to improve the functioning of team members.

Two functions of staff feedback can be distinguished. First, it provides information for staff on whether they are actually implementing the rehabilitation plan in the intended way. Secondly, it has a motivational function in providing recognition of staff functioning. It is in this connection that the effects of feedback are enhanced if they are accompanied by verbal expressions of appreciation. This does not necessarily imply a dominant role for the person who provides this positive feedback. A particularly effective pattern is one in which medical staff are non-dominant in their approach to nursing staff, but are nevertheless clearly motivated themselves and praise the nursing staff for their work. Ellsworth *et al.* (1971) found that this pattern characterized units with a good record in early discharge and stable community tenure.

### Promoting Staff Cohesiveness and Resolving Conflicts

In addition to such methods of structuring the work of the rehabilitation staff, a policy is needed for increasing the cohesiveness of the staff team. Back (1951) has distinguished various possible bases of group cohesiveness, such as that membership of the team carries prestige, or that people are personally attracted to other members of the group, or that the group enhances effective performance. It is unlikely that membership of a rehabilitation team will be prestigious enough for that alone to create cohesiveness. Neither can it be assumed that initially the members of the team will like each other much, though liking may be increased as a result of working together. The only plausible basis for the rehabilitation team is that the members have a common task to perform that can be carried out more effectively if they work together. In fact, successful performance is the most important determinant of a task-oriented group such as a rehabilitation team (Anderson, 1975).

In view of this it would be sensible to build cohesiveness around this natural basis of the *working* relationship. Sometimes attention to staff relationships leads to a preoccupation with personal and emotional relationships which is not the natural basis of the cohesiveness of a working group such as a rehabilitation team. The resolution of disagreements within the team provides both the critical test of team cohesiveness, and also the anvil on which cohesiveness can be forged.

The interrelationship between cohesiveness and disagreements is probably quite complex (Gerard, 1953). Too much disagreement can undermine team cohesiveness, but on the other hand a relatively cohesive team is more likely to be able to resolve disagreements. If the resolution is successful, it will probably enhance cohesiveness further. But it would be naïve to assume that provided communication is adequate it will always be possible to resolve disagreements (Etzioni, 1960). Whether cohensiveness facilitates the resolution of disagreements or whether disagreements undermine cohesiveness no doubt depends on their relative strengths.

Unfortunately, the resolution of disagreements tends to be a time-consuming business. The first requirement is the structural one of providing staff with sufficient opportunity to explain their own points of view and grasp those of the other team members, though it may be prudent to limit the time taken by these discussions. In such discussions it is possible for key members of the team to foster cohesiveness. Liberman (1971) has reported some research on group therapy showing that when therapists explicitly elicit 'cohesive' comments from group members and reinforce them with attention and approval, the level of expressed cohesiveness in the group increases. Presumably the same kind of process can operate in team meetings. In this context, 'cohesive' comments will be such things as pointing out previously unrecognized commonalities in the positions of different team members, taking an interest in other people's views, and so on. In this way the team, or even just a few key members of it, can create an atmosphere in which mutual understanding is stronly reinforced.

All that is necessary is that staff should understand each other's orientations enough to be able to work out an integrated plan. It is not necessary that staff should always *agree* with each other. Indeed, if they do, this really means that the range of viewpoints, which is one of the main potential assets of a team, has been lost. It is not desirable to foster a culture in which expression of divergent viewpoints is regarded as disloyalty to the team!

Another problem that can develop with a cohesive team is that the 'boundary' of the team becomes too sharply defined. The team learns to understand and respect its own members, but finds it hard to do this with people outside the team. It is inevitable that rehabilitation work will bring the staff into contact with staff working in hospital wards on the one hand and community agencies on the other. The rehabilitation team must be capable of achieving effective working relationships with the large network of people on the periphery of the team.

If the divergent viewpoints within the team are to be integrated into a coordinated plan, it is necessary to conduct discussions in a way that ensures these different viewpoints do not become polarized through internal debate (Myers and Lamm, 1976). It is possible that when disagreements are expressed 'psychological reactance' can take place, and the differing views can become even more strongly held and sharply divergent (Brehm, 1976). If psychological reactance is not to take place, it is essential that there should be no coercive pressure on people to abandon their views. It is also necessary to approach points of conflict gradually, starting from issues on which there is least divergence of view, or on which opposing views are least strongly held (see Varela, 1971, chapter 7).

It may also be helpful for the team to have a conceptual model that enables them to integrate the different emphases in rehabilitation policy into a single programme. For example, if the rehabilitation team understands the importance of combining 'demands' and 'supports' in socialization processes it may be able to see that those who want to take 'hard' and 'soft' lines with a patient can each have a useful part to play. Provided they understand each other's contributions and can work together, their differing views need not be bad for the patient. Skynner (1975) describes the use of a concrete form of this conceptual model (in terms of 'fathers' and 'mothers') in his account of a staff group at a rehabilitation-orientated day hospital.

There may be a case for providing staff with some explicit training in techniques of communication. Alston (1974) reports the use of a communication training programme for the staff of a correctional rehabilitation team. The results indicated significant improvements in communication skills and in favourable perceptions of other staff. To some extent regular team meetings called to discuss particular problems can also serve as indirect training in communication and problem-solving skills, at least where the meetings are reasonably effective at resolving disagreements. It can be especially valuable for new staff in a team to watch how the established members resolve disagreements. Because of this, team meetings can be especially important at times when a team has new members.

## Leadership Functions

There has been a tendency in organizational psychology over the last 20 years to polarize two different styles of management and to present them as alternatives. The choice has been presented as between a clear, efficient organizational structure or one that develops human resources. But it is becoming increasingly clear from the empirical literature that this is a false dichotomy (Bryman, 1976).

Perhaps the most important empirical basis for this view comes from work on the two basic dimensions of leadership. The Ohio leadership studies (Fleishman, 1973) showed that there are two independent dimensions, of consideration and, of provision of structure, and that the optimal pattern of organizational leadership was a high level of both. Though this is the general finding, it should be pointed out that it does not apply in an invariant way in all situations, and it increases the empirical clarity of the theory to focus on some of these moderating factors (Kerr *et al.*, 1974). High levels of structure are most likely to increase staff satisfaction when staff are working under pressure, when they lack information, and when they are at a low level of the organizational hierarchy. The many empirical studies of consideration and structure include a number that have focused on nurses in mental hospitals (Nealey and Blood, 1968; Nealey and Owen, 1970; Pryer and Distefano, 1971). The effects of structure on satisfaction at different levels of the nursing hierarchy has been one of the main issues investigated in these studies, but the results have not been entirely consistent.

The effect of structure is especially dependent on the level of consideration with which it is combined. Structure is more likely to be helpful when consideration is also provided (Fleishman and Harris, 1962). The most critical aspects of support in the rehabilitation team probably are that the leaders of the team should be available and approachable, should show that they understand the positions of the various people in the team, and should be able to give expert help when it is required. One of the marks of the considerate, supportive leader is his attitude towards his 'least-preferred co-worker' (Rice, 1978). Supportive and non-supportive leaders differ most widely in their attitudes to their least-preferred member of the team. It is a key aspect of effective support that all the members of the team should feel valued by the leader. When members of the team disagree, the leader can play an important part in resolving the conflict by displaying some understanding of the positions of both parties, and by showing that he can tolerate dissent. He should not use his disapproval as a sanction against people he disagrees with or who open up uncomfortable issues.

Just as the support of the leader determines how useful task structuring is to the team, so it can determine how much stress is caused by role conflict. Kahn and Quinn (1970) have discussed the moderating effects of psychological support, both for the leader and for the group as a whole, on role strain. They draw attention to the helpful effect of experience in coping with role strain. It may well be the longer serving members of the team who are able to exercise leadership in helping others to cope with strain. However, there is also a danger of very long serving members becoming so 'locked in' to their roles that they lose the capacity to adapt to new problems.

The leadership functions that need to be exercised in a team are very varied. Attention has already been given to the structuring of tasks and to the provision of support. In addition, there are other functions associated with charismatic leaders (House, 1976) such as demonstrating effective involvement with patients, communicating high expectations of other staff and showing confidence that they can be met, articulating a grasp of the overall goals of the team and providing a broad view of the nature and significance of rehabilitation.

None of these leadership functions needs to be exercised by a single person. When leaders are allowed to emerge in groups it often happens that leadership functions are shared between two or more people (Secord and Backman, 1964). In a rehabilitation team there are usually several people who have the experience and ability to exercise some degree of leadership. Normally a team will function better if there is more than one person who is prepared to assume some leadership responsibilities for the general level of functioning of the team. There are many ways in which leadership functions can be distributed. One person can be concerned with the organization of day-to-day work, another with working out long-term aims and developments, and a third with maintaining the cohesion of the team. Any one of these types of leadership can also be shared. Each team will evolve its own pattern of distributed leadership. In general, however, it can be said that the more people are able to make a contribution to the leadership functions that need to be exercised within a team, the better integrated the team will be.

Finally, there are leadership functions concerned with the relationship of the rehabilitation team to the larger institution in which it works. Normally there will need to be a single person who can be identified by the institution as having this function. There are particular problems of role conflict associated with this role. On the one hand, it involves representing the team to the institution and explaining why it may want to operate in ways that seem divergent or even incomprehensible to those outside. On the other hand, it involves representing the larger institution to the team (explaining, for example, why it is useful for rehabilitation records to be kept in a form that can be integrated into the general record system, why financial resources are not available for some development, etc.). It is difficult to exercise this double function in a way that retains the confidence both of the team and of the institution. The person who has the job of doing this has an exceptionally difficult management role.

The most important objective here is to secure the maximum amount of autonomy for the rehabilitation unit. There is converging evidence relating to the care of alcoholics (Otto and Orford, 1978) and the mentally handicapped (Raynes et al., 1979) that the quality of patient care is better in relatively autonomous units. This is a more important variable than the overall size of the institution. Where a unit has maximum autonomy staff tend to increase the amount of time they spent with patients, and provide a kind of care that is better geared to the needs of individual patients. It also needs to be recognized by the institution that individual units need autonomy if they are to function well. Ways need to be found of achieving coordination on essential matters, while delegating as much freedom of action as possible to the rehabilitation team.

## Conclusion

Teamwork has suffered from being misrepresented in various ways. It has been presented as a panacea for all problems and as a soft and comfortable option for the staff concerned. Also, it has frequently appeared to be merely a piece of fashionable but unsubstantiated ideology. It is none of these. We have endeavoured to present it as a style of work that has a sound scientific basis and is simply necessary if an effective rehabilitation service is to be achieved. We do not suggest that good teamwork can be brought about quickly or easily, or that it is not without cost to those involved.

## References

Alston, P. P. (1974) Multidiscipline group facilitation training: an aid to the team approach. *Rehabilitation Counselling Bulletin*, **18**, 21–25.

Anderson, A. B. (1975) Combined effects of interpersonal attraction and goal-path clarity on the cohesiveness of task-oriented groups. *Journal of Personality and Social Psychology*, **31**, 68–75.

Back, K. W. (1951) Influence through group communication. *Journal of Abnormal and Social Psychology*, **46**, 9–23.

Band, R. I., and Brody, E. B. (1962) *Archives of General Psychiatry*, **6**, 307–314.

Bass, B. M., and Valenzi, E. (1974) Contingent aspects of effective management styles. In J. G. Hunt and L. L. Larson, eds, *Contingency Approaches to Leadership Behaviour*. Illinois University Press, Carbondale.

Bowen, W. T., Marler, D. C., and Androes, C. (1965) The psychiatric team: myth and mystique. *American Journal of Psychiatry*, **122**, 687–690.

Braga, J. L. (1972) Role theory, cognitive dissonance theory and the interdisciplinary team. *Interchange*, **3**, 69–78.

Brehm, S. S. (1976) *The Application of Social Psychology to Clinical Practice*. John Wiley, New York.

Brief, S. P., and Aldag, R. J. (1976) Correlates of role indices. *Journal of Applied Psychology*, **61**, 468–472.

Bryman, A. (1976) Structure in organizations: a reconsideration. *Journal of Occupational Psychology*, **49**, 1–9.

Burnham, D. C. (1966) The special problem patient: victim or agent of splitting. *Psychiatry*, **29**, 105–122.

Burns, T., and Stalker, G. M. (1966) *The Management of Innovation*. 2nd edn. Tavistock, London.

Cartwright, D., and Zander, A. (1968) *Group Dynamics*. 3rd edn. Row, Peterson & Co., Illinois.

Cossiart, A., Hall, R. V., and Hopkins, B. C. (1973) The effects of experimenters' instructions, feedback, and praise on teacher praise and student attending behaviour. *Journal of Applied Behaviour Analysis*, **6**, 89–100.

Davis, M. K. (1974) Intrarole conflict and job satisfaction on psychiatric units. *Nursing Research*, **23**, 482–488.

Doyle, M. C. (1977) Egalitarianism in a mental health centre: an experiment that failed. *Hospital and Community Psychiatry*, **28**, 521–525.

Ellsworth, R. B. (1973) Feedback: asset or liability in improving treatment effectiveness. *Journal of Consulting and Clinical Psychology*, **40**, 383–393.

Ellsworth, R. B., and Ellsworth, J. J. (1970) The psychiatric aide: therapeutic agent or lost potential. *Journal of Psychiatric Nursing*, **8**, 7–13.

Ellsworth, R., Maroney, R., Klett, W., Gordon, H., and Gunn, R. (1971) Milieu characteristics of successful psychiatric treatment programs. *American Journal of Orthopsychiatry*, **41**, 427–441.

Etzioni, A. (1960) Interpersonal and structural factors in the study of mental hospitals. *Psychiatry*, **23**, 13–22.

Fleishman, E. A. (1973) Twenty years of consideration and structure. In E. A. Fleishman and J. G. Hunt, eds, *Current Developments in the Study of Leadership*. Southern Illinois University Press, Carbondale.

Fleishman, E. A., and Harris, E. F. (1972) Patterns of leadership behaviour related to employee grievances and turnover. *Personnel Psychology*, **15**, 43–56.

Foster, S., McClanahan, L. D., and Overley, T. (1974) Mental hospital staff attitudes as a function of experience, discipline and hospital atmosphere. *Journal of Abnormal Psychology*, **83**, 569–577.

Gardner, J. M. (1972) Teaching behaviour modification to non-professionals. *Journal of Applied Behaviour Analysis*, **5**, 517–521.

Gerard, H. B. (1953) The effect of different dimensions of disagreement on the communication process in small groups. *Human Relations*, **6**, 249–271.

House, R. J. (1976) A 1976 theory of charismatic leadership. In J. G. Hunt and L. L. Larson, eds, *Leadership: The Cutting Edge*. Southern Illinois University Press, Carbondale.

House, R. J., and Rizzo, J. R. (1972) Role conflict and ambiguity as critical variables in a model of organizational behaviour. *Organizational Behaviour and Human Performance*, **7**, 467–505.

Janis, I. L., and Mann, L. (1977) *Decision Making: A Psychological Analysis of Conflict, Choice and Commitment*. Free Press, New York.

Kahn, R. L., and Quinn, R. P. (1970) Role stress: a framework for analysis. In A. McLean, ed., *Mental Health and Work Organizations*. Rand McNally, Chicago.

Kazdin, A. E. (1977) *The Token Economy*. Plenum, New York.

Kerr, S., Schriesheim, C. J., Murphy, C. J., and Stogdill, R. M. (1974) Towards a contingency theory of leadership based on the consideration and initiating structure literature. *Organisation Behaviour and Human Performance*, **12**, 62–82.

King, R. D., Raynes, N. V., and Tizard, J. (1971) *Patterns of residential care*. Routledge & Kegan Paul, London.

Kushlick, A., Felce, D., Palmer, J., and Smith, J. (1976) *Evidence to the committee of inquiry into mental handicap nursing and care*. Dawn House, Winchester, UK.

Liberman, R. P. (1971) Behavioural group therapy: a controlled replication. *British Journal of Psychiatry*, **119**, 534–544.

Mager, R. F. (1972) *Goal Analysis*. Lear Siegler, Belmont, Pennsylvania.

Main, T. F. (1957) The ailment. *British Journal of Medical Psychology*, **30**, 129–145.

Meehl, P. E. (1973) Why I do not attend case conferences. In *Psychodiagnosis: Selected Papers*. University of Minnesota Press, Minneapolis.

Myers, D. G., and Lamm, H. (1976) The group polarization phenomenon. *Psychological Bulletin*, **83**, 602–627.

Nealey, S. M., and Blood, M. R. (1968) Leadership performance of nursing supervisors at two organizational levels. *Journal of Applied Psychology*, **52**, 414–422.

Nealey, S. M., and Owen, T. W. (1970) A multitrait–multimethod analysis of predictors and criteria of nursing performance. *Organizational Behaviour and Human Performance*, **5**, 348–365.

Noble, M. A. (1971) Organizational structure, ideology and personality in psychiatric nursing. *Journal of Psychiatric Nursing and Mental Health Services*, **9**, 11–17.

Otto, S., and Orford, J., *Not Quite Like Home: Small Hostels for Alcoholics and Others*. John Wiley, Chichester.

Pryer, M. W., and Distefano, M. K. (1971) Perceptions of leadership behaviour, job satisfactions and internal–external control across three nursing levels. *Nursing Research*, **200**, 534–537.

Rabkin, J. G. (1972) Opinions about mental illness: a review of the literature. *Psychological Bulletin*, **77**, 153–171.

Raynes, N. V., Pratt, M. W., and Roses, S. (1979) *Organisational Structure and the Care of the Mentally Retarded*. Croom Helm, London.

Rice, C. E., Berger, D. G., Klett, S. L., and Sewall, L. G. (1966) Measuring psychiatric hospital staff opinions about patient care. *Archives of General Psychiatry*, **14**, 428–434.

Rice, R. W. (1978) Construct validity of the least preferred co-worker score. *Psychological Bulletin*, **85**, 1199–1237.

Schuler, R. S. (1975) Role perceptions, satisfaction and performance: a partial reconciliation. *Journal of Applied Psychology*, **60**, 683–687.

Secord, P. F., and Backman, C. W. (1964) *Social Psychology*. McGraw-Hill, New York.

Shepherd, G., and Richardson, A. (1979) Organization and interaction in psychiatric day centres. *Psychological Medicine*, **9**, 573–579.

Skynner, A. C. R. (1975) The large group in training. In L. Kreeger, ed., *The Large Group: Dynamics and Therapy*. Constable, London.

Stanton, A. H., and Schwartz, M. S. (1954) *The Mental Hospital*. Basic Books, New York.

Stoffelmayr, B. E., Lindsay, W., and Taylor, V. (1979) Maintenance of staff behaviour. *Behaviour Research and Therapy*, **17**, 271–273.

Varela, J. A. (1971) *Psychological Solutions to Social Problems*. Academic Press, New York.

Wallace, C. J., Davis, J. R., Liberman, R. P., and Baker, L. (1973) Modelling and staff behaviour. *Journal of Consulting and Clinical Psychology*, **41**, 422–425.

Wilkinson, G. S. (1973) Interaction patterns and staff response to psychiatric innovations. *Journal of Health and Social Behaviour*, **14**, 323–329.

Wing, J. K., and Brown, G. W. (1970) *Institutionalism and Schizophrenia: A Comparative Study of Three Mental Hospitals, 1960–1968*. Cambridge University Press, London.

Theory and Practice of Psychiatric Rehabilitation
Edited by F. N. Watts and D. H. Bennett
© 1983, John Wiley & Sons, Ltd.

# 16

# Planning the Rehabilitation of the Individual

GEOFF SHEPHERD

This chapter is concerned with the practical problems of how to plan and implement individual programmes of rehabilitation. Of course, not all patients want, or will be prepared to follow, a planned programme. Nevertheless, a clear plan at least offers staff the feeling that they know what they would like to do, even if what they eventually end up doing turns out to be something different. This is important since, as was made clear in the previous chapter, the morale of the staff is at the heart of the rehabilitation process. So, how should we start in the construction of individual plans? Let us begin with a case:

John is 24 years old; he has been referred to a day hospital from outpatients for 'assessment and rehabilitation' at the request of his parents. The main problem seems to be that John has great difficulty in holding down a job for longer than about 6 months. His instability in work has been markedly worse in the last 4 years. Since leaving school at the age of 17 he has actually had seven jobs, the longest, as a clerk in the Post Office, lasting 18 months. He has usually been sacked and his employers have complained of his slowness and repeated instances of 'childish behaviour'. At the initial interview he seems quite a pleasant young man; he looks a bit nervous and tends to smile rather a lot when asked about his problems. His parents are present at this interview. Father seems rather quiet and mother does most of the talking. She seems very worried about John's failure at work and keeps asking what will be done to help him.

In some ways John's case is an unusual one. He does not fit the traditional stereotype of the psychiatric rehabilitee, i.e. he has not already spent long periods in hospital and he seems to show little in the way of recognizable

Table 16.1    Problem checklist

1. *Basic attachment*

| | |
|---|---|
| Is patient attending *regularly*? | YES/NO |
| Is patient attending *punctually*? | YES/NO |
| If there are problems with attendance or time keeping, do we know why? | (Comment) |
| Could anything be done to improve these? | (Comment) |

2. *Physical and psychiatric symptoms*

| | |
|---|---|
| Are there any problems with the patient's current *physical health*? | YES/NO |

If yes, specify:


Please note if the following have been recently checked:

| | |
|---|---|
| Eyesight | YES/NO |
| Hearing? | YES/NO |
| Teeth? | YES/NO |
| Is any action required regarding physical health? | YES/NO |

If yes, specify:


Please check for the following psychiatric symptoms:

| | |
|---|---|
| Psychotic experiences? | YES/NO (Comment) |
| Depression? | YES/NO |
| Manic symptoms? | YES/NO |
| Anxiety or fears? | YES/NO |
| Obsessional or compulsive symptoms? | YES/NO |
| Organic problems? | YES/NO |
| Drug abuse? | YES/NO |
| Suicidal attempts? | YES/NO |
| Other symptoms? | YES/NO If yes, specify: |

What action should be taken regarding psychiatric symptoms?
Specify:


3. *Attitudes and defences*

| | |
|---|---|
| In general, what attitude does he/she have regarding his/her difficulties? | (Comment) |
| Does he tend to deny? | YES/NO |
| avoid? | YES/NO |
| use the 'sick role'? | YES/NO |
| Is he realistic in his aims? | YES/NO |
| What is his attitude towards medications? | (Specify) |
| Does he have any *motivation* to change? | (Specify) |

4. *Accommodation and self-care*

Are there currently any problems regarding
  *accommodation*?                                       YES/NO
If yes, specify:

What is his current *financial situation*?
Does he have any outstanding financial commitments?     YES/NO
If yes, specify:

Are there any problems regarding basic educational
  skills?
  Check: Basic literacy?                                 YES/NO
         Basic numeracy?                                 YES/NO
Are there any problems with ability to handle money
  and budget?                                            YES/NO
Are there any problems with *basic self-care*?
  Check: Personal hygiene and appearance?                YES/NO
         Clothing reasonably clean and tidy?             YES/NO
         Able to do simple cooking?                      YES/NO
         Able to cope with basic housework?              YES/NO
         'Survival skills' in the community?
           (e.g. crossing roads, using public transport,
           shops, post office, etc.)?                    YES/NO
Any other problems?


5. *Work*

What problems does he present regarding the work role?
  Check: Attendance?                                     YES/NO
         Time keeping?                                   YES/NO
         Task Performance?                               YES/NO
         Supervision?                                    YES/NO
         Social interaction?                             YES/NO
         Realistic aims for the future?                  YES/NO
Any other problems?


6. *Family and social supports*

What is his current *family situation*? Are there
  problems regarding:
  Roles and responsibilities? (Who does what?)           YES/NO
  Conflicts and decision-making? (Who decides and how?)  YES/NO
  Power and autonomy (family structure, alliances, (etc.) YES/NO
  Communication of feelings (Content and clarity)        YES/NO
  Myths and stereotypes? (for one another)               YES/NO
  Attitudes to 'outsiders'?                              YES/NO
Does he have *supportive figures in the community*?      YES/NO
How does he use his 'supports'? (Comment)
How does he organize his spare time? (Comment)
Is he already engaged with supportive services? (Comment)

psychiatric symptoms. John represents a new kind of patient for psychiatric rehabilitation. His difficulties are not hidden under the effects of institutionalization and his problems seem to be due to social and environmental factors rather than to 'illness'. Irrespective of whether John is a chronic schizophrenic or simply a rather inadequate young man, we have to begin with a thorough assessment of his difficulties.

Assessments should be both valid and reliable. That is, they should measure adequately whatever it is that we are interested in and they should do this in a reproducible way. So, the first thing that we need is a comprehensive list of the possible areas. Such a list is provided in Table 16.1. (This problem checklist has been developed specifically for use in a day hospital, although it could be modified for inpatient settings.) It is organized around basic roles (self-care, work, social, etc.) and aims to provide a preliminary screening of the problem areas. At this stage comprehensive coverage of the possible problems (content validity) is what is most important; then, when specific problems have been identified, more detailed and reliable measures can be taken.

The first questions are concerned with the patient's engagement in the services. This is particularly important in community-based rehabilitation where poor attendance and high dropout rates are relatively common (often up to 50 per cent; see Beard et al., 1978). In John's case attendance was not a problem but writers like Davis et al. (1972) have emphasized the need for 'an aggressive delivery system' to cope with marginal and poorly motivated clients. This means that staff must be alert to absenteeism and be prepared to act. The need to respond quickly means that this is a task which cannot easily be left to one specialized professional group (e.g. social workers or community nurses). All staff involved in rehabilitation must be prepared (and encouraged) to go into the community and find out what has happened when patients do not attend. This in turn implies having good contacts with the patients' families, and it will be noted that John's parents were invited to his initial interview. By this means a relationship can be built up between the staff and significant others in the patient's life so that, at the very least, staff will have an idea of what might be happening to the patient when he is not attending even if they cannot always do a lot about it. (This need to involve families will be returned to later.) An understanding of why an individual is not attending may lead to a negotiation about various aspects of his/her programme. For example, some kind of part-time arrangement may be necessary for some patients in the initial stages. Similarly, special working conditions (e.g. working alone), temporary exemption from an aspect of the programme (e.g. groups), or special attention from certain staff members on arrival may all help an anxious or withdrawn patient to settle down and become attached.

The next section concerns physical and psychiatric symptoms. It is important to check the physical condition of those patients who have spent long periods in hospital, since they have often been neglected (Hall et al., 1977).

Basic physical functions like sight and hearing, and condition of the teeth, also need to be examined if one is thinking about how the patient is going to manage in work or in the community. The provision of appropriate prosthetic devices such as spectacles, hearing aids, and dentures can be just as crucial as the control of symptoms. A brief checklist of psychiatric symptoms is used next and here the doctor in the team obviously has the central role to play in assessment. However, other members of staff may be able to give the doctor information about how the patient appears in other contexts, e.g. at work or at home, which may be very important in arriving at an accurate diagnosis. For example, the patient may appear withdrawn and apathetic in one setting but relatively lively and outgoing in another. Similarly, a man who, when interviewed, may deny any obsessional problems, but may be observed by staff to avoid touching certain objects in the workrooms and be seen to wash his hands once or twice an hour.

These are both examples of behaviour problems which seem specific to particular situations, and it is now recognized that many problems show 'specificity' in this sense (Mischel, 1968, Chapter 2). This phenomenon has important implications for assessment because it means that problems often cannot be validly assessed unless we have an opportunity to observe them directly in the setting where they occur. This may be contrasted with an assumption of 'generality', i.e. that problems are not specific to situations but rather they show themselves irrespective of the situational context. This has been the more usual assumption in psychiatry and is reflected in all the traditional models of personality and illness. The pathology is seen as something that the person carries around inside him and therefore its effects will be apparent whatever the situation. As indicated, this view can now be questioned and we can be suspicious of the extent to which problems do display this generalized influence. In fact, both specificity and generality seem to be important (Wiggins, 1973) and the extent to which either one dominates depends on the nature of the problem and on the individual (Alker, 1972). So, we should be cautious about assessing psychiatric symptoms, or any other problems, by interview alone and we should aim to incorporate observations from other sources. In John's case very few symptoms could be elicited by interview; his problems were evident in other situations.

The next set of questions concerns the patient's attitudes towards his illness. Wing et al. (1964) used the term 'secondary disabilities' to refer to those handicaps not consequent upon the primary symptoms of the illness (hallucinations, delusions, depression, retardation) but related to the person's reaction, and the reactions of others, to the fact of having been 'ill'. For many patients the 'meaning' they find for their illness can represent more of an obstacle to their rehabilitation than any primary symptoms, or indeed any loss of skills. Patients may wish to deny the reality of their difficulties and maintain fixed and unrealistic expectations. At the other extreme, they may come to see themselves as completely disabled and capable of nothing but a permanent, dependent, 'sick' role. Sometimes, the existence of these secondary disabilities can only be inferred from the patient's behaviour, for example by repeated avoidance or by non-compliance with treatment plans. On other occasions, as in the refusal to take medication, the wish to deny and avoid the reality of difficulties may be much clearer. Some patients may be so frightened of becoming 'ill' again that they wish to avoid all stress and are therefore not cooperative in any treatment programme. Although John had never suffered a psychiatric illness as such, he did not seem particularly interested in examining why he was having difficulties or in looking at ways in which he could change. His parents were genuinely perplexed; they were asking whether he should be labelled as 'ill' and what implications this would have for what could be expected of him. These problems of motivation and the attitudes of key relatives to illness are important to assess.

We come next to the problems associated with the resources and the skills necessary to survive as an independent person in the community. The adequacy and the stability of the patient's current accommodation need to be considered, as does his financial situation. Money is an obvious factor in motivation, especially as far as work is concerned, yet it can easily be overlooked. We also need information about basic educational skills and this is one of the few areas in which formal psychological tests are useful. The patient needs to be assessed with regard to basic self-care skills, e.g. personal hygiene and care of clothes; we need to know if he can cook for himself, if he can look after his accommodation, if he can find his way about in the community and use public transport, shops, the post office, etc. Training programmes in these basic 'survival skills' have already been described in the literature by workers such as Goldstein et al. (1976) and Priestley et al. (1978). All these kinds of problems require assessment by direct observation. They are aspects of functioning which are obviously almost entirely dependent on specific situational influences and which therefore cannot be assessed by interview or self-report. Again, they depend on staff who are able to observe the patient directly in the community or in a realistic, simulated environment in hospital, e.g. supervised 'home-management' areas. It is also important with these problems to try to separate what are deficits in skills and what are deficits in motivation. For example, John was basically able to look after himself, his educational skills were good and he had few problems in coping with all the basic aspects of self-care when he was asked to perform under supervision in the day hospital. However, when he and his parents were questioned it became clear that he actually did very little for himself. His parents managed all his affairs for him including his money, even buying his clothes. His problems were thus not due to lack of skills, but lack of motivation. This is an important distinction for, as we shall see later, it has very clear implications for what kind of intervention one might consider.

The next area to consider is work. The nature and importance of work have already been discussed elsewhere (see Watts, Chapter 11); suffice to say here that the same principles of assessment still apply. We need valid schedules which cover all the relevant aspects of work behaviour, including the important social ones, and we need clear and realistic expectations so that the assessments can be made reliably. It must be remembered that the reliability of assessments is determined by the extent to which the observers share a common frame of reference as well as by the characteristics of the assessment instrument. (Hence, if observers share a commonly mistaken idea of what they should be looking for they can agree and therefore be reliable, but still be 'wrong' in the sense of not being valid.) To provide valid assessment of work performance we therefore not only require a realistic physical environment, we also require a realistic social environment in the sense of realistic expectations. Mental health professionals may find it difficult to provide these kinds of expectations, since they often lack the necessary experience. Thus volunteers, or other professionals from industrial settings, may need to be recruited to staff such work environments in order that the valid assessments can be made.

John was set to work in the office. (We may note here, in passing, that as clerical jobs come to occupy an increasing part of the general economy so clerical work will become increasingly important to provide for rehabilitation.) When John was observed at work his problems really began to become apparent. He quickly established himself as the office 'fool'. He was slow and repeatedly made careless errors. He failed to carry out instructions and created a general impression of slackness and unreliability. Although initially both staff and patients were vaguely amused by this behaviour, after a short time they became irritable and lost patience with him. When confronted with his problems he admitted his mistakes but just grinned nervously. In his social interactions with both peers and supervisors he seemed timid and unassertive and seldom initiated any contact. He tended to ask unnecessary questions, repeat what others had said, and make inane comments. He was seldom observed to put forward a personal opinion or state a personal goal for the future. In order to rule out the possibility that John's behaviour could be explained by intellectual deficits his intelligence was assessed and he was found to be functioning towards the top end of the average range. There was no evidence of any other cognitive problems. In order to assess his social difficulties in more detail John was asked to take part in role-play sessions with one or two of the staff. To everyone's surprise he demonstrated that he could produce appropriate social behaviour, including assertive responses, in these role-play sessions. This contrasted markedly with his behaviour in actual work and in general social situations around the unit. This reinforces the 'specificity' of some patient's difficulties. (It also demonstrates the possible unreliability of role-play assessments for social difficulties; see Shepherd, Chapter 13.)

By now, we were gradually building up a picture of John's difficulties, of what they were and of where they occurred. We were beginning to see how they interfered with his functioning and we had some clues as to what interventions might be necessary. But, there is one important area that we have not yet considered: this is the nature of the family situation and social supports outside the treatment setting. It is now clear that for many patients what happens in these areas profoundly affects their ability to function in other areas, e.g. self-care and work (see Birley and Hudson, Chapter 9; Bennett and Morris, Chapter 10). John's parents were invited to be involved right from the beginning and this illustrates what Bennett *et al.* (1976) refer to as a 'family approach' to rehabilitation. A family *approach* is not the same as family *therapy*. It does not necessarily set treatment goals. Rather, it simply recognizes that the family is important (most patients spend the majority of time with their families, even those at work), and whether or not the family can be 'treated' it is still useful to have a good idea of what is going on at home. Contact with the family can therefore be seen primarily as an important source of information, perhaps useful in a preventive sense, perhaps to keep one alert to impending crises. Of course, if treatment is possible, and attitudes or behaviour can be changed, then this is to be welcomed. But even if change is rather unlikely (and this is often the case) that does not mean that continued regular contact is of no value. Families may be seen within the treatment setting or, bearing in mind the arguments in favour of direct observation, it may be preferable to see them in their own home.

We decided to see John and his family at home and two members of staff (a doctor and a nurse) made a series of visits. Assessing family functioning is a difficult and controversial area. Theories abound and it is not at all clear which theory provides the most useful conceptual framework. The problem checklist provides a minimum list of the possible problems that might be considered. First, there is the issue of roles and responsibilities—the question: who does what? This is obviously important, and there is evidence that in families which contain a member with psychiatric problems the role structure is affected (Collins *et al.*, 1971; Orford *et al.*, 1976). It is important to know in some detail who does the various chores, who cooks the meals, puts out the rubbish, takes care of the children, etc. What are the roles and does everybody have one? The next question, which follows on from the first, is how did this particular pattern of roles and responsibilities arise? In any family there are bound to be conflicts and disagreements and these often focus around who is responsible for which tasks. How these conflicts and disagreements are resolved is therefore an important area to be examined. Different researchers have provided ways of conceptualizing these problem-solving processes: for example, for a behavioural approach see Vincent *et al.* (1975), or for 'systems' analysis see Alexander (1973). If one examines in detail what behaviour is actually being described by these two different approaches, in fact they seem quite similar. They discuss positive ('supportive') problem solving as making constructive suggestions, offering alternatives, compromising, etc.; negative ('defensive') responses include criticizing, complaining, denying responsibility, etc.

We can move on next to consider the family structure in terms of power, 'alliances', and the recognition of individual autonomy. These dimensions have been particularly emphasized by therapists like Minuchin (1974); he provides helpful diagrams to illustrate different family configurations.

The communication of affect is the next question and this is a topic that has received a great deal of attention in recent years. It is now quite clear that certain levels of expressed emotion can have a direct effect on patients' symptomatology (see Birley and Hudson, Chapter 9). In addition to the nature and amount of emotional expression, it is also important to consider its clarity. Although the evidence for the 'double-bind' hypothesis does not suggest that this is a specific aetiological factor in schizophrenia, there is some reason to suppose that lack of clarity may still be an important dimension (Jacob, 1975). More recent research has focused on possible discrepancies between the intended content of communications and their received impact (Gottman *et al.*, 1976). It has been shown that in distressed couples communications are often received much more negatively than was intended. This suggests the influence of cognitive 'sets' or 'stereotypes', filtering the information prior to it being perceived. These stereotypes are the family 'myths', e.g. 'he's hopeless', 'he's unreliable', 'she's the clever one', etc. They are built up over the years and may be highly resistant to disconfirming evidence.

Finally, we need to consider the attitude of the family towards 'outsiders'. What are their attitudes to people outside the family and to professionals? Are they relatively welcoming and open or rather suspicious and self-sufficient? (e.g. 'in this family we believe in sorting out our own problems').

John's family was a very interesting one. We have already seen how in the area of self-care he did little for himself. On seeing more of the family a picture soon emerged of over-protection and over-involvement with his mother and with his elder sister who was now absent. This was evident in the way the household was organized, who took the decisions, and the kinds of feelings expressed by the mother towards John. Father said little, but when he did speak he tended to be very emphatic, making his point in an uncompromising, even angry way. He was perceived by the family, particularly by John, as a rather remote, mysterious man, a bit frightening and possibly even capable of being violent. The family was a relatively 'closed' one, having little contact with outsiders, and it was therefore especially upset by the departure of John's sister who had emigrated to Australia some 4 years before. This coincided with the worsening in John's work record.

In his case the last questions on the checklist, those concerning social supports, were nearly all answered in the negative. He had few friends outside the family and few social supports, clubs, hobbies, or other activities that would take him outside the home. The concept of 'support' is a difficult one and as yet we have no clear understanding for whom, and under what conditions, 'support' is most helpful (see Bennett and Morris, Chapter 10). John was someone for whom social contacts and activities were likely to be helpful and thus he was given a careful interview to try to build up a picture of what kind of social 'network' he did have and the areas in which this might be improved. Although research instruments have been devised to investigate social networks (e.g. Henderson 1977; Henderon et al., 1978; Falconer, 1979), no easy and quick method exists for routine use in rehabilitation. This seems an important priority for the future.

All the information which is gathered using the checklist provides the basis for a formulation of the patient's difficulties and the construction of an individual plan. The process of assessment is therefore not like a simple, 'one-off' administration of a test or interview. It can take weeks, even months, to collect all the relevant information and any assessment or formulation is bound to be provisional and reflect only the current state of knowledge about that particular patient. It may change over time as the outcomes of further investigations and interventions become available. With John it was possible to make a provisional formulation after 3–4 weeks. The assessment suggested that the reasons for John's failure to maintain stable employment were not due to intellectual deficits, or primarily to task performance problems. The difficulties seemed to be mainly social and motivational. Although he could show that he possessed adequate social skills, for some reason he was unable or unwilling to use them. It was hypothesized that he had adopted his childish way of relating to others as a result of differential reinforcement by his mother and elder sister. It was further reinforced by the fact that it enabled him to avoid meeting many of the expectations of independent, adult behaviour; something which he obviously lacked confidence in doing. It was even partially successful in getting people to like him (at least initially). Of course, it was only successful in the short term and there was a price to pay. People soon lost patience with him and it also obviated any opportunity for constructive self-expression, i.e. asserting his own wishes, needs, and aims. He was unhappy with himself but took some satisfaction in displacing this frustration onto others. (In this sense he could be described as 'passively aggressive'.) As indicated, family factors were seen to play an important role in the aetiology and maintenace of his problems and his functioning does seem to have deteriorated since his sister's departure. Perhaps his sister had played a mediating role; they were certainly close and she seems to have been supportive. Father remained a distant, fearful figure and a poor role model for the expression of feelings.

There is much speculation in this kind of formulation and one may wish to disagree with all or parts of it. But its function is to bring together the information that we have about John and to give a plausible account of his difficulties. Furthermore, it directs attention to specific aspects of his functioning where interventions might be attempted. This is the next stage in the process.

His basic involvement with the services was good. There were no problems with his physical health and little in the way of psychiatric symptoms. In other cases the assessment might lead to attempts to treat symptoms by either pharmacological or psychological means. As indicated earlier, observations from the whole team of behaviour across a range of settings are important in evaluating such interventions. In the area of self-care the problems have been described: some deficits in skills, but mainly deficits in motivation.

Skills can be improved by what is now a fairly standard 'skills training' or 'social learning' approach (see Anthony, 1977). This approach employs basic psychological learning theory to improve specific target behaviours. The target is first identified and detailed measures are taken of baseline performance, e.g. daily ratings of personal hygiene or appearance; ratings across a number of specific items concerned with cooking a meal; etc. There are no fixed rules as to what constitutes an adequate baseline, but it must be stable enough for subsequent progress to be reliably judged. Next, the new target or skill is described. This may involve simple verbal instructions or the therapist may actually need to 'model' (i.e. demonstrate) the new response. When the patient fully understands what he is being required to do, he is then asked to practise the new response, e.g. 'now tomorrow please try to remember to comb your hair properly/brush your teeth/not cover your jacket with cigarette ash'; or, 'the next time you cook the meal try to remember to take the sausages out to thaw a bit earlier'. After practising he is given feedback and/or reinforcement. The effects of reinforcement are now clear, although the mechanisms are still not well understood (Elliot et al., 1979). There is at least one indication in the literature that feedback and social attention are just as important as a tangible physical reinforcer, e.g. a token, (see Hall et al., 1977). After feedback or reinforcement the next step is to practise again, and again, and again, until a succession of correct responses is achieved.

There are a number of basic points which should always be borne in mind when carrying out this kind of procedure. (a) If 'modelling' is used always direct the patient's attention to that aspect of the model's behaviour that you want him or her to notice (otherwise they won't). (b) Always set the level of a new response at just above the baseline towards the desired response. This minimizes the danger of arranging yet another failure situation. (c) Reinforce with praise, don't punish. Punishment is rarely effective and it is much better to take a 'constructionist' approach (Goldiamond, 1975). i.e. build on the positive. (d) Try to reinforce or give feedback immediately and continuously, especially during the acquisition phase. Once established, a new response can be successfully maintained as a more 'partial' schedule of reinforcement. (e) Always use 'overlearning', i.e. repeated practice beyond the first correct production of the response.

It should also be remembered that the arguments for direct, *in vivo* assessment apply just as well in the treatment phase. Most psychological treatments have some problems with 'generalizing' improvements, in other words in helping the patient to transfer the gains from an artificial treatment setting to everyday life (Goldstein and Kanfer, 1979). If the treatment can also take place as far as possible *in vivo*, these problems of generalization can be reduced. For example, some of the treatment of self-care problems can be carried out in the patient's home and in his local community, as well as in hospital.

So, to a consideration of motivational problems: these are obviously much more difficult to 'treat', but again it will depend on an understanding of just what each problem is. In John's case one aspect of the problem was that he seemed to lack confidence in his skills. This was put to him and it was suggested that the only way to improve his confidence was for him to practise those skills and to find out that he really could manage. Another aspect of his problem was his parents' attitudes. Again, this was explained to them and the extent to which they would encourage him to do more and take more responsibility at home was explored. Finally, he was given individual sessions to discuss his general frustrations and his ambivalence about 'growing up'. Motivation *is* a difficult area, but a good assessment and sympathetic counselling can at least leave you with some understanding of what the problem is, even if you are not successful in eradicating it.

This discussion of skills and motivational problems also applies to the area of work difficulties. John's problems at work were again mainly social, and so an individual programme was constructed with the aim of decreasing his childish behaviour at work and increasing appropriate social interactions. This used individual sessions of modelling, role-play, and feedback which were then generalized to the actual work settings involving other staff, even other patients, in the reinforcement of appropriate behaviour (see also Shepherd, Chapter 13). John's behaviour was observed and rated every day and he was given bi-weekly feedback on his progress. At the same time some of his problems with social motivation were also discussed. As for the family situation, the assessment and formulation again suggested a number of goals for treatment. John was encouraged to develop his 'problem-solving' skills at home. He had to learn how to put his point of view across and to express his needs to his parents. They had to learn how to accept it. Mother needed support in order that she might be less over-involved and over-protective. Father needed encouragement to express his needs more openly and to try to dispel the image of him as a remote, mysterious, possibly dangerous figure.

A social learning and a counselling approach can both be useful with family problems (Liberman *et al.*, 1976). 'Contracting' methods can be used to tackle problems about roles and responsibilities (Crowe, 1973), and recent technical advances make the exploration of ambiguous communications a much simpler and more practical proposition (Margolin and Weiss, 1978). Family therapy is another difficult area, but progress is possible if we can identify *specific* processes, and apply *specific* interventions, using *specific* outcome criteria. The final area to consider for treatment is that of social supports and the most important point to appreciate here is that no attempt can be made to increase a person's range of social activities unless one knows not only what his needs are but also what facilities are available in his local community. Local information is therefore the key, and the rehabilitation service must be in a position to collect and offer that information to those who need it. (How support can best be provided is discussed at length by Bennett and Morris in Chapter 10.)

The emphasis in treatment is therefore on specific targets and specific outcomes. But how can treatments be evaluated? One approach is to use single-case 'designs' (see Shapiro, 1970, 1975; Yule and Hemsley, 1977). In essence these consist of the application of scientific methods to the investigation of individuals. The simplest design is known as A–B (where A = 'baseline' and B = 'treatment') and involves just repeated observations before and after intervention. Then, visual inspection may be used to determine whether there has been any change over the period of observations which could plausibly be attributed to the intervention. This kind of design would be suitable to evaluate any of the skills training procedures described above for self-care, work, or social problems. It is often a very useful design, especially if all that one is interested in is looking for improvement. More complicated designs can be used to clarify the relationship between a particular intervention and a particular target; these use additional reversals, e.g. A–B–A; A–B–A–B. Simplified versions of the intervention can also be evaluated to try to understand exactly what are the effective ingredients, e.g. A–B1–B2–A. Finally, effectiveness of an intervention may be examined by continuously monitoring several variables in addition to the target and showing that the target variable is specifically affected by the introduction of the intervention (a 'multiple-baseline' design). These different designs have particular strengths and weaknesses but they all offer a systematic and individual-centred approach to evaluation. They also offer the possibility of being therapeutically eclectic, i.e. being prepared to use different kinds of interventions—pharmacological, behavioural, psychotherapeutic, etc.—while maintaining a rigorous attitude towards evaluation.

An alternative approach is to use some kind of 'goal-setting' method. These are forms of problem-oriented records (see Weed, 1969; Miller, 1976), and their use in rehabilitation has been described by Austin *et al.* (1976). The original technique of Kirusek and Sherman (1968) involved formulating

Table 16.2 Examples of Goal Attainments Scaling

| Outcome Value | Goals | | |
|---|---|---|---|
| | Decision making | Dependency on Mother | Social Functioning |
| Most unfavourable treatment outcome thought likely (-2) | No new decisions taken. Still weighing same alternatives | Lives at home. Does nothing without mother's approval | Withdrawn, no friends, no social contacts |
| Less than expected success with (-1) | | | Not withdrawn in day hospital, but no friends outside |
| Expected level of treatment success (0) | Still complains of difficulty but does take decisions | Lives at home. Has some activities independent of mother | Has at least one social activity per week |
| More than expected success with treatment (+1) | Takes decisions without actually complaining | | |
| Best anticipated treatment success (+2) | Takes important decisions, e.g. re work, with confidence | Leaves home, lives independently, sees mother occasionally | Has maintained a regular friendship for at least one month |

Source: Adapted from Kirusek and Sherman (1968)
Note: Goal levels are devised.

individual goals for a number of problems and then monitoring progress through various levels of outcome which were specified in advance (Examples are given in Table 16.2.) The authors claim that progress can be standardized and compared across individuals in this way. A recent modification of this approach described by Ihilevich and Gleser (1979) attempts to standardize problem areas and outcome levels so that they need not be worked out individually for each patient. (Examples are given in Table 16.3.) This second method has obvious advantages in terms of economy of time but the content validity of Ihilevich and Gleser's problem areas could be questioned. The preset goals would also require a more detailed analysis before individual targets could be specified. Both the single-case approach and goal-setting methods therefore seem useful in evaluating rehabilitation programmes and the choice between the two would seem to depend upon whether one was primarily interested in the outcome of individuals or of groups.

So, we have our assessment and we have tried to treat our patient's problems, but that is not all there is to rehabilitation. In many cases — John's

Table 16.3 Examples of the Progress Evaluation Scales

| Goals<br>Family Interaction | Occupation | Getting Along<br>with others |
|---|---|---|
| Often must have help with basic needs (e.g. eating, dressing) | Does not hold a job, or care for home, or go to school | Always fighting or destructive; or always alone |
| Takes care of own basic needs but must have help with everyday plans and activities | Seldom holds job, or attends classes, or cares for home | Seldom able to get along with others without quarrelling or being destructive; or is often alone |
| Makes own plans but without considering the needs of other family members | Sometimes holds job, or attends some classes, or does limited house-work | Sometimes quarrelling, but seldom destructive; difficulties in making friends |
| Tries to consider everyone's needs but somehow decisions and actions do not work well for every body in the family | Holds regular job, or attends classes, or does housework (or some combination of these), but with difficulty | Gets along with others most of the time; has occasional friends |
| Usually plans and acts so that own needs as well as needs of others in the family are considered | Holds regular job, or attends classes, or does housework (or some com bination of these) with little or no difficulty | Gets along with others most of the time; has regular close friends |

*Source:* Adapted from Ihilevich and Gleser (1979).
*Notes:* Goal levels are supplied.
Goals are also supplied for the areas of Feelings and Mood, Use of Free Time, Problems (symptoms), and Attitude Towards Self.

was one—patients will not, or cannot, respond to treatment. What do we do then? In the first place, this should not be seen as a failure. Therapy may have failed to produce improvement but if we have done it systemtically then it should not fail to provide us with information. In fact, therapeutic failure is the only way in which *chronic* disabilities can be defined; i.e. chronic disabilities are those problems which do fail to respond to reasonable appropriate treatment. What will constitute 'appropriate treatment' in any particular case is not easy to define. Most therapists will assume that no one has received appropriate treatment until they themselves have had a try, and this is not necessarily an attitude to be discouraged. What it implies is that as much depends on the patience and the ingenuity of staff as on the provision of resources. (Hence, the importance of the staff in rehabilitation and of good teamwork; see Watts and Bennett, Chapter 15.)

The level of chronic disabilities will obviously be different for different individuals, and within the same individual may be different for different areas of functioning. Thus some patients will only be able to cope with a very sheltered living and working environment (e.g. as in a sheltered workshop and supervised hostel); others may require a sheltered workplace but be able to manage independent living. We therefore need to be able to fit together individualized 'packages' of care and this underlines the need for as wide as possible a range of services geared at different levels in each area of functioning. The long-term management of chronic disabilities is therefore concerned with providing different kinds of environments, tailored to meet specific needs, which will maintain functioning without necessarily expecting to improve it. How such environments can be created and maintained has been discussed elsewhere (Shepherd and Richardson, 1979; Shepherd, 1980). The process is thus one of modifying the environment (the demands and the expectations) in the face of disabilities which seem unmodifiable. Although John may not have been psychiatrically 'ill', in the usual sense, his disabilities did prove very difficult to 'treat'. Systematic evaluation, over a period of months, of his progress in the office and at home suggested that he only achieved small improvements in his abilities to interact more appropriately with others and to be more independent and assertive at home. He was eventually placed in a sheltered workshop and his parents reluctantly accepted that, for the moment, open employment was not a feasible goal for him. While he remains at home it does not seem likely that any further major changes will occur. Contact with the family is being maintained with the aim that whatever small gains have been made should not disappear. John may be reassessed at some time in the future.

From this discussion a number of general points seem to emerge.

(a) *The process of rehabilitation can be thought to consist of three basic states: assessment, treatment, and management.*

(b) *For assessment purposes the most accurate methods are those based on the direct observation of criterion behaviour.* Formal tests and interviews are of limited value. If direct observation is not possible then useful information can be obtained from a carefully taken history (see Watts and Bennett, 1977) or alternatively from standardized references, especially those obtained from peers (Wiggins, 1973).

(c) *Assessment and treatment should be carried out as far as possible in the setting where the problem occurs, or some approximation to it.* This principle of working *in vivo* is necessary to improve the validity of assessments and to minimize problems of generalizing treatment effects.

(d) *Assessment is a gradual accumulation of information about a patient, not a single administration of a test.* It is seldom possible to predict *a priori* what level of functioning an individual is likely to achieve in a particular area. This can only be determined pragmatically, by trying him out in various settings and then carefully assessing the outcome.

(e) *'Evaluation' in this sense is no different from treatment; they are both part of the procedure of assessing the limits of change.* Evaluation tells one whether or not the intervention has been successful in treating the 'symptom', but whatever the outcome the information that is obtained will still be useful in planning new interventions, or in planning strategies for the management of chronic disabilities. Assessment and treatment are thus linked as two aspects of the same process, i.e. defining disabilities.

(f) *There are limitations to the treatment model, but just because treatment fails that does not mean that one should necessarily give up.* Successful treatment may be limited for a whole variety of reasons, e.g. motivational problems such as denial or 'secondary gain'; the intransigent attitude of key relatives; the influence of life-events such as unemployment or bereavement; the unavailability of appropriate resources; etc. But the fact that treatment fails still means that the individual requires help to manage his disabilities in the long term. The provision of suitable environments which will maintain functioning in specific areas (work, self-care, social) is as important in rehabilitation as is assessing and improving functioning. This is the true legacy of trying to provide a community-based alternative to the mental hospital.

(g) *Rehabilitation must be based on individualized 'packages' of care, not on block treatment or a 'throughput' model.* Individuals are different, both from one another and within their own particular patterns of needs and abilities. Rehabilitation services must recognize these differences and create individualized programmes which contrast with the 'block treatments' of the institutional approach (Goffman, 1961). These individual programmes are more like 'packages' of care (the 'shopping-basket' approach; see Bennett, Chapter 2) than they are like a treatment model which aims at gradually improving functioning and moving the patient on to higher and greater achievements.

(h) *Conclusions in rehabilitation will always be provisional and open to change.* The rehabilitation of the individual has been depicted here as an unfolding process, where the conclusions reached in the assessment, or in relation to decisions as to which kind of sheltered environment might be suitable, are determined by the outcomes of the various investigations and interventions. These conclusions will also be affected by subsequent changes in individuals' circumstances. We are all susceptible to life-events and they can have beneficial as well as adverse effects; for example, the death of a parent may remove a long-term disabling motivational block as well as being a cause of immediate upset.

In summary, planning the rehabilitation of the individual is a time-consuming, difficult, and often frustrating exercise. It requires services which are sensitive to the practical demands of everyday life and it also requires organizations which can meet the needs of individuals. Perhaps above all it requires staff who can accept their limitations. There is nothing wrong with trying to 'treat' people, just as long as failure is met with the same enthusiasm and optimism as success. Rehabilitation is as much about failure as it is about success and the pressures to fall back on institutional practices are always very great. These pressures can only be resisted by staff who know what they are doing, and why they are doing it, and are sufficiently self-critical to change the way in which they are working if needs demand.

## References

Alexander, J. F. (1973) Defensive and supportive communications in normal and deviant families. *Journal of Consulting and Clinical Psychology*, **40**, 223–231.

Alker, H. A. (1972) Is personality situationally specific or intrapsychiatrically consistent? *Journal of Personality*, **40**, 177–192.

Anthony, L. A. (1977) Psychological rehabilitation—a concept in need of a method. *American Psychologist*, **1977**, 658–662.

Austin, N. K., Liberman, L. P., King, L. W., and De Risi, W. J. (1976) A comparative evaluation of two day hospitals. *Journal of Nervous and Mental Diseases*, **163**, 253–262.

Beard, J. M., Malamud, T. J., and Rossman, E. (1978) Psychiatric rehabilitation and long-term rehospitalisation, the findings of two studies. *Schizophrenia Bulletin*, **4**, 622–635.

Bennett, D., Fox, C., Jowell, T. and Skynner, A. C. R. (1976) Towards a family approach in a psychiatric day hospital. *British Journal of Psychiatry*, **129**, 441–447.

Collins, J., Kreitman, W., Nelson, B., and Troop, J. (1971) Neurosis marital interaction III: Family roles and functions. *British Journal of Psychiatry*, **119**, 233–242.

Crowe, M. J. (1973) Conjoint marital therapy: advice or interpretation. *Journal of Psychosomatic Research*, **17**, 309–315.

Davis, A. E., Dinitz, S., and Pasamanick, B. (1972) The prevention of hospitalization in schizophrenia: five years after an experimental program. *American Journal of Orthopsychiatry*, **42**, 375–388.

Elliot, P. A., Barlow, F., Hooper, A., and Kingerlee, P. E. (1979) Maintaining patients' improvements in a token economy. *Behaviour Research and Therapy*, **17**, 355–367.

Falconer, L. J. (1979) The social networks of the relations of psychiatric patients. MPhil thesis, University of London.

Goffman, E. (1961) *Asylums: Essays on the Social Situation of Mental Patients and Other Inmates*. Anchor Books, Doubleday, New York.

Goldiamond, I. (1975) Alternative sets as a framework for behavioural formulations and research. *Behaviourism*, **3**, 49–86.

Goldstein, A. P., and Kanfer, F. H. (1979) *Maximising Treatment Gains*. Academic Press, New York.

Goldstein, A. P., Sprafkin, R. P., and Gereshaw, N. J. (1976) *Skill Training for Community Living: Applying Structured Learning Therapy*. Pergamon, New York.

Gottman, J., Notarius, C., Markman, H., Bank, S., Yoppi, B., and Rubin, M. E.

(1976) Behaviour exchange theory and marital decision making. *Journal of Personality and Social Psychology*, **34**, 14–23.

Hall, J. N., Baker, R. D., and Hutchinson, K. (1977) A controlled evaluation of token economy procedures with chronic schizophrenic patients. *Behaviour Research and Therapy*, **15**, 261–283.

Hall, J. N., Baker, R., and Jones, G. (1977) *Clinical Applications of Behaviour Modification Techniques with Long-Stay Psychiatric Patients*. Final Report from Department of Psychology and Psychiatry, University of Leeds and Stanley Royd Hospital, Wakefield, Yorks.

Henderson, S. (1977) The social network, support and neurosis. The function of attachment in adult life. *British Journal of Psychiatry*, **131**, 185–191.

Henderson, S., Duncan-Jones, P., McAuley, H., and Ritchie, K. (1978) The patient's primary group. *British Journal of Psychiatry*, **132**, 74–86.

Ihilevich, D., and Gleser, G. L. (1979) *The Progress Evaluation Scales*. Shiawassee County Community Mental Health Services Board, Owosso, Michigan.

Jacob, T. (1975) Family interaction in disturbed and normal families: a methodological and substantive review. *Psychological Bulletin*, **82**, 33–65.

Kirusek, T. J., and Sherman, R. E. (1968) Goal attainment scaling: a general method for evaluating community mental health programs. *Community Mental Health Journal*, **4**, 443–453.

Liberman, R. P., Levine, J., Wheeler, E., Sanders, W., and Wallace, C. (1976) Experimental evaluation of marital group therapy behavioural vs. interaction-insight formats. *Acta Psychiatrica Scananavica*, Monograph Supplement.

Margolin, G., and Weiss, R. L. (1978) Communication training and assessment I: A case of marital enrichment. *Behaviour Therapy*, **9**, 508–520.

Miller, E. (1976) Growing weeds: a problem-oriented approach to patients' records in clinical psychology. *Bulletin of the British Psychological Society*, **29**, 359–368.

Minuchin, S. (1974) *Families and Family Therapy*. Tavistock, London.

Mischel, W. (1968) *Personality and Assessment*. John Wiley, New York.

Orford, J., Oppenheimer, E., Egert, S., Hensman, C., and Guterie, S. (1976) The cohesiveness of alcoholism—complicated marriages and its influence on treatment outcome. *British Journal of Psychiatry*, **128**, 318–339.

Priestley, P., McGuire, J., Flegg, D., Hemsley, V., and Welham, D. (1978) *Social Skills and Personal Problem Solving: A Handbook of Methods*. Tavistock, London.

Shapiro, M. B. (1970) Intensive assessment of the single case: an inductive–deductive approach. In P. Mittler, ed., *The Psychological Assessment of Mental and Physical Handicaps*. Methuen, London.

Shapiro, M. B. (1975) *The Assessment of Self-Reported Dysfunctions: A Manual with its Rationale and Applications*. Parts I & II. Department of Psychology, Institute of Psychiatry.

Shepherd, G. (1980) Day care and the chronic patient. Paper presented at the Annual Conference, MIND (National Association for Mental Health), London.

Shepherd, G., and Richardson, A. (1979) Organisation and interaction in psychiatric day centres. *Psychological Medicine*, **9**, 573–579.

Vincent, J. P., Weiss, R. L., and Birchler, G. R. (1975) A behavioural analysis of problem solving in distressed and nondistressed married and stranger dyads. *Behaviour Therapy*, **6**, 475–487.

Watts, F. N., and Bennett, D. H. (1977) Previous occupational stability as a predictor of employment after psychiatric rehabilitation. *Psychological Medicine*, **7**, 709–712.

Weed, L. L. (1969) *Medical Records, Medical Education and Patient Care*. Case Western Reserve University Press, Cleveland, Ohio.

Wiggins, J. S. (1973) *Personality and Prediction: Principles of Personality Assessment.* Addison-Wesley, Reading, Mass.

Wing, J. K., Bennett, D. H., and Denham, J. (1964) The industrial rehabilitation of long-stay schizophrenic patients. Medical Research Council Memo No. 42, HMSO, London.

Yule, W., and Hemsley, D. (1977) Single case method in medical psychology. In S. Rachman and C. Phillips, eds, *Advances in Medical Psychology.* Pergamon, London.

# Subject Index

349

# Author Index

*Note:* Page numbers in italic indicate the pages on which the full references appear.